PENNING POISON

PENNING POISON

a history of anonymous letters

EMILY
COCKAYNE

OXFORD
UNIVERSITY PRESS

OXFORD
UNIVERSITY PRESS

Great Clarendon Street, Oxford, OX2 6DP,
United Kingdom

Oxford University Press is a department of the University of Oxford.
It furthers the University's objective of excellence in research, scholarship,
and education by publishing worldwide. Oxford is a registered trade mark of
Oxford University Press in the UK and in certain other countries

Published in the United States of America by Oxford University Press
198 Madison Avenue, New York, NY 10016, United States of America

British Library Cataloguing in Publication Data
Data available

Library of Congress Control Number: 2023933778

ISBN 978–0–19–879505–6

DOI: 10.1093/oso/9780198795056.001.0001

Printed and bound in the UK by
Clays Ltd, Elcograf S.p.A.

'For you. You know who you are.'

Acknowledgements

Increasingly, it is very difficult for academics to write on top of a 'teaching-only' contract. I have had no opportunity to present any of this material at conferences, or to apply for any funding, or ever take any research leave. All those on academic 'scholarship' contracts must decide either to give up research entirely or to conduct all their research and writing in their annual leave and other spare time. This book is dedicated to all academics on similar contracts.

Luckily, academia is filled with people who help others—including the late (and much missed) Richard Deswarte. I have benefited much from advice from and discussions with Helena Carr, Joel Halcomb, Jayne Gifford (who also read drafts for me), Emma Griffin, Geoff Plank, Milla Schofield, Becky Taylor, Eliza Hartrich, Jacquie Burgess, and Jennifer Wallis. Various anonymous readers for Oxford University Press crafted reports which have been invaluable in shaping my arguments. Thank you also to Leon Jackson for generously supplying me with unpublished material, and to Christopher Hilliard, both for his correspondence and for publishing two exceptionally useful books.

Archivists across the country have been very helpful, especially in the difficult pandemic times, particularly Bristol Archives, Dudley Archives, East Sussex Record Office, Gloucestershire Archives, The National Archive, Northamptonshire Archives, Staffordshire Record Office, Worcestershire Archives, the Shakespeare Birthplace Trust, the British Motor Museum, and the Wellcome Library.

My parents have, as usual, been involved, with my father, David, supplying encouragement and reading the whole draft, and my mother, Yvonne, providing invaluable help with genealogical researches. My agent, Clare Alexander, yet again provided perfect support, and my editor, Luciana O'Flaherty, suggested wise corrections and alterations. Thank you also Louise Larchbourne, Vasuki Ravichandran, and Tara Werger. Maud Webster created three beautiful diagrams, all done efficiently and with expertise. Especial thanks go to Wendy Roderick for responding to my out-of-the-blue query with candour and kindness.

I am conscious that some families may come across ancestors in these pages, or even people they once knew personally. I am sincerely sorry if telling their stories causes any distress. I have tried my best to trace living relatives, but that is not always possible; some may have been missed. In some cases, I have anonymized or semi-anonymized individuals to protect living relatives.

On my own street neighbours have received nasty letters from a house on a street behind us, complaining about the behaviour of their cats, so thank you to Kevin and Genghis for not being so badly behaved that you have drawn any unwanted attention to yourselves. To George, my writing this book coincided with your brave decision to leave academia and forge a new career—I could not be prouder (or more jealous!) of you. Finally, to Ned and Maud—you know the drill by now, again your mother has written about things she wants you never to do!

Contents

Abbreviations		xi
List of Figures		xiii
Note about Anonymity		xv
Introduction:	Dear Madam	I
1. Gossip:	Major Eliot's maiden sisters	19
2. Tip-offs:	Undermined coalmasters in Staffordshire	44
3. Threats:	Lord Dorington's in danger	64
4. Obscenity:	Peer's perversion uncovered	90
5. Libels:	'er at number 14 is dirty	109
6. Detection:	Detectives say	139
7. Media:	Herbert Austin robs men's brains	163
8. Local reaction:	And Winifred Simner sows discontent	189
Conclusion:	[unsigned]	209
Endnotes		225
Bibliography		273
Index		291

Abbreviations

BA	Bristol Archives
DA	Dudley Archives
ESRO	East Sussex Record Office
GA	Gloucestershire Archives
IB	Investigations Branch (Post Office)
LMA	London Metropolitan Archives
MOA	Mass Observation Archive, Mass Observation Online, Adam Matthew, http://www.massobservation.amdigital.co.uk
NA	Northamptonshire Archives
OB	*Proceedings of the Old Bailey*
OED	*Oxford English Dictionary*
PC	Police Constable
PS	Police Sergeant
SRO	Staffordshire Record Office
TNA	The National Archives
WA	Worcestershire Archives

List of Figures

1. Anonymous letter to Mary Cokayne, Exeter House, Roehampton, postmarked Sutton 10 November 1894, Northamptonshire Archives Service, C 637   2

2. Anonymous letter to Mr Burn 1847, Shakespeare Birthplace Trust ER21/4 recto   11

3. Anonymous letter to Mr Burn 1847, Shakespeare Birthplace Trust ER21/4 verso   12

4. Hagley murder anonymous letter, Worcestershire Archives, 010:18 BA 14908/3/1/1-2, with permission from West Mercia Police   16

5. Major Eliot letter 1829 recto, author's own item   20

6. Major Eliot letter 1829 verso, author's own item   21

7. Copy of a letter sent to Peggy, Countess of Coventry, c.1815, Worcestershire Archives 705:73 BA 14450/289/18(1) recto   24

8. Copy of a letter sent to Peggy, Countess of Coventry, c.1815, Worcestershire Archives 705:73 BA 14450/289/18(1) verso   25

9. Letter from Peggy, Countess of Coventry, Worcestershire Archives 705:73 BA 14450/289/7 (1)   29

10. Anonymous letter [from Thomas Hill] re: Jane Bell, North Shields, 1821, author's own item   39

11. Anonymous letter [from Thomas Hill] re: Jane Bell, North Shields, a second letter from 12 June 1821 recto, author's own item   41

12. Anonymous letter [from Thomas Hill] re: Jane Bell, North Shields, 1821 verso of the second letter from 12 June, author's own item   42

13. Letter to 'Master Heberard', 1849, Dudley Archives DRBC/7/8/8, with permission from Mr David Williams-Thomas   45

14. Map of the Moor Lane Colliery area, by Maud Webster   56

15. Anonymous letter to the Dorington family of Lypiatt Park threatening murder, 1864, Gloucestershire Archives, D5344/1, recto   65

16. Anonymous letter to the Dorington family of Lypiatt Park
    threatening murder, 1864, Gloucestershire Archives, D5344/1,
    verso   66

17. Anonymous letter to the Dorington family of Lypiatt Park
    threatening murder, 1864, Gloucestershire Archives, D5344/1,
    envelope   74

18. Mock-up of classified advert from *Loughborough Echo*,
    3 November 1916, 1   90

19. Anonymous postcard sent to Sanitary Inspector, Hounslow,
    1915 recto, author's own item   110

20. Anonymous postcard sent to Sanitary Inspector, Hounslow,
    1915 verso, author's own item   111

21. Location of Eliza Woodman's house in relation to Mary Johnson's
    house, Redhill, 1910, by Maud Webster   121

22. Numbers 43–49 Western Road, Littlehampton, a plan by
    Maud Webster   136

23. Extract from Charles Chabot and Edward Twisleton,
    The Handwriting of Junius Professionally Investigated (1871), 37   139

24. Anonymous postcard to Herbert Austin, 1935, © British Motor
    Industry Heritage Trust, recto   164

25. Anonymous postcard to Herbert Austin, 1935, © British Motor
    Industry Heritage Trust, verso   164

26. Letter to Marie Stopes, Wellcome Library Collection Creative
    Commons—Attribution-NonCommercial 4.0 International—CC
    BY-NC 4.0   166

27. Anonymous letter to Charles Hohenrein, 12 May 1915, L
    DBHR/1/1/13, page 1, recto, Hull History Centre   167

28. Anonymous letter to Charles Hohenrein, 12 May 1915, L
    DBHR/1/1/13, page 2, verso, Hull History Centre   168

29. Envelope for anonymous letter to Charles Hohenrein,
    12 May 1915, L DBHR/1/1/13, Hull History Centre   169

30. Letter from Father O'Halloran, from Mattock Lodge, Ealing, to
    Father Thomas Jackson, 8 September 1902, author's own item   180

31. Envelope for letter from Father O'Halloran, from Mattock Lodge,
    Ealing, to Father Thomas Jackson, 8 September 1902, author's
    own item   182

32. Photograph of Winifred Simner, courtesy of Wendy Roderick   193

33. Anonymous letter received in Yately, *Daily Mirror*, 25 October 1926,
    p. 24, permission from Mirrorpix   198

Note about Anonymity

Where cases occurred within the last century, some individuals have been anonymized, especially those who were victims of letter campaigns which revealed private details and those who were either acquitted of writing libellous letters, or dispatched to an asylum immediately after their court appearance, or shortly after any incarceration.

Introduction
Dear Madam

Perhaps in a trance or coma, don't bury yet—the other Curate was reported dead—some time since.[1]

A t the heart of this book is the experience of receiving and first reading a note of this kind. If you have never been sent such a letter, then it is likely the confusion you felt on turning to the one above will be as close as I can bring you to the first moments of that experience. It was received by someone about to bury their son. Mary Dorothea Cokayne, wife of the genealogist George Edward Cokayne in 1894, would have received it about three days after her son, Morton Willoughby, passed away. Morton, an assistant curate at All Saint's Church in Carshalton, was twenty-eight years old. The letter implies that Mary was about to bury him alive.

Why would someone send a note like this to a grieving mother? Her husband George (author of the eight-volume *Complete Peerage*) kept a diary, but he gives us no clues about his wife's reaction to it. As was usual for the time, his journal is more of an outline of the day, and we are given but little sense of Cokayne's emotional state around the time of the illness and death of his son. In the months before his death, Morton visited his parents, regularly staying over to help out with gardening tasks.[2]

Morton was struck down by illness on 28 October 1894, while George was working on the 'R' section of his *Peerage*. Morton had been at Carshalton, but made his way to his parents' residence, Exeter House, in Roehampton, where a doctor diagnosed typhoid fever.

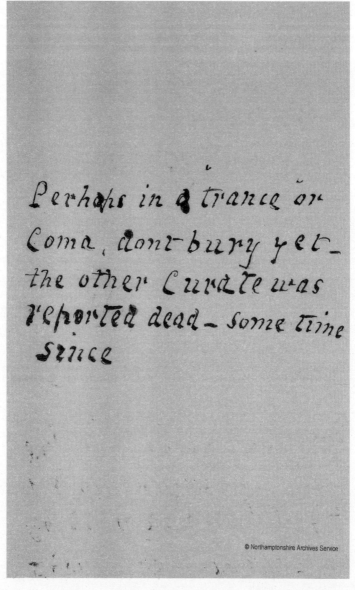

Figure 1. Anonymous letter to Mary Cokayne, Exeter House, Roehampton, postmarked Sutton 10 November 1894, Northamptonshire Archives Service, C 637

Within two weeks Morton was dead. Funeral arrangements were made. Morton's coffin would need to be screwed down to contain the spread of illness. The funeral took place in Morton's church at Carshalton, and then the cortege moved to Putney cemetery. George transcribed a copy of Morton's medical certificate into his diary, which stated that his son had died from exhaustion induced by typhoid fever.[3]

Once the moral shock of the letter has been registered, perhaps the next question is not 'Who wrote it?' but instead 'What other curate?' Finding that answer is complicated by the split locations: was it a curate in Carshalton, or in Roehampton? However, it is possible that the note was written by someone with a long memory, recalling and alluding to a dark moment in the Cokaynes' family life. George's nephew, the Reverend George Hill Adams, absconded in 1877 while on bail for a serious sexual assault involving three very young girls in Cheltenham. One account described Hill Adams as 'a Ritualistic clergyman'; part of the second generation of the High Church revival of the nineteenth century seeking to reintroduce a range of Roman Catholic liturgical practice into the Anglican Church.[4] Many rumours circulated about him afterwards: was he in Spain? Was he in France? Was he in a foreign mental asylum? Was he dead?[5] The truth was unclear, which is perhaps what the anonymous author is alluding to. Then there are even more fundamental questions about the document itself. Why did Mary Dorothea Cokayne retain it? It must have brought her sadness. Was it kept as evidence, in case future letters arrived? The vast majority of such messages, throughout time, were destroyed or hidden. The reason why certain letters appear in the historical record at all is often an important one.

★★

This book is about letters sent anonymously (i.e. unsigned, or signed with initials, a symbol or a pseudonym) with the aim, or apparent aim, of unsettling the person they were sent to. In his *Anonymous Letters* (1933) Robert Saudek, an influential, Czech-born graphologist, categorized anonymous letters as: those signed with an initial only; letters signed pseudonymously as 'A citizen', or 'An old friend'; letters signed with symbols such as X or a dagger; letters signed with the 'name of an acquaintance of the addressee, to set the two at variance'.[6] This includes a range of letter types, including: obscene or threatening letters; and letters accusing a person, or people, of doing something, sent to someone else, who might use the information to make life harder for the person(s) mentioned. Many letters defy simplistic categorization, including saucy letters which were considered obscene by the person who intercepted them, but were not considered so by the intended recipient. *Anonymous Letters* also discusses anonymous tip-offs and libellous correspondence. This sometimes includes the decoy letter— penned or typed by someone who then sent it to themselves.

Anonymity and pseudonymity in publishing are very well-researched fields. By contrast, anonymous letter writers have received little attention.[7] This is surprising given the way such campaigns appear, from our current perspective at least, to prefigure some of the most concerning tendencies of the Internet age. Putting a more positive spin on anonymous letters for *London Society* in 1886, Frederick Arnold found much to praise in anonymous letter-writing, and that some letters had 'a very agreeable character'. He suggested that the 'principle of anonymity is one which has taken deep root in the shy, reserved, island-like British character'. Arnold draws attention to notes which accompanied anonymous donations to charity, and notes sent between lovers which made people's lives happier and more interesting.[8] The intentions behind sending letters anonymously could be positive or negative. The focus here is generally on the latter, but Arnold's point should never be entirely forgotten.

There is a compelling argument to count malicious, anonymous letters quite separately from other correspondence. The interaction contained in them is very different. Replies to anonymous letters are usually impossible because of the lack of return address. The historian Leon Jackson has contrasted blackmail and threatening letters with the usual 'polite' forms of correspondence. He observes that they are hard to interpret, because 'they do not fit readily into the recent and influential historiography of epistolary practice.' By not following the same conventions, they did not 'invite epistolary reciprocity, or create social bonds'.[9] One way of categorizing them is as forms of impolite behaviour, giving them more things in common with riot, assault, spoken intimidation, stalking, and verbal haranguing than with other letters. Despite being a one-way form of communication, anonymous letters *were* often written in the hope of getting a response, either in observable behaviour or in a newspaper advertisement. Occasionally, a perpetrator might even entertain semi-realistic hopes of a physical encounter, although (as we will see) on such occasions the police would often be waiting. Although they are often written in the hope of getting a reaction, such messages are not generally written in expectation of a reply. In this they often seem closer to graffiti than to letters. The closest they come to 'polite' forms is when they overlap with unsolicited and unreciprocated love letters. The key difference appears—again—in the lack of specified sender, since unwanted love letters can be unsettling enough.

Back in the late 1980s I anonymously sent a single Rolo (a truncated cone-shaped, chocolate-coated toffee) through the post to a boy I liked. It was my last Rolo: a gesture of my fondness for him. A successful advertising campaign for Rolos had pushed this idea—'do you love anyone enough to give them your last Rolo?' We were good friends. In the following days he spoke of many things, but never of receiving this small confectionery gift. This left me hungry for a reaction. Did he get the Rolo? If it had arrived, did he have any suspicions as to the sender? Switch the Rolo for something else and the nature of the situation can shift suddenly or subtly. But the sender in most cases would still hunger for a reaction, an observable response. The anonymous letter is actually an inefficient means of eliciting a reaction, especially if sent to people beyond the immediate neighbourhood or social circle. This is, perhaps, why many senders of anonymous letters have targeted their neighbours, because they might be in a position to observe, or overhear, to fetch out some response. In retrospect, receiving a crushed or melted Rolo anonymously in the post could have been more frightening than charming. Cruel letters circulating in small communities such as villages could create paranoia and suspicion—damaging the social fabric very quickly. For this reason, many people never talked about such incidents.[10] The rector of a small village in Essex took to the pulpit in 1962 in an attempt to ferret out the person who had sent letters to several members of the community over a two-year period. He told the *Guardian* that nerves were fraying in the village, and that 'minds are broken, one actually having to go into a mental hospital because of these letters'. After he spoke in church about the matter, two more villagers came forward as victims.[11]

Receipt of an anonymous letter (and possibly also, anonymous chocolate) has always been more common than people suppose. Exact figures are elusive, however, because people respond in different ways to receiving these missives. It is worth emphasizing again that many people who received anonymous letters destroyed them. Many recipients would not have wanted to be connected to the letters, either because they *did* expose a secret, or because they feared that revealing the content might make people think them guilty of things they had not done; hiding the letters could prevent shame or embarrassment. Shame—most of it hidden—may be the real subject of this book, but as far as the record goes it is practically indistinguishable from prudence. In 1928 the criminologist Harry Ashton-Wolfe declared all anonymous letters to be 'cowardly, treacherous, vile things' which 'should be burned'.[12] Citizens were advised to single out any item of mail without a signature, and to 'consign the communication to the fire unread'.[13] The destruction of a majority of the letters renders the full extent of malicious letter-writing unknowable.[14] It also means that the source material is relatively scarce and difficult to locate. This is probably why they have been little studied by historians, despite important exceptions such as an essay, 'The Crime of Anonymity', by E. P. Thompson in *Albion's Fatal Tree* (1975).[15] They are often quite poorly catalogued; there are many hidden cases out there. The words from many letters survive today only because they were included in newspaper accounts (often with foul words and names redacted); actual documentation is scarce.

The wartime diarist Nella Last received an anonymous, 'pathologically venomous' and 'wildly malignant' letter in May 1940. She found the experience 'upsetting and unpleasant'. Pragmatic Nella 'decided to burn it and say nothing to anyone' (besides writing about it in her diary), explaining that it would 'upset my husband to no purpose if I had told him'. Nella justified her actions to herself by remembering what her grandma used to say—'nothing could hurt unless we let it'—although she did vow to take any subsequent letters (if they arrived) to the police.[16] Other people also followed Nella's path. The recipients of letters sent by a mother and daughter to neighbours in Morpeth in 1944 burned them (at least at first), and this was a common response. The matter was only taken to the police when more letters arrived. In recent discussions surrounding the abuse of anonymity in cyberspace, some commentators have advised a similar response— offensive tweeters, they say, should be blocked, but not necessarily reported. This is, of course, a controversial and important topic in contemporary public discourse.

As I have mentioned this project to my acquaintances, four have voluntarily told me they have received anonymous mail through the post. Only one kept a copy (not the original). One was sent to a university lecturer by a disgruntled student; one was sent to newcomers to a small Yorkshire village; one—a postcard—was dispatched following a house sale; the last was received by the owners of a cat:

Regardless of whether or not we had cat allergies, we should be able to leave a window open without then having to scrub and repaint walls, or change all the bedlinen, and vacuum/mop the house. We do not have time or money to take on this extra work which has come with your cat entering our house.

In each case the person who received a letter was upset, shaken, and confused. The effect was lessened where the writer's identity could be ascertained. The effect of malicious anonymous letters varies greatly, of course, depending partly on the resilience of the recipient of the letters at the time they were received, but also on an infinity of circumstantial factors. Charles Babbage, the nineteenth-century polymath, was himself the receiver of anonymous threatening letters, at a period of time when he was already hypersensitized to external threats, in the form of street noises which hindered his study. His reaction to these noises made him the target of abuse, and he 'received constantly anonymous letters, advising, and even threatening me with all sorts of evils', including arson and assault.[17]

Some people were deeply affected and frightened by poison-pen letters, but others (like Nella Last) thought that a letter was impotent unless the receiver dwelt on the contents. Some letters were dismissed as lunatic rantings. Letters that alluded to deep secrets had the potential to terrorize their recipients and could cause mental breakdown and suicide. In 1938 a woman in Streatham Vale, London, miscarried shortly after receiving a letter which included this passage:

... You are lowering the value of our property by hanging out washing on the Sabbath. Unless you cease we, the neighbours, will inform the borough council or your landlord, and you would not like him to know.[18]

In close-knit communities, such messages had power. Nella Last described her feelings on receiving the poison-pen letter and detailed some of the contents in her diary. On opening it, Nella felt her heart as it 'nearly stopped beating', she felt fearful and unwell. The letter alluded to her son's cowardice for not enlisting in the army, and for taking a safe job instead. The writer insinuated that she and her son were mad. Most people receiving letters like these will work through memories and try to think who would bear them enough of a grudge to write in this way. Regaining her composure after the initial shock, Nella reread the letter—and concluded it was from a woman (because it was 'calculated to wound'). Nella noted that it was printed to disguise the handwriting, and that some of the details suggested only historic knowledge of the pair, as some of their circumstances had changed. This helped her to settle on a person who knew them 'between two and four years ago', and she surmised that it must be from one of Arthur's former girlfriends—'a fascinating little thing with soft boneless hands with which she pawed everyone in reach—particularly male things!' That relationship had foundered after Nella had gently intervened. With typical magnanimity (even empathy), Nella Last reasoned that the writer 'must feel better to get that filth out of their system!'[19]

The line between self-expression and criminal malice is not always easy to draw: it is a complicated field in moral and political philosophy. In *On Liberty* (1859), printed in the same year that Post Office pillar-boxes became standard nationally, the philosopher J. S. Mill established a 'harm principle' as a way of setting a boundary to individual liberty; we can do what we want as long as 'what we do does not harm'.[20] One might think that hate mail came to be treated in terms of harm, but for the period in Britain under discussion this was largely not the case; it was very rare for such letters to be considered under tort law, for instance. Of course, it was not (and is not) an offence per se to send an anonymous letter: anonymity itself is not illegal. The law instead judged other, no less complicated aspects of such communication—such as whether it was 'indecent', 'obscene', 'threatening', 'extorting', or 'libellous'. The laws used to deal with letters also varied according to how they were delivered. Letters, variously known as 'hate mail' or 'poison-pen letters', might be left on street furniture, slid under milk bottles, into hedges, or put straight through a letter box. If sent through the Royal Mail, an exposed sender could be tried under legislation empowering the Post Office to interdict socially harmful communications. Until the passing of the Communications Act (1988), poison-pen letters could become the focus of a criminal libel case in a civil court, but some slipped through the net, and in that Act provision was made for 'the punishment of persons who send or deliver letters or other articles for the purpose of causing distress or anxiety'. Henceforth the sending of a threat; a grossly offensive message; false information; or an article which was 'indecent or grossly offensive', was easier to prosecute.[21] What is very clear from the record is that anonymous letters slip into grey areas of the law; the law had categories of obscenity, defamation, and blasphemy, but the anonymous authors of some letters committed none of these. Yet their words still caused harm by upsetting or unsettling the people who received them, and despite the different charges brought in court this idea often seems at some level to have impelled the prosecution of such writers. If threats to kill, damage property, or make demands with menaces are made by letter, a person might take them to the police or to their employer (if received at work). Letters with no specific threat were unlikely to have been shown to the police.

★★

The academic investigation of these letters involves a certain degree of nosiness; more than one case caused me ethical discomfort. Although the content of the worst letters is still shocking, those campaigns which disturbed me most often involved individuals suffering from severe social alienation, neglect, injustice, and disempowerment. The missives sent by Winifred Simner in Wimbledon in the 1930s (Chapter 8) were unexpectedly unsettling in this regard, as I was able to construct some of Simner's character from her campaign. Many of her targets had indeed been acting in ways which a person of Simner's background would have found shockingly corrupt. Simner probably felt powerless and that she had no other outlet for the bitterness of a woman thwarted all her life by men like those she wrote to and wrote about. It was Simner who ended up being the person in trouble—but in her mind she was upstanding and moral. I could not fully warm to Simner, especially on reading her will, but I did start to understand her perspective, and how she had created a fiction, a coherent moral universe in her mind, in which what she did appeared completely righteous. By contrast, I was not always able to understand why some men wrote obscene letters to much younger women, or why they wrote bitter and rancorous letters to erstwhile employers. In general, I concluded that such psychological excursions, while sometimes irresistible, were very rarely fruitful.

The aims of my research here were various and not every case or campaign has been treated in the same way. In some cases, I wanted to explore who might have written the letter and how this could be found out. In others, I wanted to establish the context for writing anonymously. Sometimes I was able to ascertain the emotional response to receiving a letter, but (again) it was much more difficult to come by certain knowledge of the emotional motivations for sending letters. Indeed, many authors may not have been entirely sure themselves what motivated them to write anonymously to a particular person at a particular time. Perhaps they felt compelled by circumstances, or triggered by crises, which are now partly or wholly lost to us. All the historian can do is recreate the context and suggest likely scenarios. Still more important is the wider reception of such letters when they were published, as often this casts light on the role of such communications in British society. The history of detection and forensics supplies a kind of subplot to the book.

Here is another letter:

Sur

I have re[a]d in the papers about the mulbery would and has I think you is a man with a tidy cheek i think we could due bisnes. but atween ourselves I don't think doctor Dod ever sor Shakespeare, so how cud Ee hav[e] yur hit imbut i say, i am a fancier off silk wurms an i av a tre[e] in my gardin – Nou coud yu and i work the horrible the wod w[oul]d be grene of corse but not greener than the flats he he.

If you like tu send a line you can tu

    Mulberynose Snooks Esq

    To be left til cal[le]d for.

This strange letter was sent on 20 September 1847 to Jacob Henry Burn. Burn lived at 8 Great Newport Street, off St Martin's Lane in London. He was an essayist, publisher, and numismatist.[22] I imagine he had more idea than I do about what 'Mulberynose Snooks' is proposing. That is often the case with anonymous letters; they work by tapping into our own private paranoias. There were several newspaper accounts of Shakespeare's mulberry tree, to which the author could be making reference.[23] One paper noted that

Shakespeare planted a mulberry tree with his own hands on his ground, at Stratford-upon-Avon; and Garrick, Macklin, and others, were entertained under this mulberry tree in 1742. Shakespeare's house was afterwards sold to a clergyman of the name of Gastrel . . . he pulled it down and sold the materials. He had previously cut down the mulberry tree for fuel; but a silversmith purchased the whole of it, which he manufactured into memorials of the Poet.[24]

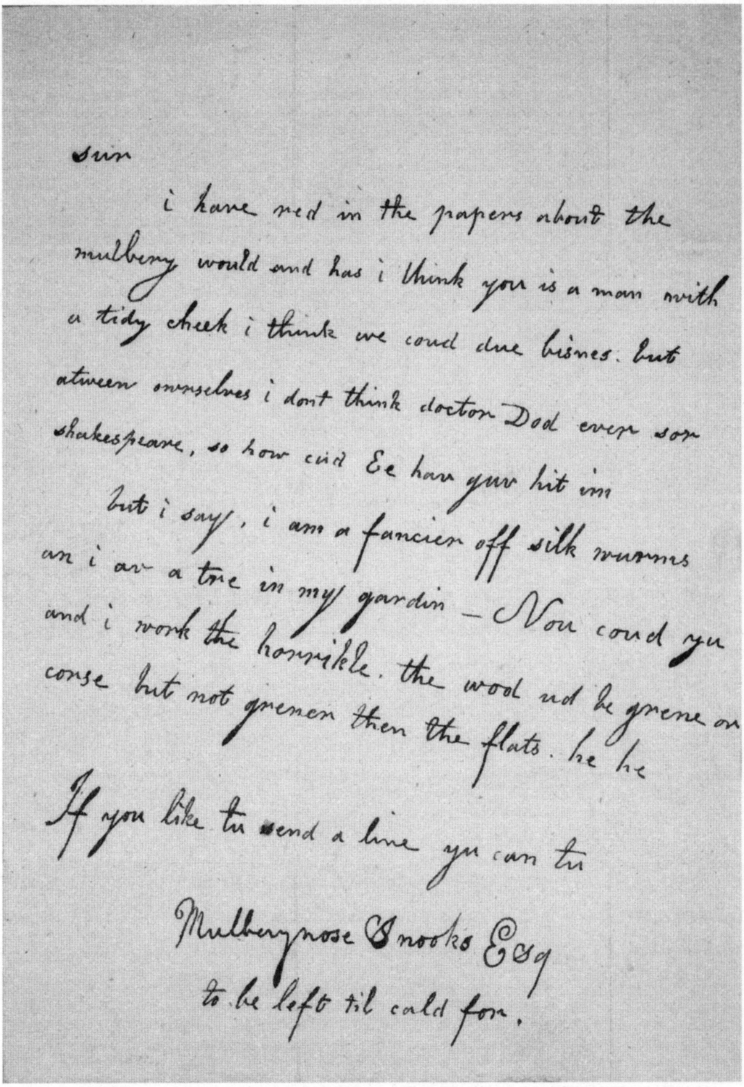

sun

i have red in the papers about the mulberry would and has i think you is a man with a tidy cheek i think we coud due bisnes. but atween ourselves i dont think docton Dod ever sor shakespeare, so how cud Ee have gur hit im

but i say, i am a fancier off silk wurms an i av a tree in my gardin – Now coud yu and i work the honnikle. the wood ud be grene on conse but not grener then the flats. he he

If you like tu send a line yu can tu

Mulburynose Snooks Esq
to be left til cald for.

Figure 2. Anonymous letter to Mr Burn 1847, Shakespeare Birthplace Trust ER21/4 recto

Figure 3. Anonymous letter to Mr Burn 1847, Shakespeare Birthplace Trust ER21/4 verso

Items from Shakespeare's house had been recently auctioned, and there was speculation about the vast number of articles, all apparently made from one tree.[25] The implication, perhaps, is that the mulberry tree items—secular relics—symbolized fraudulent or doubtful business. Perhaps 'Snooks' is implying that Burn had dirty hands.

Among the most exciting archival materials are those letters for which the envelopes or wrappers have been retained. We have this for the Mulberynose Snooks letter to Burn, because, as was common in 1847, the address was written on the reverse of the letter, which was then folded and sealed. This side (above) supplies various clues. The 62 in a dashed oval shape over the one penny red stamp shows that it went through a London postal district office, where it was stamped with a particular cancellation mark: this one South Tottenham. These marks were added to letters which had been posted at suburban sorting offices, and to letters from other districts on the same route which had not passed through the chief sorting office.[26] There is also a stamp in the shape of a compressed square with rounded corners, in red, at the top in the image, which provides the date. Victoria on the Penny Red stamp looks at Tottenham [Office?], stamped in red, to her left. Great is spelled 'Grate', possibly a deliberate error. Many anonymous letter writers tried to appear less intelligent than they actually were, a common technique of obfuscation.[27] Burn may have known the author personally.

Anonymous letters often leave things dangling, to imply the writer knows more about the recipient than they reveal. Some authors would have wanted to wait for a reaction to the first letter before deciding on a next move—hence the invitation to reply here, which is not uncommon in one form or another. The story about the mulberry tree could have been a trick to provoke Burn, by someone wanting to unsettle him for a reason unrelated to green mulberry wood. The date on which the letter was sent is interesting, as Burn gave evidence at the Old Bailey on 25 October 1847, in a case taken against Thomas Hellyer, for obtaining one sovereign from Mary Ann Sevenoaks, by false pretences. Giving evidence, Burn stated that he had met Hellyer on Fleet Street in early September, and allowed him to arrange orders for coal (in addition to his literary work, Burn was also a coal dealer). 'I told him he was not to collect any money on my account, I particularly told him I would collect it myself.' Hellyer arranged for Mr Sevenoaks to have coal, but procured payment himself, while telling Burn that he would still be paid by Mr Sevenoaks, in October. Fraud of this sort was a capital offence, punishable by transportation. Found guilty, Hellyer was transported for seven years.[28] The letter arrived with Burn between his meeting Hellyer and the Old Bailey trial. How might Burn have interpreted this? Could it have been seen as a proposal to work together in another fraud, like making relics from a mulberry tree? Would it have created an atmosphere of tension, which caused Burn to question how he might give evidence? Perhaps the author knew something that would be damaging if they disclosed it in court?

When malicious letters were taken to the police, their judgement was often that there was insufficient evidence to proceed with a case.[29] The seriousness with which letters are treated by their recipients or by the police depends on the context and the content of the letters. It took the police quite a while to get a handle on anonymous writing. There were several infamous false accusations and miscarriages of justice in the early twentieth century—especially in cases involving women. By 1940 there were signs of some improvement, and even a softening of approach. Reginald Morrish, an ex-chief inspector at the Metropolitan Police, wrote a guide to crime detection on his retirement. In this, he described anonymous letters as a 'scourge', and felt that they were 'cowardly, and very frequently the result of a disordered mind, of inhibition or repression; and the writers of such missives need treatment rather than punishment'.[30] The police themselves have, historically, received many anonymous 'tip-offs'. As Frederick Arnold noted in 1886, two years before the Metropolitan Police started to be engulfed by Jack the Ripper missives, much valuable information comes to the police through anonymous sources.[31] Even further back, Lord Monteagle received a letter sent on 26 October 1605, warning him to avoid being in attendance in Parliament, which was set to 'receive a terrible blow'.[32]

Hundreds of hoax letters were written in the aftermath of the Ripper murders in the East End of London in 1888, and they continued to arrive until 1896. Many documents relating to this serial killer went missing from the police archives for many years, but were returned, anonymously, in 1987. These included the infamous first 'Dear Boss' letter from 25 September 1888, while the atrocities were continuing. Written in red ink and signed, 'Jack the Ripper', it was sent to the Central News Agency, a London-based news distribution service. Like many of the anonymous letters which followed, the letter was purported to have been written by the killer himself. This letter was followed up with a postcard signed 'George of the high Rip Gang'. The Metropolitan Police issued facsimiles of these two pieces of correspondence on posters asking for more information, resulting in a welter of anonymous letters. The Ripper letters include bloodstains, fake and real; some are written in red, as though inscribed in blood, others have sketches—some simple, some very elaborate, of knives, skulls and crossed bones, poison bottles, guns, people (including a man in a uniform and a Pearly King, as well as crude stick characters wielding weapons). Some included press cuttings, either as separate words to make up sentences, or written over clippings.[33] These are of dubious authenticity, and in fact a key theme in the history of messages to the police following more serious crimes is the red herring. A fake tip-off sent concerning the death of a student from Sidney Sussex College in Cambridge in 1931, falsely 'admitted' to involvement in the mysterious death. Other letters were also sent, all of which the police dismissed.[34] While some material sent anonymously helped the police to solve crimes by providing vital information, chasing leads in anonymous communications often hampered investigations as the police were sent on wild goose chases.[35] Police investigating the 'Yorkshire Ripper' case in the 1970s–1980s were 'hampered severely' by tape recordings by 'Wearside Jack', claiming to be the perpetrator of the crimes.[36] On the other hand, they were also hampered in that case by their own enthralment to the voice—rather than by any especially clever subterfuge.

At other times the police have been more attentive. In 1944 the Birmingham City Police received this note, written on a torn-up envelope front inserted into a similar envelope. It bears a Kidderminster postmark with the time and date of 1.15 p.m., 11 April 1944:

> Hagley Murder
> what woman was
> signalman Edginton
> with up the Hagley
> road one Sunday night
> near midnight.
> came through
> Blakedown. 5 oclock
> next morning. going
> up the Birmingham
> road Kidderminster.
> where he then lived
> very fishy[37]

The 'Hagley Murder' was a national sensation; in 1943 the skeletal remains of a woman had been found in a wych elm in Hagley Wood in Worcestershire. The body was thought to have been placed there around 1941, and in 1944 graffiti started to appear locally, asking 'Who put Bella down the Wych Elm?'[38] 'Signalman Edginton', referred to in the note, was Arthur W. Edgington. In his late fifties, Edgington was employed by the Great Western Railway and lived in Blakedown, near Kidderminster (and less than five miles from Hagley Wood). Richard Skerratt of Clent police station, one of the officers who attended the scene when the body was discovered, established that Edgington had been separated from his wife, Ada May, since 1942, and that Ada lived in Worcester. He also ascertained that Ada was 'a woman of peculiar mentality for she has frequently written to her husband and the people with whom he has been lodging, accusing him of all kinds of silly things'.[39] The file recording this information included a couple of

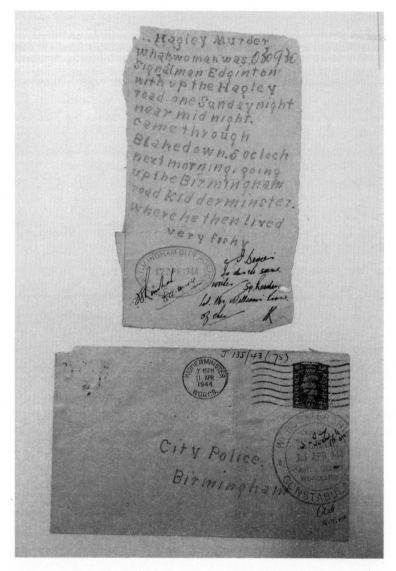

Figure 4. Hagley murder anonymous letter, Worcestershire Archives, 010:18 BA 14908/3/1/1-2, with permission from West Mercia Police

these notes, and a postcard addressed to Arthur's landlady in Blakedown, written in pencil in 1943. Although the postcard was written in capital letters, the similarity of the hand to the later note is very striking. In the postcard, Ada implied that Arthur was a criminal, 'AS HE DONE ANY PINCHING LATELY', she asks, before making a further accusation: 'WE KNOW IT WAS THROUGH YOU HE BROKE HIS HOME UP. NO <u>DIRTY</u> WOMEN THERE WOULD BE NO BAD MAN (LIKE YOU)'. Another letter, sent to Arthur himself, implied more wrongdoing, and included the line, 'you deserve being shown up': 'very fishy', indeed.[40] The case remains unsolved to this day, but Edgington was never considered to be a credible suspect.

My study focuses on letters sent between 1760 and 1939. Study of anonymous communications after 1940 is increasingly complicated by burgeoning methods of dispatch: the telegram, the telephone, and, much later, the Internet. Additionally, there was such an efflorescence of anonymous letter-writing from the late 1930s that the subject in those years probably warrants a separate study. In the early to mid-twentieth century there seemed to be a 'plague' or 'epidemic' of these letters. During the peak, in 1946, the vicar of Holy Trinity, Malvern, in Worcestershire, remarked glibly that 'almost everyone receives an anonymous letter from time to time'. The vicar had himself received 'a fairly large number'.[41] This uptick could have been triggered by a reaction to popular works of fiction and dramas. Agatha Christie's *The Moving Finger*, published in the UK just around the time Ada May was libelling her estranged husband in 1943, may have been one of these. Interestingly, the letters at the heart of the novel's plot also turn out to be red herrings. Although such fictional works undoubtedly concentrated public attention on poison-pen writers, I will argue that such letters were already much more common than one might think. As the century progressed, there was of course a shift away from the hand-written; letters were increasingly typed. A parliamentary report of 1985 noted a lack of statistical evidence as to the incidence of poison-pen letters, but it did suggest that receipt of them was 'by no means a rare event'.[42]

There is a more pressing consideration in choosing to halt the study around the 1930s. This is a subject that involves secrets, slanders, and intrusions upon intimate space. Many anonymous letters attack reputation. Around the letters themselves one often finds all kinds of speculation as to identities and motives. The work of researching such cases is often haphazard, and in the course of trying to explain significance it is next to impossible to avoid conjecture and insinuation. There is a good chance that some cases after 1940 involve individuals with living relatives; in a few cases some of the authors and recipients may still be alive themselves. It is both prudent and sensitive to address earlier cases before and after the Victorian postal reforms rather than more recent affairs which contain more potential to aggravate harm.

I

Gossip
Major Eliot's maiden sisters

Sir, A Gentleman on Blackheath is just returned from Brighton where he heard a Certain Lady spread a report that your sisters two maiden Ladies were kept out of Charity by General Mann and that your Family endeavours to marry into Familys to live and spunge on them.

As things go, this letter may seem mild: it is neither obscene nor obviously libellous. Appearances can be deceptive, for the letter would very likely have hurt Major Eliot, to whom it was sent in May 1829. It purportedly warns Eliot about gossip circulating in fashionable Brighton circles: his sisters are reported as freeloading from the father of his first wife, who had died seventeen years before the letter was sent. It tells him that his 'Family' at large were known parasites, and did not live honestly. By passing on the gossip, the letter reinforces and amplifies it; possibly it is created out of thin air. The letter poses a deeply uncomfortable question to Eliot: what can he do about this? In this it targets anxieties about reputation, which once lost was regained only with great difficulty. In one way or another, most malicious anonymous letters concern themselves with reputation. Reputation is diffuse and remains a very abstract notion, especially from this distance where we don't have detailed knowledge of the community or communities in which it operated.[1] To grasp why the contents of this letter might hurt its recipient, to investigate why they would care about the letter at all, means investigating who they were and who they knew.

Major Eliot was William Granville Eliot, formerly a Lieutenant Colonel in the Royal Regiment of Artillery. He had seen action while

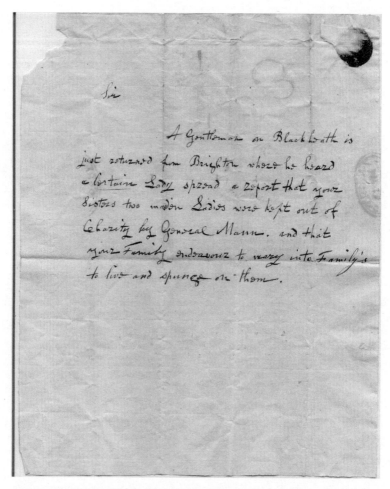

Figure 5. Major Eliot letter 1829 recto, author's own item

in command of two 'rocket troops': forces armed with what was known as the Congreve rocket. Eliot's first wife was Harriet Ann, the daughter of the 'General Mann' mentioned in the letter. General Gother Mann was a military engineer, who by 1829 was eighty-two years old. Eliot was now married to Anne, daughter of a lawyer called Samuel Heywood, but he still kept up a close connection with his first father-in-law General Mann. Around fifty years old, Eliot had retired from service owing to ill health the previous year.[2] The letter refers to

Figure 6. Major Eliot letter 1829 verso, author's own item

the behaviour of two of Eliot's sisters, both 'maiden ladies'. They were Elizabeth ['Eliza'] Mary and Ann Cathrina, both in their early forties.[3]

The 'certain lady' to whom the writer alludes was almost certainly Eliot's wife, Anne. In 1828, the year before the letter was written, Anne's father had died. When Anne and William married in 1813, her father drew up an agreement during the dowry negotiations stipulating that property that Anne would eventually inherit should not be controlled by her husband. Although it was not uncommon for the lineage and financial independence of wealthy heiresses to be protected in some way, this particular agreement may have been unusual.[4] It later provoked a drawn-out legal process which was only resolved seven years after this letter was sent: Anne was to have control and benefit of her own inheritance, and her interests would not revert to Major Eliot.[5] Lasting acrimony between the couple may be evident from his will. Anne died in Paris in 1857, two years after William, without his wife by his side, had perished in East Sussex. He made no mention of Anne in his will, and also slighted his youngest daughter, Isabella Frederica, who was the only surviving child from his second marriage—the will giving preference his two eldest daughters.[6] Anne lived in Brighton in 1830, and might feasibly have been there in 1829 also, at the time of the anonymous letter's writing.[7] It is therefore feasible that its author had overheard Anne gossiping about her sisters-in-law in Brighton, and picked up a pen either because they felt duty bound to inform Eliot so he could take measures to protect his reputation or because they wanted to rub Eliot's nose in his wife's gossip.

Anthropologists and evolutionary psychologists generally agree that gossip was important in the earliest human communities as a tool of social bonding required for the creation of larger groups.[8] Although the boundaries of gossip are hard to define, it can be called a kind of communication relating to a person who is absent. It helps maintain the status quo because it usually implies some sort of normal behaviour by describing deviancy.[9] One reason gossip is attractive is the way it 'allows one (implicitly) to compare oneself favourably with others'; 'it is the evaluative and comparative nature of gossip that allows it to be used as a vehicle for enhancing self-satisfaction'.[10] Sometimes it seems gossip is not only compulsory but compulsive. Can a letter such as the one above rightly be considered a form of gossip? If the writer possessed only limited access to a community in which they could enjoy gossip, it is feasible that contacting the target of the gossip anonymously was an outlet for a basic social need. On the other hand, such an action could be that of a person for whom the usual gossip was simply not enough. In any case, the letter to Major Eliot may at least have procured for its writer a sense of superiority. Perhaps that is enough of a motive.

This chapter examines some roles played by the anonymous letter in gossip, secrecy, scandal, and marriage in the late Georgian and early Victorian years. An obsession with privacy, secrecy, and revelation created a natural breeding ground for anonymous letters and their malicious abuses of information. Notions of honour had secrecy at their heart; zones of intimacy and trust could only be created and maintained by close control over private information.[11] As historian Deborah Cohen has written, 'protecting oneself and one's family from incursions' into privacy during the nineteenth century 'toppled the wall between private character and public conduct that the Georgians had sought to erect'.[12] Just as gossip more noisily stood at the boundary between private character and public conduct, anonymous letters flitted silently back and forth beneath and around it. These letters had the power to undermine carefully devised constructions of selves, and many letter-writers knew this, and tried to use it to their advantage or pleasure.

Friendly blackmail

The 'gossip' involved in the next letter is more obscure than the news sent to Major Eliot. It eventually turns out to be a subtle kind of extortion, but to understand it fully we must plunge into an aristocratic scandal with a plot (if not a telling) that reads like a Wilkie Collins novel. In 1815 the Countess of Coventry received a letter from 'a well wisher' who knew she was already 'acquainted with the gaiety of [her] husband'. The Countess—Peggy—was the daughter of Sir Abraham Pitches, a wealthy brandy merchant. She had married George William Coventry, then Viscount Deerhurst. Her husband later become the 7th Earl of Coventry. The anonymous writer alludes to the Earl's 'generous liberality', and declares that they should not like to see him 'imposed on'. They claim to have witnessed a recent scene of import to the Countess. They saw that 'that seafaring Gentleman (who I have often seem with his Lordship)' was with a mistress of the Earl 'an hour before' the Earl's arrival at the house in question: 'for I am sure he is as well with her as your own husband'. According to the letter-writer, this was not the first such occurrence.[13] The Countess interpreted the writer's insinuations as an indirect demand for money. On the back of the copied letter, she summarized its contents: 'L[et]t[e]r exact pecuniary sacrifices from his fondness & his folly'.

Hon[ourable] Madam
   Knowing you are acquainted with the gaiety of your husband, & I also knowing his generous [superscript 2] liberality [superscript 1] and ways— I lament to see him imposed on, as I did the other day when I witnessed that Seafaring Gentleman (who I have often seen with his Lordship) being with her an hour before his Lordship came—but this has not been the first time—I will

let your ladyship know more for I am sure he is as well with her as your own
[deleted] own husband. a well wisher

Directed to

April the 22nd   The Countess of Coventry
Piccadilly

The letter was sent to the Countess's London address, Coventry House
in Piccadilly. It is not the original. It is a copy made by the Countess
herself. Peggy's husband George, the Earl, had been blind since a hunt-
ing accident in 1780.[14] As a consequence, his wife acted as his secretary,
writing and signing letters on his behalf.[15] It is not possible to know
how the Countess reacted to the letter. Maybe she did not retain or
pass on the original at all but destroyed it immediately; there is a chance
that the extant document was a copy of the letter recreated from
memory alone, including its postal details. That could explain some
amendments to the text: 'my Lord' has been changed to 'my Lordship'
five lines down, and 'sure' and 'her' have been added in superscript to
the seventh line of the text. Still, Peggy would have had a prodigious
memory to be able to retain the level of detail here and it is more likely
the copy was made from the original. The postal details are interesting.
There is a large '2' near the bottom right-hand corner and the recreated

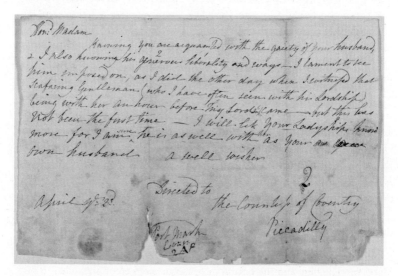

Figure 7. Copy of a letter sent to Peggy, Countess of Coventry, *c.*1815,
Worcestershire Archives 705:73 BA 14450/289/18(1) recto

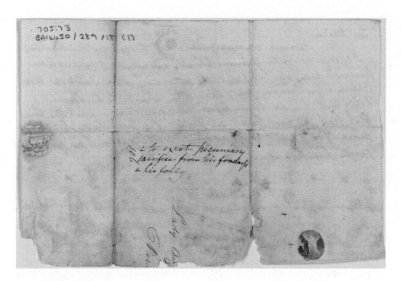

Figure 8. Copy of a letter sent to Peggy, Countess of Coventry, *c*.1815, Worcestershire Archives 705:73 BA 14450/289/18(1) verso

'Post Mark'. Inclusion of the postmarkings in this copy suggest that the Countess was preserving details which might prove useful later. As was her habit, the frugal Countess reused a wrapper for a letter sent to her daughter, Augusta, who married Lieutenant General Sir Willoughby Cotton in 1806, quite a few years before this copy could have been made.[16]

For the Earl to be able to arrange and conduct the sexual affairs hinted at in the letters he would have needed help. Some of that assistance appears to have been supplied by Dr William Battine, a 'very learned but eccentric man'. Battine was a Fellow of the College of Doctors of Law; a Fellow of the Royal Society; Chancellor of the Diocese of Lincoln; the Advocate-General in the High Court of Admiralty; and other things.[17] Battine had been the lead barrister of the late Lord Ellenborough, who had promoted him to various sinecures.[18] Solicitors' bills from 1815 reveal that the 7th Earl was threatened with an indictment, along with Battine, for

a conspiracy to effect and effecting the seduction of Doctor Battine's servant Mary Ann Kitching and she having in consequence thereof pretended to be with child by my Lord Coventry and having threatened to filiate the same upon his lordship.

It is likely Mary Ann is the nameless woman in the letter.[19] This back-story strongly suggests that the letter from the 'well-wisher' concerns an incident from 1815: the birth of William George Kitching on 10 October 1815 in Marylebone, London. The register records the parents as Mary Ann Kitching and The Right Honourable George Earl of Coventry.[20] The anonymous letter throws William's actual paternity into some doubt, which is key to unlocking its meaning. Could the 'seafaring Gentleman' have been the father, and not the Earl? In unpicking the confusions of the case, it quickly becomes apparent that at its heart is a matter of family honour.

Coventry and Battine were accused of attempting to 'suborn the Girl to swear the child to Cornelius Walker, late groom to Doctor Batine'. When Mary Ann refused to do this, Coventry and Battine were charged with 'attempting to persuade Cornelius Walker to make an affidavit that he has had a criminal intercourse with Mary Ann Kitching and was the father of the child'. Items listed on the solicitor's bill suggest that Mary Ann's father, Joseph, a cordwainer, had made the accusations against Battine and Coventry. The two wealthy men were advised not to concede any payment; they were also told not to initiate their own proceedings against Joseph Kitching.[21] Yet Coventry paid up 'to preclude an indictment'. He paid £300 on 11 September, a month before William Kitching was born, in a seeming attempt to suppress the scandal. Joseph Kitching signed a release and quit claim, waiving all rights and promising not to bring any legal actions.[22] The agreement included quarterly payments to young William, who attended school in North Wykeham.[23]

Although there can be no certainty, there is strong circumstantial evidence that William Battine was behind the letter of 1815—written during the first heat of the scandal of the Earl's illegitimate son. Battine possessed significant leverage as a co-conspirator in the cover-up. Indeed, Dr Battine had full knowledge of the entire affair, in which it sounds as if he exploited and abused his servant Mary Ann. His financial dealings appear often to have left him desperate. Correspondence kept by the Coventry family suggest him to be unreliable, self-serving, and manipulative. Battine was not good with money; he seems to have got by in trading in favours, information, and influence. When in his prime as a lawyer, he was considered 'a most eloquent pleader'—but by the end of his life he had 'squandered the acquisitions made in his profession'.[24] By 1819 Battine's finances had collapsed. He was described as being 'lately discharged from the King's Bench Prison, under and by virtue of an Order of the Court for the Relief of Insolvent Debtors'.[25] In July 1822 he was again in a predicament and wrote to Lord Coventry—presumably in perfect knowledge that his letter would be read aloud to the Earl, possibly by Peggy. The letter he sent then perhaps ties into the anonymous and more direct attempt at blackmail in 1815.

Battine's story in the letter of 1822 overflows with convolutions and insinuations. He wrote as follows. A man by the name of Gilbert had visited him at his house on Quebec Street, off London's Oxford Road, and made some demands of him. For complicated reasons, on which Battine dwells unnecessarily, he was unable to pay. Gilbert had connected Battine to Lord Coventry. Battine pretends surprise at this, assuring Coventry that he had never taken any credit for this connection; Battine could 'solemnly declare that I cannot account for his knowing that I was acquainted with you or your family'. He then states that Gilbert was angry about something involving not only Battine but also the Earl. After this cut-short revelation, Battine digresses, ranting about the general crisis of the times, the state of Ireland, and the failures of the government and the nobility. He singles out the 'Enacters of the Act for the Relief of Insolvent Debtors' for criticism. Returning to himself, Battine mentions his own health; his frugal routines. He gives further false assurances as to his solvency, falsely claiming to be 'not indebted to any individual, not indeed for the loan of a single shilling'. He ends with a reprisal of the insinuation: 'I beg you, my Lord, to believe me That I never mentioned your name to Mr Gilbert or anyone.' What was the nature of this obsequious letter? It made an indirect request for money and allusions to a shared secret.[26]

The pattern seems to continue in 1826, as Battine works this connection for all he can. Writing to the Earl once more, Battine again makes reference to his straitened circumstances. He first expresses gratitude toward the Countess for some game, claiming that (in the name of frugality and his poor health) he had abstained from meat and wine for four years. The letter contains a passage concerning Battine's housekeeper, possibly Sophia Carr. Carr would be the executrix of Battine's will, in which she was described as being known to him since she was a little girl. In his letter, Battine alludes to her as an attendant of thirty years' service 'whom your ladyship knows'. As in the earlier letter, Battine's intent in this seemingly casual aside may have been to cause anxiety and remembrance in the Earl's mind. The housekeeper would remember the events of the 1810s, which sparked the Kitching affair. As in other Battine letters, he comes across here as self-indulgent and sly.[27] He makes room to gossip about his sisters—one 'an ancient virgin'—and claims to have outlived all his friends. Again, the subtext to the last complaint was that Battine expected 'friendship' from those whose secrets he kept; he clearly felt he was not receiving it. Later, Battine was back in King's Bench Prison for debt.[28] Obituaries following his death in September 1836 dwelt on his erstwhile good connections to King George IV when he was Prince of Wales. Battine's will grudgingly forgave his married sister, presumably another whom he entreated for assistance and money, and 'all others who have ignored me'.[29]

If Battine was the author of the 1815 anonymous letter, which may explain his expectation of further payment in later, more cordial correspondence, then who was the 'seafaring gentleman' it mentions? It may have been Peggy's nephew, Frederick Boyce—the son of her sister Jane. Frederick made the rank of Lieutenant in the Navy in 1810: he really was a seafaring gentleman. His uncle, the 7th Earl, made unsuccessful efforts to fast-track his promotion in the Navy; Frederick appears to have been very close to his aunt. 'Fred' wrote to his aunt Peggy on 23 March 1826—the year of one of Battine's letters—about the scandal and its legacy. He explained that he had hatched a plan to which all parties agreed but had been scuppered in his efforts to execute it. Fred worried that 'to the end of the Chapter poor Lord C's pocket is still to be picked until the family compel the removal of the concern from Quebec St [Battine's address]', which had 'now become more notorious than any house in London'. The whole matter gave Fred a day-long headache, and he promised to talk about it when he and his aunt next met.[30] The Countess replied to Fred, returning to him some bills which needed settling, and apologizing for being 'fool enough to give you any trouble upon the subject'. Peggy vowed in future to leave things up to those 'who have hitherto managed the unfortunate business'.[31]

Frederick was twenty-six years old when Mary Ann Kitching gave birth to William. So far we have been making sense of the 1815 letter kept by the Countess in terms of her husband's reputational liability in the scandal. If we return to this letter from the 'well wisher', however, the involvement of Fred might give an even more solid explanation for why Battine (if indeed it was he) could have expected his efforts at blackmail to work. For the letter implied a threat not only to the reputation of the Earl, but also to the reputation of the 'seafaring gentleman' involved in the scandal. If the seafaring gentleman was Peggy's own beloved nephew, with the world at his fingertips, the vulnerability of the Countess was much greater.

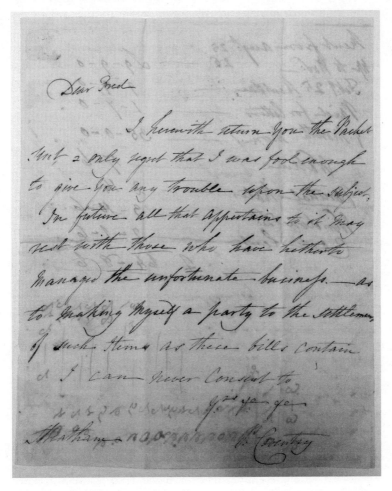

Figure 9. Letter from Peggy, Countess of Coventry, Worcestershire Archives 705:73 BA 14450/289/7 (1)

Why was the scandal of 1815 still raw in the 1820s? The quitclaim signed by Joseph Kitching in 1815 had become the source of continued dispute. A decade after it was drawn up, the Kitchings—perhaps cognizant of the Earl's failing health—sought to change the terms of the agreement. The Earl's attorney, Blackiston, wrote to Joseph Kitching, reminding him of the release and quitclaim signed in 1815, and explaining that it was deposited at the Coventry family seat of Croome, in Worcestershire. It was, wrote the family lawyer, 'impossible for his lordship (at present) to take a journey himself tither to procure it, and he should not chuse to depute any person to look over his private concerns'. This statement is odd, given that the blind Earl would necessarily have to delegate someone to the task in any case. Blackiston requested instead that Kitching send his counterpart of the disputed document 'to ascertain the particulars to which you allude' (i.e. the terms of any agreement, which were still in doubt).[32] Lawyers for the Coventry family concluded that the Kitchings were being manipulative, that a letter disputing the terms 'is evidently a threat for it seems that very little can be had for him [Kitching] by law', and so was relying on 'exposure and publicity' to exact money.[33]

The quarterly payments for the care of the boy continued, but the matter was still unresolved. Following Mary Ann Kitching's death around March 1826, her widower John Howard enters the scene. Mary Ann had been married to him for less than a year. After her death, Howard wrote to the Earl from Gainsborough (on black-edged notepaper). He informed him of Mary Ann's deathbed wish that Howard should care for her son, and requested that the quarterly payments be made to him.[34] The Coventry family argued that the arrangement set up when William was born 'was intended as a provision for Miss Kitching and to avoid legal proceedings which were then threatened', and that 'no reference whatsoever' had been made to 'arrangements which might after the birth of the Child be required'.[35] There was still uncertainty in the family about what to do. One of their solicitors, Thomas Lloyd, advised that although Howard's request was 'preposterous', it should be humoured a little 'to prevent abusive fabrications...in the Press which might distress the whole family'. He suggested that no further money be paid after 1826, 'as the family were aware of the gross imposition Lord C has suffered upon the occasion'. Lloyd also urged his clients to think about the 'poor lad' William, who was 'innocent of all misconduct': he ought to be allowed 'a few pounds until he was 21 years of age'.[36]

Further letters came from John Howard, who requested the quarterly payments in 1827. Howard stressed his care of William, that the boy was in good health, and that money was needed for his education. The Countess wrote a brusque note to Howard in February 1829, signing off as 'P.C.'. The Countess supposed that Howard was 'aware [that] Lord Coventry has not attended to any kind of business for the last two years' (her husband being very ill). In a ragged tone, the Countess once more reminded Howard that the last payment was intended to be final, but agreed 'for the last time' to pay. Howard replied, again addressing his correspondence to the Earl, and still pushing for more money, pointing out that William was too young to be 'put forward in any respectable way of life'. In August of 1829, Howard was informed that the half-yearly 'gratuitous donation' had been paid, and would not be paid again. In May 1830, when he was about fifteen years old, William Kitching wrote to the Countess directly, 'trusting you will pardon the liberty I have taken in addressing your ladyship'. He explains that she had given him 'reasons to hope that if ever I should be placed in the situation I now am I might look to you for protection'. William was aware that the Earl was suffering from a 'Malady', but his grandfather Joseph Kitching's trade had suffered owing to 'the pressure of the Times' and could not support them both. William and his grandfather had come to London with the hope of finding work. William wondered if the Countess might help with this, 'which would enable me to provide for myself; without which we must be under the painful necessity of applying to the Parish of Marylebone'. To save the young man from the workhouse, an account was set up with Coutts Bank. It was managed by a solicitor, George Capron, for the purpose of settling bills 'for a specific purpose'. So William was set up as an apprentice, apparently in Hull. On the back of one note connected with this arrangement, the Countess has written in pencil: 'Set a Watch O Lord before my mouth & keep the door of my lips'.[37]

The matter rippled into the next generation in another way too. Capron addressed his correspondence to Lord Deerhurst, the 7th Earl's son and heir. On a reused wrapper presumably used to contain these letters, in what looks to be the Countess's hand, is a note recording the bundle's contents: a letter from Capron, and 'inclosures from Kitchings as to never troubling the family in a pecuniary way after the arrangement now in completion'. A further note continued in the same vein: 'Terms to get rid of the incumbrance of Kitching—in the most honourable manner Mr Capron and Lord Deerhurst can suggest £200', dated

18 September 1830. In October 1830, Joseph Kitching wrote to Capron from Grimsby, stating that it was 'expressly understood both by myself and grandson & I do hereby pledge myself that we will in no other instance trouble the family of Lord Coventry in any pecuniary or other way'. Joseph promised that his grandson would also write to this effect, in the next post. William obliged, with a beautifully written letter reiterating his grandfather's statements. The letters were forwarded to Viscount Deerhurst. A rather hopeful note on the reverse of a letter from Capron to the 8th Earl concerning apprenticeship indentures records it being 'as to completion of Kitching's business'.[38]

In fact it was not the end of the 'Kitching business', and over the following years further monies were sought from the Coventry family, even after the Earl died in 1831.[39] But in July 1838 Henry Pytches Boyce, the Countess's nephew and Frederick's brother, informed George William, the 8th Earl of Coventry, that William Kitching—'my poor Brother'—had died in Calais after a long illness. William (or some would say the Coventry family) had left behind five children and 'a woman (not their mother)' in a state of destitution. 'My poor brother' is a figure of affection (Henry's father was long dead by the year of the affair involving Mary Ann Kitching). Henry notes that the Earl's 'friendly subscription is of course at an end'. Requesting some final money for funeral expenses, the letter concludes poignantly: 'Events here long separated me from my Brother but I can assure you that I feel acutely what has happened.' A postscript asks the 8th Earl to inform his mother, Peggy, of events. Henry felt the information might be better coming from her son in person, 'as it might plague her to receive a letter on such a subject'. The responsibility of travelling to Calais to make funeral arrangements fell to Frederick Boyce.[40] Why would Frederick rush off to Calais when William died? Perhaps he was not the Earl's illegitimate son after all—but Frederick's? This deeper secret would explain Battine's insinuation in the letter of 1815, Frederick's continued involvement in the case, and the Countess's lasting anxiety. Perhaps her blind husband mistakenly believed William to be his: remember Peggy's pencilled statement: 'Set a Watch O Lord before my mouth & keep the door of my lips': her husband could not see it; and she should not say it.

The case of the Coventry family over these two decades—1815 to 1835—reveals that some anonymous letters can be understood as variations on other kinds of overt and attributed communication.

If Dr William Battine was really the author of the anonymous letter discussed above, it can be understood as just one tool among several which he used over a longer period to apply pressure to the Coventry family. Rereading the 1815 letter, it only becomes intelligible as black-mail when put in this context: possibly Battine expected the Countess to surmise his identity but did not care, because that was indeed his aim. He was showing that he had knowledge of the kind of secret that would make the Coventrys vulnerable to blackmail—and showing them that he would stop short of it as long as they maintained their friendly relations with him. The letter has features of amicable coer-cion similar to those that one also finds in Dr Battine's *signed* letters to Peggy. It may have been through the gentle application of knowledge to maintain and exploit existing connection that Battine acquired the great social influence he enjoyed at that time before his debts overtook him. The 1815 letter is implicitly transactional in nature; it is not involved in upholding moral norms even though it disguises itself as that sort of gossip.[41] In a society such as this, where the appetite for scandal, sensation, and disclosure was matched only by fear of them, secrets had great currency. Anonymous letters were just one way in which people used and abused them. Anonymous letters played a part in the maintenance of advantageous and extortive connections with and within the English aristocracy. However, the nature of (vigorously defended) family secrets means that the stories behind some anonym-ous letters cannot be easily uncovered. As the sensitivity to moral impropriety increased over the course of the century, matched by increased use of the postal network, such situations may have become more common.[42] In 1830 a struggling upholsterer and cabinetmaker based in Bury St Edmunds approached the 7th Earl of Coventry to sell him a 'confidential letter case'. Apparently, the Marquis of Bristol and Baron Cougham had both put in orders for one.[43]

Disrupted engagements

A different anonymous letter blighted the next generation of the Coventry family; it was received by Viscount Deerhurst (who would later become the 8th Earl) in 1814. The letter warned George (named like his father) about the activities of his wife, Lady Mary Beauclerk. It claimed she had seduced his younger brother William, who was 17.[44]

When she was confronted with this accusation, Mary reminded her husband that he had often said anonymous letters 'deserved no attention' as they 'must be ashamed of their name who refuse to sign it'. She hoped that he would not be swayed by the judgement of others. Describing the intentions of the letter-writer, Mary wrote of the 'wicked designs of these hideous enemies who are so constantly working to overthrow the happiness' of others. Requesting that her husband 'not mention the unpleasant' accusations again, Mary stated that she did not want to be separated, or to have the 'contents of an anonymous letter' annoy George's 'mind or temper'. An enclosure in her hand states, 'Mary Deerhurst: I give my word of honour I will not mention your Brother's dishonour or my own to any Lady whatever.'[45] In a later letter Mary asks if his mind had been quieted 'concerning the vile anonymous letter' and repeats her innocence, contrasting the kindness of her husband with the maliciousness of the letter-writer.[46]

Matters of the heart and emotional feelings (both positive and negative) such as love and jealousy were commonly the focus of anonymous letters. Indeed, Valentine's Day messages were perhaps the most frequently sent anonymous communications, especially after the introduction of the Penny Post in 1835.[47] Simple spite could hijack the form of a Valentine's wish, or another love note, and ruin a young person's peace of mind. Martha Smith, aged eighteen, lived in Little Waltham in Essex and was described as a 'rosy cheeked village beauty'—she received an anonymous letter in 1830, with 'rhyming words, like valentine nonsense'. She burnt the letter but became increasingly withdrawn and 'presented a picture of melancholy'. Smith's suicide by drowning was reported in the *Stamford Mercury* and set against rising concern about the increasing circulation of similar letters.[48]

It can safely be assumed that anonymous letters alleging adultery within marriages were far more common than the record suggests.[49] Marriages were also vulnerable to disruption during the period of engagement. The public were acquainted with legal suits for breach of promise to marry both through a series of notable cases and for the representation of such procedures in fiction.[50] 'The maid reports that her mistress is apparently very much agitated by a letter that she has received this morning', one reads in Wilkie Collins's *Woman in White* (1859): 'There is some underhand villainy at work to frighten my sister about her approaching marriage.'[51] A key theme in fiction and in stories presented in newspaper reports is the way breach-of-promise cases were used to bolster ideals of female virtue in wider society and query the morals of particular women involved.[52] In the famous case *Smith v The Earl Ferrers* (1846), Mary Smith's action against Washington Sewallis Shirley—the 9th Earl Ferrers—hinged on a number of love letters she claimed she had received from him. But the Earl had also retained four anonymous letters sent to him during the alleged courtship, and these were produced by his barrister at the climactic moment of a widely publicized trial. Mary's own mother was compelled under hard questioning in open court to admit that they were written in her daughter's hand. In one, written in March 1844 when she claimed in her suit they were preparing the wedding celebrations, Mary confessed her deep love—she was aware it was 'unmaidenly thus to write; but you know not the writer'.[53]

The Earl claimed indeed that he had received another letter 'on the very day on which he was married' to another woman, but destroyed it—'not contemplating that, so soon after the event, he would be called upon to defend himself against an action of this description'. Resting his case, Sir Frederick Thesiger, the Attorney-General and counsel for the defence, discouraged the court from any further forensic examination of the handwriting: 'Look at the internal evidence to be extracted from these anonymous letters, and tell me whether you scarcely require distinct and direct proof of the handwriting.' The circumstances of the case were manifest enough, he claimed; all could see now plain as day that the suit was a scheme by Mary Smith, 'artful and ingenious as she has shewn herself to be'.[54] As the legal historian Saskia Lettmaier observes in her more detailed analysis of *Smith v The Earl Ferrers* and the popular interest it aroused, the narrative given to the court by Thesiger was 'about solving the puzzle of a woman's secret identity'.[55] As we will see in later chapters, this fascination with what anonymous letters might reveal about private female lives can be traced all the way into the next century.

The *Smith* case was somewhat unusual among breach-of-promise suits in that the gulf in social status between Smith and the Earl was very great (Mary was a farmer's daughter). A case that came before the Court of King's Bench in 1802 has similar features, but with the gender roles reversed. The defendant was Esther Mellish, twenty-three. Esther had broken off an engagement to Joseph Forster, a medical man.[56] The court was 'most uncommonly crowded with ladies, who were anxious to hear the trial, it being rather singular for a gentleman to bring his action against a lady for a breach of promise of marriage'. Mellish was a woman of fortune. Forster had recently purchased a business from an apothecary and surgeon in London. Mellish and Forster had met at the end of 1799, after which they enjoyed secret assignations whenever they could. Then, in August 1801 everything changed; Mellish received an anonymous letter. It urged her to hasten the marriage plans, calling on her to protect her reputation and desist from illicit meetings with Forster.

Dear Madam, from motives of friendship I am induced to inform you, that attempts are made to destroy your character. As your sincere friend, I would advise you to put an end to them as soon as possible. You have gone too far to retreat with honour. It is publickly known, that you have had meetings, during the night, at Mrs Gowland's,[57] in Bond-Street, and in Lincoln's Inn. This is the talk of the whole west end of the town. If it is in your power, instantly silence it, by marrying Mr. F. Putting off longer will only enable your brother to counteract your schemes, and to deprive you of all opportunity to retrieve your reputation. Hasten and have courage: this concludes a friend, who for the present conceals her name.

Mellish's brothers thought that Forster himself had written the letter—they suspected he was impatient to get his hands on her money. An indignant Esther shared their suspicions and broke off the engagement. Eventually, the couple became reacquainted, but Esther again called a halt to things. Evidently the trust between them was gone.

Forster, seeing all this as capricious and injurious, sued for damages of £10,000. The anonymous letter was important to his action and pivotal to Mellish's defence. The court aimed to determine whether Forster had indeed written it in an attempt to manipulate Mellish. Some witnesses swore it was not Forster's hand. Thomas Coleback, 'the Inspector of Franks at the Post Office', was called in to give expert testimony—it was considered that his occupation 'particularly enables him to detect forgeries and distinguish a disguised from an ordinary flowing hand-writing'. After 'looking minutely at this letter' Coleback had no doubt that Forster had written it and noted several letters 'which were exactly similar in shape'. Perhaps it is therefore surprising that the jury returned for the plaintiff anyway, awarding Forster £200 damages, for costs he had incurred getting ready for marriage.[58] The judge in the case had decided that the handwriting evidence could not safely be shown to a jury—to do so at that time would have been considered a novelty outside mainstream legal wisdom.[59]

In 1824, the Court of King's Bench was busy with another case involving a breach of promise to marry. Again, it hinged on the receipt of an anonymous letter. The plaintiff was Amelia Ann Wharton, twenty-six, the daughter of a former innkeeper in Bicester. She had been engaged to the defendant, William George Frederic Lewis, a lieutenant in the India service, son of a retired London hosier. Lewis had proposed to Wharton in June 1822, but later broke off the engagement, alleging impropriety. Letters sent between the erstwhile couple were read out in court, to the amusement of observers. In these Lewis was 'Willy' and Amelia 'Milly': 'Will Milly resign everything and follow her Willy [to India]?', he asks in one. Lewis courted Amelia with presents too: raspberry vinegar; a 'pot of cherry-paste for the teeth'; six lemons; 'some things for curling the hair'; pink ribbons; lozenges. He was a catch.[60] Lewis presented Wharton to his father as a wholesome girl—of a sort that would fit nicely into British colonial society in India. But before a meeting with her future father-in-law could take place, Old Mr Lewis received an anonymous letter. The letter, signed 'Your well wisher', began:

I think it my duty, as one who sometimes visits your house, to acquaint you with the character of Amelia Wharton. She was formerly a milliner at Oxford, in partnership with a lady who is now in keeping; and they become bankrupts, in consequence of their infamous conduct with the Oxonians. She came to town only to get a situation as bar-maid, not having sixpence; and her brothers, who are so much delighted with the match, can do nothing for her, one of them being a shopman, another a town traveller, and the brother with whom she is staying, a banker's clerk with three children.

Her family had implied that Amelia's time in Oxford had been under the chaperonage of a respectable older woman, not as a disreputable milliner. Wharton's brother was invited by the court to detail his sister's unrespectable past; he did confirm that—as the anonymous writer had claimed—there were indeed financial difficulties in the family such as make Amelia's affections suspect.[61] The Lewis family were spared a bad match; the bride-to-be was awarded £150 damages for their breach of promise.[62] Here an anonymous letter has abetted the court in clarifying and reinforcing social difference, with compensation if not happiness on both sides.

On a few occasions, the plaintiff sought compensation directly from the anonymous writer—moving the issue into the province of action for libel. In North Shields in 1822, one Jane Bell sought compensation for the 'loss of matrimonial engagement' between herself and a man called William Sissison, a currier from Hull, 'in consequence of an anonymous letter'. The case in fact centred on two letters which 'came by successive posts', but the second was not entered into evidence. The case is unusual firstly because Sissison was not the defendant; secondly, because of its tortuous repercussions. Thomas Hill, a Methodist minister, was accused of writing the anonymous letter. His main aim seems to have been to drive a wedge between Bell and Sissison. Jane Bell was born around 1784, and owned a glass and china shop with her brother John. John was a local Methodist preacher; Hill was the superintendent of Methodist churches in the Shields district (a presiding elder in a supervisory position). After he received the letter, Sissison showed John Bell the letter. Bell was able to compare the writing to other letters by Hill. The watermark and the way the letter was folded also pointed to the author's indeed being Hill. Crucially, Sissison did not initially believe in Hill's guilt. The role of his own gullibility in the affair would haunt him for many years. The first letter, dated 12 June 1821, asked that Sissison excuse its 'haste, brevity and obscurity'. It was indeed obscure, informing its recipient that if he married Jane Bell 'you had better end your days in prison'. It hinted at some improper relationship with a 'Dr O'—Dr William Oxley, a local physician and prominent member of the Methodist congregation—and invited Sissison to 'ask the Methodist preachers; ask any respectable person in North Shields for the truth of this letter'. Sissison claimed in court that it was the letter which made him reconsider his engagement, but it was only upon further inquiry that he ended it.[63]

The case was dismissed ('non-suited') on the grounds that it was not the letter itself which had led to the breaking of the engagement, but the investigation which came after it. The letters were deemed to caution the receiver, but not to libel Bell.[64] As the judge put it, 'I see no imputation on the chastity of the plaintiff in the letter.'[65] The effect of this outcome may have been to legitimize and amplify doubts about Jane Bell's virtue. The letters had been read in court in York and were picked up by newspapers; although Bell had almost two dozen character witnesses prepared, her counsel did not make use of them because the object was only to prove Hill's authorship.[66] In England, then as now, an action for libel was not restricted to false statements as it concerned harm not truth; and anyhow the legal matter here focused on the injury caused by the end of the engagement, not on libel per se.

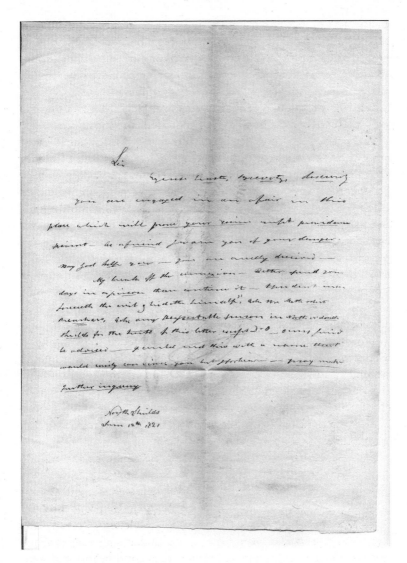

Figure 10. Anonymous letter [from Thomas Hill] re: Jane Bell, North Shields, 1821, author's own item

Bell 'retired, almost broken-hearted' in 1822, her good name presumably ruined. As had already been suggested by her advocate at the beginning of the trial, 'her prospects in life had been blasted'.[67] After the non-suit she stood in an even worse condition. Her health was bad, she was anxious, her mind 'considerably deranged at times'.[68]

Jane was yet to enjoy at least a measure of satisfaction, for Thomas Hill could not contain himself. He had written a self-satisfied letter to Sissison, who now noticed similarities in the handwriting when compared with the anonymous letters. Previously Sissison had withheld the original letters from the Bells' legal case because he believed them to be true. Now he passed them on to the Bells, writing sorrowfully in August 1822 that 'I have most unhappily been made the channel and instrument of irretrievable injuries.'[69] A fresh legal action was started against Hill. As well as helping with handwriting comparison, the text of the second letter was also very relevant because it established a more direct connection to the further enquiries which ended the engagement:

Dear Sir,

Is it you for whom this dreadful pit is dug in Shields—o Sir, for God's sake, make inquiry before you take such a desperate step. What[?] a methodist join himself to infamy and poverty. Ask the methodist preachers, whether you ought to take such as step – ask any body in North or South Shields, except Dr O.l.y—Fly. Fly from danger—bury yourself in a prison rather than take a—a—a—&a—for better for worse

Your sincere Friend

N Shields
June 12th 1821

<u>do make inquiry</u>

Just as in the first letter, Sissison was implicitly directed to seek further confirmation and advice from the Methodist clergy—or rather, from Hill. Sissison had naively followed this advice and written to Hill. Hill had responded with a signed letter in which he wrote:

She, her sister, and her brother are generally considered a dangerous and disreputable family, buried in debt, always squabbling, and deceiving, full of religion, and calumny . . .

Now there was a case to be heard, because the letters and what the first trial had ruled was separate information were in fact all part of the same conspiracy. Bell won this case and was awarded £300 in damages.[70]

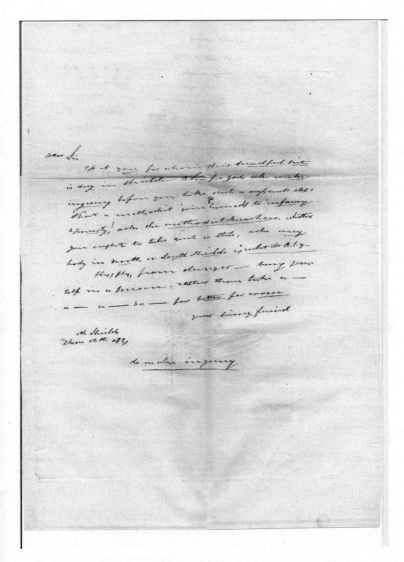

Figure 11. Anonymous letter [from Thomas Hill] re: Jane Bell, North Shields, a second letter from 12 June 1821 recto, author's own item

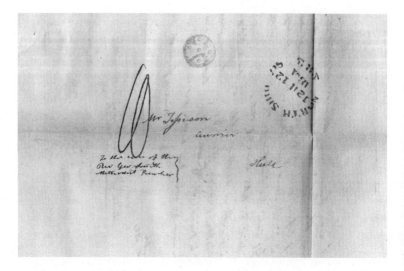

Figure 12. Anonymous letter [from Thomas Hill] re: Jane Bell, North Shields, 1821 verso of the second letter from 12 June, author's own item

Bell's reputation, however, was not yet restored—that would require the circulation and publication of her story, in order for the truth to be recognized in the circles she moved in. But Hill's religious position gave him opportunity to keep up a campaign of disinformation; he appealed to the Methodist Conference, who published a vindication of his innocence and an assertion of Jane Bell's vice in their annual minutes. Bell, in her turn, received help from friends, including Dr Oxley, to confront this injustice, and a pamphlet complete with detailed facsimiles of the letters, called *The Cause of Truth Defended*, was published in 1827. Its preface described Bell's grief, caused by 'fruitless applications, numerous long journeys, tedious days and sleepless nights, loss of relations and property, injured health and depressed spirits'. By that time her brother John, on whom she had become 'wholly dependent' as a result of the libel, was long dead; *Truth Defended* implies his death was the result of stress.[71]

The case caught the attention of the novelist Sir Walter Scott. He and Jane Bell met in February 1826. Scott wrote of her 'odd visit' and noted that her case against Hill had 'made some noise'. Finding Bell 'prepossessing', Scott gave a description: 'brunette, with regular and pleasing features, marked with melancholy'. It was a cause of consternation to Scott—and no doubt still more so to Bell—that the Methodist Church merely demoted Hill, degrading him from first- to second-class preacher. 'This calumniator was actually convicted of guilt morally worse than many men are hanged for', thought Scott. He decided against working the story up into a novel because he wanted to avoid any contest with the Methodists, who he thought 'do infinite good' despite being prone to hypocrisy and 'spiritual ambition'.[72] The case illustrates how difficult it was to restore a reputation once impugned—*The Cause of Truth Defended* painstakingly details the many complicated actions, over many years, required to spread news of Hill's culpability through the communities in which Jane Bell's reputation had meaning. Sissison's long letter in 1824 to the President of the Methodist Conference—another attempt, born of his own guilt, to make things right—aptly summarized how hard it was to counter 'fake news':

It is exceedingly painful to me to have to bring forward such shocking proof of the depravity and falsehood of a person, holding the highest office with which a mortal can be invested, viz. as a messenger of reconciliation from an offended Deity to a guilty world. But how must it enhance the poignancy of shame and sorrow, not merely in my mind, but in every breast where there is a spark of feeling for the honour of true religion, when the whole country shall ring with the hateful and degrading subject from one end to the other?[73]

Hill's motive is unclear, but a small detail given by a witness in the court report of the first case raises the possibility that his chief target was not Jane Bell at all, but Dr Oxley: Dr Oxley had not been attending the meetings of the Methodist leaders in a manner befitting the rules.[74]

One account of the Jane Bell story, published in 1827, was called *The Cause of Truth Defended*, but the truth is often inconvenient, and there were other accounts published at the time. Walter Scott, a man with more cultural capital than Bell (an obscure woman), was intrigued by the story, but himself drew back from making it more famous, on account of the potential for damaged relations with the Methodists if the truth came out. Throughout the entire period covered by this book, people read newspaper reports as truth, but the vast majority of those reports were anonymous. What were people supposed to believe?

2

Tip-offs
Undermined coalmasters in Staffordshire

Master Heberard
> You look after those "Butchers and Softly Jack" at Moor-Lane – they be very near Master Honeyborns Garden if not under—You must not give them any notice before sending any one down their Pit—If you do they will stop up their Roads and cheat You

Veritas[1]

This letter was sent by post in 1849 to a Stourbridge lawyer, Henry 'Harry' Eberhardt, manager of the Moor Lane glassworks, owned by William Stevens and Samuel Williams in Brierley Hill, Staffordshire. 'Veritas' ('Truth') probably signed off with a pseudonym because he or she did not want to be identified as a snitch, but another important possibility is that they were themselves invested economically in the matter or bore a grudge from earlier business. No doubt it took Eberhardt far less time than it took me to identify the 'Butchers' and 'Softly Jack'. As I will show, the inclusion of these names is only one of the ways in which the letter deeply embeds itself in local concerns. The letter is a warning that certain parties had extended their coal works beneath the glassworks; and that the same parties would prevent this being discovered by blocking up parts of the mine (its 'Roads') to make the possibly illegal parts of it inaccessible to survey.

This chapter details how anonymous letters in the nineteenth-century Black Country interacted with emerging cultures of expertise, trust,

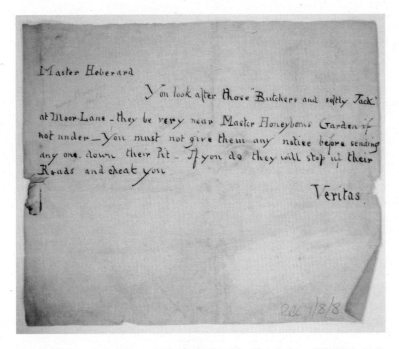

Master Heberard

You look after those "Butchers and softly Jack" at Moor Lane – they be very near Master Honeybons Garden if not under – You must not give them any notice before sending any one down their Pit – If you do they will stop up their Roads and cheat you

Veritas

Figure 13. Letter to 'Master Heberard', 1849, Dudley Archives DRBC/7/8/8, with permission from Mr David Williams-Thomas

and class or socio-economic status in an area of Britain that was undergoing rapid change. As we shall see, part of the potency or potential potency of anonymous letters such as the one from 'Veritas' arose from the fact that landowners were losing touch with what was going on underground. In the eighteenth century, aristocratic landowners tended to oversee directly the exploitation of resources on their property. By the early nineteenth century, there was a growing tendency across the country for landowners to give over control of coal extraction to lessees. Rapid developments in infrastructure and coal-extraction technologies empowered some of those with mining experience and mining knowledge, those with the 'knacks' of the trade. This was because such developments made the acquisition of deeper coal both feasible and desirable. Excavating deeper coal required landowners without close knowledge of the business to place trust in men with the experience and expertise to undertake such work. In the nineteenth century, the stock of capable mine superintendents, agents, and surveyors rose significantly.[2]

Letters like the one to Eberhardt were concerned with the more attenuated relations of trust that had developed in the course of the previous decades. Entrepreneurs operating within this space formed agreements and partnerships that would have seemed unlikely in the pre-industrial era when social stratification was more rigid. Many of these partnerships and businesses required skill in both mining and mollification of landowners. Consequently, it was not uncommon for individuals of quite different socio-economic backgrounds to go into business in order to exploit leases from landowners. In such a context, anonymous letters alleging malfeasance and breach of trust would expose class tensions that were only too close to the surface.

Early rumblings at Moor Lane

Staffordshire was experiencing great changes in 1849: a network of canals had increased transport options for local businesses, like the glassworks, and also for those extracting raw materials from underground. Stourbridge, just south of the county border, in Worcestershire, was an important centre of glass production, which benefited from abundant coal and fireclay deposits nearby. The West Midlands overall was a hive of industrial development—with carpets coming from Kidderminster and glassware from Brierley Hill, taken via canals to houses warmed by local coal. 'Those who will face the dirt and dinginess of Brierley Hill and Tipton will...see a scene of industry and wealth where, within the memory of man, little else was to be found but open waste and common', wrote *The Daily News* in 1849.[3]

The Moor Lane coal shafts described by the anonymous letter accessed the southern tip of the South Staffordshire Coalfield, sometimes referred to as 'the great black cake' in contemporary sources. Locally extracted coal, fireclay and dolomite fuelled nearby production. The market for inland collieries had been very localized owing to the weight of the commodity: it was rare for a market to extend further than ten miles from the pit.[4] Industrialization, in particular new forms of transport, produced dramatic topographic and economic shifts. The introduction of a new canal could make a disused pit suddenly profitable again, as more distant markets became available and compensated for the expense of digging deeper. Later, railways streaked across this landscape, encouraging still further exploitation of the earth.

Coal had been mined for a long time by the 1840s, but the seams were not exhausted. Many pit shafts had been abandoned when miners had hit layers which were not then viable to work. The top layer, the brooch coal, which was of very good quality in this area, was taken first. Canals permitted the movement of coal to local industries—the Stourbridge Extension Canal opened in 1840. The arrival of railways made the extraction of even deeper 'thick coal', which was inferior to brooch coal and harder to extract, profitable.

At the time of the letter, the landscape around the Moor Lane glass-works was punctured by many pits, shafts, and quarries. It was undergoing constant change—the ground quite often literally moving and changing underfoot. Subsequent modern geological surveys suggest that much if not most of the surface soil between Stourbridge, West Bromwich, and Wolverhampton is two-metre deep 'made ground': excavated rock and soil; rubble; refuse.[5] In the mid-nineteenth century, new sinkings unsettled the ground and unsettled the locals. New businesses emerged in rapid succession. Their new masters employed new workforces and new technologies, but they were judged by existing expectations of good behaviour. The men denounced here, 'Butchers and Softly Jack', were colliers and entrepreneurs: pseudonyms were not just the preserve of the letter-writers. 'Butchers and Softly Jack' undermined the land upon which a glass factory sat: 'Veritas' undermined them.

Disputes above and beneath the surface around Moor Lane had a long history by 1849. Thomas Honeyborne—'Master Honeyborn' in the 1849 letter—described the changing situation in the 1800s, explaining how his father had 'a lease of the surface of the Moors Estate'. Nearby he built a house and outbuildings; these were 'always kept very neat'. The 'garden' mentioned in the letter was appended to this house. The presence of thick coal under the estate was well known—as already noted, the whole area is known for its thick coal or 'Ten-yard Coal'[6]—but it was 'so deep as not to be worth getting'; 'the only demand for Coal was for the supply of the Neighbourhood & its vicinity, the roads intolerably bad' and 'scarce passable'.[7] Other mines, on the massive estate belonging to Lord Dudley, saturated the local market. Honeyborne, fearing that the coal might eventually be taken from under lands near to his property, made legal arrangements to try to limit the impact on his buildings. To do this, Honeyborne relied on the principle that mining rights were forfeit once workings had been abandoned for a certain time.

Thomas Honeyborne kept up a long battle with two local mine-owning families, the Brettells and the Piddocks, concerning the coal under his property. In 1806 Honeyborne had purchased the rights to work it carefully, in order to prevent Brettell and Piddock causing structural damage above ground through greed or negligence. In the early 1800s, mine owners were apt to stop working a mine, and then try to return to it within a legally permitted interval. A mine abandoned for a year was considered to be discontinued, and at this point the land was to be returned to a ploughable state with mine equipment and pumping engines removed. Much of Honeyborne's energy went into worrying about the implications of the year-long interval for his property. In 1809 he issued an order to prevent Benjamin and Thomas Brettell and Thomas and John Piddock from entering or being on his land near Moor Lane. Their pits would be filled, the land made ploughable.[8] Speculation in mining increased 'surprisingly rapidly' in the area, responding to increased demand and improved transportation.[9]

Shaky partnerships

Before unpacking more details from the 1849 letter, let us first examine two letters from 1847 which also concern the behaviour of colliery agents, this time in nearby West Bromwich. This will make the social background of the 1849 dispute more intelligible. These earlier letters were likewise aimed at the interests of a landowner—the Earl of Dartmouth. Dartmouth forwarded them to his mine agent, William Willis Bailey. By 1847, Bailey had spent nine years travelling from his home in Kilburn, Derbyshire, to check on the collieries leased by the Earl. Bailey comes across in his correspondence as mild-mannered, diligent, and measured. So what induced him to conduct 'himself in a very violent manner to a constable' in October 1847?[10] To understand this, we need to consider Bailey's reaction to three anonymous letters sent to the Earl.

The first of these letters was not kept, but we do have Bailey's detailed response to it. He had immediately headed to the colliery, where he arranged interviews, asked questions, and generally investigated the letter's claims despite his belief that 'the greater part' of the allegations were 'false'. In summary, Bailey picked through the various claims to assess their validity. One claim, that coal was left lying and wasted, was determined to be wrong: 'the anonymous writer is, therefore, on this point, a very great story-teller', wrote Bailey. Bailey also dismissed claims that bills went long unpaid, stating that he would be able to look over the accounts at a later date.[11] He also contested the letter's accusation that supplies of bricks and timber had been misappropriated. Bailey found that materials were shared with other companies: 'I make out also that your Lordship had some Bricks from the Victoria Pits.' Reflecting on the potency of such letters to generate new liabilities and disputes, Bailey quipped, 'I presume the anonymous writer did not intend to bring in your lordship "guilty" with the rest of us.'[12]

When it came to the Heath Colliery, however, Bailey did find evidence of mismanagement or worse. He observed a 'want of cordiality between the Partners'. The colliery at that time was managed by the lessees: James Eaton, William Salter, and William Raybould. Eaton, Salter, and Raybould paid royalties on the coal they dug from the Earl of Dartmouth's land. Bailey found Eaton, a navy man who had served at the Battle of Trafalgar on HMS *Temeraire*, to be agitated when questioned. Thus Bailey reassured him that, 'from his rank and standing in her Majesty's Navy', the Earl found him 'utterly incapable of doing a disrespectful thing'.[13] On 27 March 1842 Bailey got Joseph Bird and James Moss, two of the colliery's doggies, to sign with an 'X' documents in which they stated that no coal had been left unfairly or forgotten or lost through neglect.[14] A 'doggy' was an underground supervisor in charge of setting shifts, tasks, or 'stints' for the miners; sometimes called 'a corporal'. On the same day, Richard Peggs, a clerk at the Heath Colliery, signed a statement asserting that the colliery owed him money, but that he did not know if others were also owed. The document made by Peggs implies that Peggs had been cited in the lost anonymous letter, and he denied having said 'there was a great deal of roguery going on' amongst the partners, or that the partners were attempting to deprive the Earl of his rights. 'They have always shown great anxiety to do what was right or fair', he said.[15]

Although Peggs denied knowing that the partners were regularly drunk, Raybould confessed to Bailey that he had been intoxicated 'a few times'. He 'expressed contrition and promised to amend for the future.'[16] Bailey was unable to confirm the allegation that beer was sold on the premises: 'Raybould Brews beer for the workmen at the expense of The Company', stated Bailey, 'saving them money from the costs of buying from brewers.'[17] In 1843, Raybould claimed to have been working with coal for twenty-four years, which (if true) would mean he started when he was twelve. If we are to believe his story, Raybould became a manager in 1826, in his teens. He probably always worked with the thick coal, as he was located throughout his career in collieries around Dudley, near Rowley Regis and West Bromwich. Of the three partners, Raybould was the only one to have had close experience of the trade. His social standing as a business partner rested on his having the 'knack' for coal work needed for supervision of the day-to-day operations. Eaton and Salter were of a 'better' sort: much of the mistrust arising from the letters and the subsequent legal business can be traced back to the dependence of the other partners, and in turn the dependence of the Earl and his agent, on Raybould's goodwill.

Raybould and the topic of drinking at the mines were at the heart of the next anonymous tip-off letter to be forwarded to Bailey from the Earl. That letter was written on 9 August. The year is not recorded, but it must date to sometime between 1842 and 1847. The letter was signed by 'A well wisher to all parties' who claimed to write 'by the request of a Large body of the inhabitants of Westbromwich'. The well-wisher singled out 'the most unmanly and infamous conduct of one of your lordship's lessees, Wm Raybould' for attention. According to the well-wisher, Raybould was brewing ale and selling this to the colliers at his pit, compelling them to pay more than they would get it for elsewhere. Further, the well-wisher observed, 'if any man is heard to express his dissatisfaction he is forthwith discharged with a bad character'. Not only was this 'unprincipled proceeding…nothing short of a robbery of the poor', it also was 'a great injury to the Publicans who are compelled to pay licences heavy rents and other expenses and depending upon the Public trade for a bread'. It is (of course) possible that the well-wisher was a publican. The anonymous author claimed the scheme used bribed doggies. Each doggy paid Raybould for the beer, and then collected money from the miners on Saturday nights. This meant that Raybould could avoid responsibility for any swindle. The 'well wisher' provides the names of several persons from whom the Earl could request further information. Explaining his or her anonymity, the author notes that if Raybould 'were to know it, he would discharge every man under his employ, from laying out a farthing with me, or any family'. This again suggests the writer was connected to the beer trade.[18]

A parliamentary report from 1843 had highlighted a common practice in other Staffordshire mines, where butties (charter-masters who supplied miners with tools and equipment and paid their wages) kept beer shops and public houses. This was a device 'for inducing men to spend their wages' by paying their wages while they drank, with deductions for the beer exacted on their pay. But the parliamentary report of 1843 noted that at the Heath Colliery doggies performed this task instead because, unusually, no butties were employed there. Raybould argued that in other systems 'nobody but the butty profits', and that when bailiffs and butties operate in the same mine, they 'play into each other's hands; they'll seem as obstinate as possible, and all the time they'll fit together as nicely as a cup and ball'. The report suggests that the system which ran without butties was safer, because butties were thought to take risks in order to maximize profits. In fact, the point was mainly semantic: in the Heath Colliery, the doggies acted like butties; in fact, as they were working the coal on behalf of the Earl, Raybould and Salter were themselves closer to butties than masters. Nonetheless, Raybould and Salter presented their business as more focused on safety and fairness. 'Our doggy', they claimed, 'receives fixed wages, and therefore is not interested in oppressing the men.' In the pits of their competitors the butties 'require the same uniform stint, though the quality and hardness of the coal varies much'. The compilers of the report interviewed workers at the colliery; a pikeman called Simeon Smallman thought that his current masters were the best he had known, and that his wages were fair. Both Raybould and Salter were also interviewed at the Heath Colliery for this parliamentary report. Their management was described as exemplary.[19]

By April 1844, Bailey himself was more acquainted with the Heath Colliery accounts. He wrote a convoluted letter to the Earl, detailing a disagreement concerning accounting irregularities.[20] Partway through his letter, Bailey digressed into a discussion of whose name ought to front the business. Eaton had left, and Bailey claimed to have a 'distinct understanding' that the firm be styled 'Salter & Raybould'— in that order. 'For Raybould is no favourite of mine, nor do I consider him entitled to stand first in his Form as lessees of the Heath Colliery', the agent remarked. Bailey's respect for Raybould had 'been much lowered, whether viewed as a Husband, a Father, or a Citizen of the World'. Bailey feared that Raybould's 'immorality will & must ultimately interfere with his duties and responsibilities', and suspected that his character and the colliery's 'pecuniary difficulties' were connected. Bailey hinted that Salter had fallen out with his partners because he had stretched his interests, borrowing money to invest in other collieries (one of the concerns Bailey had investigated in 1842 was that funds from the Heath Colliery were being diverted to the Lewisham Colliery). With Eaton gone, Salter appeared to Bailey to be the most active of the partners, but Bailey ends his letter with a note of caution: 'Mr Salter is not an experienced or Practical Coal Miner.'[21] In other words, Raybould was the only person in a position to really know what was going on at the pits.[22]

The campaign of the anonymous 'well wisher' continued in late September 1847; a third letter arrived. In the same handwriting as the second one, the writer accused Salter and Raybould of avoiding tollage by transporting coal disguised as manure. Again, the 'well wisher' supplies names for corroboration. He goes on to claim that Raybould left to buy horse corn from a 'Mr Badger' in Birmingham but went instead to a brothel for two nights and was robbed of £35. The claims made in this part of the letter are difficult to assess, but the writer's assertion that three people were each transported for two years for robbing Raybould seems unlikely because transportation for only two years was no longer a common sentence for such crimes. Contemporary newspapers are silent about the episode. At the end of this third letter, the 'well wisher' casually drops in another detail about the partners: 'They have also been getting lawyer Caddick's Coal.'[23]

There was truth to the final claim. Salter and Raybould gave evidence at the Wolverhampton Public Office at the end of October 1847 after being accused of feloniously getting 945 tonnes of coal from underneath property owned by Mr Elisha Caddick, a solicitor based in West Bromwich, who owned land near the mines of Salter and Raybould.[24] In late August that year, Caddick had noticed that cracks had formed in the walls of his house; some of his windows cracked or shattered. He called for Raybould, who argued that the sandy foundations on which the house was built had given way. Raybould refused to acknowledge that the actual cause was subsidence caused by his removal of coal below or a collapse of the works themselves. Caddick requested that he be allowed to go down the pit to see for himself, but

Raybould refused, offering only the reassurance that his workings were 'yet at a distance' from Caddick's land. When more damage became evident on Caddick's property in early October, he again repeated his request to go down the pit. This was again refused, with a vague statement asserting that Raybould's lease prevented this. Eventually, Caddick was able to send a mine agent underground to check whether any part of the shaft had collapsed.[25]

Many of the coal workings in the area were developed using the pillar and stall method pioneered in the seventeenth century:

From the main roads, termed gate-roads, each side of work, unless commenced near the outer boundary, is accessible only through a narrow opening, cut, like the gate-road itself, in the lower part of the seam. 'Stalls' are then driven out in the coal, each of them eight or ten yards wide, and are crossed again by similar galleries, leaving between them pillars of eight or ten yards square, but varied of course in dimension, according to local circumstances.[26]

In such a system and its variants, the pillars bore the whole weight of the earth above the shaft. Even if the pillars did not collapse over time, the ceiling between them could sag and fail, producing disturbances on the surface capable of affecting any built structures present there. If any of the pillars themselves collapsed, often this would produce a chain reaction as greater stress was quickly added to pillars and supports nearby. Modern research has shown that the collapse of many pillars in such a mine can produce shallow subsidence over a large area of the surface. These so-called 'sags' develop quickly, with the first significant shifts happening over the course of a week.[27]

In 1847, at the same time as Caddick was investigating whether Salter and Raybould's works extended under his damaged property, Bailey stated that he had not seen any plans of the mine to suggest that Salter and Raybould were stealing Caddick's coal. Still, Salter admitted to Bailey that they had indeed got Caddick's coal, but asserted that they had not been aware of this at the time.[28] The contradiction points up the fact that mine workings in this area were being developed more quickly than plans or maps could be produced for them.

When the case was heard at the Wolverhampton Police Court in October 1847, a few weeks after Bailey had received the third letter, plans made by 'a competent mine agent' were presented. Such moves were part of attempts to circumvent Raybould's monopoly on knowledge of what was going on under the surface. The plans showed various gate-roads and wide workings driven through Caddick's property. The prosecution also called Isaac White, formerly a ground bailiff of the company. White confirmed that gate-roads had been driven through Caddick's land at the direction of his masters. Apparently, the partners had reassured their subordinates that they intended to buy Caddick's land. Workings continued 'for some time' and good-quality thick coal was extracted. Perhaps wanting to keep the Earl's name out of the affair, Bailey refused to attend the initial hearings in Wolverhampton. He claimed he could not spare the time, and 'conducted himself in a very violent manner to the constable at the time the summons was served'.[29]

Salter and Raybould were 'anxious to settle the matter'. They had a lot on their plate at this time, having also to defend themselves against accusations of neglect after a terrible accident at their pit.[30] Early in 1848 negotiations led to a resolution by 'amicable arrangement': Caddick would get royalties for his coal.[31] Following the sudden death of Bailey in April 1848, the Earl installed William F. Gordon as his new mining agent. Gordon expressed concern that legal arbitration would set a high figure for Salter and Raybould to pay in royalties to Caddick, enough to affect his employer's business.[32] Gordon suggested that the Earl consider ending the lease of the mines before the case was final-ized, to avoid being drawn into any financial reckonings.[33] By 1850 Caddick had received £2,170 in compensation from William Salter, who, by then, had ended his partnership with Raybould.[34] £2,170 was over thirty years of wages for a Staffordshire collier at that time.

At the start of that year, Salter wrote a desperate letter of apology to the Earl, detailing his remaining debts, which included legal fees aris-ing from the Caddick case. Salter asked the Earl if he could use the reserve fund from the old partnership (totalling £1,130) so as to avoid mortgaging or selling his remaining property. Salter reiterated his remorse: 'the keenest & most enduring pangs have arisen from the thoughts of having incurred your lordships displeasure'. In a reflective mood, Salter reproached himself for ever entering business with Raybould. The Earl refused his request.[35] Perhaps reflecting the social stratifications at play, Caddick and Salter do not appear to have fallen out in the aftermath of the incident. Salter seconded Caddick for nomination to the West Bromwich coroner position in 1852.[36] Salter died in 1854, in his sixty-first year; it was reported that his death was 'deeply regretted by a large circle of friends and relatives'.[37] Raybould appears to have focused on beer-selling after quitting the mines.[38]

Softly Jack and the Butchers

Let us now return to the 'Butchers and Softly Jack' letter from 1849. Like Salter and Raybould, these mysterious figures were also being charged with undermining a neighbour's buildings.[39] In early March 1849 it arrived at the lawyer Eberhardt's office after travelling to Stourbridge from a sub-post office in Claverley, via the head post office in Wolverhampton. The writing is stylized, perhaps disguised, suggesting the hand might be known by the recipient, whose name is spelled incorrectly—perhaps another ruse to throw the lawyer off the scent. Eberhardt had a partner, Charles Roberts: they owned a mine together.[40] With his knowledge of the local coal trade, Eberhardt might well have known which individuals 'Veritas' was referring to as 'Butchers and Softly Jack'.

Around 1824, Joseph Silvers and Joseph Stevens, brothers-in-law, leased the glassworks on Moor Lane as tenants of the Honeyborne family. Silvers and Stevens manufactured utilitarian glass goods. In 1802, Robert Honeyborne had left the land and property to his brother, Thomas. When Thomas died in 1831, the estate went to a relative in Ireland.[41] In the 1840s, the glassworks were taken over by sons-in-law of Silvers: William Stevens and Samuel Cox Williams. Eberhardt was clerk to the Moor Lane glassworks. In other words, Honeyborne's garden was part of the property owned by the glass company Stevens & Williams in 1849.[42]

In 1845, Joseph Silvers had written a reference for the wife of one of his employees, addressing his remarks to 'Messers Roberts & Heberardt'—adding an H just as the writer of the anonymous letter sent about four years later had. It would, however, be strange for Silvers to have written the 'Softly Jack' letter, as it pertains to his own property and was addressed to his own clerk. This detail does, however, suggest that Eberhardt's name might have been pronounced with an 'H'.[43]

Eberhardt (or 'Heberard') had already been having a strange time. Just over a week before the letter arrived at his office, he had been witness to a fracas in Mrs Webb's drinking establishment in the town,

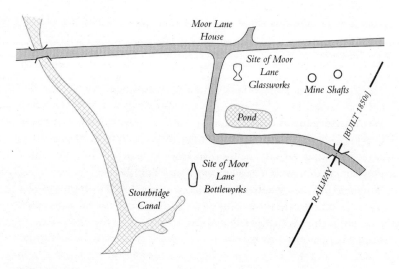

Figure 14. Map of the Moor Lane Colliery area, by Maud Webster

when a man followed him inside, kicking the door open and shouting about the quality of Mrs Webb's drinkables.[44] Moreover, on the night of 17 February, over a dozen fowls had been stolen from the hen pen of Joseph Silvers, to be later discovered in a pool 'a short distance from the house'. Silver's neighbour, James Noden, was burgled when 'three ruffians ... unroofed the brewhouse': bacon, sugar, hams, clothing, 'eighty silver tea-spoons', and other things were taken. But Noden's daughter, Mary Ann, captured one of the gang of thieves by grasping him 'firmly by the collar'. Handed to the police, this prisoner was found to have 'about fifty skeleton keys in his possession'. Noden, a coalmaster, lived in one part of the large house formerly occupied by Honeyborne, and Silvers lived in the other part.[45] So when Eberhardt read the letter a short time later, he might have wondered whether the letter had anything to do with the other strange events.

But the anonymous letter does not refer to overground crimes. It concerns instead an underground theft and underground negligence to compare with what was alleged against underminers of Caddick's land. As has already been noted, the 'Roads' referred to in the letter were underground gate-roads. Who might have been undermining the garden of the glassworks? An invoice headed 'Moor Lane Colliery, Brought of Darby, Higgs & Pickering' appears in a file of notes detailing legal opinions about mining, focused on the interests of the Honeyborne family. The invoice lists purchasers of coal by type in 1845. Silvers & Stevens bought common coal for their glassworks. The reverse of the sheet of accounts displays the address: 'Messers Roberts & Eberhardt, Solicitors, Stourbridge'. A handwritten note records 'Darby & Higgs, 1845'.[46] Until 1845, Joseph Darby and Joseph Higgs were in partnership as coalmasters and ironstone-dealers with Thomas Pickering.[47] Joseph Darby, a maltster by trade, owned lots of property nearby, including various malthouses. He also leased coal mines: one such lease encompassed 180 acres in the Forest of Dean.[48]

Joseph Darby had written to Roberts and Eberhardt from his home on the Delph, nearby, on 21 August 1847. This letter refers to an old shaft next to the Moor Lane Road, and thick coals in the vicinity that he and Higgs wanted to extract immediately, 'as there is our men at liberty now and the weather [is] fine'. Darby promised not to interfere with the railway under construction nearby.[49] A week later Darby wrote another letter to Roberts & Eberhardt, having examined the exterior of Moor Lane House (presumably at the solicitors' request). In this letter Darby stated that 'there is not one pennyworth of damage', and that the partners are 'ready to meet you any time you appoint to go into the matter'.[50] Later, in 1852, £18 was spent repairing doors and a porch.[51] A report for the Oxford, Worcester & Wolverhampton Railway compiled in February 1845 had described Moor Lane House as 'some time one Gentleman's Mansion but now converted into two and totally unfit from the works surrounding it for a Gentleman's residence'.[52] The Moor Lane House was still subject to undermining as late as 1867: a surveyor for Honeyborne's heir found evidence of roads underground being driven further east and south beneath the property. There were 'signs of damage' on the large barn attached to the Moor Lane House.[53] When Stevens and Williams moved to other glassworks in 1870, they left the old site 'very dilapidated'.[54] At the same time, and also due to undermining, the nearby Brierley Hill Station was in danger of collapse—possibly suggesting that the mine run by Darby and Higgs did indeed affect the railway despite their assurances.[55]

Darby and Higgs are therefore the prime suspects in the escapades mysteriously alluded to by the 1849 letter. Their works extended under the garden of Moor Lane House. So how might they have got their nicknames? Darby's family history may explain the link to 'butchery'. Nearly a century before, in 1759, three of his ancestors were found guilty of murdering a bailiff at their house near Halesowen. The bailiff, John Walker, had been at their house distraining goods: the Darbys had fallen behind on the rent. The sons beat Walker with 'a Broom-Hook and Bludgeon', stripped him naked and whipped him 'almost in pieces'.[56] Darby and his two sons, Joseph and Thomas, were executed. The Darby boys were left hanging in chains to set public example. Joseph's body was taken by surgeons for dissection.[57] If the Darbys were not 'Butchers', then Higgs could have been one: members of his family worked in the butchering trade.[58]

'Softly Jack' is still stranger and more difficult to tackle: 'Jack' is of course a common folkloric name and includes no individualization.[59] There was once a highwayman called Rowley Jack, who had an accomplice, Rebecca Fox, the daughter of a rich local. Both disappeared in 1754—it was rumoured they had died when the roof of their secret hideout collapsed. Rowley Jack was said to have shod his horses with shoes put on backwards, giving the impression of movement in the opposite direction to his actual course and throwing pursuers off his track.[60] Softly Jack is perhaps derived from Rowley Jack: both Darby and Higgs were born in Rowley Regis, and they were stealing coal softly (that is, quietly, stealthily).

Such conjecture must remain unsatisfying, as must speculation around the identity of the author. Thomas Pickering, the erstwhile partner of Darby and Higgs, left the company in March 1845. He can probably be ruled out, as he signed the document marking the dissolving of the company with an 'X': he was probably illiterate.[61] Both Joseph Darby and Joseph Higgs were connected to recent mining deaths in the 1840s. Darby also owned a colliery near the Five Ways in Rowley Regis: it was the scene of a 'frightful' explosion in 1844 that killed eleven men. Higgs was the ground-bailiff at the same works, 'one of the most dangerous in the neighbourhood'. Conveniently for Darby and Higgs, official blame was laid at the feet of 'one of the unfortunate sufferers'.[62] Accidents at the Moor Lane Colliery in 1847 also led to deaths and injury.[63] Lots of people could have carried grudges against the men. The lease for the Moor Lane Colliery expired in 1851, and the plants and effects were auctioned off. Higgs, who had been a beer-shop keeper in addition to his mine work, became the licensee of an inn.[64] Joseph Darby died in June 1856. His sons all focused on the malt trade, and so his coal interests were auctioned.[65] The Moor Lane Colliery was leased to

Thomas Crew, in partnership with Eberhardt's erstwhile partner, Charles Roberts.[66]

Let us take stock by returning to the letter:

> Master Heberard
>   You look after those "Butchers and Softly Jack"
> at Moor-Lane—they be very near Master Honeyborns Garden if
> not under—You must not give them any notice before sending
> any one down their Pit—If you do they will stop up their
> Roads and cheat You.
>   Veritas[67]

As in the letters of two years before written by the 'well wisher' to the mine agent Bailey, the letter by 'Veritas' to the lawyer Eberhardt is powerful because of the way it targets links in an increasingly complex chain of trust and supervision between landowners and mining lessees. 'Veritas' draws attention to the possibility that fraudulent and irresponsible mine operators could use their expertise to prevent effective third-party oversight of the quality and extent of mining operations ('they will stop up their Roads and cheat You'). A letter like this also exploited or exacerbated inter-class mistrust within these networks. The names given to the underminers may have appealed to the middle-class Victorian fear of the 'criminal class' and its frightening mythical characters.[68]

On the other hand, the criminality exposed by the letter does not appear to have been fictitious. The entrepreneurialism of Darby and Higgs shows many signs of irresponsibility and greed; their fraud and carelessness may already have led to the deaths of several people working for them. So, the letter about them can also be read against the background of social and geological turmoil in which men prepared to get their hands dirty would ascend and become rich. Even in this small area of the Black Country, the industrial and consequential topographical developments of the 1830s and 1840s would have been unsettling. Local power relations could shift quite quickly, and the social and political backdrop was undergoing massive change. In this context, letters such as those from 'Veritas' and the 'well wisher' can be understood as informal techniques of moral regulation and supervision, compensating for the failure of the state and its laws to constrain the actions of coal-hungry entrepreneurs. Some of those men undermined social norms and legal contract; in the cases examined so far, they literally undermined the very ground on which their neighbours stood.

Public wrongs

New state infrastructure and the officials that came with it were also subject to censure by anonymous letter-writers. With the establishment of novel welfare systems following the 1834 Poor Law Act, there were new duties for officials employed on behalf of local authorities and boards. Of course, not all of this work was undertaken diligently. Again, one informal method of redress was to write anonymously about malfeasance. The issue of trust is sustained in these letters in a different way, being directed not at private but at public interests.

One person, with untidy, probably disguised writing, bombarded Somerset House, where the Poor Law Commission was based, with at least five anonymous letters between December 1848 and June 1849. The letters all focused on the alleged wrongdoings of James Lamb Barker, clerk to the Guardians of the Tynemouth Poor Law Union. After the first letter arrived, enquiries were apparently made 'into the statement contained in this communication which do not appear to rest on any certain foundation'. A letter sent in 1849 was dismissed by an official: 'No attention need be paid to these anonymous communications if the writer has any specific charge to make against Mr Barker he ought to come forward in his proper character and proffer it openly.'[69] In the county of Somerset, brothers John and William Rees Mogg were clerks to the Guardians of the Clutton Poor Law Union in 1846. They were forced to respond to an allegation made anonymously to the Poor Law Board, that the workhouse used skimmings of bacon fat from cooking pots (dripping) in place of butter. The Rees Mogg brothers did not deny the allegation.[70]

A different sort of letter was sent to the Poor Law Board at Somerset House in February 1849. It came from the neighbour of a woman who died suddenly in Kidderminster. The letter intimated that the woman's death was suspicious. Although the author did not name her, the victim was Elizabeth Nash. Nash was the widow of a boatman and was thirty-five years old when she died in Kidderminster. On her death certificate, Nash was recorded as dying at 'Pratt's Wharf', which was along the Staffordshire canal at Falling Sands in the Oldington area of

Kidderminster.[71] The Staffordshire canal bearing some of the coal mined in the Heath and the Moor Lane collieries ran to this wharf, and it was there that cargoes were unloaded when the canal was closed in the evenings.[72] This was a little-populated area; the letter-writer, describing him or herself as 'a neighbour', could only have been one of just a few people unless he or she was using the word 'neighbour' in its wider, Christian sense.

The letter, dated 6 February, stated that an inquest was held in Kidderminster that very day; Elizabeth Nash had died the previous Sunday. A newspaper report concerning Nash's death corroborates this. According to the letter, Nash was 'beautiful and in perfect health' until she drank her coffee, at which point she 'suddenly expired', after an illness of a 'few minutes'. The newspaper report narrates Nash's final moments after she

rose on Sunday morning about the usual time .... She sat down to breakfast with the rest of the family, ate heartily, sat a few moments, rose up, walked towards the door, said a few words, and fell down dead.

Concerned that no post-mortem examination had been carried out, the anonymous neighbour states that 'this is a case demanding inquiry'.[73] The coroner was Ralph Docker. Docker was a solicitor with eleven years' experience as a coroner, but this was not the first time his judgement had been challenged. His verdict was that Nash had died by 'Visitation of God': natural causes.[74]

Ralph Docker was not a very conscientious coroner. When in 1848 skeletons believed to be of two boys were found in a property previously owned by a surgeon, the local press wondered if the discovery was evidence of bodies used for anatomical training. Docker conducted some brief interviews and concluded that further enquiries would be fruitless.[75] Docker had got into some trouble previously for his reliance on his deputy, Edward Moore, a surgeon from Halesowen. Moore had continued and signed off an inquest that Docker had begun on the body of a woman in October 1844. Docker had been present, but 'did not sum up, or sign the inquisition, nor did he view the body'—leaving most of the business to his deputy. As in the Elizabeth Nash case, the verdict was also 'death by visitation of God'.[76]

It is questionable, however, whether Docker's methods were far outside what was expected. A discussion of coroners' fees that took place at the Quarter Sessions in Worcester suggests that in cases where a person died suddenly, and not as a result of fever, apoplexy, 'or other Visitation of God', coroners 'ought not...to obtrude themselves into private families for the purpose of instituting enquiry, but should wait till they are sent for by the Peace Officers of the place'. Moreover, the coroner should use 'sound discretion' and not proceed without a reasonable ground of suspicion that there had been a violent or unnatural death. Another local coroner had been praised for declining to hold inquests in two cases of sudden death near Worcester. The implication behind the report was that some coroners were apt to interfere in order to secure a fee: this does not seem to have happened in the Nash case.[77]

The author of the letter about Elizabeth Nash did not communicate their concerns to the correct body. Annotations made by Poor Law Board officials on the reverse of the letter conclude that it 'does not state anything which brings the matter within the sphere of the P.L.B. [Poor Law Board]', as Nash had not been a pauper. The systems of local government and welfare were complex and not fully understood at the time. Perhaps the neighbour also communicated their concerns to other authorities; this is unknown. The Poor Law Board officials marked the letter as 'Anonymous'. Like other unsigned letters received by the Board, it would have received scant regard.[78] Some anonymous tip-offs might have accused coroners of wrongdoing—but many more were sent to coroners themselves, with testimony relevant to cases. In 1856, after numerous accidents at the Brandy Bottom Colliery in South Gloucestershire, the local coroner received an anonymous letter asking him to inform the government inspector of mines to investigate the deadly works. The manager of the mine was later found guilty of three counts of dangerous working conditions as a result.[79]

A further episode of anonymous letter-writing from 1858 coincidentally connects Elizabeth Nash to Joseph Darby—by way of not the canal but the coroner. Thomas Darby, Joseph's brother, was a wealthy coalmaster and maltster; he died suddenly at his home in Rowley Regis in 1863. Joseph's sons (William, Thomas, and Joseph) claimed that Thomas had been poisoned. It was the coroner, Ralph Docker, who carried out the examination, involving exhumation, 'to silence such reports'. In December 1863, Thomas Darby's body was put in a tent erected in the churchyard at Quinton, where he had been buried, attracting many spectators. An inquest jury was sworn in and Moore,

Docker's deputy, conducted a post-mortem. Moore sent samples to be examined by a Birmingham-based analyst. Docker reported 'nothing to lead me to suppose that deceased had met his death by unfair means'. Joseph's sons were censured for 'the manner in which they had acted', as it was not until after the will was read that they had considered such proceedings necessary.[80] They were unhappy that their uncle had bequeathed some £10,000 of their presumed inheritance to Birmingham General Hospital. Thomas Darby stated in his will that he considered it his 'duty for many reasons to be the benefactor to some charitable institution'. His benefaction provided tickets for outpatient care in the parish, each to have these words 'printed conspicuously' upon them: 'Presented gratuitously in conformity with the Will of the late Thomas Darby formerly of the parish of Rowley Regis'. Local vicars were tasked with advertising the scheme.[81] It was noted in a report from October 1863 that someone (presumably Thomas) had been writing anonymously to the hospital board in 1858—enquiring about the costs and the various privileges of being a donor.[82]

Lots of relationships in the mid-nineteenth century brought together people, often in business, who would previously not have worked together. Dubiousness about the trustworthiness of partners, or of managers, or officials, developed into suspicions about specific activities. People sending tip-offs, and even people trying to seek information about how to give charitably, had various reasons to be cagey and to write anonymously—they might not have wanted people in positions of power to take revenge, or hide their tracks. Thomas Darby might not have wanted his nephews to know that their inheritance was insecure, hence his anonymous enquiries. All of the anonymous letters here have signalled the ways in which trust had become fractured in the new social, economic, political, and even topographical landscapes at the time.

3

Threats

Lord Dorington's in danger

Sirs,   Feb 1864

I hope you will not be surprised when you read this short note merely pointing out to you the position you both stand in at present. Your lives are in danger and will very shortly meet with a sudden surprise for your behaviour in trying to enclose the Commons of Bisley Parish. You think that all things are quiet and smoothe on your sides But you shall soon know to the contrary. Recollect Mr D[orington] that you are robing the working class of the Parish and their offsprings forever in fact you are not Gentlemen but robbers and vagabonds, however if it is enclosed you shall never receive any benefit thereby as there are several on the lookout for you both and so help my God I am on the Alert for you and if I have one chance of you I will shoot you as dead as mortal—instead of trying to do good for the working people of this Parish you want to deprive them of the little benefit they have. I most solemnly hope that an opportunity will come soon and I will willingly resign my life for the sake of yours.

      I Remain Sirs, your obedient Servant

      J. C. I. H

      P.S. I shall be happy to visit upon you soon.[1]

This polite death threat was written in 1864. It was addressed to John Edward Dorington, the local lord of the manor who had lived at Lipiatt Park since 1847, as well as to his son of the same name. The family were incomers; Dorington senior had made money in the civil service and served as a local magistrate. On the whole, the family may have enjoyed good relations in the community. A local historian would later describe Dorington junior as 'a kind and beneficent landlord' who took 'an active part in parochial matters'.[2] Beyond the letter,

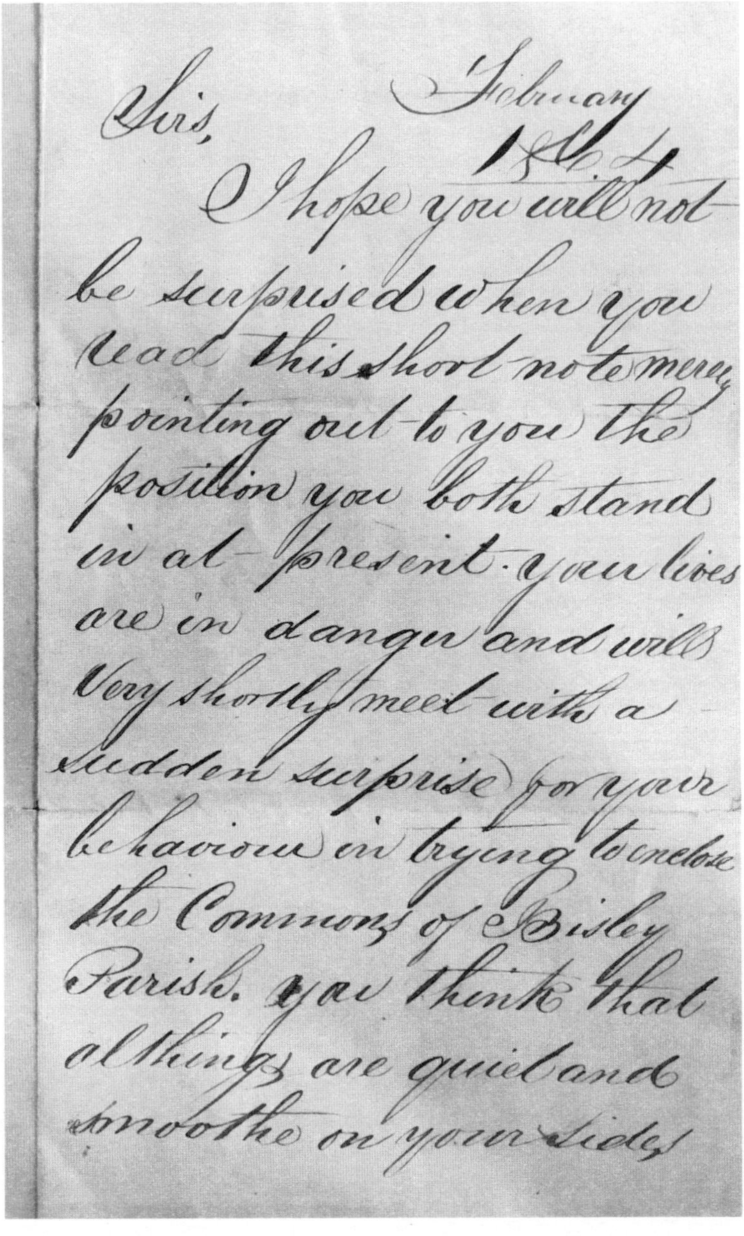

Figure 15. Anonymous letter to the Dorington family of Lypiatt Park threatening murder, 1864, Gloucestershire Archives, D5344/1, recto

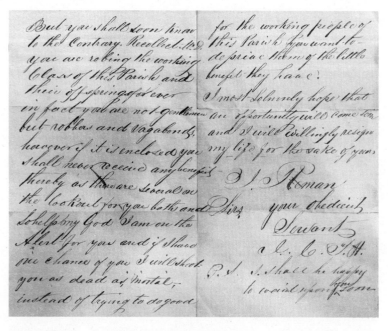

Figure 16. Anonymous letter to the Dorington family of Lypiatt Park threatening murder, 1864, Gloucestershire Archives, D5344/1, verso

however, there is reason to doubt that they were universally popular. The letter is a strange mix of murder threat and polite observance of epistolary rules: the ironically deferential sign-off indicates a knowledge of the form. It also lacks the spelling quirks common in earlier letters and letters of this sort and is beautifully penned. The handwriting does not appear disguised.[3]

It's helpful, once again, to consider the groundbreaking work of historian E. P. Thompson when trying to understand this letter. Using notices for rewards placed in the *London Gazette*, Thompson analysed 284 anonymous letters considering both the nature of the threats and the status of their recipients, regarding the letters as a 'characteristic form of social protest' in societies where 'forms of collective organised defence are weak, and in which individuals who can be identified as the organisers of protest are liable to immediate victimisation'. Unlike many of the anonymous letters written between 1750 and 1811 that he analysed, the letter to the Doringtons does not use the pronoun 'we'. Although it alludes to communal interests it is written by an individual, not a group. Thompson found that these letters split into two broad groups: those addressed to the rich; and those addressed to a crowd.[4] The 1864 letter to Dorington would have to slot into the first group. Thompson argued that anonymous letters of the late eighteenth and early nineteenth centuries were 'intrinsic to protodemocratic forms of organisation'. Such an interpretation was consistent with Thompson's other work. For example, in his famous essay 'The Moral Economy of the English Crowd in the Eighteenth Century', he deployed anonymous letters as sources on the assumption that they were 'expressive' of wider communal 'grievances' or dialogue between classes. Later, in *Customs in Common*, Thompson referred to 'the anonymous letter' as one of those 'acts of darkness' common in rural societies where open defiance was quickly identified and punished.[5]

In his writings Thompson traced the legal response to the sending of anonymous threatening letters. After the Black Act of 1723, sending letters 'without a name' or pseudonymously, 'demanding money, venison, or other valuable thing', was a felony. Uncertainty about how to apply this law led to further clarifications in 1754: letters which threatened lives or arson were then brought under the purview of the law. Three years later its reach was extended to absorb blackmail and extortion (but with a maximum sentence of transportation for seven years). According to Thompson's analysis, murder was the most common threat in letters triggered by a private grievance, and arson was more common in those letters reflecting or connected to social protests.[6] Possibly the key difference was that in the latter case the violent sentiments were directed against property and seemed to include the letter-writing more clearly in a politics of contested space. Although the 1864 letter to the Doringtons appears to belong to this latter group, it also included a decidedly personal murder threat. It is possible that the author harboured a personal grudge against the two men, in addition to this anger about the enclosures. Of course, Thompson's distinction is hard to maintain here. This chapter will focus exactly on this tension and ambiguity in anonymous letter-writing—the question of how private interest and political affiliation intersect in such letters—and will attempt to refine Thompson's important insights. The most influential historical works on anonymous threatening letters tend to read them always as expressions of wider social movements, and by implication as manifestations of class identity and incipient class consciousness.[7] Yet the reasons for writing anonymously in a paternalistic and deferential society were manifold. Anonymity was a reasonable precaution for many. These letters formed part of the arsenal available to the subordinate members of society. They would number among what the anthropologist James C. Scott termed 'weapons of the weak'.[8]

Many letters were sent between 1766 and 1767, a time when rural settlements were struggling with food shortages.[9] Thompson identified twenty-seven anonymous letters reported in the *London Gazette* during this period that 'indicated some social or economic grievance of a general character'.[10] In 1766 an 'anonymous incendiary letter' was found in the doorway of a shop in Norwich, threatening grocer James Poole ['Mr Pooll Grocher'] that his house would burn down unless the butchers, bakers, and market-people lowered the price of their commodities to a 'reasnabell rate'. Another letter—found in the ashtray at the Rose Tavern—threatened that the entire city and its inhabitants would be destroyed 'by fire and sword' unless the prices of 'most Eatables' were immediately reduced. Like the majority of the social protest letters, the threat involved arson attack.[11] The following year, a letter dropped in the high street of Hereford signed by '3 parts starved' was addressed to the city magistrates:

I am a freeman and a Citizen of Hemsfarth but the dear times has almost Ruined me & hundred beside are Starveing for want of Bread: 'dis is give Notice that if you do not make the farmers bring the Grain to Markey and Sell it a 5 Shillins a Bushell that we shall destroy both them and you theirs and yours by soord or gun. Within this fortnight trades people Shopkeepers are Redy to take up Arms, for we Cant live if such Villiany is carried on for to Starve and famish us in Plenty tis better to Undergo a forriehn Yoke than to be used thus We Cant bear it no longer So look to it if Mischief befalls you or them blame nobody but yourselves far We Are above 7 Hundred Cancerned And as Many more redy to Assist so looke to it & do it Spedile...[12]

Here, the threat is less specific than the Norwich letter; 'if Mischief befalls you' is a vague threat, bolstered by the suggestion that the author has the backing of more than seven hundred people, who are 'Redy to take up Arms'. Although it starts with 'I', the author swiftly switches to the pronoun 'we', to reinforce their message. Thompson describes letters like these as the 'saddest' type of anonymous letters, bearing 'the testimony of men driven to fury by the humiliation of the poor law, low wages, the abuse of charities'.[13]

During the nineteenth century the quantity of anonymous letters increased, partly because literacy increased. There was nothing new about the letters themselves, even if their quantity and their specific targets deserve careful explanation.[14] Taking a long view, the letters of the nineteenth century should be understood as in some ways consistent with letter-writing of the medieval period. A key factor to highlight here is the consequences of changing delivery mechanisms and opportunities. The meaning and effect of a letter could vary depending on whether it was slid under a neighbour's door or arrived in the post. In both cases, the messages entered the victim's property, bringing the violence, symbolically at least, not only to the receiver's doorstep but beyond it.[15] As a tool of protest and grudge, such letters had long possessed great power and potential. Many of the anonymous letters sent during the first half of the nineteenth century were threats written by people (usually men) with relatively little power, to people (usually men) in positions of power. Most of these letters expressed resistance to social change of various kinds, but especially developments that posed threats to livelihood (and, directly or indirectly, to labouring communities). In the majority of cases, their authors have not been identified. Such letters often concerned the price of provisions, or the use of apparatus which increased unemployment—but they could also detail aspects of local politics.

There are many new and concrete things to say about threatening letters in the period, filling in the picture created by Thompson. Our social-historical understanding of anonymity and power during this time needs to be more nuanced. In a fascinating article about Thompson's research assistant Edward Dodd, Carolyn Steedman exposes a methodological bias in Thompson's approach to anonymous letters. Thompson, Steedman discovered, insisted that Dodd should send him only letters with 'social significance'. As Steedman notes, this 'gives some insight into what [Thompson] *wanted* from eighteenth century anonymous letter-writers and the poor in general: he wanted their own conscious articulation of antagonisms towards an inequitable social and legal system'—and, so, Dodd found these letters for him. Communal motives were the key to the inclusion in Thompson's analysis—but 'personal and neighbourly grievance about the inequalities of everyday life was far less interesting to him'.[16] This is important to highlight as Thompson's research has been immensely influential. However, examining the local contexts of letters—even those written in the most communal and national of spirits—can sometimes reveal that their intent, purpose, and effect are not exactly what one might have assumed on first reading. Anonymous letters are not easy to classify. The protest genre could be manipulated for social gain in numerous and complex ways. Letters were not only tools used by the weak—as I will show, they were also open to manipulation by the powerful to shore up or defend their interests.[17]

Thompson was aware of the partiality caused by his source selection, noting that his approach gave 'only an erratic indication' of the state of anonymous letter-writing. As he put it: 'What survives in the *Gazette*s is only what is left after much else has drained through the sieve.' The authorities were not alerted to the existence of many letters. Many were ignored or kept secret. In some cases, their recipients would have complied with their specific demands and the matter would have remained completely private.[18] The range of the sources used here does not obviate such problems, which are discussed elsewhere in this book. However, the selection of sources I have used (combining local newspaper accounts, documents in local record offices, and Home Office material) draws attention to certain kinds of letter which are relevant to the social-historical understanding of such writing in general. Thompson's approach stressed the quantification of letter types. This helped to unmoor such letters from the local social contexts in which they are often best understood and present them in terms only of a national moral economy.

Anonymous writing and the Bisley Commons

Enclosure saw plots of thitherto publicly owned land enclosed and allocated to local landowners, proportionate to the value of their respective pieces of land. Between 1750 and 1850 the process of enclosure had converted more than six million acres of open, common land to private fields.[19] The decision to enclose the commons in the Gloucestershire village of Bisley near Stroud in the 1860s—the ostensible occasion of the letter at the head of this chapter—was a relatively late one. Other enclosures had also attracted anonymous letters.[20]

The Bisley commons extended far over the local area, taking in parts of Chalford Hill (just over two miles to the south of Bisley) and Bussage (two miles to the south-west of Bisley). There had been previous, failed attempts to enclose the commons: in 1733 and 1815.[21] In a parliamentary report of 1840, Bisley had been described as 'one of the poorest and most distressed parishes in the manufacturing districts of

Gloucestershire'. One of the local major farmers argued at that time that a system of allotment (whereby the common land was sold into allotments parcelled out to people of the parish) would be detrimental, as it would encourage allotment-holders to eke out a subsistence living and not seek supplementary waged work. The report from 1840 makes it clear that plans were afoot nonetheless to enclose the entire common and allocate small allotments to the local poor. The Assistant Commissioner for Gloucester argued that Bisley 'would ultimately suffer by such a plan . . . the population would ultimately become . . . more impoverished than at present'. Other objectors noted the difficulties encountered by people trying to grow plants without manure from grazing animals, which objection was countered by calls for allotment-holders to make compost heaps. Another suggestion was that as the sizes of gardens would be increased following partial absorption of the bordering commons, pig-keeping could be expanded in the area.[22]

The Commons in Bisley occupied about nine hundred acres of land and was split into four parts of the parish. One hundred acres were scrubland, but the rest was easier to cultivate. Taking into account the costs of seeking an Act of Parliament to enforce enclosure, and the building expenses, a local landowner based in Chalford Bottom, just south of Bisley, calculated the advantages and argued for enclosure on the grounds that there would be 'a considerable increase of produce; which, with the chances of a foreign war gathering around us, makes it a matter of [national] importance', despite the local effects.[23] In July 1863 a Bisley resident who signed off as '[a] freeholder who possesses common rights' wrote to the editor of the *Gloucester Journal* describing the common as a 'large tract of land' which had been unproductive for a long time, especially for freeholders without animals to set to graze there. Under the Act of Parliament, those freeholders were now set to gain, either through the allocation of allotments or by compensation. The writer looked forward to advantages: increased productivity, which would benefit labourers and local tradesmen, and he expected there to be building on the site. It was hoped that the scheme would be followed through 'at the smallest possible expense, and in the short-est possible time', and that a surveyor would be appointed 'at the least charge'.[24] This letter firmly expressed the views of the local elite; a very similar letter, signed by 'W.C.', was sent at the same time to the editor of the *Stroud Journal*.[25] John Bravender, a land agent and surveyor, was engaged for the task. Bravender proposed a meeting in

December 'for the purpose of receiving Claims in writing from all Persons claiming any Common or other right or interest' in the Commons.[26]

An anonymous poem was published in the *Gloucestershire Chronicle* in November 1863. It was entitled 'On hearing that Bisley Commons were to be enclosed'. It noted how the Commons were the place people went to when wearied with work, and concluded with these lines:

> And who will be the gainers?
> Not the sickly, not the poor,
> But those who have already
> So much that—they want more.
> Well good bye Bisley Commons.
> Perhaps when it is too late
> Those who now wish to destroy them
> Will be sorry for their fate.[27]

The Commons were used for more than just grazing and recreation. Brushwood, teasels, and thorns, timber, hay, and manure could be gathered from them. They provided space for tenterhooks to dry cloth; this was especially valuable to the many local workers in cloth trades. Local tension was evident in a heavy-handed response to the cleaning of a pool on the edge of the Common in April 1864. A 'lad' was summoned and charged with committing 'damage, injury and spoil to Bisley Common, by digging and taking away a quantity of earth and turf'. There is evidence of a lack of local knowledge in this reaction, or at least a lack of insight into the lives of neighbours and their attitude towards common land. Later investigation revealed that the boy lived in a house near the pool, and that the 'drift of the common' frequently ended up in the pool. In fact, it required cleaning out—which activity the 'lad' was engaged in.[28]

In early 1864 newspapers made fun of Levi Davis's spelling. Davis was a local churchwarden and lime-burner. He had put up a notice on the church and chapel doors concerning a meeting about the Bisley Commons enclosure. The note read:

Notice Year by Given that the Lotments Will be Set out on Manday, 22 Febuay, and All Persans as Wants a Lotment is requested to be thear if Posebel to Lock out the Best Plase fort. Order by the Caushwrns.[29]

The spelling in the death threat sent to the Doringtons suggests that we can rule Davis out from any list of potential writers. From the postmark, we can see that the letter was posted in Chalford on 11 February 1864; Chalford was among the most depressed parts of the area. The letter was written of behalf of the poor: 'you are robing the working class of the Parish and their offsprings forever'.

In addition to its distinctive style, there are other clues suggesting that it may have been written by someone with greater social status than would be considered usual for a complaint about the Commons. For instance, the author implies they own a gun. Another question is whether or not the issue of common land was covering up a different concern. One possibility here is tensions caused within the parish by religious change. The vicar of Bisley throughout the period of enclosure was Thomas Keble, whose brother, John, was 'the great Tractarian leader'. Thomas himself developed a great sympathy for Tractarianism, a movement associated with the University of Oxford, whose adherents argued for the reinstatement of older Christian traditions of faith and their inclusion in Anglican liturgy and theology. Finding the Church to be 'sinking into a ruinous state' on beginning his duties in 1827, Keble tried to improve the parish church and associated buildings over the next three decades. His restoration of Bisley Church was 'carried through in the face of great opposition from many of his parishioners'. Many from the huge parish attended Dissenting meetings at the chapel instead.[30] The Chalford Episcopal Chapel, built in 1724 for a congregation of 500, had never been consecrated. In 1840 Thomas Keble proposed to have the chapel enlarged.[31]

The area was described as being 'in an extremely impoverished condition' as a consequence of the depression in the cloth trade. Keble sought subscriptions towards the costs of enlarging Chalford's chapel, and although he donated more than £10 himself, such efforts in this context seem to have fostered significant animosity.[32] Perhaps the Doringtons had become involved, inciting the wrath of a parishioner who took close notice of ecclesiastical developments. The evidence is slight, but such possibilities show how muddy the waters could become in local politics and how difficult it can be to assign letters a social origin with real confidence. The local newspapers are quiet about the letter; its threats were apparently not made good. The letter was later retained by Dorington Junior's land steward.[33]

Figure 17. Anonymous letter to the Dorington family of Lypiatt Park threatening murder, 1864, Gloucestershire Archives, D5344/1, envelope

Just desserts

Other threatening letters belong even more obviously to very particular circumstances and contexts. However, many were consistent in at least some respects with the moral economy of those other letters. For instance, they often alluded to natural justice and found their occasions in deals and duties unhonoured by the powerful—the letters help us to understand certain economic activities as viewed through a moral lens.

A good example comes from 1767. Thomas Parry, an agent, was warned by an anonymous letter 'of the Danger you are in fir so often promising payment of the Prize Money for the Galoone—and not keeping your word'. The letter details plans to set his house ablaze, but informs him that it was abandoned in case his 'inisent Neighbours' were harmed. Here again one sees how even threats could be presented as moral claims. In place of the plan to burn him to death, Parry was told of a plot to keep watch on him until he could safely be kidnapped, after which event he was to lose his tongue, eyes, and right arm. The letter-writer claims to have thought this was going too far—and presents the letter as a neighbourly warning. The postscript contains the real meat: 'Sir I would advise you to give them Satisfaction if you can or elce make your escape before next Week.' Parry put up a £50 reward for information, to be paid upon the conviction of one or more of the offenders.[34] The letter is written as though sent from one person, but suggests that there were divisions among the conspirators; the letter itself appears an emblem of these divisions.

The 'Galoone' in question was the *Santissima Trinidad*. She was a large vessel used to carry luxury cargoes from Manila in the Philippines to Acapulco in Mexico. In October 1762 the *Santissima Trinidad* had been taken as a prize by two warships of the Royal Navy. They were *Panther*, commanded by Hyde Parker, and *Argo*, commanded by Richard King. In addition to the great ship herself, her cargo was also captured; it included three million pesos. Escorted back to Plymouth, the *Santissima Trinidad* reached port in June 1764. She was greeted by crowds, amazed at her quaint appearance and mass. The *Annual Register* described her as lying 'like a mountain in the water'.[35] But to those who had captured her, such wealth remained long a mirage. The process of realizing the ship's wealth was initially delayed by appeals from the Spanish Ambassador, and by a report from the Advocate General suggesting that the ship and her cargo might not be legitimate prizes of war.[36] Probably a certain reluctance to dissolve this wealth in the customary way existed in the halls of the Admiralty and the British government at large. The cargo was eventually auctioned, on behalf of Benjamin Vaughan & Son, Brokers, at various London coffee houses. It included vast quantities of cloth from India and China, including nankeen, various silks (as cloth and as thread), cottons, silk and cotton stockings, ribbon, cinnamon, cloves, nutmeg, pepper, and other spices.[37] Plans to turn the *Santissima Trinidad* into a ship to transport timber from North America were abandoned, and the ship was broken in the summer of 1765—salvaged for the timber used to make her. The workmen were instructed to check her construction, as it was suspected that there might be treasure hidden among her timbers—a similar find had been made in Portsmouth a few years before, when cases of Mexican gold dust, diamonds, and coins were found stowed in a secret part of the ship.[38]

Captains Hyde Parker and Richard King both became extremely rich on the back of their exploit. But many men aboard *Panther* and *Argo* (the officers, companies and supernumeraries), who had been promised a share of the 'bounty money' made by the sale of the cargo in 1765, had still not been paid two years later.[39] In 1766, a second payment had been made, with midshipmen and other petty officers receiving £45 each—but lower-ranking men waited still longer.[40] In June 1767, Thomas Parry—the agent who received the letter threatening him with torture and worse—put out a notice in the *Gazetteer and New Daily Advertiser*, concerning the third and final distribution of prize money from the sale of the *Santissima Trinidad* and her cargo. Parry explained that two distributions had been made following auctions, but that some goods remained in warehouses, unsold. Consequently, they would be unable to make timely payment of the next shares. They also noted the annoyance of a suit in Chancery that had been brought by the East India Company's officers on behalf of themselves and their troops; these had served in Manila and wanted a share of the ship and cargo. This had further delayed sale of the cargo and distribution of the prize money.[41]

The letter to Parry about the 'Galoone' was certainly targeted at him for breaking his word—but it clearly expressed also the frustrations and grievances that had arisen over a longer time as various parties appeared to conspire to deny the sailors their rightful dues. There were various motivations to write these anonymous letters in the 1760s, mostly concerning the economy; they expressed a desire for fairness, or for the people in power to act in a morally correct fashion. The same tool was employed for different reasons, by different people, but behind all of them was a sense of anger, expressed by people who felt their situation unfair. The letter to Thomas Parry does not fit into Thompson's scheme. It is directed at an agent who worked on behalf of richer people. It appears to express the anger of a group of people who had a financial predicament in common. It concerns a maritime matter, and lies outside the familiar territory of rural unrest and industrial dispute. It threatens arson—but it does not come from the same place as other incendiary letters.

Arson was rapidly destructive, left little evidence, and fostered animosity with neighbours. Fire also had potential symbolism as a kind of purification. Thompson noted that after 1790 it became increasingly common for anonymous writers to threaten arson. The 1790s were a decade when liberation seemed to be a possibility and many old ways were engulfed in flame. In the wake of the American and the French Revolutions, many people in Britain were inspired by revolution. The price of basics—food and clothing—was subject to public debate. But this took place while other developments changed the economic fortunes of the country and its citizens. Fossil fuels were increasingly harnessed to industrial developments, and machinery that made many workers redundant was increasingly adopted. On the night of 15 March 1792, the 'weaving factory' of Robert and John Grimshaw located in Knott Mill in Manchester burned down. There was reason to believe that this was intentional, as the Grimshaws had received through the post a month before an anonymous threatening letter, which began: 'Sirs, We have sworn together to destroy your Factory if we dye for it, and to have your Lifes for ruining our Trade.' Arson in a city like Manchester was a completely different thing from setting fire to a hayrick in the countryside—in cities there was a much greater chance of death.[42] The threat of arson, especially, caused 'prodigious alarm' in the countryside, but in built-up urban areas, this might have led many to comply with instructions and demands in anonymous letters.[43] Francis Haywood, a Manchester cotton merchant nearby on Deansgate, was threatened by anonymous letter two days after the fire:

Sir,…you have a deal of Warehous's full of Cotton if you dont lesson the Prices very much in next week they shall all of them be in flames depend on it since we have begin our design we intend to carry it on and have less proud Devils in the town that impoverish us so ill by keeping up the prices of Cotton Wool your life shall go also depend upon it with 4 others we intend—A Weaver. P.S. if we are hanged for you we will be better off than as we are.

Large rewards were offered for information in both cases.[44] The Grimshaws seemed preoccupied with the menace posed by what they saw as undesirables. Just days before the fire, they had used the local paper to warn people in the locality about delinquent servants. They were said to include a Welshman called John Jones and his three sons, none of whom spoke English well, and one Thomas Pollitt, scarred by smallpox.[45] The worst fears of the Grimshaws came true; perhaps they pushed their realization along a little themselves. The business of Grimshaw & Sons, jointly managed by Robert and John, who was the younger brother, did not survive the attack—the mill was all but destroyed by the fire. The Grimshaws had been in the process of installing power looms, of Cartwright's design, when their business burned down. The property was put up for re-lease in April 1792, 'so much damaged by Fire as to be necessary to be re-built'.[46] Robert and John Grimshaw went bankrupt in 1799, and Robert committed suicide the same year. At the time he was in King's Bench gaol for debt.[47] The brothers and their ill-fated business are remembered in an old song: 'Grimshaw's Factory Fire'.[48]

In 1795, after harvest failures and poor weather, there were food riots. The main complaint was the price of bread and this continued into 1796. The controversy extended to the question of whether it was too expensive to maintain Corsica, whether much grain was being sent owing to the British occupation of the island.[49] During the French Revolution and the Napoleonic wars, a civilian corps was used for defence of Britain in case of French invasion. Members of this volunteer guard were given allowances and certain exemptions. In some areas these associations created tensions.[50] In 1800 the Commanding Office of the West Bromwich Volunteer Association was passed a letter from one of his men, who had found it, dropped in his garden. The note was found folded: writing on the exterior directed the person who found the note to give it to someone from the corps, with the threat of a 'good thumping' if they should not. The letter was directed to both the officers and to the privates. The officers—the 'monky looking dum christian rougenation [meaning unknown]'—were further described as 'damned red faced devils that have your lessons taught you'. The authors, claiming to be part of a group of 'about 44 in number', stated that 'we dont care a dam for you big Devils as wear that damnation bloody bloody rag about your damnd paunch bellys' and threatened that 'blood shall be spilt from you like a butcher sticking a pig'. The writer[s] claimed to be 'well provided with weapons', and asserted that the privates ('poore fellows') would not protect the officers in the event of attack: 'you think you will try to make them but wee will set them right'. A line separates this threat to the officers from a section aimed at the non-commissioned men. Again reiterating that they are 'poor fellows', the writers claim that the privates were only there to protect their officers' 'liver & their ill gained property & to dam you to death, and when you have done all you are able you may goe to hell for all as they care'. The privates are then given a choice: the authors will be their 'well wishers' if they leave the corps—but they will face consequences if they remain.[51]

The letter was sent on to the Home Office by Earl Gower, the Lord Lieutenant of Staffordshire. A letter from Richard Jesson, the Commandant at West Bromwich, was enclosed. In the latter, Jesson expressed his fears that the anonymous letter might represent the sentiments of many people in the area where the corps was garrisoned. He suggests that a reward be offered for information leading to a confession, and notes that some of the privates had been threatened while out drinking. Clearly, Jesson was worried that some of the men would quit the corps.[52]

Dropped in a garden, the letter was different from letters pushed under doors or sent through the post. It charged whoever found it with a responsibility to act and backed up that demand with threats of physical violence. The main threat was aimed at members of the volunteer guard. The letter emphasized social divisions—between citizens outside the guard, and between officers and privates within the guard. Again, it's not clear whether the letter was truly representative of a wider and deeper social feeling; or whether its author was exploiting existing fears for the purpose of amplification.

Many seditious letters were dispatched at the start of the period. Thompson notes that until the later Ludd, Swing, and Rebecca letter campaigns, the year 1800 was 'undoubtedly the *annus mirabilis* for threatening letters'. (It was also the year soup kitchens were established in London.) Thompson (or rather: Dodd) found thirty anonymous letters in the *Gazette*, more than in previous years, when there had been widespread food rioting.[53] Anonymous letters containing threats of arson and murder against millers and farmers were sent to people in Saffron Walden in 1800.[54] In March 1800 a fire destroyed the brewery of Messrs Williams in Bath; the whole neighbourhood was illuminated by the immense fire. The maltster was presumed dead. Williams was only partially insured, and it could not be established if the fire had been accidental. Anonymous letters threatening arson had been received by another brewery in the city, and strenuous efforts were made to discover who had written them.[55]

In November 1800, three millers—William Hetley of Alwalton, Huntingdonshire; William Hardwick of Market Deeping in Lincolnshire; and Messrs J. and W. Rickett of Lolham Mills—each received letters in the same handwriting threatening them with violence if they did not reduce the price of flour.

Sir. If you dont fall your flowers to 3s 6d / stone next Saturday we will pull your mills over your heads and take your flower a way we will pull you about the Market Place on Saturday next your Jacknipps

[To Rickett, signed with a squiggly pattern]

Sir. If you Dont fall your flower next Saturday to 3/6 per stone we will pull
your mill down over your head a take your flower away we will Dragg you
about the Market Place on Saturday next
                    [To Hetley, signed with two different squiggly patterns]

Sir. If you Dont fall your flower next Saturday to 3/6 per stone we will pull
your mill down over your head & take your flower away we will Dragg you
about the market place on Saturday
                    [to Hardwick, signed with a squiggly pattern very similar
                              to one in the sign-off for Hetley's letter][56]

Letters sent in a rural context often insisted that stocks were sold at set
or reduced prices. The letters were sent locally; each bore a Peterborough
postmark. Hetley owned much property including at least two bake-
houses, and common rights.[57] The millers offered a reward, £20 from
each business. To this was added £40 from the Peterborough magistrates, who were 'convinced that the due and regular Supply of the
Market depends on the Security and Protection of all Persons trading'.[58]
As in the 1790s, threatening letters were not just a concern in rural
settlements. Anonymous letters threatened 'fire and destruction to the
clothiers' in Bradford, Westbury, and Warminster.[59] Arson and threats
of arson meant something quite different in cities: letters invoking
arson in urban contexts cannot be linked automatically to the sensibilities
and anxieties reproduced in those letters linked to the large protest
movements in rural areas.

Luddites, inspired by the frame-breaker Ned Ludd, promoted
frame-breaking between 1811 and 1816 in response to the mechaniza-
tion of the textile industry. Their campaigns were sometimes accompanied by letters signed 'Captain Ludd', or 'Ned Ludd'. The 1810s saw
further economic misery; unemployment increased after the soldiers
were demobilized in 1816. The introduction of corn laws in 1815
blocked the import of cheap grain—boosting profits for landowners
and immiserating many more. William Hetley of Alwarton, one of the
millers targeted by anonymous letter in 1800, went bankrupt.[60] Hunger
in the countryside saw an increase in prosecutions for poaching. In
1814, John Nicholson, a Staffordshire poacher, was convicted of having
sent an anonymous threatening letter to Theophilus Levett of Wychnor
in Staffordshire, the High Sheriff of Staffordshire. Having been expelled
from Levett's land at Wychnor Park, Nicholson sent a letter suggesting
that Levett watch out lest he get a ball through his head. Justice Dallas
sentenced Nicholson to death and did not refrain from commenting
upon the 'demonlike' offence of putting someone in constant fear of

murder. Nicholson was described as having a 'most hardened physiognomy' and was said to show no emotion during his trial. But he burst
into tears on hearing his fate. Levett, having heard Nicholson was too
poor to pay for counsel, had provided him with the money for legal
assistance. To his further credit, Levett later requested mercy for the
man. Nicholson was reprieved.[61]

Many of these cases—however personal—should be situated within
the wider context of social protest. After the Peterloo Massacre in 1819,
when protestors gathered to demand the reform of parliamentary representation were fatally charged by mounted yeomanry, the government tried to tighten the rules surrounding the organization of protest.
Some political tensions had been brewing for decades by then. George
Bellamy, the irascible mayor of Plymouth in Devon, received anonymous threatening letters, some from Dublin, after he had antagonized
members of the local Irish community in speeches rich with anti-Irish
rhetoric.[62] One letter, from August, warned 'Beware of Your life
Bellamy. *You must inevitably die.*' A £500 reward was offered.[63]

In December 1820 Thomas Griffin Phillpotts, the mayor of Monmouth
in Wales, received two threatening anonymous letters. One read:

> You blodshy villan
> remember the victim Bellingham
> You deserve and will have his fate
> Mr Humphry is persecuted and will be
> revenged

The reference to John Bellingham, who in 1812 had assassinated Prime
Minister Spencer Percival, reveals this to be a death threat against
Phillpotts ('You . . . will have his fate'). Despite the reference to national
political drama, Phillpotts knew that the letters originated in a private
grievance. He had recently prosecuted Charles Homfray at King's
Bench for 'an outrageous assault' on him, on the high road. Homfray, a
political rival, and the adjutant of the East Monmouthshire Militia
(where Phillpotts was a captain), was currently serving a two-month
prison sentence. Homfray had powerful friends; these were also
enemies of Phillpotts. One, Joseph Price, was an acting magistrate. He
ensured that Homfray's stretch in gaol was a comfortable one. Phillpotts
was certain the letters had been 'manufactured' by Homfray, who was
in prison 'without any manner of restraint'. The background to this
clash lay in local politics, which was dominated by those faithful to the
Somerset family on one side, and old Monmouthshire families who

had been sidelined locally, like the Phillpotts, plus the radicals, supported financially by local merchants, on the other.[64] Phillpotts wrote to Viscount Sidmouth, hoping for extra money to increase his offered reward. In order to advertise the reward, he had handbills printed to be posted around the city.[65] His benefactor Sidmouth had himself received anonymous letters, connected to the Cato Street Conspiracy of 1820. That was a plot to assassinate British cabinet members, organized by people angered by the Peterloo Massacre, by economic depression, and by political attempts to suppress protest.[66]

Large social movements and high political intrigue could inform and intersect with the manifestation of personal grudges. But what weighed most heavily in an individual's motivations for writing could be very unclear. Certainly, many people of high social standing lived in fear of organized revolt—but how far anonymous letters justified their paranoia, and how far they simply played on them, is less certain. What is clear is that many letters of this time were backed up by action, and that in turn the letters themselves acquired more and more power to frighten, extort, moralize, and upbraid.

In addition to a cotton factory, David Bellhouse had a steam sawmill, situated by a branch of the Rochdale Canal, along Oxford Road in Manchester. The mill was set ablaze on 27 February 1822. Many of the buildings had only recently been erected, following a devastating fire the month before. Arson was suspected as the cause of the second fire, and a reward was offered for information which would lead to the arsonist. But—as will now be unsurprising—the reward was also promised for information about an anonymous letter sent earlier that month. The letter had warned that Bellhouse's life (and the lives of his family) were in danger, as was his house, and cotton factory, 'for you being so illnatered against the poor sawyers'. Bellhouse's sawmill was described in the letter as stopping 'a hundred familys Ceep [keep]'. This was the reason, the letter informed its unhappy recipient, why townsfolk 'have such a spite at you'.[67]

In *Captain Swing* (1969) Eric Hobsbawm and George Rudé traced the development of the Swing riots, agricultural uprisings and attacks that swept across the country in 1830, noting that there was often 'an opening phase of fires and threatening letters'.[68] The death penalty for anonymous letters like these had been abolished in 1823, and the maximum sentence reduced to seven years' transportation. Labourers rioted over the loss of livelihood cause by the introduction of threshing machines (horse-powered apparatuses which took work from men). People were already struggling after recent bad harvests. Protests spread, especially in the south and the east of the country. Hayricks were torched; machines were damaged. Many letters were signed 'Captain Swing'. Swing was an umbrella figure who stood for the hard-working tenant farmers forced into destitution. Using this pseudonym implied organization and could protect individual local protest leaders. The Swing persona allowed individual letter-writers to attach themselves to the broader movement. Where this decision was not made by the writer, one should be more circumspect before attaching a given letter to a larger movement.

That such circumspection could itself have a political character is obvious from responses at the time. John Thomas Huntley, the vicar of Kimbolton in Huntingdonshire, was shaken by an anonymous letter he received in November 1830. Huntley believed he had always shown kindness to farmers and labourers in the parish: 'I have no reason to conclude that my Character either as a landlord or a Clergyman is offensive'. In a letter to the Home Secretary, Huntley suggests that the letter was sent by 'a Tribe of Gypsies whose encampment I had broken up on Monday last'. Huntley had read in the papers of the important national protests, 'imbued with the revolutionary Spirit of the Times'— but he argued that his local community was not riven in this way. Huntley claimed that his parishioners were not greatly represented in the protests locally. They, he thought, were bulked out by 'Gypsies' and vagrants.[69] The Swing movement probably provided, for some anonymous writers at least, a convenient way to develop their own arguments and alarm people with whom they had fallen out. In December 1830, Dr John Lamb, the Master of Corpus Christi College, Cambridge, forwarded two anonymous letters to the Home Secretary, both written in the same hand, and signed 'Swing Head Quarters'. One had been sent to Lamb; the other to Dr Charles Simeon, the Dean of Arts at King's College. The letter to Lamb suggests some playfulness and education—addressing him as 'Dr Agnus' (*agnus* is Latin for 'lamb'). Both letters warned that the two colleges would soon be in flames.[70]

Anonymous threatening letters could be easily manipulated for personal gain and can never be automatically identified as outcroppings of the moral economy. An anonymous threatening letter written to William Brown of Long Benton, Northumberland in 1797 shows the way that the language of despair, common in the social protest letters, could be appropriated without any loss of meaning. Its author demanded that £20 be put under a stone in Barrack Lane, Tynemouth, a large town at the mouth of the River Tyne. The money would facilitate emigration to America: 'me famalry are now starving the Butchers will let them have no more meet, the Bakers will let them have no more bread what must we do, I'm resolved now to go to Immirica'. The writer claimed he had once been a servant of Brown's 'but was turned away for no reason'.[71] This letter departs from the pattern set by the social protest letters and shows that some people shifted the message on their unsigned letters, so they become not generalized requests to make life easier for people in the community, but requests for themselves—simple extortion, really—with an element of personal grievance against the recipient.

Building Jerusalem

When John Thomas Huntley read the 'Captain Swing' letter he received in 1830, he assumed it was 'a general denunciation of the Clergy in the Neighbourhood', because these were so common. Clergy were often the targets of anonymous letters. Some men were steered away from pursuing a career in the Church on receiving one.[72] In 1828 'a Brother Presbyter' dropped in on Reverend Arthur Atherley's service, in St Michael's and All Angels Church, Heavitree, in Devon. He then addressed a letter to 'Rev Mr Hatherley' complaining about the content and structure of the service. Apparently, Atherley gave scant attention to Jesus' sacrifices, and paid too much heed to the 'common blessings of life' for members of the congregation. In a long and detailed letter of reproach, the anonymous author noted scornfully that Atherley had read his sermon from a printed book, and steered him to make better choices, avoiding 'those half hearted essays which keep back many vital truths, & pervert others'.[73] In 1825 Reverend Broderick of Banstead in Surrey was accused via anonymous letter of drawing out christening and burial services, exhausting the parishioners and making mourners stand in the cold 'longer than there is any occasion for, without their hats'.[74] Clergymen were often the symbolic focus of community life—they often bore the brunt of local anger about national religious changes. And they were easy to find: the addresses of clergymen

('The Rectory', 'The Vicarage', 'The Church', et cetera) rarely required much effort to establish, and indeed many parish clergy would have welcomed written communication from their parishioners.

One significant letter-writing campaign took place in the 1860s as part of the 'Tractarian Crisis', which was also interwoven into the Dorington story (and, later, seems potentially part of the letter to Mary Dorothea Cokayne in 1894). The crisis came about when attempts to move the Anglican Church to a midway point between Catholicism and evangelicalism—by emphasizing ritual, bringing back some sensory paraphernalia, and introducing more elaborate garments—were attacked by those who saw Tractarian developments as an ecclesiastical regression. Thomas Keble junior, the son of the vicar of Bisley, whom we have already met, was at Sidmouth in 1858. The church in Sidmouth wanted to expand, but the High Church architectural design was interpreted as 'semi-popish' in the local newspapers. The expansion was intended to accommodate incomers sympathetic to Tractarianism, so local resistance also developed along social lines emphasizing the usurpation of the parish by outsiders. New seating plans upset long-held customary hierarchies and privileges.

Anonymous handbills were posted, signed 'Ratepayer'. Some of the anonymous letters were published in the *Exeter & Plymouth Gazette*. A new vicar, Frederick Luttrell Moysey, replaced the Tractarian-leaning Reverend Hamilton in 1861. The change of incumbent caused controversy. The Earl of Buckingham, who backed Moysey, was sent 'a grossly abusive and threatening letter'. As so often in those cases where the receipt of the letter is known, a reward was offered. In the following years 'a large number of scandalously disgusting and obscene letters' circulated—eventually Moysey departed.[75] The letters in Sidmouth were part of a wider campaign of protest which highlighted differences within a small community, but they reflected national concerns. Elsewhere one comes away with the impression of the anonymous letter as a weapon wielded by those with little alternative power. But those in the best position to abuse the medium of the letter were still the educated—those already in possession of significant cultural capital. Indeed, people in positions of power—including clergymen—could manipulate the tensions of the time to use the fears surrounding anonymous letters fraudulently, for personal gain.

On 17 January 1811 the parsonage adjoining Maresfield churchyard in East Sussex burned down. The curate Reverend Robert Bingham and his family were home when the fire started—two Bingham children were thrown clear from a window. In 1810 the parsonage stables had burned down,

as supposed, because he [Bingham] had endeavoured to check the disorderly conduct of some of his parishioners, in consequence of their encroachments in Ashdown forest, being resisted by the proprietors, respecting which anonymous letters had been sent, containing the most outrageous and audacious threats.[76]

A local farmer, Richard Jenner, had received a letter threatening that his house would be set on fire.[77] The contents were made public but a 200-guinea reward had gone unclaimed. Headed 'Fire! Murder! And Revenge!', the letter claimed that fifty people intended to

keep our lands and have revenge. Therefore Parson Churchwards and Farmers your Barns and Houses shall burn if you take our Lands your Luves two shall pay Your sheep we will eat Your Oxen we can mame your Stacks shall blaze and DICK [Richard Jenner] you shall be shooted as you return home from the market or fair. We are united and sworn to stand by one another 50 good fellows.

The letter appeared to come from one of the 'Foresters', local people who had enclosed parts of Ashdown Forest a few months before, but whose enclosures had been torn down on the order of the Duchess of Dorset. Threatening statements had been uttered at the time; the parish was on the alert.

Eventually, however, suspicion settled upon the curate himself—and the possibility that he had exploited the Foresters' grievance to cover his own mischief. On 22 January Bingham was arrested by a Bow Street Principal Officer, 'Adkins'. He was charged with writing an incendiary letter to Jenner, and with arson. Since 1810 the contents of the parsonage had been insured by the Union Office, and insurance fraud was supposed. Bingham, who was set to acquire over £1,000 from the scam, was seen acting suspiciously—burying and hiding belongings and documents before the fire. He claimed that he could not access any water to extinguish the fire, despite there being a pond nearby and a bucket to hand.[78] Bingham had taught many in the community how to write: he had founded a Charity School for the Poor. Many people were familiar with his handwriting and swore that the writing in the anonymous letters looked like a disguised version of his writing. It was noted that the 'J' of Jenner had been amended to look like a 'G'. However, if Bingham had taught many people to write, then it also stands to reason not only that his handwriting could have been recognizable to many of those people, but that some of them could have possessed a handwriting style rather like his. Jenner said he had known Bingham for five or six years, and that they had a friendship.[79] Investigations even centred on the watermarks on paper sold locally.[80]

Jenner's sons claimed to have seen the letter drop from Bingham's pocket on the road, but they had been ignored at the time. Indeed, many parishioners had considered Bingham so respectable as to be beyond suspicion, and everyone was on the lookout for a Forester. But Bingham had been seen moving stacks of wood the day before, and had planted a flower over his copybooks, buried in the garden, 'for better concealment'. Bingham conducted his own defence during the trial, which lasted just twelve hours. A London stationer was called in to state that the whole region was awash with paper bearing the watermark 'Evans & Sons'. Bingham's brothers—the Reverend Richard Bingham and Captain Joseph Bingham, a naval man—asserted that the value of Bingham's lost books alone amounted to about £1,000. Others spoke of opulence in the house. Bingham's main defence was: why would he do such a thing? What had he to gain?[81] One of his upstanding brothers and character referees was later found to have some sins of his own. Reverend Richard Bingham was found guilty of various offences from 1813 to 1818, including 'fraud of the revenue', theft of surplice fees, and assault. In 1818 he was forced to sell property, including a little empire of houses called 'Bingham Town' in Gosport, from which he secured tithes. He was struck off as a magistrate and made bankrupt in 1822. At that time, he was described as having been 'in distressed pecuniary circumstances since 1807'.[82] In 1811 his brother Robert was found not guilty of writing the letter to Jenner, and not guilty of arson. The judge was swayed by the robust character references, and by Bingham's status as a clergyman.[83]

The evidence in the case was mainly circumstantial, although circumstantial evidence can be compelling. Robert Bingham's burial of his belongings before the fire did seem powerful on the face of it. Bingham published a pamphlet in 'his own vindication'.[84] Moved out of the Maresfield parish, by the summer months Bingham had taken up a residence in Cockeringham near Louth.[85] Writing to her brother in Leicestershire, one Mary Frewen of Brickwall House in Northiam,

Sussex—about thirty miles from the Maresfield parsonage—referred to
the case. She had been reading about it in a newspaper. 'On examining
the premises', Mary noted, the search had 'some fresh turned up mould
in the garden dug into & there was found put as a place of safety the
Curate's Books'. 'Who could do it but himself!!' she exclaimed.[86]

Who indeed? If Bingham was in fact guilty, what had been his intent
in writing the letter? He had hoped to pin the crime on the Foresters.
He had hoped to divert attention from such secrets as the buried stash
of valuables by invoking fear of radicalism, common land disputes, and
national protest.

Figureheads and signatories

E. P. Thompson put a decline in the number of anonymous threatening letters sent after 1830 down to their being 'displaced by the Radical
or Chartist printing-press'.[87] This may explain a reduction in the volume of letters sent as part of wider social protest movements; but it
may also mislead as to the actual scope of anonymous letter-writing in
the period. Thompson's explanation reflects his sources and method-
ology more than any actual decline in anonymous letter-writing. His
focus on letters deemed to be of 'social significance', defined by his
own narrow view, saw much else that was also socially significant slip
through the net. How anonymous letters connected to social power
remains the central issue—but the letters themselves are often unreliable witnesses in this respect.

Many of the letters discussed here participated in the setting or
upholding of moral norms, holding the recipient to account based on
a public standard of behaviour. Some of this could be connected to
Thompson's concept of the 'moral economy'.[88] Anonymous letter-
writing was a way in which people from very different backgrounds
could link their particular grievances to wider notions of justice and
accountability. However, the terms on which different letters attached
to larger communal values appear highly varied when each letter is put
in its local context. Additionally, the concept of 'moral economy' has
many possible meanings overlapping with the sense in which
Thompson used it.[89] One thing that such letter-writing in this period
does suggest is that there were many ways of invoking and using public
injustice in private letters. Linking public and private concerns in this

way greatly increased the potential power of threatening anonymous letters. Their actual effect is very hard to judge for many reasons, the most important of which is that the most effective anonymous letters might be those that did not make it into an archive or newspaper. Suffice it to note that in the years following the letter they received in 1864, the Doringtons took a close interest in their reputation in Bisley. They opened their garden to communal festivities, involved themselves in parish charity—and paid for a new courtroom.[90]

4

Obscenity

Peer's perversion uncovered

ENQUIRER.—Yes.

Figure 18. Mock-up of classified advert from *Loughborough Echo*, 3 November 1916, 1

In February 1917, a Liberal agent in Darlington pleaded guilty to sending five anonymous and pseudonymous obscene letters to a woman in Loughborough, the writer's home town. John Peer, sixty-seven, had been trapped by a police operation involving the cooperation of his victim, Mrs Merishaw. The first letter received by Merishaw had appeared to come from a woman in Loughborough, because Peer had arranged to have a letter sent first from Darlington to Loughborough, and thence to its target. Merishaw, disgusted by the contents, took it to the police. Peer had known Merishaw in the past, probably through local politics, but Peer had moved to Darlington and they had not met for sixteen years. In his letter, Peer requested that Merishaw respond to the letter by placing a notice in the *Loughborough Echo*: 'Enquirer, Yes'. This she did.[1] An 'equally offensive' letter followed the publication of the reply in the newspaper. It was typed this time, suggesting new caution (if not disbelief). It asked for the same response to be repeated. Peer eventually requested a meeting. A rendezvous on the Midland

Railway bridge was set for 6.55 p.m. on 12 January 1917—and this is how the writer came to be arrested by the police. He tried to excuse his behaviour on the grounds of illness and the stress of war work. Combined with a medical operation, these factors had caused him to 'become unhinged...[and] not responsible for actions'. The court did not accept his explanation and the letters were deemed to have been written by someone in possession of their senses. Peer was fined £50, a fairly hefty figure at the time.[2]

'When it is considered how much the religious, moral, and intellectual progress of the people, would be accelerated by the unobstructed circulation of letters', Rowland Hill had written in 1837, 'the Post Office assumes the new and important character of a powerful engine of civilization.'[3] John Wilson Croker, in a review of Hill's proposals, was less optimistic about the moral good of cheaper post. He took a more mixed view. 'Even admitting—what it would be hard to prove—that there should be a preponderance of good', wrote Croker, 'can it be shown that the preponderance will be so great as to compensate the other, as we think, inevitable disadvantages?'[4] The Penny Post came into being in January 1840, with a variety of immense social consequences. Among these were the greater opportunities for privacy of posting afforded by pre-paid stamps.[5] These opportunities became still more meaningful in the 1850s when pillar-boxes were introduced.[6] Their presence meant that a sender no longer had to go into a post office or give their letters to their postman, having once acquired some stamps. This made the process much more impersonal, especially in small communities. Earlier letters might have been associated with particular individuals by the postman. The introduction of cheap, accessible, and potentially anonymous communication enriched the lives of many. As with the introduction of Internet communication in the 1990s, these changes also removed some of the earlier disincentives that had existed when the technologies of delivery were more expensive, inconvenient, or personal. The Post Office reforms of the nineteenth century made it much easier for unwanted anonymous letters to enter the homes of their targets, while the interpersonal connection remained almost as intrusive and intimate as if the message had been delivered directly by a half-known neighbour.

As was normal in almost all such cases, the letters received by Mrs Merishaw do not survive. They were probably destroyed by the police. Many people like her would have destroyed the letters immediately—if not out of shock or disgust, then for more complicated reasons of shame that can only be lightly sketched in this chapter. The concept of obscenity is a tricky one. As a legal idea, it had undergone expansion and change in the second half of the nineteenth century. The Obscene Publications Act of 1857 empowered police to seize materials and request permission to destroy them.[7] It was aimed at suppressing the trade in pornography by superseding provisions in the Vagrancy Act of 1838 that required that some element of public display be included in the offence.[8] The law of 1857 targeted commercial sale of obscene materials that did not involve the public display previously needed for prosecution. At the heart of the 1857 Act's intent was the belief that such material caused a corruption of morals in those exposed to them. This presumed effect was central to the policing of private letters too; the focus of the cases presented here.

The relevance of the new law to such letters is hard to assess. This is reflected in the fact that pornographic traders took advantage of improvements in the postal system to circumvent the new police powers of 1857, transmitting obscene material to buyers without using a commercial venue that could easily be found and raided by the police.[9] Mailing of letters increased by 62.5% between 1850 and 1860, reflecting not only an expanded postal network but also increasing literacy rates. Much unwelcome material could hide within such quantity even if organized interception efforts had been made. The Customs Act of 1846 prohibited the import of 'indecent or obscene prints, paintings, photographs, books, cards, lithographic or other engravings, or any other indecent or obscene articles'. This was linked to a vague belief that foreign sources of corruption and pornography were a significant problem in British society. Such provisions did not always bear directly on obscene letters sent within the British postal system.[10] Still, the possibility of interdiction at the Post Office remained quite consistent in theory. Nasty, libellous details written on postcards might in any case be read by employees of the postal service, or by servants and family members.[11]

The 1908 Post Office Act also permitted Post Office regulations 'for preventing the sending or delivery by post...letters, newspapers, supplements, publications, packets, or postcards having thereon, or on the covers thereof, any words, marks, or designs of an indecent libelous, or grossly offensive character'.[12] Peer was described as being charged with 'sending through the post five indecent letters, three of which contained indecent postcards'. In other words, he was charged under Section 63 of the Post Office Act, which prohibited the 'sending by post of...indecent prints, words &c'.[13] The detection of such crimes often relied on the participation of Post Office workers. The methods used to catch abusive letter-writers kept pace with technological change. Such efforts can be seen as allied with the intent behind the Obscene Publications Act, aimed at the suppression of pornographic traders and 'immoral' art and literature. However, that law related to the possible destruction of the offending article rather than to direct punishment of the author or trader. Its focus was on the intent to profit by obscenity; the motivations of anonymous letter-writers were obviously more diffuse and varied. Prosecution of such people was usually handled as a criminal matter that relied on legal provisions to fine and imprison for libel.[14] The Obscene Publications Act of 1857 nonetheless reflected a growing anxiety about the spread of obscene material in Victorian Britain. The same moral thinking and belief in the efficacy of obscene material is of high significance in how the cases that follow were handled.

Publications

The legal definition of libellous publication was quite broad. For instance, taking an individual into a back room to show them an obscene print was considered publication.[15] Much later, in a significant 1932 case, the prosecution argued that 'it is a publication to put [an obscene article] into anybody's hands' (this was conceded to be plain legal fact by the defence in the same prosecution).[16] Throughout the period covered here, any obscenity sent privately to another in the post could have been considered published. This was an old paradox in libel law: to bring the libel to attention, the recipient needed to publish it again by handing it to another.[17] For example, Mrs Merishaw needed to publish the 'indecent' letters from Peer to the police in order to pursue justice. Although no actual legal risk was assumed in such cases, the moral context of Victorian and Edwardian society probably meant that for many people it would have seemed unwise to reveal their own possession of obscene materials—even if they had not chosen to receive them. Possibly many of the men (they are overwhelmingly men) who sent obscene letters relied on this vulnerability, especially when they were targeting individuals who were already socially marginalized. But it was a worry that could transcend class and status. A case from 1896 has the editors of The Lancet claiming to be saving their readers from blackmail by publishing the names of various writers hawking pornography as science (often 'anthropology'). It was thought that innocent scientists and medics might be exposed to blackmail if they came into possession of such works because they were unadvised of their obscene nature.[18]

In 1865 the Society for the Protection of Women and Children initiated a legal case against a Church of England clergyman. The case is especially interesting as it illustrates some of the complexities involved in publication, possession, and consent. The cleric was accused of sending obscene letters to a nineteen-year-old woman. She had become an adoptee of the Royal Patriotic Fund after her father had died in the Crimean War. Two years before the case in question, she had found herself a ward in Dalston, which is where she met the clergyman. Later, after she had moved to Chelsea, a bundle of letters was discovered in her room by an aunt. All had been received in Dalston. The aunt, 'on perceiving the contents of those filthy missives, written in love strains', confronted her niece. The young woman 'flew into a passion at the discovery, showing the demoralising effect of the letters'. An Inspector Raymond would testify that the letters were in the handwriting of the vicar. The Bishop of London conducted some enquiries, having been forwarded the letters. He concluded there were insufficient grounds for action. Likewise, a court summons was not granted, on account of the fact that the receiver of the letters had not objected to their contents.[19]

Anonymous letters considered to be obscene by those who intercepted them, but not necessarily by their intended recipient, created headaches for the courts. Doubts were entertained about whether there was an obscenity case to be made, with regard to letters opened under such conditions. Potentially obscene letters that were misdirected or read by someone other than the intended recipients constitute many of the letters which survive in the historical record. In July 1914 Bertram Stonell, thirty-two, was found guilty in a Lambeth court of 'unlawfully attempting to solicit and incite Susannah Meader and a certain woman unknown to procure and attempt to procure a certain girl not being a common prostitute or of known immoral character'.[20] However, Stonell was not tried on the crime of 'unlawfully writing and publishing certain false defamatory and obscene libels' concerning Meader, for which he had also attended court. The month before, a letter addressed to 'The landlady' had arrived at the wrong house in Camberwell. After it was opened and read, the police were involved. That Stonell was the author was confirmed by handwriting comparison.[21] In this case, the fact that the letter had been read by another (any other) constituted publication of the libel. However, a different crime (solicitation) was added to the sheet and used as the basis of the prosecution. The fact that Stonell was bailed caught the notice of a Suffragist reporter, who wondered why men charged with such serious offences were bailed while Suffragettes were kept in remand and force-fed.[22]

Moral panics created conditions in which transgressive letters could draw power from publicity. Among the most famous (and most misogynistic) pseudonymous letters ever written were penned in the late nineteenth century. The 'Dear Boss' letters, purportedly written by 'Jack the Ripper', may also have encouraged other people to write letters with wicked intent and disturbing content. Indeed, by the close of the nineteenth century the circulation of malicious letters was increasing. Only a tiny fraction of them made it to the pages of newspapers. (The historian must often rely on problematic newspaper sources in order to get any sense at all of the Victorian traffic in obscene and abusive letters.) The involvement of print media in the transmission of the case details and the capture of the perpetrator could be multilayered and complex. It is important to keep in mind that newspapers had their own agendas and shaped and policed such stories accordingly. Legal authorities were often only part of the picture in response to such incidents—given the ambiguous legal status of these crimes and their deeply personal intrusions, there was quite often a vigilante component to the search for the author. In 1844, a father published 'a caution' in the *Exeter & Plymouth Gazette* warning the sender of an anonymous letter addressed to his daughter, to 'send no more of his filthy and obscene letters to the ladies of this neighbourhood'. This anonymous father added darkly: 'There are men in Exeter as keen to detect and resolved to punish such odious depravity. Let him look to it!'[23] Likewise, the moralistic language of the journalist did not always dovetail neatly with the lawyer's contemplation of obscenity.

One of the first major cases of serial obscene letter-writing to be examined by the Post Office authorities concerned a wealthy man:

Walter Frederic Mason.[24] A married Ipswich engineer, Mason was a respectable Victorian. By 1877, when he was twenty-nine, he had already been 'in the habit for years past of writing disgusting letters to members of a great many of the leading families in the neighbour-hood'.[25] The *Ipswich Journal* records his court charge:

He unlawfully, wickedly, maliciously, and scandalously did write and publish and cause and procure to be written and published, certain lewd, wicked, scandalous and obscene letters to the corruption of morals and good manners, for the purpose of contaminating, vitiating, and corrupting the liege subjects of Her Majesty, and bringing the said liege subjects to a state of wickedness, lewdness, debauchery, and immorality against the peace, &c.[26]

As the language here indicates, Mason was being prosecuted under old libel and sedition laws.[27] Note also how the charge assumes the recipi-ents would be corrupted by Mason's words. The victims were all female, aged between twelve and thirty-five; they were sent 'the most revolting and disgusting obscenity'. That the letters were written in the same hand and sent from the same post office, all at the same time of the day, allowed the police to catch Mason red-handed about to dispatch letters to five women at once.[28] A special sitting of the Ipswich Borough Magistrates was arranged in late June because in the interim Mason had jumped bail and then surrendered himself. Mason, claiming to feel unwell, was allowed to sit down in the court. He was described as the 'proprietor of the Eagle Engineering Works' in Ipswich.[29]

The court heard how Mason's offence was uncovered. In early 1877, the Post Office and the police had heard from 'different ladies' that letters had been received. These were analysed, and it was determined that many of them had been posted at the Wet Dock Post Office, usu-ally later in the day. Marked stamps were issued from that office in order to snare the sender. The Post Office set a watch in the afternoon and evening to see who posted letters at that time, and to see whether the handwriting could be detected by comparison on site. If it could be, the person on watch was instructed to signal the police officer. On an evening in March, a plain-clothes policeman asked Mason for his name and address. Mason refused, but eventually blurted out that he had no letters, only a newspaper. Mason had not been asked about let-ters at all. At this point, Constable William Garnham brought his ten years of policing experience to bear. He asked Mason to stand under a gas lamp and write his name in the officer's pocketbook. Meanwhile, employees of the Post Office had delivered the stamped letters posted by Mason to their intended targets. These letters were opened and returned to the Post Office official. The sample of handwriting in Garman's notebook was compared to the obscene letters. Crucially, comparison could also be made with a letter sent by Mason to the Ipswich Postmaster back in November 1876, requesting that his mail be forwarded to the Eagle Iron Works. George William Darken, the head clerk at the Ipswich GPO, confirmed the similarity. Darken was considered to be qualified because he was 'extremely well versed in handwriting', having been a clerk for nearly a quarter of a century. The nearest post office to Mason's premises was the one at Wet Dock.[30] On confessing his guilt, Mason claimed that he had not been 'master of his own mind'. When he returned to his seat in court 'he buried his face in his hands and wept bitterly'.[31]

The law appeared to assume that only the poor would commit such crimes. This is more or less what early critics of the Penny Post had also assumed.[32] In a scathing attack on the local magistrates, the *London Evening Standard* argued that Mason had been treated differently from other men accused of sending obscene letters, because he was rich and from a respectable family. Despite Mason's having been a scourge of innocent young women and children in Ipswich since 1868, his case was initially heard preferentially *in camera*. Bail—which he jumped— was set at £500. Half was to be paid by Mason's father, half by his employers. This agreement was reached against a backdrop of rumour that Mason was planning to flee abroad: 'No measures seem to have been taken to prevent his absconding, and his non-appearance did not elicit much surprise.' Noting that the sacrifice of hundreds of pounds was 'as nothing' compared to the avoidance of criminal penalties, the editorial suggested that this was bound to rankle with the working class, who could not fail to conclude that there was one law for the rich, another for the poor.[33]

The *Ipswich Journal* leapt to the defence of the local magistrates, arguing that they 'could no more forbid Mason bail than they could prevent his breathing'. It was noted that 'they fixed the bail so high that the man might reasonably have been expected to remain and stand his trial'. To the *Standard*'s complaint that Mason's trial had been held behind closed doors without good reason, the *Journal* rejoined:

From the nature of the case it was not the accused but his victims who would have suffered the most severely from the ordeal of a public examination. The only losers are those who have an itching ear for prurient details.[34]

The *Bury & Norwich Post* described Mason as 'a young man of gentlemanly appearance' and his position as 'business of an important and remunerative kind'. 'All that is gone', the paper seemed to lament—he was 'a ruined man'. Justice Brett told Mason that his actions were 'most monstrous, wicked, and abominable', especially so for being a married man 'of some position in life, with no temptation'. The judge thought it 'impossible, until one had seen what you had written, to conceive that any human being could write such abominations'. Mason was sentenced to fifteen months in prison and fined £100.[35] This was not Mason's last run-in with the law. In 1880, while his wife was managing five young children, he was imprisoned for 'wickedly and scandalously' exposing himself to various women on two separate occasions.[36] The *Eastern Daily Press* described Mason as being 'connected with one of the foundries of the town', and alluded to the 1877 case: 'Now he is in trouble again.' Mason was convicted and sentenced to eighteen months' hard labour (punishment through heavy manual work).[37] By 1891 the Masons had moved to Lambeth. His wife Rosa was listed as head of the household in the census of that year. The family had moved on to a large house in Balham by 1901.[38] I have not managed to find any unsolved obscene letter-writing campaigns from these places, so perhaps that was the end of his criminal career.

The difference between an obscene and a threatening letter is not always clear. Obscenity can obviously contain implied threat when sent to somebody out of the blue. Threatening letters written by a butler in 1885 were glibly put down to 'excitement, jealousy and spite', but there was likely a more complicated motivation. George Lennard was a butler for a rich wool dealer and JP, Charles Frederick Tanner. He worked in Stowford House, Harford, near Ivybridge in Devon. He was acquitted of sending obscene letters but found guilty of writing threatening letters to magistrates and others, including Lord Haldon. In one letter, Lennard demanded that Haldon use his influence to discharge a man called John Lee, a butler, who had recently been found guilty of murder of his employer. Lennard wrote: 'If you hang him we will serve you . . . We intend to work destruction among you.' Another letter went to Peter Bourne Drinkwater, a JP involved in the Lee case.

William Mallet, the keeper of the London Hotel in Harford, was also singled out; Lennard threatened to kill him if he spoke about Hugh Shortland's involvement in the drowning of his wife. Lennard threatened to murder all three men.[39]

Presiding, the Right Hon Lord Clinton remarked that Lennard's was 'a very unusual offence'. He noted that the problem did not lie in determining whether the letters were threatening or obscene, but in proving who sent them.[40] The postbox in Ivybridge was watched, and Lennard appeared to be aware of this—yet still risked posting his letters there. He was apprehended posting into the box and George Smith Inglis, a London handwriting expert, was called in to verify that the letters were in Lennard's hand. Lennard confessed and attributed his actions to 'jealousy, so that he was bordering on insanity'.[41] It is unclear what he meant. Evidence regarding the threatening letters sent to Drinkwater and Mallet was not introduced, but Lennard was found guilty of sending threating letters to Lord Haldon and sentenced to eighteen months' imprisonment with hard labour.[42]

Excuses

The Victorian moral order was challenged not only by obscene language itself, but by the complexes of gender, money, power, and community or family propriety in which such language could erupt. We looked at the role gossip letters played in relationships at the start of the nineteenth century in Chapter 1; similar letters continued to be sent throughout the century. In 1893 a husband was informed of his wife's infidelities by anonymous letter—this was probably not very uncommon even though it is not fully reflected in the historical record. In the Wigan home of plasterer Thomas Livesey and his wife Mary Jane, the ripples caused by the information led to divorce later that same year. The Livesey household consisted of the couple and their adopted daughter, plus several lodgers. Earlier in the year, one of the lodgers started a relationship with Mary Jane. Being notified by anonymous letter, Thomas charged his wife with misconduct, sold the property, and left.[43]

Minor celebrities were also targets. In 1887, Ada Morgan, a nineteen-year-old actress, appeared as 'Susy' in *The Silver King*, at the Britannia Theatre in Hoxton. A review in the weekly newspaper *Era* noted that

Morgan played the role 'neatly'.[44] Other reviews described Morgan as 'pretty'. When she appeared in another play at the theatre in April, a reviewer noted: 'Although too quiet to be really boyish, Miss Ada Morgan...is always so intelligent in her ideas and expressive in her business that she is very much liked.'[45] Ada was too well liked by one man; she had been receiving anonymous obscene letters at her home in Hackney. She guessed these were probably from a strange man who had been pestering her on the street. On the night of Wednesday 23 November, the man escalated his stalking by approaching Ada from behind and calling out, 'don't be afraid; I won't hurt you'. Ada was walking the fifteen minutes home from work. The man followed her and tried to engage her in conversation. She hastened her pace, but 'her foot slipped and she nearly fell, when he made an insulting observation'. Eventually Morgan found a policeman and called out to him. The officer took the man into custody. His name was Philip Lazarus, a twenty-five-year-old commercial traveller specializing in drapery who lived with his parents and siblings less than half a mile from the theatre. Lazarus was charged with following and annoying Morgan. However, Ada did not feel it could be proved he wrote the letters, so that charge was dropped.[46]

In the summer of 1895, at the Bolton Borough Court, William Garbett was charged with writing 'objectionable and disgusting letters'. He was a married man in his late twenties. Garbett was said to have disguised his identity by writing in capital letters. His victim was Elizabeth Pollitt, a nineteen-year-old cotton-mill worker who occasionally attended the Daubhill Primitive Methodist Chapel, at which Garbett played the harmonium. The chapel was just a short walk from his home, over the tramway. Pollitt's father was a police constable. An erstwhile colleague of his, Thomas Wood, managed to get a sample of Garbett's handwriting. This was compared to the hand in the anonymous letters by Harold Mather, a local accountant. Mather thought they were the same.[47] It was reported that Garbett's 'conduct in sending the letters periodically and anonymously was inexplicable', and he was fined 40s plus costs.[48] As with many of the reports in the local papers, the *Manchester Courier and Lancashire General Advertiser* had no qualms about providing the full address details of the victim. As happens more and more frequently on modern social media, this opened the door to anyone inspired to write copycat letters. Curiously, a notice had appeared between two musical notices in the *Bolton Evening News* back in January 1895: 'WILL THE PERSON WHO SEND THE ANONYMOUS LETTERS STOP WRITING, or send direct to the lady's house, otherwise all letters will be burned unopened.'[49] If this was addressed to Garbett, it highlights that newspapers had become the only practical means of reaching anonymous letter-writers. It is also a curious reply in kind, as it uses typed capitals to catch the attention just as Garbett used capitals to avoid it.

By the Edwardian period, victims could be found not only at the nearby theatre or church, but also in the burgeoning world of print media. Authors became targets. In 1913, William Burke, a forty-two-year-old barrister from Camden Town, was indicted for sending 'a postal packet containing an improper letter' to the writer Evelyn Underhill, the wife of another barrister. Evelyn's husband had lectured Burke when he was a student; but she had written 'a number of books in her maiden name'. Burke, having read some of these works, began stalking Evelyn Underhill. She was sent around eighty letters: a sustained campaign of harassment. Since some letters were addressed to 'Mrs Willie Burke', the case moves out of the domain of anonymous letter-writing and therefore will not be treated in detail here. It is nonetheless an interesting case for the way it arose and for the defence offered by the perpetrator. Burke later apologized, claiming that his 'letters were written during some aberration of the mind'. At trial, Burke claimed that he had been under hypnotic influence, and so was not responsible for his actions. Consequently, he could not promise to halt the letters, as he could not be sure he could abide by such an oath. Burke was found guilty but held to be insane. He was confined indefinitely.[50]

Print media also became a significant venue for emerging techniques for the detection, identification, and capture of malicious letter-writers. In 1907, after 'certain grossly obscene letters' had been circulating in Hastings for two years, the *Hastings and St Leonard's Observer* took the unusual step of publishing snippets of the clean parts, to see if a reader might recognize the handwriting. A £5 reward was offered by the Chief Constable.[51] Such activities had already received public attention in the town. A year before, a doctor had been convicted of sending 'divers false, scandalous, malicious and defamatory matters' concerning a young woman. In that case, Andrew Dunn Turner, who was described as new to the town and 'not widely known', was caught in an operation designed by the police. The case began when the father of one Kate Austin, a solicitor called Edward Austin, arranged to have an advert published in the 'situations wanted' section of the *Hastings and St Leonards Observer*.[52] A reply was collected from the *Observer* office. It bore a Hastings postmark and was 'a very long and grossly obscene letter containing immoral proposals'. The letter, offering money in exchange for various 'acts of gross indecency', was taken to the police. Its recipient was informed that if they 'entertained' the lewd idea contained in the letter, they were to walk up and down from 'Metcalf and Kirkpatrick's in Wellington-place, to the picture shop' while holding 'a red book in [their] left hand' on the following Tuesday and Wednesday afternoons. The recipient was also requested to place another advert in the local paper, addressed to 'C' (from 'K'): 'Young lady wishes light occupation, eager to learn and quite willing'.

These elaborate prompts did not achieve the kind of compliance their author clearly hoped for. Heloise Beatrice Maud Walmsley, the married daughter of a policeman, was instructed to walk the street as per the instructions from 'C'. Heloise pretended to be 'K'. Her activities were observed by the police. Eventually the 'quarry was caught'. Turner approached Mrs Walmsley and said, 'I am C', to which he received a reply: 'I am K'. Questioned by the police, Turner claimed to have a doppelganger and denied all knowledge of the newspaper adverts. Similar stationery to that used to write the letters was found to be in Turner's possession: 'greyish paper' and white notepaper watermarked with an 'Imperial Crown'. The same materials had been used in the letters sent to the *Observer* office. Described as being fifty-six years old, and in a 'delicate state of health', Turner pleaded guilty at the Sussex Assizes in November 1906, and was sentenced to six months' imprisonment for 'publishing to Edward Thomas Burnett a letter containing divers false, scandalous, malicious and defamatory matters concerning the character of Kate Austin'. Turner had an explanation: 'I must have been under the influence of drugs at the time.' His defence argued that his actions were the 'result of a disordered mind' and recounted how the doctor had been seriously injured some years ago, had undergone several operations, and had become addicted to morphine, causing 'moral and mental derangement'. A respectable medical career spanning 1877–1903 was described.[53]

In 1858 a Dudley watchmaker called Andrew Hellmuth was charged with sending 'numerous anonymous letters, containing very obscene and abusive language', to Elizabeth Still, a neighbour who kept a millinery shop. One enclosed a picture. Hellmuth, a German by birth, was in business with his brother, Markus, who came to court to testify that the letters were not in Andrew's hand. Unimpressed by this line of defence, the bench of magistrates bound Hellmuth over for *sending* the letters rather than for writing them.[54] A more dramatic case the following year centred on Colonel John Alexander Forbes of Lonach Lodge in Bath. Forbes had been committed to trial for sending over a dozen letters 'of the most filthy and obscene character' to Adelaide Fenton. Some came with enclosed obscene material. As Fenton had no reason to suspect Forbes, his involvement might never have been uncovered. However, Fenton had not been his only victim. At the end of 1858, Llewellyn Watling, wanting to secure a position as a language teacher, advertised his services in *The Times*. A man replied, signing off as 'Francis York' and directing replies to be sent c/o the Post Office in Bath. The two men corresponded until Watling brought a stop to things, having been offended by some 'remarks and suggestions' made by this 'Francis York'. He re-advertised, but 'Francis York' again replied 'in terms still more annoying'. Watling forwarded the letters to the police. A policeman noticed the similarities of hand between 'Francis York' and the letters sent to Fenton and alerted the Bath Post Office. It was Forbes who collected mail addressed to 'Francis York'.[55] Adelaide Fenton, one of Bath's fashionable ladies, was 'not in the least acquainted' with Colonel Forbes. The letters were not considered to be libellous, but Forbes was sent to trial at the Somerset Assizes on the charge that he intended to 'debauch and corrupt' Fenton. He absconded from bail and fled to France.[56] A £50 reward was offered for information leading to Forbes's apprehension. The wanted man was 'about 64 years of age, 5 feet 9 or 10 high, florid complexion, stout made, grey hair, thick bushy whiskers, which he sometimes dyes, walks very erect, with a short quick step, usually wears a silk hat with flat brim placed much over his eyes'.[57]

Postcards

Postcards became a particular concern in the late nineteenth century. In 1870 attention was drawn 'to the nuisance that the new half-penny post was likely to become by mischievous persons sending obscene, slanderous, or grossly offensive remarks on the open cards'.[58] People wanting to write postcards which could not be read by a casual or curious reader as they passed through the postal system could write their communications using 'Luntley's Invisible Postal Ink', which could be obtained from 30 Fore Street, EC London. The words remained invisible until heated by a strong flame or fire, when they surfaced in a 'deep and permanent black'.[59] The issue sharpened awareness of the less desirable consequences of cheaper postage and remote pillar-boxes. The *Dover Express* fulminated in 1890, looking back to fears when the postcard system was first introduced, declaring that 'the anticipation has been released to a considerable extent', because people think that

a post card is a very handy way of venting their spleen, and that they may with impunity write offensive things on these missives, provided they keep within the law of libel and avoid indecency; therefore it is very important that it should be known that there is a special enactment which provides that mere abuse (which perhaps might with impunity be written in a closed letter) subjects the writer to a serious penalty if the vehicle be a post card, which could be read by anyone in the household, even servants, or by an official in the post office.[60]

The paper was responding to reports of obscene letters written by Elizabeth Sarah Brown (discussed below). Obscene letters by a woman appeared to have provoked much more consideration of the anonymous postcard system than other prompts. Still, in 1865 a writer for the *London Review* had warned that cheap anonymous valentines would become 'an outlet for every kind of spiteful inuendo, for every malicious sneer, for every envious scoff, and...the foulest libels and the fiercest threats'.[61]

Percy Hamilton Farnfield, a right-handed batsman, was a sadly unsuccessful cricketer. He was bowled for a duck in his only first-class innings, when he played for Worcestershire in 1925.[62] But Percy had been at a still lower ebb earlier in his life, in 1918. Then, as a schoolmaster working in Sidcup, Farnfield was charged with 'publishing obscene libels' over a two-year period, to 'a number of respectable young women' in the town, and also in Bromley, signing himself off as 'Jack' or 'Billy'. The postcards and letters he wrote came with photographs attached or enclosed ('libels in the form of objectionable photographs'). Farnfield was a married man in his late thirties who taught boys in a preparatory school. Like Frederick Mason of Ipswich, Farnfield began his epistolary habit when his wife was pregnant with her first child. He was reported to have told his wife, 'I have been writing beastly letters to a lot of girls; I don't know why I did it.' *The Times* decided that the 'most charitable view to take of the defendant's conduct was that he must be suffering from some form of sexual mania, for no man in his senses could have done what he had done'. When arrested, Farnfield said, 'I must go and tell my wife. I have been an awful fool...I have prayed to God every night to give me a clean heart.' Farnfield explained that 'for years this kind of thing has been an awful bugbear to me—a natural passion'. He also admitted to varying his medium: 'I have never spoken to ladies on the subject, except over the telephone.'[63] Farnfield was found guilty of publishing obscene libels, but it was held he was 'insane at the time of commission of offense'. The Prison Calendar for 1918 reports that he was to be 'kept in custody as a Criminal Lunatic' in Brixton 'until His Majesty's pleasure be known'.[64]

Albert Lomax of Hornby Street in Bury came up before the Police Court in December 1892 and was fined for sending several obscene letters to Mrs Devey, who was a pork butcher. Like other men on this roll call of abuse, Lomax had been caught red-handed sliding a letter into the postbox. Devey did not know Lomax, and he offered no explanation for his actions.[65] In 1895, William Boyle, a twenty-four-year-old labourer, was convicted of sending anonymous obscene and libellous letters to a Mrs Hudson of Wandsworth; as well as to his own sister in-law, who lived in Mitcham. 'The evidence rested in the main on the opinion of an expert in handwriting, together with other circumstances which were relied upon as proof of the prisoner's connection with the libels.' Boyle got eighteen months' imprisonment (which was a comparatively steep sentence).[66] Frederick M. Browne—'an artist'—was gaoled for sending obscene postcards through the post in October 1897. The affair caused the village of Springfield, just outside Chelmsford, to buzz with whispered gossip. Sentenced to six months' hard labour, Browne refused to do any labour in prison, where he 'raved' and tore his hair, and was eventually sent to Brentwood Asylum.[67] Just before Christmas 1904 seventeen-year-old Enoch Robinson was found guilty of sending obscene postcards. Robinson, a factory packer, sent a package to a 'certain young lady. To him she was a perfect stranger.' He followed this up with a 'grossly indecent letter' and was 'found out by the writing'. Unable to pay the £5 fine (which would have been over a month's wages), Robinson was committed to prison for a month's hard labour.[68]

Reports of Robinson's sentencing were accompanied by details of the quantity of obscene materials estimated to be making their way through the Post Office at the time. They match the picture that has been slowly coming into focus in this chapter. The obscene stuff was described as being 'so prevalent' that 'every week nearly one hundred' postcards were stopped at the Nottingham Post Office alone.[69] Not much was made of any of these cases in the newspapers—they are presented as regrettable and inevitable, but neither mysterious nor sensational. In her classification of anonymous letters in 1943, Letitia Fairfield, the sister of the novelist Rebecca West, and a doctor with a background in law, described letters like these as being 'the result of pure sexual exhibitionism', judging that their writers were 'seeking some means of expression'—she underplayed the emotional and psychological effects on recipients, just as the press in the late nineteenth century had.[70] Although it was feared that poorer people with ill intent—a group which might be said to include Albert Lomax and Enoch Robinson—would abuse the halfpenny post, or be more liable to send abusive anonymous mail, most perpetrators in this chapter were in fact fairly affluent men. They appeared, outwardly at least, to be respectable members of their communities. The types of people who were in control of the medium: the male, the respected, and the rich, were those who appeared to abuse it.

By 1958, one Home Office document examiner was confident enough to state that an indication of male authorship in cases of anonymous obscenity was 'where the sex act is described in detail and with evident relish'; they thought that letters to young girls were 'almost invariably written by elderly men'. Grossly indecent letters received by young girls were apparently 'almost invariably the work of men in their fifties' (probably considered elderly at the time).[71] At the end of the nineteenth century there was less confidence and less interest in such connections, but there was still an expectation that obscene letters were written by men to women. This was regarded less as a serious social blight than as a simple reflection of gender roles. Consequently, there was press interest in the 1890s when at least two cases came to light in which the prime suspect was female. The woman accused of sending obscene postcards from an upmarket part of Sheffield in 1898 was acquitted.[72] In an earlier case, from March 1890, Elizabeth Sarah Brown, a widow, was found guilty of sending offensive and obscene postcards to three men in Dover and fined more than £17. The case was initiated by the Postmaster General, as being contrary to Section 4 of the 1884 Post Office Protection Act. That law set penalties for items sent through the post bearing indecent or offensive marks or words, in common with later iterations and variations on the same Act. Brown was described in newspaper accounts as being 'of respectable appearance'. She sent one 'grossly obscene' postcard to the home of Alexander Bottle, a magistrate, in December 1889. When asked about her motives, Brown claimed that Bottle had insulted her in the street as she passed by him (an accusation which Bottle denied). Bottle suggested that the grudge arose after he encountered Brown in the course of his duties as a magistrate, in a case concerning payment of a rate.

The next recipient of Brown's writings was John Vidler, who worked in the office of the clerk to the magistrates. Brown explained that Vidler was a target for an offensive (but not obscene) postcard because he had perverted justice: he had allowed one Mr Atkinson to escape punishment for damaging one of Brown's walls. The final victim was George E. Toomer, a magistrate, to whose address was sent an obscene postcard addressed confusingly to 'Mrs Ottaway'. Mrs Ottaway was likely to be Jane Ottaway, the wife of surgeon and erstwhile mayor of Dover, James Ottaway. Brown had also sent a postcard with the same addressee to Bottle. Sending these was deemed to be 'an offence calculated to wreck the peace of households for ever'. Brown asserted that 'no one leads a quieter life than I do. I am a respectable woman.' Unlike the many cases involving men discussed above, Brown did not claim mental defect or similar excuse. Instead, she claimed to be seeking justice on her own terms.[73] An editorial in the *Dover Express* thought that the large fine meted out to Brown was too lenient for the offence, and that the perpetrator of such 'inexcusable wickedness' ought to be imprisoned. It was here that the general condemnation of cheap postcards can be found.[74] A decade before, Brown had been cautioned at the 'request of a gentleman' for having sent indecent and offensive letters through the post.[75]

The episode from 1890 was not the end of things either. In July 1891 Brown was again up before the magistrates in Dover, having been charged once more with sending offensive postcards to magistrates and other men of the city. The state of her mind was queried.[76] In 1906, when Brown was picked up 'wandering', she was charged with being a person of unsound mind. Two doctors suggested she should be detained in the workhouse, but they dismissed concerns raised by the sanitary inspector about the state of her house.[77] It is difficult to judge whether such concerns were legitimate. To at least some extent, they formed part of a discourse in which Brown's sanity was judged according to her ability to meet gendered expectations (moderating her language; keeping a good house). Over the next century, writing obscene, malicious letters would come to be thought of as a characteristically female crime. However, in most of those cases the obscene element was included by the writer so as to throw suspicion onto another. That third party was usually considered less respectable than the sender, and the question of sexual gratification appears somewhat more obscure. In Brown's case, too, any sexual motive seems (at first sight, at least) to be more closely tangled with concepts of respectability, justice, and social exclusion than it is in many of the cases involving men.

English law did not recognize the psychological harm caused to recipients of such letters. Instead, the harm caused by anonymous letters was said to involve reputation and public morals (the 'peace'). Newspaper reports reflect a greater interest in the alleged mystery of a respectable man's motivations than in the toll extorted by his campaigns on the recipient's life. It is hard to estimate the scale of letter-writing of this kind, as (again) many of those targeted with such letters would not have taken any action past destroying them. It is also impossible to chart general trends in the obscene contents in such mail. Still, the evidence which does survive suggests some conclusions: unsolicited obscene letters were likely to have been on the rise throughout this period, matching the expansion of the postal system; such activity was apparently considered in itself quite ordinary at the time; the obscenities travelled on the whole from men to women. For these reasons, the link between obscene abuse and postal technology can be seen as an important precursor of the contemporary problems of anonymous abuse encountered more often by women than men on social media.[78] Misogynist obscenity may simply increase in proportion to efficiencies of communication. The effects of the democratization of media in the nineteenth century afforded women increasing opportunities in the public sphere; the period considered here ended with women's suffrage. Entrance into public view (for instance as an author or an actress) was matched by a greater likelihood of private harassment, increasingly in the form of obscene anonymous letters.[79]

5

Libels

'er at number 14 is dirty

In the early twentieth century one genre of anonymous letter became so prominent it was given a name: the 'poison pen' letter. Coined in America, the term 'poison pen' was first used in 1911 in a headline for an article in the Maryland *Evening Post*. The press popularized the term in Britain in the 1920s.[1] Poisoning was the form of murder most connected to women, and these letters were regarded as a form of social poisoning more often than not perpetrated by women. Designed to cause trouble, the letters were, in some ways, a continuation of neighbourly over-the-fence gossip, defamation, and rancour.[2] Some were libellous, some were obscene, some were threatening, some were all three. Others were very banal.

Will the Sanitary Inspector when he has time have a look through 14 Myrtle Rd. [Sent to The Sanitary Inspector, Council House, Hounslow, 23 March 1915]

This pithy message, written on a Christmas postcard previously addressed to (but presumably never received by) a 'Mr Townsend', arrived at the office of the Heston and Isleworth sanitary inspectors in March 1915. It draws the inspector's attention to an address on Myrtle Road in Hounslow, West London. The inspector is not invited to look at any particular issue.[3] Sanitary inspectors often received anonymous communications. They had oversight of local issues associated with public health and nuisances, much as environmental health officers today have. They were sent letters on all sorts of issues, including communicable diseases; drainage faults; dampness; accumulations of rubbish; and pigs, rabbits, and poultry kept on-site.[4] Complaints could

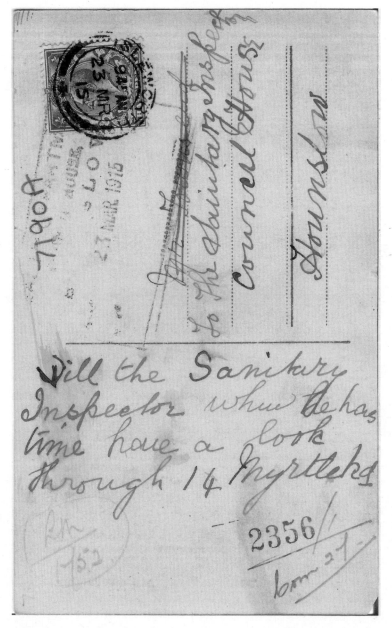

Figure 19. Anonymous postcard sent to Sanitary Inspector, Hounslow, 1915 recto, author's own item

Figure 20. Anonymous postcard sent to Sanitary Inspector, Hounslow, 1915 verso, author's own item

be submitted by council officials, doctors, policemen, or anyone aggrieved. Already it was known that some complaints were 'frivolous' or made for 'vexatious reasons', but it was not always clear which could be ignored.[5]

The writing does not look strikingly similar to that of the Myrtle Road residents who filled in their census returns for 1911, but most of those were entered by male household heads, and I suspect that this postcard was written by a woman. The Lawrences lived at number 14 in 1915—a family of five, headed by Richard, in a house of three rooms plus a kitchen. In 1911 Richard Lawrence's brother, Sidney, lived at number 8. Sidney's wife, Fanny, was the sister of the Lawrences' lodger, Alfred Morley. Mary Ann Morley, the widowed mother of Fanny and Alfred, also lived at number 8. It is possible that the postcard relates to some family spat; although Sidney and his family had moved away from the street shortly before 1915.[6] Communications like this post-card were usually designed to rectify a problem, after informal discussions had broken down. Perhaps the author did not sign their name because they felt awkward about the situation, or feared repercussion, or simply because they wrote in malice. The postcard probably relates to an issue with neighbours; at this time relationships with neighbours were among the most important, particularly for women.[7]

By the start of the twentieth century, female literacy rates had increased to almost match those for men, especially outside rural areas. Chapter 3 demonstrated some ways in which men without authority attempted to gain power through anonymous letters at the start of the nineteenth century. An apparent increase in women writing anonymously at the start of the twentieth century may have followed similar lines: a weapon in the arsenal of the weak. However, anonymous letters written (mostly) by men in the eighteenth century were generally dispatched to male social superiors and contained threats. The letters sent by women in the early twentieth century, by contrast, were mostly sent to their social peers, people within their immediate community, often next-door neighbours, often women. These letters were more obviously connected to the frustrations of community life for women who felt trapped in particular roles; they do relate to power, and powerlessness, but less overtly than some of the letters already examined.

Once again, the only letters for which we have records were those which were taken seriously and became the focus of investigation. It is possible that lots of anonymous letters written by men were, for some reason, not taken seriously, and never became the focus of investigation, with the gender of the author therefore never exposed. It is likely, for example, that many disgruntled male employees wrote letters to erstwhile male employers at this time, which letters were destroyed and not acted upon, partly because this would not conform with expectations around masculine responses to threat. Societies determine their own preoccupations—some types of anonymous letter were ignored, others were investigated. The circumstances in which the letters came to light, and the moral values and legal procedures brought to bear upon them, are often as significant as the texts themselves.

This is certainly true of the five cases I will discuss in this chapter. All played out in the area around the Weald in the south-east of England, in the counties of Sussex and Surrey, during the 1910s and 1920s. All feature female writers. Most feature innocent people deliberately framed for libel. In some of them, the actual writer had initiated proceedings as the prosecutrix. The first campaign takes us to the leafy suburbs of Surrey.

Annie Tugwell

In the summer of 1910, Annie Tugwell from Sutton was imprisoned for twelve months for 'unlawfully and maliciously writing and publishing certain false and malicious and defamatory libels' concerning various people.[8] Tugwell's victims were not her immediate neighbours but were part of a different community: members of her local Catholic church. Back in March 1909 it seemed a very different story would play out. Then, Annie Dewey, the housekeeper to a Catholic priest, Canon Henry Taylor Cafferata, in Wallington (two miles away), had been accused by Tugwell of publishing a defamatory and malicious libel, and accused also by Louisa Wesley, another member of the congregation who lived in Carshalton, about a mile from Sutton. Anonymous letters had circulated among Catholics in the area, all containing 'scurrilous charges', and the writing looked strikingly like Dewey's. A handwriting expert, Thomas Gurrin, had no doubts, and Dewey herself admitted that it seemed to be 'a very good imitation' of her own hand. The case against Dewey fell apart at the Assizes.

The prosecution was ordered to pay the costs for the defendant.[9] Shortly afterwards Tugwell was charged with sending letters, which accusation she contended, claiming to be the victim of a 'Catholic conspiracy'.[10]

Tugwell's letters were too salacious to be read aloud in court; reporters dangled some of the words into their accounts, including 'troll', described at the time as 'an old word but a foul one'.[11] Canon Cafferata had been sent a postcard with a 'vulgar joke' purporting to be a huge order for ale; another included the lines: 'You really must keep up your payments for your child. It is growing very much like you. It even calls "Daddy".' Wesley was crudely connected to Gilbert Measures, an old friend of hers. Before the letters started circulating, Tugwell had gained access to a sample of Dewey's writing, and seemingly learned to imitate it.[12]

At the end of July 1910, Tugwell arrived at the Surrey Assizes in Guildford 'fashionably dressed in deep mourning'. Peering through her large veiled hat, she saw a court heaving with spectators, mostly women. Archibald Bodkin and A. S. Carr appeared for the Public Prosecutor and Travers Humphreys observed for Wesley. On the stand, Tugwell repeated her emphatic denial of guilt.[13] Her sister-in-law, Emily Jones, gave a character statement; Tugwell was 'a most exemplary woman; a pattern to others in the way she keeps her home'. Tugwell's defence asked the jury to imagine a woman of previously 'irreproachable character' committing a foul crime to frame Dewey, 'a person practically a stranger to her'. Evidently, the jury could imagine that. A 'guilty' Tugwell, taken from the dock, exclaimed: 'As there is a God, He will prove me innocent. I hope so.'[14]

I like to think that Annie Tugwell coped well with her one-year imprisonment, which was without hard labour. When she was younger Annie (née Doré) born in Ireland, had arrived in Melbourne, Australia sometime in the 1880s. There she met Harry Warren Tugwell, and there she gave birth to their first son, Leslie, in 1887. The small family came to England, settling in 1888 in Sutton, where Harry eventually became the registrar. They were wealthy enough to employ a live-in servant.[15] Harry abandoned Annie when she was taken to prison in 1910. He also retired. A portion of his pension was insufficient for Annie, so she worked as a costumier in the West End.[16]

Thought to be busy with her writing again in August 1913, Annie was charged with 'sending through the post a postal packet of an offensive and grossly indecent character contrary to the Post Office

Act'. This time the key targets were her sister-in-law, Emily Jones (who had spoken in her defence previously), and also Jones's solicitor.[17] Questioned at the end of August, Tugwell 'most emphatically' denied the allegations, claiming that she was being impersonated by her husband's mistress.[18] 'In fact', Tugwell asserted, 'I am a second Beck.' (This is a reference to Adolf Beck, who had been wrongly convicted of a crime through mistaken identity in 1896. Gurrin, the handwriting expert, had also advised in the Beck case.)[19] Tugwell repeated her denial in the dock, stating: 'I have been too good a woman to do that. I am not depraved... I am not a low woman.'[20] In October Tugwell was sentenced to a year of hard labour at Holloway Prison.[21]

At least one of Tugwell's writing episodes followed emotional upheaval. It may be merely coincidental, but Tugwell, often preoccupied by matters of the Church, lived in Sutton in 1894, when the letter to Mary Dorothea Cokayne was sent (with a Sutton postmark), in the wake of her son's death, so she could even be a suspect in that case too: Morton Cokayne was the curate at a church nearby. Tugwell's campaign in 1913 followed a period of discontent, abandonment, precarious living, and grief. It started less than three months after tragedy. In May 1913 her youngest son, Cyril, an apprentice on board a three-mast steel ship, had been 'washed overboard' and drowned. He was fifteen years old.[22] From their involvement in 1909 the local police had failed to grasp the complexities of this case. Assumptions and circumstantial evidence even cast doubt on the validity of Tugwell's guilt: Emily Jones, her sister-in-law, a target of the 1913 campaign, believed those letters were in Harry Tugwell's hand—Emily's own brother. A servant for the Tugwell family stated in 1912 that she thought Annie Tugwell was innocent. The police assumed the campaign was merely an extension of 'the gossips and jealousies of a number of women connected with the local Catholic Church'.[23] Catholicism also features in the next case, from the seaside resort of Hove.

Kathleen O'Brien

Colonel Charles Henry Gardiner[24] did not appreciate that Kathleen O'Brien at 62 Brunswick Place in Hove left the front door open. He unsettled her with his glares.[25] Gardiner and his family occupied the four upper floors, while O'Brien and her employers, the Woodward

family, occupied the ground floor. There were plenty of opportunities
for the two households to clash, as they shared not just the front
entrance, but also the basement space, where there were two kitchens,
from one of which food travelled via a lift up to the Gardiners' con-
servatory on the first floor. Waste was also dealt with in the basement,
and the coal was stored there.[26]

Gardiner's tenants, the Woodwards, had employed O'Brien as a governess since September 1913. In the spring of 1914, O'Brien fell out with
a maid. The police were called. Nasty letters started arriving shortly
afterwards, mostly during the night. One advised Kate Woodward to 'rid
the house of the presence of Miss O'Brien'. Another, slid under a door,
was addressed to 'Miss O'Brien, Prostitute'.[27] One warned that Kathleen
would soon be murdered.[28] Significantly, one letter, giving notice of
O'Brien's 'character, drunkenness, thieving' and 'vileness', referred to
'Pou', the nickname used by the Woodward children for their father.[29]
Suspicion fell upon the Colonel.

A detective claimed that the letters were in the Colonel's handwriting. Gardiner argued that he had been too busy correcting proofs to
transfer his attention to writing 'that awful stuff', but the evidence all
pointed his way. He was completing his pamphlet, *Soldiers and Civil
War* (1914), a confused and tangential treatise written in opposition to
the Irish Home Rule Bill, intended to provide self-government within
the United Kingdom for Ireland. On 4 May, Gardiner was arrested 'in
the open street' and charged with defamatory libel and remanded to
nearby Lewes Prison. During the process, Gardiner felt humiliated and
ill-treated: 'had I only been a suffragette', he commented peevishly,
'food and other luxuries would have been forced upon me'. Gardiner
used his pamphlet to draw attention to his thirty-five-year career in
service in the army, with certificates for gymnastics and Eastern languages and a testimonial from Florence Nightingale in which she
praised him for his moderate drinking. While out on bail, forty miles
from home (as per the condition of his release), Gardiner claimed that
his house was broken into; 'a whole tray of visiting cards left by friends'
were taken, but nothing else. One of his many tenants took the opportunity to do a moonlight flit.[30]

The case against the Colonel soon crumbled to nothing. G. F. Donne,
acting for the prosecution, had been made privy to evidence that
O'Brien had previously written similar letters to herself and to others;
a Plymouth priest had retained some of these earlier letters written by

Kathleen 'to protect any possible victim' in the future.[31] Donne hoped that, 'when the vividness of the trial' had worn off, then the Colonel would 'be able to forget it and remember that it is only due to a curious construction of the human mind—to circumstances which I can only described as being demonical'.[32] Newspaper reports dwelt on the Colonel's agony at the hands of this 'cunning woman'.[33] In June 1909, while a governess in Brussels, Kathleen had written a letter to a friend, on the pretence of it being written by someone else. The letter was designed to 'enlighten' the friend about Kathleen's 'true character'. It stated that she had been 'denounced' in her previous post 'for being constantly with a man' and implied that Kathleen was hellbent on seducing a 'young monk...possibly easily duped by a prostitute so young'. Kathleen was 'suspected of being in a certain condition'.[34]

Kathleen had been under the care of Dr Hugh Nethersole Fletcher, the assistant-surgeon at Sussex County Hospital, a non-specialist, who diagnosed hysterical neurosis. Others suggested that Kathleen was suffering from a 'dual personality'.[35] Kathleen was admitted into St Luke's Hospital in London on a voluntary basis in June. Case notes from her time there survive. They point to a woman in a complex mental state. Kathleen was a 'healthy looking young woman very thinly nourished', her appetite was poor, and she slept badly. Like Fletcher, the doctors at St Luke's classified Kathleen according to the parlance of the time as 'neurotic and hysterical'. Kathleen confessed that she remembered 'quite well' writing the letters 'which got Gardiner into so much trouble', explaining that she wrote them during the night, and felt compelled to send some during daytime. She was unsure why she wrote them. When asked, Kathleen showed remorse and regret that Colonel Gardiner had gone to prison as a result of her actions. Previous episodes of mental instability were recalled, including an occasion (while a governess in Nantes) when she wandered in a confused state into the streets in her nightdress.[36] In one session, led by Dr Needham, the Commissioner for the Board of Control, Kathleen was 'very silent, depressed, saying that she wished to die' and she was unable to account for her actions. Kathleen seemed of unsound mind, but Needham was troubled by inconsistencies in her story.[37] Observing this session, Dr William Rawes, the resident medical superintendent at St Luke's, wondered if Kathleen was trying to manipulate Needham: 'It struck me', wrote Rawes, 'that a good deal of her depression was assumed.'

In June 1914, an agitated Kathleen claimed to see blood oozing down the walls and ceiling.[38]

The letters kept coming. In July 1914, while still at the hospital, Kathleen wrote two anonymous letters, one addressed to the Sister, the other to Dr Gilmour, the assistant medical superintendent. In these she accused herself of drunkenness, theft, prostitution, and of giving birth to an illegitimate child a year previously.[39] Note that, whilst herself having committed what would be defined as a 'malicious offence', in her letters Kathleen accuses herself of crimes more commonly committed by women. At the time 25% of female prisoners were convicted for sexual offences; 45% for drunkenness; 10% for theft. Only 6% of female prisoners had committed malicious offences.[40]

Transcript of letter:

Rec[eive]d July 3rd—1914 Dr Gilmour is informed that one of his present patients is nothing less than a prostitute & that a year ago she had an illegitimate child: also that she is a certified drunkard & thief & he is advised to have no more to do with her.

In October Kathleen wrote anonymously to Rawes in a style more similar to her usual handwriting. It started, 'Dr Rawes is unknowingly encouraging Kathleen O'Brien in her vileness.' Writing about herself in the abstract, Kathleen suggested she ought to be punished, and noted that she had long been an outcast, a contaminating presence who had done 'many queer things'. Signed letters written to Rawes by Kathleen reveal details about her state of mind. One from mid-September 1914 repeated her assertion that she did not know why she wrote the letters. Confessing to writing similar letters in Brussels, Kathleen described, 'an awful grief that I have been lugging for the last 5 years'. The letter closed with a sense of self-pity, that 'nobody would possibly think worse of me than I do myself' and that it was 'small wonder' that her head ached all the time. In an undated letter to her doctor Kathleen explained that she had been upset the previous Sunday because her great-aunt [Margaret Hancock] had visited, and then she had been disturbed while undressing, and had cried, and made herself ill, and sat in church feeling 'wicked and spiteful'. Hancock had told her that the doctors were keen to find a home for Kathleen. In this letter, Kathleen, who was Catholic, requested to see the Bishop of Westminster, whom she claimed to know personally ('he was awfully nice to me and promised to help me all he could').

Self-pity winds up this letter too: 'I hate the idea of leaving here, I dread it, I don't trust myself.'[41]

Transcript of letter:

Rec[eive]d 11 Oct—1914 Dr Rawes is unknowingly encouraging Kathleen O'Brien in her vileness. She is known to be a thief, drunkard, prostitute, altogether lawless. Why would she be taken care of & kept from the punishment she so well deserves when she is only awaiting a chance to act in the same way? She has been an outcast for many years past & brings only trouble to whoever has dealings with her.

I have done many queer things in my time & am a low down wretch but still think it too much to let her mix with people who would not want to be contaminated by her & cannot allow you to be in ignorance of the character of a person to who you are being kind + waste your valuable time.

In late October she made a 'half-hearted' suicide attempt, cutting her throat with a piece of broken crockery, and also made a superficial cut on her hand using glass from a tumbler.[42] On 27 October Kathleen was certified. A month later, the case notes record that she had sat on a needle (whether by accident or not was unclear); removal of a part which broke off in her buttock required a small incision. Kathleen also 'feigned blindness for a considerable period'.[43] Doctors considered the possibility that O'Brien's condition was, at least partially, hereditary in nature. Her father, Theobald John O'Brien, had died in the Devon County Asylum in 1891. Back when it seemed that she was being defamed by the Colonel, Kathleen was reported to have said that had her father been alive, he would 'wipe the floor with whoever sent them [the letters]'. But Kathleen would not actually have remembered her father; he died when she was very young. She claimed that he was a naval doctor, but records suggest he ran a cafe, and was formerly a seaman and a coastguard.[44] Kathleen was discharged, uncured and suicidal, to the care of the Devon County Asylum, the very place where her father had died. She remained there as a 'pauper lunatic' until August 1916.[45]

In 1929 Kathleen again caught the attention of newspaper reporters and again it was suggested that she suffered from a 'dual personality'. Now working as a secretary, under the alias Nora Harrison, Kathleen was accused of getting money by false pretences from the 'Professional Classes Aid Council'. Having written various letters of reference herself and forging the signatures of two Plymouth doctors, Kathleen had tried to defraud the society of £24. The defence described Kathleen as 'a very dangerous woman'. Her mother remarked, 'things are so terrible', alluding to illness in the family. Dr John Hall Morton at Holloway Prison examined Kathleen, concluding that she was 'very intelligent' and 'well educated', but that she was 'a neurotic, sensitive woman, and has had a lot of illness'. The case from 1914 was repeated by the reporters at this time.[46]

O'Brien, like Tugwell, did not stop at writing letters that implicated another person: both women were prosecutrix in court cases against those people. It is hard to say how such activity and attention relate to their secret epistolary life—perhaps it was the goal or perhaps something else—but certainly it adds new dimensions to the picture. Tugwell framed Dewey by mimicking her handwriting. O'Brien used details in her letters that she could expect would throw suspicion on Gardiner and may likewise have copied his handwriting. Unlike letters written by Tugwell, all of O'Brien's letters were about just one person: herself. From the peculiar self-focused activities of a single woman in Hove, we now shift attention to another repeat offender, and consider the 'extraordinary and unnatural behaviour over a period of years of an apparently normal and respectable married woman' from Surrey, quite a short distance away.[47]

Eliza Woodman

It all started in Redhill during the damp and gloomy summer of 1912, with the discovery of a dead, skinned kitten left in a parcel on the doorstep of the Woodman house on St John's Road. An adult cat later died having eaten a poisoned fish-head.[48] Ellen 'Eliza' Woodman had found a letter attached to the gruesome parcel and had taken it to her husband Albert ('Alfie'). Eliza complained to the police about obscene letters and death threats; some through the post, some left in her garden. One threatened, 'I will blow you and your lot to blazes.'[49] Eliza Woodman hoodwinked three juries. She convinced them that her neighbour, Mary Johnson, was the author of these threatening letters sent between 1912 and 1914. Johnson was sentenced to a total of eighteen months in prison, eventually to be pardoned and compensated, when Woodman herself was revealed to be the author. Alfred Bucknill, counsel for the prosecution in two of the four Johnson trials, later

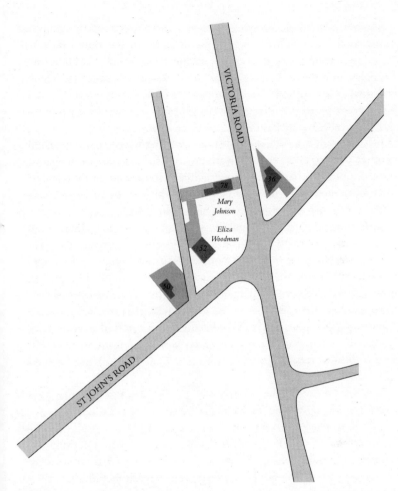

Figure 21. Location of Eliza Woodman's house in relation to Mary Johnson's house, Redhill, 1910, by Maud Webster

wrote about lessons he had learned from the experience, chiefly that 'people who appear to be sane occasionally do such very odd things'.[50]

Mary Johnson's back garden ran perpendicular to the Woodman house, from which it was separated by a narrow space containing a passageway.[51] Between their gardens lay a triangular piece of land, so that the ends of the two gardens were pretty close to each other.[52] The back of the Woodman house 'almost faced the side of the prisoner's house', with a vacant space between them. One of the Johnsons' windows was, according to the local landlord, 'the only one in the neighbourhood where it was possible to see into the Woodmans' kitchen window'.[53] As in other cases, this inescapable neighbourly intimacy fostered suspicion and hate.

Letters sent in 1912 were taunting. The newspapers described them as 'very abusive and very foul in their terms'. The worst parts were redacted.[54] 'To read even one of the letters' was, apparently, 'sickening, to read a number of them had almost the physical effect of sickness' on account of their being 'seasoned with the filthiest abuse imaginable'.[55] Their author described the local police as 'too sleepy' to stop them, and Woodman was threatened: 'in the brook you go, so you shall and soon, but the quickest and best way out of your misery will be to give you a gentle knock on the head. I will swing for you.' The writer threatened to set fire to the Woodman house by crawling underneath it; they claimed to have eavesdropped on the household from there already. Some letters were signed by 'Ikey the one-eyed woman'.[56] The local police did not entertain the idea that Woodman could have written these terrifying letters herself, and so, assuming that Johnson must have done, charged her with sending letters threatening murder. She was called to trial in the same court that Annie Tugwell had been tried in two years before.

Mary Johnson cut a diminutive figure in court in October 1912. It must have been a very intimidating experience. John William Goss was a witness. The landlord for the Woodman family, Goss had previously leased property to the Johnsons. They owed him money.[57] Like others, Goss asserted that there was no obvious animosity between the neighbours. Johnson claimed to have received two letters herself, one containing a threat to kill her horse (used in the greengrocery trade).[58] Key material evidence for the case against Johnson included a 'stylographic pen' found in a bedroom drawer. PC Kendrick had 'formed the opinion that some of the letters were written by such a pen'. Johnson said the pen was broken and had been found in that state by one of her children. Under cross-examination, Kendrick admitted that he had not tested the pen and was unaware it was broken.[59] With the negligence and collusion of several parties, and without having her handwriting analysed, Johnson was found guilty of sending letters threatening to kill—and imprisoned for six months. In the chair, Sir Charles Walpole, summed up: 'To send anonymous letters was the meanest thing anyone could do. It was cowardly, it was low, it was mean and it was cruel.'[60]

Shortly after Johnson returned home from her prison sentence in 1913, the campaign resumed. Seventy-nine letters circulated within a month, some went to Woodman, some to various policemen and others in the locality, including Goss and Harry Lane Robinson, who occupied property between the Woodman and Johnson gardens, and was a rival greengrocer to Alfred Johnson. All included threats to murder.[61] Mary Johnson found herself back in court in May 1913, charged with 'maliciously sending letters threatening to kill and murder'. Again, she lacked funds to engage her own counsel. According to her witness statements, Woodman claimed that stones were thrown at her house from the direction of the Johnson house. Robinson claimed to have been getting letters since he fell out with Alfred Johnson in April 1912. After retiring for a quarter of an hour the jury returned their verdict: Mary Johnson was again guilty of writing anonymous letters. Their threats were not considered to be credible, but the letters were deemed abusive. Sergeant Kendrick spoke in Johnson's defence, stating that although she had already served six months for such an offence, she was a respectable woman, no frequenter of public houses, with no associations with bad people. Again, the evidence against Johnson was circumstantial and again the key witness was Woodman. Johnson received a further twelve months in prison.[62] The conviction was quashed on appeal and a retrial commenced in July 1913. It explored two of three original indictments which had not been raised at the previous trial, one concerning threats to Robinson, the other threats to Goss. Again, Johnson could not afford legal counsel and was refused legal aid, again the evidence seemed compelling and yet again she was found guilty and sent to Holloway for a third time.[63]

This was a very strange time in the prison's history, owing to the recent intake of suffragettes who were credited with improving conditions for all classes of female prisoner, but who also brought some moments of crisis. Accounts left by suffragettes help us to understand the conditions endured by Johnson, and also a fellow inmate at the prison, Annie Tugwell, who was there on her second imprisonment. Their uniforms were ill-fitting. Johnson was under five feet tall, and although the skirts fitted her (they were designed to fit short women), she would have been swamped by her bodice (designed to fit 'big tall' women). Their undergarments were 'so big that one is obliged to use hairpins to make large pleats in them'. Johnson and Tugwell were known by the three numbers painted above their cells.[64] On 18 December 1913 suffragettes detonated a bomb from a nearby garden, smashing windows in the prison. Emmeline Pankhurst had been an inmate until a few days before, but there was only one suffragette in Holloway at the time of the bombing.[65] One can only wonder what Johnson, the greengrocer from Redhill, a mother missing her five daughters, made of this situation. For Tugwell it might have been the final straw—she was transferred to Colney Hatch Asylum within a fortnight.[66]

The suffragettes were released from imprisonment on the outbreak of the First World War in the summer of 1914, but for Johnson there was no release; the pattern of returning home and finding the letters appearing continued. Just as the war started, she moved to Croydon, 'so as to live in peace'. But as threatening letters continued to circulate, evidence against her mounted.[67] A letter in the possession of Eliza Woodman, dated 4 May 1914, included the lines,

I am going to burn you all out. I was quite happy at Holloway . . . I shall kill you burn you out. I shall come and settle you, you shall surely suffer death.

It was claimed that some letters were left on the doorstep, others were thrown into the Woodmans' backyard, some attached to stones. One stone had struck her eye, Woodman said.[68] Sergeant Kendrick testified to seeing Woodman with a black eye on 12 May 1914.[69]

But now the evidence began to seem shaky. Johnson had a water-tight alibi; a Catholic priest had arranged for her to stay in a convales-cent home in Hanwell between 4 May and 18 May, and thereafter she had lived in Croydon. The response of the authorities to this problem was to charge both Mrs *and* Mr Johnson with writing threating letters. In the witness box, Eliza Woodman stated that she had seen Mr Johnson climbing over fences to evade the police, who were regularly watching the Woodman house. PC James Spain said he saw letters come over into the Woodman yard while he was on watch, and that one had been wrapped in a handkerchief initialled 'MJ' (in ink). Another letter came over in a pincushion cover. One letter, which arrived after Woodman claimed her house had been broken into, threatened: 'I have a key to open your door.'[70]

The prosecution argued that Mr Johnson had taken over the pen-manship once Mary moved away, but he was illiterate. Indeed, Goss had stated in an earlier trial that Mr Johnson had not been able to sign his name on the tenancy agreement, adding an 'x' instead. Goss had never seen Johnson write.[71] James Melville, defending the Johnsons, finally got through to the jurors by asking a simple question: was it likely that the Johnsons had written these letters? Why would they deliberately concoct evidence against themselves which would affect their reputations and destroy their livelihood? Why would either of them send over a message contained within a handkerchief marked with their own initials? Melville went further. Might Eliza Woodman herself have sent the letters? After all, Mrs Johnson hadn't been in the locality and Mr Johnson couldn't write. Such seemingly obvious questions had never been aired before. Importantly, it was only when Mr Johnson was also prosecuted that the defence counsel met this minimum standard; previously, Mary Johnson had stood in court alone. The jury halted the case.[72] The Johnsons were acquitted, but their business was ruined. Mary complained that as her husband 'went on his round with his greengrocer's lorry the finger of scorn was pointed at him'. He took work as a dustman.[73] Nasty letters were sent from Redhill to the Johnsons' new landlord in Croydon, informing him that Mary 'was nothing better than a common convict'.[74]

Meanwhile, Melville's active defence of the Johnsons had shone a new light of suspicion upon Woodman. Some of the circumstances described in the letters could only be known by Woodman and Johnson; if Johnson had not been their author, then Woodman must have been. Traps were set, including stamps marked with invisible ink. Woodman fell into the net; she tried to extort money from a policeman, writing to him using the marked stamps and notepaper. She was charged with perjury then committed for sending indecent material through the post.[75] Her case attracted considerable interest; the public galleries were crowded to watch 'fashionably-dressed young ladies' occupying seats in the body of the courtroom.[76] They heard about bouts of hysteria Eliza had suffered as a teenager. Alfie stated that his wife had recently complained of headaches, and had fallen in 1912. He also recounted details of an incident which saw parts of a needle emerge from Eliza's arm, but he 'could never discover how they got there'. (This is oddly, and coincidentally, similar to O'Brien's incident from 1914. It is probably not surprising that needles were a tool of choice for self-harm at the time.) Eliza had 'not been so cheerful as late', irritable, he remarked, adding that he supposed this was on account of the letters.

Dr F. C. Forward, the Medical Officer at Holloway Prison who assessed Eliza, found no family history of insanity. Eliza herself was described as being of general good health (apart from a stroke around the turn of the century, which was mentioned in a casual fashion). Eliza had 'slow mentality, pains in the head, and disturbed speech' and 'there might be some deviation from the normal'. According to Forward's assessment, Eliza knew what she had been doing, but did not grasp the gravity of her actions, owing to the abnormal state of her mind. He thought she was certifiable. For the prosecution in 1915, Travers Humphreys described Eliza as a 'thoroughly cute-minded and clever woman, who understood the case against her'. The jury did not accept that Woodman was insane. She listened, unmoved, as she was sentenced to eighteen months' hard labour.[77]

To grasp how the story had changed means thinking back to the kitten. Either the dead kitten was a red herring, killed by someone unconnected to the letters—or Eliza Woodman had killed and skinned her own kitten (and poisoned her own cat). She had been the servant in the house of a vet in 1891, perhaps she had become hardened to the sight of animals in pain?[78] Other details were glossed over in the earlier trials, when it was assumed that Mary Johnson was the writer. Giving evidence in the first trial, Edward Blundell, a bricklayer, said that when the Woodmans had lived with him in Common Road in 1905, anonymous letters had arrived; 'some were left on neighbours' doorsteps, and some on hedges'. Mrs Woodman and her friend, Mrs Whitmore, had accused each other of sending them.[79] The weight of evidence against Mary Johnson back in 1910 had resulted in this detail's slipping through.

Other evidence seems tainted in hindsight. James Hugh Daughfery, an employee of Robinson (a rival to Johnson in greengrocery), had stated in May 1913 that he 'saw a hand and arm protruding from Johnson's window and a parcel was thrown'.[80] Robinson himself, witness for the prosecution in the 1914 trial of the Johnsons, claimed to have seen 'something' pass over his yard, from the Johnsons to the Woodmans. Local policemen also appear to have perjured themselves. Perhaps riled by taunts in the letters, their stories include many inconsistencies. In the witness box in July 1914, PC Attwood claimed to have heard something fall when watching the Woodman house before finding new letters. Similar evidence came from PC Sturt. PC Spain claimed to have seen a letter come over into the yard, wrapped in the initialled handkerchief.[81] It is possible that Woodman was involved in an elaborate plot which involved the throwing of evidence to convince the police. It is also possible that evidence was constructed to fit a narrative and secure a conviction. In his evidence in 1914, PC Spain repeated what must have been a lie told to him by Eliza Woodman, namely that on 'Whit-Sunday [Mrs Woodman] was standing in the backyard with her baby in her arms and was struck on the forehead with a stone which came from Johnson's way'.[82] When stated by a policeman in court, the story was bound to be prejudicial.

At the root of all of this was the way men in Redhill made assumptions about the likely or normal behaviour of women. Police investigations were not thorough, despite the length of the letter-writing campaign and the real moments of horror and human peril involved. Investigators had not followed up on Blundell's statement about Woodman's involvement in a previous campaign. Recidivism in anonymous letter-writing was assumed to be rare, but, like Kathleen O'Brien's, Eliza Woodman's life had been marked by several episodes. A remarkably similar campaign, and a similarly blinkered response, blighted a seaside resort in the following decade.

Edith Emily Swan

Rose Gooding from Littlehampton, a seaside resort on the West Sussex coast, was ensnared just as Colonel Gardiner and Mary Johnson had been. Gooding had at one time been friendly with her neighbour, Edith 'Edie' Swan. Edith had come across as ingratiating when Rose moved next door. Later she wrote out a pattern for socks and a recipe for marrow chutney, passing these to Gooding in a neighbourly gesture. Then, in May 1920, the thirty-year-old Swan accused her twenty-nine-year-old neighbour of sending her an obscene letter. The timing of the letter coincided with a report Swan made to the National Society for the Prevention of Cruelty to Children (NSPCC), falsely accusing Gooding of maltreating one of the children in her house: '[f]rom that time Miss Swan and Mrs Gooding were undoubtedly at daggers drawn'.[83] Eventually, Swan prosecuted Gooding for criminal libel. After being on remand in Portsmouth Prison for two and a half months, Gooding was found guilty and committed for a further two weeks.[84]

Released for the Christmas of 1920, Gooding must have felt worried when it was reported that letters had started circulating at the start of the new year. In one letter Swan was called a whore and the Swan family branded 'a dirty drunken lot'.[85] Gooding was in court again. After hearing the evidence, the jury (which included one woman) deliberated for eight minutes and then requested sight of Gooding's handwriting. They were informed this was not possible.[86] Later, the Director of Public Prosecutions expressed dismay about this lack of scrutiny in 'a case which, from its commencement to the end of it, was a case of handwriting'.[87] Indeed, initially, the handwriting of the key suspects was never really probed, just as in the Woodman and Johnson case.

As before, the case against Gooding was built on a tissue of circumstantial evidence and dubious witness testimony.[88] Found guilty, Rose went back to Portsmouth Prison for a twelve-month stretch with hard labour. There, she was stripped, examined by the doctor, bathed and supplied with an ill-fitting, crudely cut uniform, a Bible and prayer book, and basics such as bedding, a towel, a comb, and a brush. For months Rose arose from her board bed at 6.30 a.m. and started work before 7 a.m., possibly, ironically, sewing or mending mail bags.[89] Only her husband Bill visited, once in March and once in June 1921. Bill and Rose met in a 'visiting box', separated by metal mesh or caging. Prisoners and visitors found the conditions of visits so humiliating that they often kept them to a minimum.[90] An appeal failed—despite new material coming to light.

Notebooks and reutilized commercial stationery bearing obscene comments, in handwriting that matched the letters, had been found in Littlehampton; but Gooding was in prison. The possibility that members of her family had distributed them was explored and dismissed. Archibald Bodkin, who had appeared for the prosecution in Annie Tugwell's case in 1910, intervened at this stage, just after the failed appeal. 'Sir' Archibald Bodkin (he was knighted in 1917) was the Director of Public Prosecutions and he brought Inspector George Nicholls of Scotland Yard onto the case in June 1921. Nicholls suspected Gooding had been wrongly accused. The only other candidate was Swan, but she could hardly have written such 'indescribably filthy' letters to *herself*. Nicholls described Swan as 'not only a peculiar woman in appearance and behaviour, but would seem to have a remarkable memory—especially for filthy phrases—for she has apparently got these letters by heart and is enabled to reel them off without any hesitation'.[91] His first impression of Swan is also instructive: 'Edith Swan is a person who from the stony expression of her face, and peculiar stare in her eyes struck me as being possibly wrong in the head.'[92] The local police did not see Swan in the same way, as she was thought to be respectable (not rough, like Rose Gooding), but incriminating evidence was found at her home. Swan was found guilty of sending the letters.

There was speculation about possible motivations at the time. Perhaps Swan was sexually suppressed or was jealous of Rose Gooding's fun-loving lifestyle? Gooding was described by a contemporary commentator as 'an exceptionally attractive young woman' (her photos reveal a girlish charm), whose looks contrasted with those of Swan who, although only a little older than Gooding, had the appearance of a 'typical spinster'. The case has one very odd detail. A soldier called 'Boxall' was Swan's fiancé. One letter, written by Swan to this supposed fiancé, was written as though it was from the wife of a police constable, Mrs Russell, who lived next door to the Swans. In it, Boxall was informed that Mr Russell had gone away with Miss Swan, who was alleged to be carrying Russell's baby. Boxall was still in the army in 1922, and their relationship (such as it was, seemingly mostly conducted via correspondence) did not survive.[93] The importance of the letter stems from the conclusions that were drawn from it, since it made it look 'extremely improbable that Miss Swan is herself the author of the libels or that she had instigated them', because consequences of the letters seemed to affect only Swan.[94] Like those in Sutton, in Hove, and in Redhill, the local police failed to anticipate the depths of malice and cunning employed by the letter-writers.

Eliza Woodman had been given the same total sentence delivered to Mary Johnson over the course of several years, with no extra sentence for perjury for framing her neighbour.[95] Despite her obvious perjury, Edith Swan was sentenced to twelve months in prison: the same length of time that Rose Gooding served. Swan was taken to Lewes Prison.

Marie Lucinda Lee

A final short case also includes a reinvention of self; someone living another life through letters, but now we are in different circles, focused on a rich wife who pretended to be much younger than she was, and, in her letters, pretended to be much less respectable than she was.

Marie 'Molly' Lucinda Lee, the wife of Arthur Herbert Lee, a solicitor, pleaded guilty at the Old Bailey in November 1920 to publishing defamatory libels in letters' concerning Edward Webber, a furniture manufacturer, and the family of another solicitor, Charles Lewis. All parties lived at Rutland Park Mansions, on Willesden Green: the Lees occupied number 17, the Lewis family lived at number 18, and Webber at number 20. In the summer of 1920, local businesses were sent dozens of letters in disguised handwriting, accusing Webber and the Lewis family of being criminally in league, members of a gang of burglars who received and melted down stolen jewellery:

I am an old lag, and ust to be with the gang that are now in Willesden. No dout you ave eard of Robinson of Folkeston well e is a friend of 18 and 20 Rutland Park-Mansions, they are all in it. I ust to work for them, and they did the dirty on me now I go strait, so welp me. The lags at 20 have a car to swank in. I no, because I have 'elped them. I rite to warn you. They go away when they think they are being watched. They hide stuff they steal, and I no all the karackters. They are the Dalton Club set. The daughter is a pickpocket, and the mother and farther are in the White Slave trafick. They come to your shop becos the gang are thinking of breaking in on you.

Lee herself alleged she had also received letters. Charles Lewis had some handwriting expertise, having worked with documents in the war. Comparing the letters with a letter signed by Lee, he detected similarities.[96] Lee was bound over for £50 on the understanding that she would be severely punished if she repeated her libels. She expressed regret for being foolish.[97]

The Lees moved to Brighton shortly after the incident. In 1924, Molly was described by reporters as 'the beautiful young wife of a solicitor' in reports that she had made groundless allegations against Albert and Jessie Kate Underwood. Lee had written a libellous letter about Albert to his employer, Mr Baldwin, writing that Underwood 'is in with all the coiners'. Again, she focused her attentions on immediate neighbours; the Underwoods and the Lees had occupied flats in Queen Square. Underwood's counsel played on widespread misogynistic views; Lee did not 'hesitate to give expression to her feelings'; she 'used her tongue to good effect'. He also claimed that the seriousness of the slander against Underwood amounted to more than a normal neighbourly quarrel, and that 'substantial damages' would be required to end 'this scurrilous campaign of calumny'. Underwood was awarded £250 in damages.[98]

Clean women and filthy language

What is a person worth? Home Office records show how the figure of £250 for compensation offered to Rose Gooding was arrived at in 1921. In their assessment, they weighed up her moral worth; reread disparaging letters sent from Rose's former employee, in which it was suggested that Rose 'would be capable of writing abusive letters'. Her case was compared to others, including Adolf Beck (whom Tugwell had compared herself to) who had initially been offered £2,000, but refused this, eventually settling for £5,000. But Beck was a man. Mary Johnson, charged four times, thrice convicted, for a total of fifteen months' hard labour, plus eighty-six days awaiting trial, received £500 for her wrongful convictions. The Home Office noted that Mary Johnson had 'been obliged to give up a business + more'. They also recorded that 'In that case we proposed £1000 but the Treasury w[oul] d only give her £500.'[99] So, Rose Gooding was awarded a measly £250 as compensation for her 255 days in prison, 144 of which were with hard labour.[100] This was £12 less than Inspector Nicholls was awarded after being libelled about the case in articles published by *John Bull*, a popular Sunday periodical.[101]

Women often lacked legal counsel; they were judged by men and frustrated by male assumptions. In everyday life they endured social restrictions. If some letters were cries for help, they received myopic moralistic responses which associated their letters with cold, calculated 'demonical' cruelty. Some reporters, unconvinced by O'Brien's plea of 'mental derangement', put her actions down to hysteria and 'extravagant emotionalism' connected to the suffragette movement.[102]

Historian Christopher Hilliard's rich and compelling chapter on the language used in the Littlehampton libels reveals the linguistic contortions (and repetitions) Swan used to craft her strange letters: 'Just what is a "foxy ass piss country whore"?' he asks, and picks through the terms used in the letters.[103] During the war Edith was employed by a decorating firm. This work might have exposed her to more foul language, which she misremembered in her bizarre letters. Eliza Woodman's letters to herself were particularly strange. They come across as gently threatening (the italics here are mine): 'in the brook you go, ... the *quickest and best* way *out of your misery* will be to give you a *gentle knock* on the head'. It is as though she was mixing hatred of herself with sympathy. Both Tugwell and O'Brien described their own actions, effectively, as being 'depraved'; those of a 'low woman'; or 'a low down wretch'. The fraught internalization of socially manufactured gender roles comes through in the language, and may have played a part in the choice to write such letters at all.

We have considered the letters of a wife of a registrar, a governess, a greengrocer, a laundress, and a solicitor's wife. These five women lived very different lives: Lee was the wealthiest, with good legal backing, and she was treated relatively leniently by the legal process. All of the cases centred on expectations, about the proper behaviour of people, and all the women acted out alternative personalities on paper. The cases have specific variations, but there were certain things they had in common. All writers passed off their own letters as being written by someone else, and in doing so engaged with fantasy lives on paper. On paper they created spaces to explore sexuality; to defeat or circumvent repression; to engage in mischief and express malice. O'Brien's self-penned letters focused on promiscuity; corruption of Catholic priests; theft; and drunkenness. The individual psychologies involved are obviously complex and unfathomable, and the harm caused often shocking—but it is also important to note the resourcefulness involved in finding a way to undermine restrictive social identities and express emotions and feelings that have no place in 'normal' life. With the exception of Molly Lee, all of the women used obscenities that they were never heard to utter at other times. Lee played out a different fantasy; the wife of the solicitor was acting as a low-life criminal in her letters, harnessing the language of the moll.

Although Kathleen O'Brien was briefly married in the 1930s, once widowed she returned to live in the protective cocoon formed by the older women in her family (that is, her mother and her great-aunt). Edith Swan probably lived with her older brother Ernest in Western Road, Littlehampton, until he was evicted in 1934.[104] In 1939, twenty years before she died, Swan was listed as being 'incapacitated', a resident of the nearby East Preston workhouse.[105] Molly Lee died in June 1938, leaving Arthur a widower.[106] Eliza Woodman died, aged sixty-three, in 1937. Alfie and four of their fostered children attended her funeral and left loving messages, as did all or most of her eight siblings, as did her friend, Mrs Whitmore. Woodman's was the most violent anonymous letter campaign, inflicting injury on herself (and on cats), and also the most calculating and elaborate, doggedly targeting Mary Johnson, hounding her out of the town (Mary remained in Croydon and never returned to Redhill). Even after Rose Gooding had been exonerated there was local ill-feeling against her. In files kept on the Littlehampton libels there are two anonymous letters written to the Home Office in the early 1920s, advising about how the case could be closed. One, from October 1922, suggested that Gooding and her relatives be cautioned

that should either [sic] of them be caught, the person caught would receive 3 years penal servitude . . . I believe Mrs Gooding to be the leading figure assisted by others, and deserve [sic] all she got and if she had served her time it would have checked the nuisance.[107]

The other, sent on 6 September 1923 from East London was 'A word to the wise' and claimed that Swan could supply evidence to clear herself, but she 'dare not because of the consequences'.[108] It is remarkable how some families and communities could put letter-writing episodes behind them and excuse the actual letter-writers (although, seemingly, not those who had been falsely accused).[109]

It would be impossible to make any clinical evaluations from this distance, but it seems safe to conclude that at least some of the behaviours encountered in these cases would nowadays be ascribed to conditions such as borderline personality disorder and dissociative identity disorder. All the writers in this chapter had complex backgrounds: growing up either in large families, in personal distress, or both. O'Brien was one of ten children born to Catherine (née Crumbly) and Theobald after they married in 1876. All but the youngest two, Kathleen and John, had died by 1914, of various illnesses, including tuberculosis.[110] Catherine had been widowed for less than a week when the census enumerators captured the bare details of her life in Devonport, a district of Plymouth, in 1891. She ran a beer shop. Four of her children were still alive (two more died shortly after). In an environment of distress and uncertainty, while eight of her siblings failed to thrive, Kathleen somehow managed to become proficient in French and music, or, at least, sufficiently skilled to convince others that she could teach their children. By 1911 Kathleen's mother, Catherine, had moved in with her own mother, her sister Mary, and her aunt Margaret; a household dominated by widows. Maybe this created a charged atmosphere, sparking the wanderlust that took Kathleen to Europe as a governess. Kathleen feared her great-aunt and she idealized her father; were her letters a psychological defence for her?

Edith Swan was the penultimate child of thirteen (an above-average number of children at the time); four of her siblings died before she was born. Edward, their father, was never the focus of any of the libels. Perhaps Edith could not bring herself to write nasty things about him; perhaps she feared the consequences? Inspector Nicholls described Edward as 'an irritable and excitable old man, who would not be very difficult to upset'.[111] In photographs of her accompanying her daughter to court, Mary Ann Swan looks old, careworn and exhausted. In her seventies, she took in ironing to supplement her pension.[112] In 1891 two of the Swan daughters (Elizabeth and Ellen) had lived with the Leggett family just along Western Road; perhaps the Swans had too many children to cope with in too small a space? After researching overburdened mothers in these years, the social reformer Maud Pember Reeves argued that 'the children of the poor suffer from insufficient attention and care...not because the mother is lazy and indifferent...It is because she has but one pair of hands and but one overburdened brain.'[113] The two youngest Swan children, Edith and John, had obvious emotional difficulties.

In 1911, aged twenty, Swan had been a servant for a peculiar family in nearby Rustington (less than two miles from Littlehampton.) Her mistress, Alice Walker, had been deserted by her first husband (who had had left to settle in New Zealand). Four years after her second (presumably, but perhaps unknowingly, bigamous) marriage to a clerk in holy orders who had never held a living, Alice's second husband was sent to prison for a year for an indecent assault against a boy.[114] Back with her own family by the start of the war, Edith inhabited a largely male household; sleeping in her parents' room, the youngest daughter was expected to stay back and care for her brothers and ageing parents. Her sisters had moved away before she was born, and although she kept in touch with them by letter, most of Edith's sibling interactions were with brothers. In 1921 Bill Gooding described Steve and Ernest Swan, aged forty and thirty-nine, who lived at home: '[they] go by my window nearly every night at the hour of 10 o'clock or after + use the most filthy disgusting language which is not fit for a man let alone woman or children to hear'.[115] Back when the Swan boys were at school, Mary Ann had complained that 'her little boys' were not allowed school dinners, but other correspondence suggests a laissez-faire attitude to the Swans' parenting. The headmaster wrote to them 'several times' to get them to provide 'proper glasses' for Steve, 'as he cannot see a copy on the blackboard a yard off—but they do not think it necessary'.[116] Inspector Nicholls thought that Steve was not 'mentally strong'. John, the youngest child, was epileptic and, significantly, 'had a mania for writing letters to himself'. Bill Gooding claimed that John also used to 'tear his clothes up and knock his self about and say other people were doing it'.[117]

We can also identify some conditions in Molly Lee's childhood which may have contributed to her later instability. Born at the end of 1874 and christened Mary Lucinda, she was the daughter of a famous Irish journalist and parliamentary reporter, Adam Kernaghan, and his partner, Mary. Shortly after Molly was born her elder brother died. When she was six, twins Alice and Thomas arrived, and they probably took much of her mother's attention. When Molly was eleven or twelve, her mother committed suicide by drinking carbolic acid in their house in Brixton. Molly was a widow when she married Arthur Lee; her first husband had died very shortly after marriage.[118] The banns for her second marriage just note 'of age', and her birth year is recorded as 1886 in the census of 1911, chopping a dozen years from her actual age. Clearly Molly did not want her age to be known (perhaps even to Arthur). Reports about the wrongdoings of a 'beautiful young wife' in 1924 were made when Molly was fifty years old, of a similar age to her husband. Molly's grasp on the truth was uncertain, and, like some of the other writers here, she may have woven a fiction around herself as a kind of protection. There were reasons why these women might have been in pursuit of attention through their fictious alternative lives.

Expectations were heaped upon women at the time: to be a perfect mother; to be the caring neighbour; to be the clean housewife; to be chaste. In contrast to the other four writers, Annie Tugwell gave birth to her own children, and her anonymous writing may have corresponded with moments of crisis concerning them. Envy of motherhood was possibly behind Eliza Woodman's targeting of Mary Johnson; a woman with a brood of five daughters. Woodman was a foster mother. Tributes left at Eliza's funeral suggest that she was remembered very fondly by her foster children, and in her witness statements

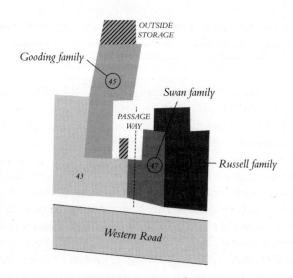

Figure 22. Numbers 43–49 Western Road, Littlehampton, a plan by Maud Webster

Woodman never missed an opportunity to present herself as an engaged and vulnerable mother; holding her baby; tending to her child in his bedroom. When she claimed her house had been broken into, Woodman added that baby shawls had been torn up; she presents the threats (that she constructed herself) as threats to her foster children, as much as to herself; she took blows from thrown stones for them.[119] A comment Mary Johnson made, when bewildered by the constant accusations made against her, might throw some light on this situation; 'Did they think that she would write these filthy letters to blacken the characters of her little children?'[120] She provided evidence to show that her girls were doing well at school. When Sergeant Kendrick spoke in Mary's defence in 1913 he added that the author 'must have spent the greater part of her time in the writing of these letters, much to the neglect of her home'.[121] The implication was that the campaign in Redhill was so elaborate that *any* mother would, inevitably, have to have neglected her children in order to have managed it.[122]

In the mid-twentieth century an expert catalogued self-written letters and concluded that most were attacks on the morality of the 'victim' but did not contain accusations of uncleanness, vanity, or neglect of children.[123] Swan's letters bucked that trend, describing the whole Swan household as 'a dirty drunken lot'. The relationships between the writers and the people their letters were about, or were sent to, or were ascribed to, were forged in neighbourhoods. Shared spaces and living in close proximity created opportunities for obsession, conflict, territorial battles, and terror. Living cheek by jowl permitted the invasion of privacy and gave access to secrets and movements, some of which were referred to in these letters. O'Brien and Gardiner shared a door and basement space. The neighbours in Littlehampton shared a store (the houses had previously shared a toilet). Ambiguous leasing contracts meant that arrangements about outdoor space needed to be established by the tenants. In Littlehampton, the question of who could use the garden (where Edward Swan grew vegetables) caused tensions. Outdoor water closets; sheds; pens for Steve Swan's rabbits; coops for Alfred Russell's chickens; drying space for laundry—they were all accommodated, awkwardly, into shared spaces, criss-crossed by neighbours privy to each other's comings and goings.[124] On top of this were other nuisances experienced by neighbours, such as bad drains and smelly bins. Letters received by the Mays (who then lived at number 49 Western Road) in September 1921 detailed these humdrum neighbourly annoyances:'You are bloody dirty or you would clean the yard sometimes you bloody rotten buggers';'It is your drain that stinks. Not our fish box' (presumably meaning an outdoor storage for fish, or for materials to catch fish with).[125]

In his handbook for sanitary inspectors, Albert Taylor remarked that 'sanitary authorities are sometimes disposed to disregard anonymous complaints', but that it was 'the duty of the authority to investigate every *specific* complaint made to them without regard to the means by which it comes to their knowledge'. Inspectors were instructed to 'exercise the greatest care when enquiring into such complaints' and that 'personal enquiry into the circumstances of such complaints is essential... otherwise the Inspector may be made the victim of much unpleasantness'. 'Inspectors should be wary', not take information for granted 'since it may be made through misapprehension or in malice'.[126] A guide published in 1915, the year the postcard that we saw at the start of this chapter was sent in Hounslow, advised inspectors to comment only on pertinent matters, but not even to 'appear to notice anything... which does not concern' them, 'for people resent any interference in their private affairs'.[127] Some unsigned letters may have come from 'tenants of poorer class houses who are anxious that their landlords should not be aware that they have made any complaints'. Perhaps that writer was 'at the mercy of his landlord or employer'.[128] At the time of the arrival there of the postcard in 1915, the Heston and Isleworth offices were home to one Inspector of Nuisances, plus two assistant sanitary inspectors.[129] Two hundred and forty-seven premises were inspected in the district following complaints in 1915.[130] Called Campo Road until 1913, Myrtle Road was a street set apart from other streets, to the north of Hounslow, close to the town station; wasteland separated it from Cecil Road to the south. The odd-numbered houses backed onto the railway line. The housing plots and gardens were small but it is likely that the wasteland was used by the street's inhabitants.[131] The Lawrences at number 14 were a family of five in a house of three rooms plus a kitchen. In 1911 they had a lodger. If this was the case in 1915, the couple, plus their twelve-year-old child and five-year-old twins, could have shared two rooms, the lodger taking the third. Cases of overcrowding were frequently raised by anonymous letters; maybe this concerned the writers?[132]

In Littlehampton, some of the letters were sent to Reginald Booker, the town sanitary inspector from 1905, and then to his successor, Charles Thomas Gardner, appointed in 1920.[133] Letters went to Booker's home address; his wife 'had been foolish enough to pay [the fine of] two pence for one of these disgusting letters which came through the post to him unstamped'. The final Littlehampton libel case, which eventually saw Edith Swan imprisoned, was actually triggered by a letter sent to Gardner in 1923. Starting with 'improper words', this letter then threatened that Gardner would be sorry for describing Edith's dust boxes as a nuisance.[134] The inspectors had made occasional visits down the passageway to the Goodings' cottage and shared spaces, after receiving complaints from one of the neighbours. In August 1920, one complaint [we can assume, penned by Edith Swan] appeared to come from Rose Gooding, drawing attention to Steve's rabbits, and also to the Russells' chickens. After his visit, Booker received an abusive letter, signed 'R.G'. He confronted the Goodings, annoyed because he thought he had inspected on their behalf, and thinking it 'not fair that I should receive this abusive letter'. Bill denied that Rose had written the letter, and when Edward Swan argued with Gooding, Booker left, not wanting to be embroiled in a neighbours' spat. He said he would report them all to the committee. He received another letter, also signed 'R.G': 'I don't care for your Fucking Committee.'[135]

6

Detection

Detectives say

In 1871 a beautiful book was published by Charles Chabot and Edward Twisleton, called *The Handwriting of Junius Professionally Investigated.*[1] 'Junius' was the pseudonymous author of letters critical of the Georgian government: they had been printed in 1772. Chabot—an 'expert', as the cover proclaimed—set out to prove on the basis of exhaustive handwriting comparison that Junius was Sir Philip Francis. The book featured hundreds of painstakingly arranged facsimiles to illustrate the process of expert comparison. Observe the loop of the *d*; make of it what you will:

Figure 23. Extract from Charles Chabot and Edward Twisleton, *The Handwriting of Junius Professionally Investigated* (1871), 37

Some were dubious. In a review of *The Handwriting of Junius*, Abraham Hayward wrote that 'listening to the evidence or reading the reports of experts, we often feel very much as if we were attending one of [those] *séances*. We are told that others see and we ought to see what we cannot see.'[2] Although such doubts about the infallibility of the professional handwriting expert persist in our own time, over the course of the period covered by the chapters here his work was met on the whole with growing interest and recognition.

The allure of deduction and the appeal of the amateur detective made fantastic partners for graphology and document analysis as the century drew near its end. Sherlock Holmes asks of his companion: 'Have you ever had occasion to study character in handwriting? What do you make of this fellow's scribble?' 'It is legible and regular', answers Dr Watson, 'a man of business habits and some force of character'. Holmes shakes his head. 'Look at his long letters,' he advises,

They hardly rise above the common herd. That *d* might be an *a*, and that *l* an *e*. Men of character always differentiate their long letters, however illegibly they may write. There is vacillation in his *k*'s and self-esteem in his capitals.[3]

This conversation appears in *The Sign of Four*, from 1890. The number of self-proclaimed handwriting experts had been gradually increasing over two decades. Among them were those who thought that a person's handwriting revealed not only identity but inner character or personality. Graphology—the so-called science of deducing character from script—also gained followers during this time. Perhaps Conan Doyle was acquainted with such works as *Character Indicated by Handwriting* by Rosa Baughan, first published in 1880.

Baughan described Florence Nightingale's 'd' as expressing 'tenderness and generosity, and sweetness'—'the first indicated by the sloping line of the upstroke, the last by the rounded and gracious curves of the final'.[4] Baughan later published works on equally dubious arts such as physiognomy and palmistry. Sherlock is close to the same nonsense when he discerns 'vacillation in his *k*'s'. What links the two texts and their liking of graphological inference is the Victorian obsession with the exposure of a person's true 'character'. As we have already seen in the previous chapter, this love of spectacular and authentic disclosure played several other roles in the history of anonymous letter-writing of the time.

Over the course of the century, more and more people—and especially prospective letter-writers—were becoming aware of the possibility that handwriting could be used for identification even when disguised. It is perhaps significant that when Conan Doyle returned to the theme, in *The Hound of the Baskervilles* (serialized in a newspaper 1901–02), the anonymous note of warning sent to Sir Henry Baskerville is largely devoid of handwriting; its words cut and pasted from *The Times*. From the choice of newspaper Holmes deduces that the sender is an 'educated' man. The method, decides Holmes, was chosen in an 'effort to conceal [the writer's] own writing', suggesting 'that that writing might be known, or come to be known'. Only the last word—'moor'—is handwritten. Holmes says this is because it was a hard word to find in the paper in a hurry (but of course Conan Doyle wanted to emphasize it for literary reasons).[5]

The fictitious scenes of Sherlock Holmes examining anonymous letters between 1890 and 1902 perhaps reflect a Victorian arms race between letter-writers and detectives—detectives of many stripes. This chapter examines how anonymous letter-writers could be identified and caught in the long nineteenth century. It covers changing attitudes and practices in respect of handwriting expertise, documentary forensics, legal admissibility, practices of surveillance, interdiction, and evasion. The vagaries of detection (and prejudice) in practice are explored with reference to cases from earlier chapters as well as to new ones.

True experts

By the time Sherlock Holmes appeared in 1887, there was already a growing rift between amateurs less gifted than Holmes and what Twisleton in the Preface to *The Handwriting of Junius* called a new kind of expert. The word 'expert', wrote Twisleton,

is often used very loosely. It is frequently used to designate lithographers, or gentlemen connected with banks, who come forward as witnesses once or twice in their lives to express their belief that a particular document was or was not written by a certain individual. The word has, then, a meaning very different from that of general experts in handwriting, recognised as such in courts of justice...I have been assured that during the last fifty years the number of such experts in London has been very few.[6]

Eventually, such expertise came to be seen as an occupation in itself. As Twisleton states, it had previously been a skill offered by other professionals when necessary.[7] The early nineteenth century had seen various experts called upon to give advice in anonymous letter cases, especially post-office officials.[8] Thomas Coleback, the Inspector of Franks who made a brief appearance in this book's first chapter, was later involved in a case in Staffordshire. In 1805 John Warburton, the manufacturer of earthenware in Cobridge, had been accused of sending 'infamous' anonymous letters to 'certain virtuous & respectable' local women. Warburton refused to sign a 'humiliating apology', worried that this would be seen as an admission of guilt and might damage his relations with the women. Discovering that the vicar of St John's in Hanley had been repeating accusations about Warburton being the author, he went to the press, to 'solicit those who have the Papers' to hand them in to be scrutinized. Warburton implored the prosecution to end 'this scandalous affair' which he felt was contrived by 'some gossiping simpleton, with intent to irritate me'. Warburton was suspected on the basis of the opinion of 'a person employed at the General Post Office': Thomas Coleback, who did not appear to have the backing of his own superior.[9]

One of the most famous of the new Victorian handwriting experts was Chabot himself. He was of Huguenot descent, and had started out as a lithographer. Chabot died in 1882 with 'a large private practice as an expert, and his skill was in much request in the Law Courts'. His evidence was used in the Roupell case of 1862–63 and also the later Tichborne case.[10] The Scottish lawyer Alexander Wood Renton argued that Chabot 'raised the expert's craft from an art', and put the profession on a scientific standing 'by showing the world that a scientific witness could give evidence without improper bias'. Chabot drew attention 'not to incidental and often imaginary peculiarities in the writings submitted to him, but to the character of the writer portrayed there, which cannot be permanently disguised'. Chabot died just as the profession he helped to establish was cementing its reputation.[11]

That Chabot should have started as a lithographer was not unusual. Lithographers were among the most common informal handwriting experts throughout the period. Lithography, a German invention of the late eighteenth century, uses several stages of application of oil and water to hard surfaces to produce highly detailed prints. This very modern printing technology became popular in England from the 1830s. Much of the work of the lithographer was in making facsimile copies for circulars for trades and businesses:

A facsimilist in full employment, as all the tribe were on the introduction of lithography, could easily do a dozen or more of these circulars in a day; and it could not fail that the eye, closely trained to follow every turn of the pen, and note every slight mannerism of letter formation, laid up a store of observation that would escape the ordinary reader. The joining of letters; the break of the pen when in the middle of the word it habitually leaves the paper and goes back to cross or to dot; the general slope of the whole hand; the formation of the capital letters; the invariable shape of a g, or an a, or an r; the flourishes and the running of words together;—all these and many other characteristics, in which all handwriting abounds, and which are as much a part of the writer as his nose or his eyes, were necessarily keenly noted by a man whose business it was to make the closest possible copy of the original.[12]

Having acquired skill in the course of their trade, lithographers gradually gained experience in anonymous-letter cases. The *Cornhill Magazine* went on to describe the usual profile: a lithographer might begin a 'small private practice', but it would not be long before they were consulted by 'recipients of scurrilous letters', forged receipts, suspicious codicils, and other questionable documents. In 1894, one commentator drew a connection between the two skills:

It is admitted by all experts in handwriting that a keen knowledge of lithography is absolutely essential to the true exercise of their peculiar craft. The eye and the hand have been trained to observe and copy all the peculiarities and eccentricities of writers—a training absolutely necessary to one who practices as an expert in handwriting.[13]

There were many 'hushed up' cases in which handwriting experts were consulted, including 'scandalous communications from disappointed suitors, secretly thrust under the front door; abusive and threatening letters', and even Valentine's Day missives, 'as to the authors of which the recipients show an angry and a lively curiosity'.[14]

Frederick G. Netherclift appears in the 1891 census as 'Expert in Handwriting'. By then Netherclift was an old man with a young wife, living in Islington. A decade before, Netherclift was described as 'Professional expert in handwriting'. In 1851 Netherclift appeared in the census as a 'Lithographic artist'.[15] Netherclift's father, Joseph, had also been a handwriting expert, and had likewise begun as a lithographer: several sons followed their fathers into handwriting expertise. When Frederick Netherclift died in 1892 his obituary observed that he had 'figured as witness in many civil and criminal trials where evidence of handwriting was required'. A sting in this eulogy came at the end: 'of course calligraphic experts are not infallible any more than other people'.[16] Another obituary of Netherclift, while acknowledging that 'his evidence was often extremely valuable', noted how handwriting experts frequently disagreed, implying a lack of objectivity in their work. Netherclift was 'often at variance' with his colleague 'Mr Inglis' in the witness box, with the result that the 'testimony of both was liable to be lightly estimated'.[17] 'Mr Inglis' was George Smith Inglis, described in the 1871 census as a 'Lithographic writer'. 'I have watched Mr Inglis at work', wrote one enthusiastic fan in 1894: 'He will watch a "t" for an hour at a time.'[18] Inglis's son, George Douglas Inglis, also went into the business, and he was a 'Lithographic transfer writer' in 1891; the same year his father was listed as 'Lithographer and Handwriting Expert'.[19] In one only slightly reported case, a young girl at a boarding school blamed a classmate for sending her abusive anonymous letters; Inglis's examination found that the victim had been writing the letters herself, left-handed.[20] Inglis was consulted in the Garbett case in 1895 we saw in Chapter 4, when the prosecution relied on the evidence Inglis supplied concerning the similarity of the writing on the letters and on other documents written by Garbett.[21]

Inglis's practice was busy in 1895. He was also called in to examine documents at the centre of a case in Birdingbury in Warwickshire. George Munslowe, a beerhouse keeper and an Overseer of the Poor, had been accused of writing libellous letters. They were not anonymous but had the appearance of being signed by other local men. Apparently motivated by anger arising from petty debts and disagreements, Munslowe sent many letters over several years. Using the Libel Act of 1843, his prosecutors were keen to make clear they would not be probing the truth or falsity of the letters—their interest was only in whether they had been written to breach the peace. They suggested that Munslowe was motivated by 'a sort of itching to abuse various people and to set everybody by the ears as much as possible'. For instance, the farmer Henry Truslove received a postcard accusing him of blaming the poor for drinking themselves into poverty—when in fact, the postcard pronounced, it was his payment of low wages that was the true cause. That the political element was simply opportunistic can quickly be shown. Martha Jane Rathbone had been troubled by letters in the same handwriting since 1891, following the death of her daughter, Edith, of tuberculosis. The letter was made heavier with a French coin, meaning that Mrs Rathbone had to pay the Post Office in order to receive it because it was under-stamped for the weight. The letter was contrived to seem as if it had been sent by Walter King, a local coachman. It instructed Martha not to bring her 'little boy' when she came 'down to our saddle-room again', but instead to bring her husband, Eli, for a kicking. It continued:

If you would take those walnut shells off your boots, as when you are walking you tumble about as if you are drunk. You and old Eli Rathbone are two bad devils. You killed that girl of yours, starving her to death on purpose to save money...You robbed the Co-operative Society.

Walter King, giving evidence, said he owed Munslowe 1s/6d, and that he had received an insulting postcard, which he burned, and then a letter, in April 1892—and then another in July 1892, which came with 'a wax vesta box full of filth' (a vesta box usually contained wax matches). The handwriting on the letters was similar and 'to some extent disguised'. Inglis stated that they were all written by the same person; the hand possessed 'peculiar characteristics' and a similarity in the formation of letters. The case rested on the handwriting, but only the prosecution had expert evidence, for the defence had not had access to the letters before the trial.[22] At the Warwickshire Assizes in 1894, Munslowe claimed that he had also been victimized. A letter he claimed to have received was addressed to 'Lord Munslow, King of Birdingbury'. It too came with a box of 'refuse'. In summation, the judge steered the jury to acquit Munslowe on the grounds that Inglis's expertise could not be deemed infallible: all of the evidence came from Inglis, he said, who 'in looking for resemblances' might have missed 'important differences'. The jury disagreed, and Munslowe was found guilty on three counts of libel.[23] Losing his licence to keep a beershop, Munslowe was committed to gaol for six months with hard labour.[24]

John Holt Schooling flirted with the occupation of 'handwriting expert' in the 1900s, but also worked as a consulting actuary (a kind of financial risk assessor), statistician, author, and journalist. In 1881 he had been a barrister's clerk, and by 1911 was listed only as a 'consulting actuary' (which might have been where the real money was).[25] Others came to handwriting expertise through law stationery and scrivening. Before getting work as a document examiner, Henry Dixon was a law stationer and 'ornamental writer'.[26] In 1890, Dixon's advice was sought on a libellous letter in Manchester. A dressmaker had been charged with making a 'false, scandalous, and defamatory libel' against her doctor. Jane Boston had been under the care of Thomas Henry Pinder for several years. Following an operation that Pinder had been encouraging her to undergo for years, Boston left his care. She still wrote hundreds of letters to him 'containing charges of...a horrible character': she did not deny writing these and they were used for handwriting samples.

Boston was also accused of sending two anonymous postcards. One had a compelling address: 'Thou blood mark faced reptile'. It mentioned a 'mother of thy child' who had been 'ruined'. Dixon's job was to compare the writing in the letters with that on the postcards. He concluded they were similar 'in a general way', but that the writing was disguised, hazarding to say that Boston was a 'versatile writer'. A different expert, Fred Smart, was sent for. A 'teacher of handwriting', Smart was based in nearby Sale. Boston was imprisoned for six months; the judge ordered that she be given medical attention, as she seemed 'not quite right in her head'.[27] Smart had been a 'Commercial and Civil Service Tutor' in 1891, but from 1901 was listed as 'Handwriting expert'; he was involved in several other cases. In 1911 his expertise was again sought in a complicated case: a schoolteacher had been accused of libelling a dressmaker in Oakmere, Cheshire.[28] The careers of Dixon and Smart show that there was work enough for two experts based in northern England.

Eventually, with more focused training and technological advances, handwriting expertise became a specialism in its own right: photography was used to enlarge letters, to permit a better critical examination.[29] Photographic analysis could also permit a closer analysis of things like the flow of ink, or the number of pen lifts. The longer an anonymous-letter campaign lasted, the more handwriting there was to analyse, and so, the more likely it became that a writer might be identified. Writers often got lax and their ability to write with 'unnatural characteristics' diminished—at least, such was the theory. Writers who kept duplicates of their letters would find the maintenance of a false style much easier: one of the neglected little details of long-term animosity.[30]

Expert witness

Notwithstanding the judge's reservations in the 1895 Munslowe case, over the course of the century English law had come to give greater recognition to experts like Chabot and Inglis. This development should be seen within the wider context of the law's evolving attitude towards scientists. Handwriting expertise based solely on documentary comparison did not exist in the English courtroom before the second half of the nineteenth century; it was, as Twisleton noted in the Preface to *The Handwriting of Junius*, only recognized in principle in criminal law after 1865.[31] Tests of handwriting similarity conducted by experts in open court gradually became more common. A guilty person might try to write in a way which was different to the letter held as evidence. Then they would be asked to do the same again, with the first version held away from them. On the second attempt, the writer would not always be able (under court conditions) to replicate their newly disguised form of handwriting; both copies made in court could vary. Innocent people writing in their normal handwriting would craft copies that looked similar. In this way an effort to deceive could be uncovered.[32]

It is sometimes stated that the opinion of experts was accepted as evidence in English courts after the case of *Folkes v Chadd* (1782), at the end of which Lord Mansfield, perhaps the most famous and influential lawyer of the eighteenth century, had seemingly allowed it.[33] Mansfield's judgment made explicit appeal to cases of handwriting: 'Handwriting is proved every day by opinion, and for false evidence on such questions a man may be indicted for perjury.'[34] The decision was not published until 1831. Mansfield's ruling was linked to the fact that the scientist in question had made on-site inspections of the harbour at the centre of the case—in other words, he was a *witness* who had seen things with his own eyes, not a partisan expert. Mansfield's reasoning in the case was distorted and used as '*post facto* rationalization' to explain how English law came to recognize expert testimony.[35] Consistent with this, the way handwriting experts came to be viewed by English courts was much messier and more inconsistent than sometimes thought.

When Mansfield's judgment in *Folkes v Chadd* was printed in 1831, his editor Roscoe added a note that cast doubt on how Mansfield's ruling would be received on such points as handwriting.[36] The most recent contrary ruling Roscoe mentioned was that of *Gurney* et al. *v Langlands* (1821). In that case, revolving around a forged signature on a legal document, the testimony of one Joseph Hume, 'Inspector of franks at the post-office', was ruled out. 'When a witness has seen another write...or become acquainted with his hand-writing', said the judge, 'he has a ground of forming a belief as to it.' Anyone who had not—with their own eyes—seen the subject write, or who had not received letters from the person in question, had no business speaking about it in a court of law. The judge, who was apparently aware of Mansfield's decision in the 1780s, drew a distinction between

connoisseurs of written documents and other experts: 'Opinions of
skilful engineers and mariners, &c., may be given in evidence in matters upon skill...Because in such cases, the witness has a knowledge of
the alleged cause.' By contrast, the expert in handwriting drew infer-
ences from, and made comparison of, effects alone. As the law then saw
it, such witnesses could never properly say who had caused the effects
to come into being, at least not without great prejudice to a trial.
Justice Best, commenting on the judgment, concurred and noted: 'It
does not appear to me necessarily to follow, that an inspector of franks
has peculiar means of ascertaining imitated hand-writing.'[37]

We have already seen similar doubts expressed in court about such
expertise. For instance, in the 1801 contest between Forster and
Mellish, Thomas Coleback, 'the Inspector of Franks at the Post Office',
was called in to give expert testimony and identified Forster as the
author of the anonymous letters at question. But the judge found such
evidence inadmissible and the court made the Mellish family pay
compensation.[38] Early nineteenth-century advice, such as that issued
to Justices of the Peace in 1814, called for comparisons of handwriting
to be left to the jury alone.[39] Nonetheless, growing appreciation of
scientific specialization meant that in the course of the century English
law would make more concessions to the concept of expertise.[40] By
1856, Alexander Mansfield Burrill could write in his *Treatise on the
nature, principles and rules of circumstantial evidence* that even where a
criminal hand had been heavily disguised, 'under all this exterior of
ingenious and labored uncouthness, the practised eye of an expert was
enabled to detect those traces of the usual and natural manner' of an
individual's own handwriting.[41] Doubts about the scientific status of
handwriting analysis have persisted. In 1989, one comprehensive
review of its merits informed a legal readership that there was no good
reason to assume it had any probative value at all: 'From the perspective
of published empirical verification, handwriting identification expertise is almost nonexistent.'[42]

Disguised hands

If the belief that handwriting could betray identity was in fact supersti-
tious, the growing respect accorded to it by the courts meant that
anonymous writers of the Victorian period and beyond had to take it

seriously. *The London Journal* carried an article about anonymous letters in 1911 which identified 'certain little tricks' used by people trying to disguise their handwriting. Such tricks included changing the spaces between characters and writing in a 'back hand' (sloping backwards rather than forwards). Clues were still thought to exist in the positioning of dots over the 'i's and other quirks. Those wanting to ensure maximum disguise would print their words.[43] Other writers tried to disguise their handwriting by changing the size of their letters or using a different sort of pen. Many writers were found out because they had changed only a few characteristics while retaining the basic quirks of their usual writing style. Another common technique was to feign semi-literacy by including spelling and grammatical errors. These habits were often exposed because the writer omitted to insert errors in 'arrangement, paragraphing and punctuation'. Handwriting experts knew that a feigned hand was 'almost certain to be inconsistent with itself in important features' and would not be 'free and rapid'. Other techniques of writing disguise involved modifying margins and spacings; the addition of flourishes; hand tremors; variations in the application of pressure; and manufactured signs of hesitancy.[44]

In addition to the written words, the examiner could focus on other comparable features, including

paper, pen, pencil, ink . . . subject matter, style, idioms, grammar, spelling, use of capitals, punctuation, division of words, titles, use of numerals or words to express numbers, corrections, erasures, interlineations, abbreviations, folding, creases, worn portions of paper, machine cut, hand cut or torn edges of paper, size and shape of paper and watermarks.[45]

The ways that women and men were taught handwriting probably introduced differences in the style and shape of letters.[46] An American forensic expert noted that, by 1910, women were 'more apt to acquire the characteristics of men's writing' simply because new jobs were available to them. By contrast, men were rarely required to adopt the writing style of women. As a result, there were more women whose handwriting looked masculine than there were men who wrote in a 'feminine' manner.[47] Fewer options for disguise were available to those with less literacy, as they could not feign a more literate style. It was of course much more common for highly literate writers to feign 'downwards'. Despite fears that it would be the uneducated who would abuse the postal system by sending abusive and offensive mail, it was those most educated who could manipulate the new anonymity of the postal system to the greatest—or at least the safest—advantage.

The examination of handwriting in practice appears to have been inchoate, ad hoc, and even entirely absent in some anonymous letter cases, especially those for which there appeared to be an obvious female suspect. Much was known (or thought to be known) about the idiosyncrasies of a person's natural hand by the 1920s. Despite Rose Gooding's handwriting appearing quite different from that of the libellous letters circulated in Littlehampton at that time, suspicion of her was as intense as if there were conspicuous similarities.[48] Samples of Rose's hand survive in the Home Office records.[49] Her style is messy, flamboyant, and a little chaotic, with varying pencil pressure. It doesn't look as if it was written by a person who would be easily capable of writing in a neat and consistent style. The handwriting in the libels was described as 'a round, bold and well formed writing', as though from 'school copy books with nicely looped Y's, G's and H's, well formed... not studied or unnatural'.[50] An excerpt from the letters was printed in the *Daily Mail* in 1922, and it does not look anything like Rose's handwriting.[51]

No handwriting expert was consulted in Littlehampton—to examine either Rose Gooding's handwriting or Edith Swan's. In Rose Gooding's first trial 'the question of handwriting did not form the main feature' of the judge's summing up.[52] In June 1921, Sir Ernley Blackwell, Legal Assistant Under-Secretary of State at the Home Office, wrote to the registrar at the Criminal Appeal Office asking to see specimens of Edith Swan's writing.[53] In her petition to the Home Office from Portsmouth Prison sent in June 1921, Rose Gooding noted that her solicitor had Swan's handwriting, which Gooding claimed 'corresponds with some of the documents'. She claimed to possess Swan's writing in a pattern for a sock, written out at Christmas 1919, and a recipe for marrow chutney. In court Swan stated these writings were not in her own hand, and suggested they were written by Gooding, using 'disguised writing'.[54]

Edith Swan's presumably undisguised handwriting, sent from incarceration in 1923, can be found in a letter in which she again repeated her innocence and petitioned to have her handwriting tested. She claimed that when she was tried, she 'had no means to provide for the services of a handwriting expert'; and that no evidence of her writing was given (which was untrue). Swan further noted that Detective

Inspector Nicholls had told her two years before that 'it was absolutely impossible for any person to disguise their handwriting', and that there were 'scientific means by which anybody's handwriting could be traced'. With little left to lose, Swan requested a handwriting test. This request, written in a neat hand, with consistent well-formed letters, is not in the same writing as the anonymous missives, but looks (to my non-expert eyes) to be written by a person very much in charge of their writing style (unlike Rose's writing), and who was clearly able to modify her writing skilfully.[55]

Obfuscations and traps

New technology made it ever easier to avoid handwriting altogether. In late 1910 a person, or persons, unknown used a typewriter to bash out a warning to some depositors of Birkbeck Bank, a combined bank and building society located near High Holborn in London. Signing off 'A Friend', the anonymous author wrote:

I beg you to withdraw your deposit from the Birkbeck Bank, as I have heard on sound authority that the company are in very low water and there may be a run on the bank any day. This has occurred through the failure of Charing Cross Bank. There may be no cause for anxiety, but it is well to be on the safe side—Yours A FRIEND.

The envelope bore a postmark from Kentish Town, marked 8 p.m., November 8. Another bank, the Charing Cross, had failed in October and the Birkbeck Bank had already weathered a run on its capital reserves back in 1892. In November 1910, as a result of the anonymous letter, queues of anxious account-holders snaked around the Southampton Buildings on Chancery Lane. Women were conspicuous in the queues; many were widows. Pickpockets took advantage.[56] Solicitors for the bank offered a £200 reward for information leading to the conviction of the person or persons responsible for writing this letter.[57] Using a typewriter was by no means an entirely safe method of evasion. The machine's alignment and the condition of the type, 'broken serifs', defective ribbons, clogged-up centres on q's, e's, R's, g's, and other letters, and overly large full stops created consistent artefacts on a typed page. These could be used as good evidence provided that the machine could be found and associated strongly with someone.[58]

Examined by experts, the letter to depositors was judged to have been typed on a Remington No. 7 typewriter, four or five years old, with a carriage which was 'running sluggishly'. The type-bar bearing the letter 'o' was bent or loose, with the result that the letter was not flush with other characters; the type-bar carrying the 'r' 'was not in proper adjustment as regards spring'; and the capital letter 'C' was 'worn'. Despite these clues, nobody was charged with writing the letter. It had been reproduced for transmission to multiple recipients on a duplicating machine, supposed to be a Roneo. This was a type of mimeograph: a stencil rotary duplicating device of the type eventually supplanted by photocopiers. An anonymous telegram which read 'Run on the Birkbeck. Withdraw immediately' was examined at the same time.[59] The Birkbeck Bank did not recover; it went into receivership in the summer of 1911.[60]

If letters and postcards could be traced through the postal system, possibly fruitless examination of their hand or type became of secondary importance. The Post Office Investigation Branch (IB) was formed in 1861, from an earlier 'Confidential Bureau' that had been established in 1843.[61] By the end of the nineteenth century the IB had approximately fifty staff. They were known within the Post Office, a little melodramatically, as the 'Men of Secrets'. The Men of Secrets were authorized to oversee postal workers and even open and reseal letters as they passed through the system. Most of their work involved investigating financial irregularities and theft, but they sometimes turned their attention to anonymous letters, especially after the implementation of the Post Office Act of 1908.[62] In 1923 the IB investigated at least two obscene postcard campaigns: both were found to be the work of outwardly respectable women. In August 1923 Cecilia Giles, a twenty-nine-year-old from East Croydon, was found guilty of posting eight 'grossly indecent postcards' after an investigation by Frederick C. Cartwright of the IB, who proved the case by keeping Giles under surveillance. Giles's father, Henry, was one of the recipients of the postcards, as was Cecilia herself (some were sent care of her employer). The bulk of the postcards went to the Reverend A. E. Wilkinson, the vicar of St James's Church, Croydon, and members of his congregation. By 1923 the cards had been circulating for three years; their handwriting was 'obviously disguised'. Cecilia, who arrived in court 'smartly dressed', was described as 'of the highest respectability'. Her father was a county court bailiff and her motives were opaque. One report suggested that the writing on a postcard posted before June 1923 was 'quite different': it is not out of the question that Giles had initially received letters sent by someone else before extending the campaign herself. Perhaps she had started to crave the attention. This possibility does not appear to have been considered at the time.[63] The other notable case in which the IB became involved that year was the Swan case from the last chapter. The Beach Post Office in Littlehampton, from which marked stamps were sold to Swan, was watched and a 'special periscope mirror' was used to watch inside the postbox.[64] The Men of Secrets who took an interest in the affair included Walter Edward Bowler, a clerk in the IB who supplied the marked stamps, and his junior colleague Cartwright, who had run the investigation of Cecilia Giles in East Croydon the same summer.[65]

The other respectable woman caught by the IB and found guilty of a similar offence that year was Diana Langham, a fifty-year-old who had lived all her life in Coleford, Gloucestershire. She was imprisoned for six months for writing 'extremely libellous' indecent postcards to two men and two couples from the town. One man, a bank official, had received thirty-two cards. Coleford was 'an old-fashioned little place nestling prettily in the hollow of the hills' near the Forest of Dean. Langham was a woman of independent means, the daughter of a mining engineer. She was a regular churchgoer and a member of the local golf club and lived a 'highly respectable life'. Langham was snared by Arthur Bishop of the IB. Bishop marked a set of stamps with the invisible initials 'D. L.', after suspicion had settled on Langham. She was caught red-handed, in the act of posting cards on which were pictographics. A house search revealed an incriminating blotting pad showing traces of the cards. At the initial hearing, Langham 'wore a heavy coat with a wide turned-up collar' and hid her face with a veil. The words on her postcards were deemed too filthy to be read aloud; they expressed the 'most horrible vulgar coarseness which must have caused the greatest distress'. Speaking 'in a low refined voice', Langham used smelling salts in the dock to regain her composure. Her motivation was unclear; the trial did not address it in detail. Prosecuting, Lionel Lane observed that 'cases of this sort occur from time to time, and for some extraordinary reason they generally occur amongst people of education and position'. Summing up, the judge described it as a 'very sad case', noting that the accused 'bore an unblemished character', and intimating that the episode may have been triggered by menopause: 'that period of life which roused a strange mental and nervous condition'.[66]

The distribution of marked or altered stationery was one of the surest techniques of associating an individual with particular letters. The technique reveals unsound members of a specific community in which material circulates. In fact, the various battles waged on a lower level by anonymous letter-writers and the Post Office had been fore-shadowed by earlier tests at a diplomatic and political level. In 1844 the British government's tampering with letters as they passed through the expanded postal network was exposed in a public scandal. An Italian man named Joseph Mazzini cleverly enclosed grains of sand, fine hairs, and poppy seeds in his correspondence, speculating that some would go missing en route; they did.[67] Similar ruses were used later in reverse to supply strong evidence in anonymous-letter cases. In Sutton, Annie Tugwell was caught out by a ruse of the postmaster: stamps marked with invisible ink were sold to Tugwell's servant and subsequently detected on anonymous letters.[68] Doctored stamps had been used on items with the same handwriting sent to Canon Cafferata, Louisa Wesley, and to Tugwell herself. A search of her house revealed water-marked envelopes like those used for the libels; and *French First Course*, a French textbook which included some phrases used in the anonymous writing.[69] Stamps marked with invisible ink were sold to Eliza Woodman in Redhill.[70] To find even more evidence a special constable called Harry Budgen, who worked as a clerk, devised an even cleverer trap. He arranged to have packets of free samples of 'Paramite' notepaper delivered to Woodman's friend, Mrs Whitmore, who lived at 74 St John's Road, as well as to Woodman herself at number 52. Papers in each pack were marked with invisible ink: '52' for the Woodman pack, '74' for the Whitmore one. Samples were sent to Whitmore in case Woodman mentioned them to her friend (although it is also possible that Whitmore had not yet been eliminated as a suspect herself).[71] Material evidence started to stack up against Woodman; one of the letters that she had gathered up to hand to the police was inscribed on the back of a picture from an edition of *Little Folks* from 1881—a copy of which was found in the Woodman family home.[72]

Material evidence of this kind was always going to be more per-suasive than handwriting analysis. Surveillance and searches—the tools of patient police work—were also tried. The Tugwell case featured a detective dressed up as a door-to-door seller of bootlaces;[73] in the Edith Swan affair, a policewoman called Gladys Moss, Worthing's first female officer, who would have been ejected from the police force the year before without the intervention of an 'influential deputation' of local women, hid in a shed to watch.[74] Blotting paper was apparently located in Tugwell's home; one piece had blotted the words 'in the stable, the trolls', another 'old gas bag'—phrases used in her obscene letters. It also featured the names 'Measures' and 'Annie Dewey', all in the curly-tailed letters familiar from the libels.[75] In a search of the Swan house in Littlehampton in 1921, police found incriminating pages and a blotting book. The blotting paper was photographed and enlarged at Scotland Yard, and 'on it in numerous places [were] found impressions of various words and addresses of recipients of these libels'.[76] Blotting paper also formed part of the evidence against Diana Langham in the same year, 1923. The collection of such evidence meant nothing if it was not treated with care. Various pieces of material evidence went missing in the Littlehampton case. The need to locate them was the subject of internal memoranda at the Home Office.[77] Other material evidence was also treated casually; the police had not checked that the stylographic pen found in a drawer at Mary Johnson's house actually worked.[78]

Once material evidence did point to a clear suspect, the police could mount surveillance and other techniques of detection—but not without risk. The investigation itself could be hijacked and steered this way or that by cunning writers. In 1913, Mary Johnson had asked if a policeman could live in their house to observe that she was not writing letters. The request was not granted; police manpower was instead directed to provide surveillance on the Woodman house, making the investigation more directly vulnerable to Woodman's tricks and diversions.[79] Police surveillance undertaken in the Hove case from 1914, where later the campaign was found to have been perpetrated by Kathleen O'Brien, is another example of naïve and misdirected patience. Colonel Gardiner wrote of being watched by detectives from the Hove police force for a fortnight: 'the Head and other detectives of this wonderful Police of Hove [did] pass their time (no wonder our rates are high!) in company with the mistress and the governess, half in resting, half in watching, also in listening at my flat door'. Gardiner additionally remarked that 'the detectives had seized upon my maids, threatening them in a semi-brutal way'.[80]

In a different case, a female police officer went undercover as a housemaid in the home of the prime suspect. The case involved the circulation of hundreds of letters, playing out in the Norfolk seaside town of Sheringham through the 1920s, gripping the entire nation. Despite an extensive criminal investigation, nobody was ever convicted of writing the letters.[81] For three years from late 1920, well-to-do townsfolk received abusive anonymous letters and postcards, all written in the same obviously disguised handwriting. In 1924, the key suspect, a young woman, was thrice tried unsuccessfully. Pillar-boxes were watched by plain-clothes police officers, and stamps were marked with invisible ink to no avail. During one of the trials, it was revealed that letters had circulated in the town thirteen years earlier, at a time when the accused was twelve years old and living elsewhere. At another time, the suspect went to live temporarily in Eastbourne. It was there that a policewoman inveigled them into giving her employment. Letters continued to circulate, but the police officer stated that she had not observed any writing or posting of letters.[82]

Despite the slightly chaotic ingenuity of some of these investigations, the police often appear a little as they do in the tales of Sherlock Holmes. Although the nature of the crime often made investigation very difficult, the record shows that the police were often duped by simple stratagems and that they took to forensic investigation quite reluctantly. Decoy letters sent by the writers to themselves often worked. Sometimes authors included themselves in the libel in a different way, perhaps by including unpleasant details about their own persons in letters to other people. Self-addressed 'decoy' letters were sent by all the women in the last chapter. Swan's letters made her appear racier than she in fact was, as did letters by Kathleen O'Brien and Molly Lee. Such tricks likely had a psychological aspect in at least some of the cases. Others have written about reconfigurations in the meanings of selfhood, and self-reconstructions of identities in the late nineteenth and early twentieth centuries, and some details in the anonymous letters appear to follow similar patterns, if not similar motivations.[83] Decoy-letter authors were inevitably involved in investigations, gaining them unusual attention. The last thing these women wanted was for the recipients of their letters to keep quiet about them—they required a reaction.

Decoy letters were especially common in campaigns involving many recipients. If only those in charge of these investigations had closely read Albert Osborn's book of 1910, *Questioned Documents*:

Another peculiar fact of great importance in connection with the investigation of the authorship of such letters [in campaigns involving many letters] is
that in a large proportion of cases, perhaps twenty per cent, the actual writer
is also one of those who receive them and is supposed to be one of the victims
of the work of some one else. On account of this fact one of the first steps to
be taken in such an inquiry is to learn the name and get samples of the writing
of every one who claims to have received similar letters.[84]

In 1933 a handwriting expert suggested that good investigative practice would be to pick out the name which was mentioned most in the
letters, noting that 'it is a favourite device of those calumniators to
include all sorts of evil gossip about themselves to throw the addressee
off the scent'.[85] When letters included details that could only be known
to the prosecutor and the person accused, the police were often gulled.
They wrote off the Tugwell campaign as part of ordinary congrega-
tional bickering, triggering a sequence of assumptions that ended with
Dewey being charged in Tugwell's place. Even when material evidence
was available, local investigators readily ignored what it plainly told
them. They were often tricked into looking further afield than was
necessary, preferring hunches which almost invariably aligned with
prejudices about persons less respectable or educated than the actual
perpetrators.

   More experienced commentators suggested that miscarriages of
justice were more likely when rural police forces were tasked with
investigating such cases. Sir Archibald Bodkin, Director of Public
Prosecutions, thought the case against Gooding merely 'inferential',
and marked by a failure of judgement in 'the country Police'. They
were 'perhaps not so alive to the mysterious occurrences which may
be met with if a woman becomes malicious towards another woman'.[86]
There is plenty of evidence that Bodkin was not wrong to doubt the
open-mindedness of parochial forces. Superintendent Peel of Arundel
admitted: 'I cannot think that Miss Swan would write to persons that
employed her with a chance of losing work.'[87] Police in the Redhill
case assumed that Mary Johnson was so lacking in guile that they
immediately swallowed Eliza Woodman's lie that she had thrown over
a fence an anonymous letter enclosed in an initialled handkerchief.
The police in Littlehampton thought that Rose Gooding was stupid
enough to send libellous letters signed 'R.G'. Some police were as
sleepy as 'Ikey' in Redhill said they could be, but it should be carefully
observed that they were especially sleepy when it came to judging
women.

Male judges and jurors also perpetrated all manner of assumptions and sometimes seem to have been given scope by the nature of the crime. Colonel Gardiner complained about the mayor, the magistrates, and also the 'detective branch of the Hove police', who wasted a fort-night observing him on slight evidence: 'The police, for whom we pay so heavily, ought to be our protection and to know something of the eccentricities of young females.'[88] Many men within the legal system assumed that certain 'types' of women were unable or unlikely to write such awful letters, but that others belonged to that 'sort' who would.[89] Alfred Bucknill remembered Woodman and Johnson in court: Woodman self-possessed and restrained, Johnson just 'a shrill little woman with a worried, angry face in a little black bonnet'.[90] Now we know the truth, it is no surprise that Mary Johnson looked fretful, but on the witness stand her demeanour deepened the impression of guilt.[91] Swan was a 'marvellous witness, cool, collected and convinc-ing', while Gooding seemed stressed, uncertain, uneducated, and coarse. A previous accusation of cruelty to her niece was held against her. Not only was it not probative, the accusation was false—it had been made by none other than Swan. There was one woman on the jury for Rose Gooding's trial in July 1921; two on Swan's jury in 1923. (No women served on juries before 1919.)[92] In his legal recollections, Alfred Bucknill, twice counsel for the prosecution against Johnson, opined: 'Surely a woman is probably a better judge of how another woman... would behave under the known circumstances than a man would be.'[93] Judge Avory, summing up at Swan's final trial in 1923, steered the jury to acquit her and complained when they did not.[94] Despite the gravity of the evidence against her, he could not reconcile it with her respectability.

The Edalji case

A long campaign of anonymous letters centred in Great Wyrley, a vil-lage in South Staffordshire in the West Midlands, reveals many of the wrong turns and paranoia that such crimes could provoke. Perhaps even more vividly than the other cases considered so far in this chapter, the sometimes nightmarish Edalji affair revealed how closely late Victorian forensic investigation—supposedly 'scientific' techniques—was a cloak for prejudice. The case has been the subject of detailed fictional and historical treatments. It was complicated by the number of letters and possible letter-writers involved. But its most conspicuous feature was the lack of willingness on the part of the police to look past the person they thought the likeliest suspect. The Edalji case can be used to underline how wrong it would be to suppose that the detection of anonymous letter-writers had benefited from Victorian advances in scientific deduction. The case also features even stronger hints of the viral dimensions of letter-writing campaigns: the way they seemed to provoke other writing, and other crimes.

In September 1888, the household of Shapurji Edalji, an Indian-born clergyman, received the first of what would become hundreds of anonymous letters at the vicarage in Great Wyrley.[95] The anonymous author demanded that Edalji place orders for a local newspaper, threatening to break windows (a threat later carried out) and to shoot Edalji (as a result Edalji felt obliged to minimize his parish activities). The Edaljis' teenage maid, Elizabeth Foster, also received letters. They were signed 'Thomas Hitchins', and the author claimed to be the person who had been threatening her 'Black master'.[96] The police discovered suspicious envelopes in the vicarage and matched paper torn from schoolbooks belonging to the three Edalji children: Horace, George, and Maud. Eventually, the maid, Foster, was charged and bound over in January 1889. She died years later, still protesting her innocence.[97]

In 1892, more letters started to arrive at the vicarage.[98] Those mentioned in the renewed campaign of letters were not just the Edalji family, but others nearby, including the family of a local grocer. Suspecting George Edalji, then still a schoolboy, the police surveilled the vicarage. Materials appear to have been planted to frame George, and the surviving letters are in several different hands, all of which were different from those used for the letters sent in 1888. From 1893 the letters darken in tone. Some contained religious rants, others death threats. The new maid, Nora, also received letters. The author offered rewards for domestic misdeeds: 'Put shit with everything you may cook for the family.'[99] One letter to Edalji himself began: 'My Dear Shapurji, — I have great pleasure in informing you that it is now our intention to renew the 'persecution of the Vicar!!! (shame) of Great Wyrley.' The writer then stated that 'a certain lunatic asylum not a hundred miles distant from your thrice accursed house' was on standby to receive him when he cracked under the pressure of the letters. To one of Edalji's neighbours, the writer said they had sent a letter 'as will make her wish her husband in the lake that burneth with fire and brimstone'. The letters, written in the first person plural, implied a larger conspiracy: a 'gang of conspirators', or a 'gang of scoundrels'.[100]

Other letters mentioned meeting young George Edalji on the train on which he travelled to school, or observing the family in church, watching 'your kid...your wife, and horrid little girl'. Some letters intimated that the local police—especially one Sergeant Upton—were in on the conspiracy. Murder threats were made, threats of 'revenge, revenge, revenge, revenge, sweet revenge'. In one, the writer declared he or she 'will be happy in hell'. One letter taunted that George Edalji and his friend (Frederick Brooks) 'will, before the end of this year, be either in the graveyard or disgraced for life (ha ha, hurrah for Upton), good old Upton...'[101] Others were peppered with incoherent ranting—or questions implying deep social and racial prejudice as well as disturbing familiarity:

What makes you always look so silly? How old are you? Are you a Pharisee or a Saducee?... Were you born in the workhouse? Is your kid mad? Is Frederick Brooks an escaped lunatic? Is your kid more ignorant than he looks...?

The author also referred to their own success in avoiding detection. They triumphed in being able to copy handwriting, and claimed to have perfected George's and Frederick's: 'Our only reason for not forging their signatures and yours is that you all write such a vulgar hand that no manager of newspapers would suppose it was written by a parson.' That vainglorious letter was signed 'God Almighty'. At other times the writer mixed triumph with a kind of despair: 'I know that I do not deserve to live. I have driven young girls to desperation and suicide...' The writer recounts a dream of themselves in hell. The inconsistencies of the discourse and tone confused the increasing number of observers taking an interest in the campaign's development. It is possible, of course, that such distraction and confusion was exactly what the campaign's author(s) hoped to produce. Looking over the case, the editor of *Truth* (a British Liberal periodical) commented on 'the religious excitement, the blasphemy, and the general incoherence of these letters, the insane expressions of hatred...and the mingled puerility and violence'—predictably concluding that they were the work of a maniac whose motives might never be comprehended.[102]

In December 1892, Shapurji Edalji wrote to the editor of the *Morning Post*, warning that 'some evil-disposed persons have been for the last six months sending me a number of letters, threatening to do a great many annoying things unless I agreed to do as they wished'. The reason Edalji wrote to the newspaper was that the author's threats included putting false adverts in the local papers. Just as in the early years of the campaign, this threat was executed. A hoax 'public apology' signed G. E. T. Edalji appeared in the *Lichfield Mercury* in March 1893. The newspaper apologized for being duped into publishing it.[103] Various inappropriate adverts were also placed, purporting to be from members of the Edalji family.[104] Hoax letters were also dispatched to clergymen outside the county. Again, they purported to be from Edalji himself. Recipients were invited to arrange funerals for parishioners who found themselves in Wyrley.[105] The postage and advertising costs involved in sustaining this harassment probably exclude poorer members of the community from reasonable suspicion. In late 1895, the letters and hoaxes ceased. The final strange contrivance was a classified advert in the *Blackpool Times* on Christmas Eve that year: it sought an Irish orphan girl for adoption by the Edaljis.[106]

Eight years later, the 'Great Wyrley Outrages' began.[107] Cattle, sheep, and horses in the area were sensationally mutilated. George Edalji had since begun a career as a solicitor in Birmingham. But he was drawn back into the affair. A postcard sent from Wolverhampton on 4 August 1903 to Edalji's office, a card 'most scurrilous' and 'unfit for publication', implied that he had committed 'habitual misconduct' with an engaged lady. It advised him to go back to his 'old game of writing anonymous letters and killing cows'.[108] Despite the fact that George had alibis, and that the evidence against him was not only circumstantial but a libel on the part of this unknown writer, the investigation fixated on him as the prime suspect for the injuries to the animals. The police had discovered that Edalji was in financial trouble. Apparently it was reasonable to suppose that the maiming of animals was connected to this circumstance.[109] Captain G. A. Anson, the Chief Constable of the Staffordshire police, had a 'jaundiced worldview', and was 'predisposed to overlook more likely candidates'.[110] The author of the campaigns only too easily enlisted the police force in the persecution. Institutional racism drove attention ever back to George Edalji. Indeed, from the very first campaign police attention had focused on his household and family as perpetrators.

In 1903 George Edalji was tried and convicted for the eighth animal outrage—an attack on a pit pony. He was given a sentence of seven years' imprisonment, on weak evidentiary grounds. Crucially, prominent in the evidence was an analysis of writing in anonymous letters that resulted in their attribution to Edalji.[111] The so-called handwriting expert consulted for the investigation and trial was Thomas Henry Gurrin of Holborn in central London. Gurrin, born in 1849, had started work as a civil service clerk. By the 1891 census, he was describing himself as 'translator of languages'. In the 1901 census Gurrin was listed as a 'Handwriting expert', but his services as such had been called upon in earlier legal cases.[112] For instance, in 1894 he had looked over evidence in a society slander suit concerning Dowager Countess Cowley.[113] He had also confessed to errors in the past that had led to miscarriages of justice: 'I very deeply regret the error,' he said of an affair which sent an innocent man to prison.[114] 'Are presumptions drawn by the "experts" from handwriting so infallible and so conclusive?' wondered the *Truth*.[115] The persecution of Edalji became a matter of public interest. Arthur Conan Doyle became involved, employing his own expert to prove Edalji's innocence. Dr George Lindsay Johnson, an ophthalmologist, used photographic enlargements to identify writing styles and 'pulse beats' (where the speed of writing and any hesitancy in letter formation could be detected)—just as Gurrin did. Trying to distinguish the true expert from the false, Conan Doyle claimed that Lindsay Johnson had deliberately avoided reading any of the newspaper reports, to ensure his findings were unbiased.[116] Partly as a result of these efforts, Edalji was pardoned in 1906. He received no compensation.[117]

These campaigns effectively illustrate the point that new techniques of investigation were no match for old prejudices. The effort to trace the emergence of Victorian 'expertise' in such matters is as much a red herring as any that Swan or Woodman could dream up. Taking this longer, more social historical view suggests that the investigation of anonymous letters is best understood, not as a separate or later undertaking, but as part and parcel of the same cultural and social phenomenon to which they responded. In this instance that was very literally the case: hoax anonymous letters were written by the investigators themselves. It became apparent that Conan Doyle himself had been the focus of a police conspiracy. Captain Anson of the Staffordshire Constabulary had fabricated letters in an attempt to discredit Conan Doyle's attempt to help Edalji. One such fictitious letter was signed 'A Nark, London'. In keeping with the malicious arrogance of the very letters written to the Edalji family, Anson dared to write of this, his own letter: 'There is a vein of humour running through it which I fear was quite lost on the somewhat obtuse recipient.'[118]

7

Media

Herbert Austin robs men's brains

In April 1935, this postcard was sent anonymously from Molesey in Surrey to Herbert Austin, the car manufacturer, at his works' address in Birmingham:

> [why are you?] continually
> having your photo shown in the News
> papers? Your face shows nothing to
> be proud of – it is a cruel, hard face –
> dishonest, satanic face.
> Only such a face, which shows <u>the</u>
> <u>man</u> could stoop to rob other
> mens brains as undoubtedly
> you did with the 'sunshine' roof.
> You are a Cad.
> For Lord's sake stop exhibiting
> your photo.[1]

Alongside Austin's address was pasted a photograph crudely cut from a newspaper. Austin also received other anonymous letters.[2] Around the time this postcard arrived, he had been embroiled in a series of legal cases, initially started by Eduard Ernest Lehwess, who claimed that Austin had stolen his invention of the sunroof—mentioned in the postcard as the 'sunshine' roof. Lehwess claimed to have discussed his ideas with Austin in 1928, before Austin patented a design. In October 1933,

Figure 24. Anonymous postcard to Herbert Austin, 1935, © British Motor Industry Heritage Trust, recto

Figure 25. Anonymous postcard to Herbert Austin, 1935, © British Motor Industry Heritage Trust, verso

Lehwess successfully sued for damages, but this was overturned by appeal in March 1934.[3] The case was considered by the House of Lords a year later, just before the postcard was sent. The original judgment was partially upheld, and Lehwess was awarded £35,000 damages.[4] Presumably not from Lehwess himself, the postcard was more likely penned in response to publicity about Austin and his case in the press.

Poison-pen letters were sent to other figures in the media in the 1930s, including prominent footballers. Some were sent to Bolton Wanderers but many were weeded out before they reached the players, the writing being recognized. Even still in December 1937, Jack Milson, who played centre forward, sought a transfer, feeling that the crowd was 'not with him'. Letters to Milson attacked his 'type of play'. Milson believed the letters to be the work of a crank, but also that they were 'well written'.[5] Signed by Manchester City, Milsom left the club in February 1938.[6] Ephraim 'Jock' Dodds, who had played centre forward for Sheffield United, wrote the following year about poison-pen letters sent to footballers, after his transfer to Blackpool.[7] Players were not the only ones singled out for attack. The Vice Chairman of Torquay United resigned from his seat on the board in November 1937 following a year-long poison-pen campaign. The writer tried to disguise themselves using various techniques, including typing, writing in block letters, or using pencil. One letter, signed 'Shareholder', read 'any wonder the team don't win with you and them drinking'.[8] Sir Francis Joseph, the Chairman of Stoke City in 1938, observed that 'anonymous letters and postcards pour in when matches are lost'.[9]

Women in the public glare were in receipt of nasty communications long before the well-publicized reports of harassment of women on Twitter and other online platforms in the early twenty-first century. Anonymous misogyny has a long history. Florence Nightingale received a 'threatening anonymous' letter after her involvement in the case for the repeal of the Contagious Diseases Acts was exposed. She corresponded with Harriet Martineau about it.[10] Other women faced different anonymous attacks—including obscene letters, and strange advances by stalkers, such as dozens of letters sent to the writer and pacifist Evelyn Underhill (Chapter 4). Marie Stopes, a palaeobotanist and campaigner for eugenics and women's rights, received anonymous letters, including the one shown on the next page, sent in July 1928. It arrived shortly after the publication of her novel, *Love's Creation*, sent by a member of the public who had been less than

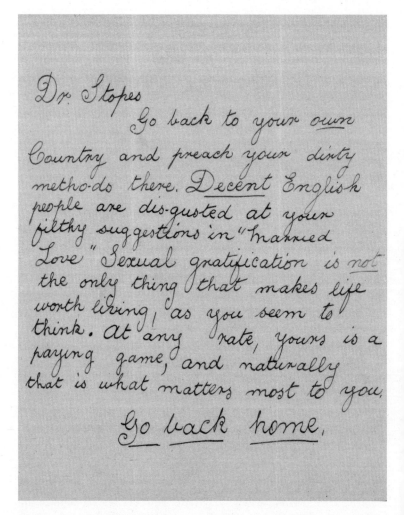

Dr. Stopes
Go back to your own
Country and preach your dirty
methods there. Decent English
people are dis-gusted at your
filthy suggestions in "Married
Love" Sexual gratification is not
the only thing that makes life
worth living, as you seem to
think. At any rate, yours is a
paying game, and naturally
that is what matters most to you,
Go back home,

Figure 26. Letter to Marie Stopes, Wellcome Library Collection Creative Commons—Attribution-NonCommercial 4.0 International—CC BY-NC 4.0

enamoured with her *Married Love* (1918).[11] Other anonymous and pseudonymous letters were complimentary about her work, signed off by 'a loving husband', a 'mother of three', and 'John Bull'.

This letter, sent c/o the Mother's Clinic in Holloway, starts and ends with the same sentiment: 'Go back to your own country'. Stopes was Scottish by birth. The writer claimed that

<u>Decent</u> English people are dis-gusted at your filthy suggestions in 'Married Love' Sexual gratification is not the only thing that makes life worth living, as you seem to think. At any rate, yours is a paying game, and naturally that is what matters most to you.[12]

Back in 1923 Stopes had appealed a case against Dr Halliday Gibson Sutherland and his publishers, who she claimed had libelled her in a book, *Birth Control*. In that case Lord Justice Scrutton had been 'pestered by anonymous communications' urging him to decide in favour of Dr Sutherland and his publishers.[13]

Other letters were sent to much less famous people, often people known locally, in response to national events. Some warned them to change their behaviour or activities—for example, not open shops on holidays. The letter below was sent to Charles Hohenrein, who ran a long-established pork butchery firm in Hull in the north-east of England, with a shop on Waterworks Street by 1889. His family business, G. F. Hohenrein & Son, was an international award-winning firm.[14]

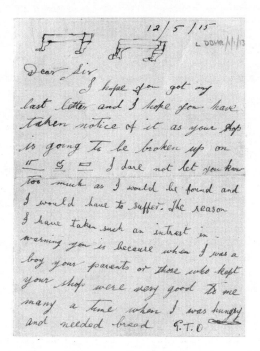

Figure 27. Anonymous letter to Charles Hohenrein, 12 May 1915, L DBHR/1/1/13, page 1, recto, Hull History Centre

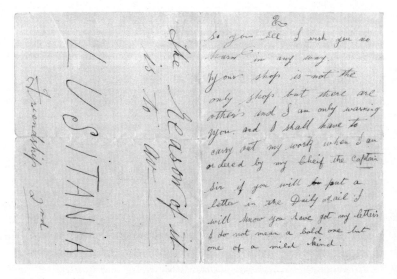

Figure 28. Anonymous letter to Charles Hohenrein, 12 May 1915, L DBHR/1/1/13, page 2, verso, Hull History Centre

[two doodles, with features like booted table-legs]   12/5/15
    Dear Sir
    I hope you got my
    last letter and I hope you have
    taken notice of it as your shop
    is going to be broken up on
    [cryptic detail, looks like 15-5-☐] I dare not let you know
    too much as I would be found and
    I would have to suffer. The reason
    I have taken such an interest in
    warning you is because when I was a
    boy your parents or those who kept
    your shop were very good to me
    many a time when I was hungry
    and needed food P.T.O.

    [doodled snake-like '2']
    so you see I wish you no

harm [ends with elaborate flourish] in any way.
Your shop is not the
only shop that there are
other's and I am only warning
you and I shall have to
carry out my work when I am
ordered by my Chief the <u>Captain</u>
Sir if you will put a l
letter in the Daily Mail I
will know you have got my letters
I do not mean a bold one but
one of the mild kind.[15]

German pork butchers, who made and sold pork pies, hams, bacon,
and sausages, were one of the largest groups of immigrants in Britain
working in the food industry and their numbers had been increasing
since the start of the nineteenth century. Most came from south-west
Germany. Pork butchers like the Hohenreins had established family
businesses in Hull during the first quarter of the nineteenth century,

Figure 29. Envelope for anonymous letter to Charles Hohenrein, 12 May 1915,
L DBHR/1/1/13, Hull History Centre

but anti-German animosity created problems for them at the outbreak of the First World War. The windows of the Waterworks Street shop had been smashed by a heavy stone in August 1914. The *Hull Daily Mail* described this as a 'regrettable instance of rowdyism': Victor Parker, a nineteen-year-old fisherman, was charged. Parker stated that he had tried to enlist, but finding the Recruiting Office closed, went to Waterworks Street, where he saw a crowd around Hohenrein's shop. He did not know that Hohenrein was a 'naturalised Englishman'. Here the *Hull Daily Mail* ought to have corrected the record: Charles Hohenrein had not been naturalized; both he and his brother George William were born in Hull. The magistrate, not wanting to prevent Parker from being able to sign up to the army, allowed bail, and Parker was committed for trial at the Quarter Sessions, where he was bound over to keep the peace for a year.[16] Crowds gathered again around the Waterworks Street shop in October. Someone signing with the initials A. J. L. wrote to the *Hull Daily Mail* describing the mob 'blocking the street and behaving in a manner suggesting the utter lack of knowledge of right and justice'. A. J. L., stating that they were 'born three doors from him', described Hohenrein as a patriotic and loyal Englishman', and argued that the 'un-English' behaviour of the crowds should be 'nipped in the bud'. The editor added: 'we hope there will be no recurrence of these disgraceful episodes'.[17]

The *Hull Daily Mail* also reported on the Hohenrein family in November 1914, on the front page, after Charles received a postcard from his brother George William (known as William), a prisoner of war. On account of his being a British citizen, he was interred in Ruhleben as an enemy alien along with his son, Willy. William had been in Germany at the outbreak of war. The paper added a note: 'This letter should correct the erroneous reports which have been prevalent that Mr G. W. Hohenrein, who is an Englishman, is fighting against his own country.'[18] Back in August the paper had let an uncorrected fact slip into the record. In November, Charles Hohenrein received a snide pseudonymous postcard from a 'Fritz' asking 'Why don't you come and see us? We're not Germans', with the address down as 'The English Pork Butcher (I don't think)'.[19]

The warning note to Hohenrein came after a German U-boat torpedoed the *Lusitania* on 7 May 1915, and a folded note was also enclosed, which read:

> The reason for it is to av[enge]
> LUSITANIA
> Friendship 2nd

Riots broke out in Hull, and elsewhere; over 200 premises connected to German pork butchery were attacked in Liverpool.[20] On 12 May 1915, the day that letter was sent to Hohenrein, a brick had been thrown through the window of another German pork butcher's shop. Similar attacks followed. The *Hull Daily Mail* expressed regret that naturalized British subjects were being subjected to this abuse, describing one of the pork butchers as naturalized for forty years and being 'known not to favour the fiendish and inhuman methods of warfare of the Germans'.[21] Apparently, women were 'the most inflamed' among the crowds, and 'some of their language was strong and threatening'.[22]

The local paper, in trying to distance itself from this reaction, was being disingenuous. In 1902, when Charles and William's father died suddenly, the paper reported from his funeral: 'The Germans form a large *colony* in Hull, judging from the numbers present yesterday' (my italics).[23] On 7 June 1915, the *Hull Daily Mail* again fanned the flames by publishing a pseudonymous letter from 'Curiosity', asking why the Zeppelin raids over England had managed to avoid damaging 'the life and property of the naturalized alien, living in sublime contentment among us'. Curiosity goes on to ask: 'Is it possible they have a secret code of signals indicating where they lie fermenting their hate, or is it that since we have proved they are in league with the evil one, he insures them as a reward for their cooperations?'[24]

Nobody from the Hohenrein family appears to have complied with the instruction in the letter in May, to 'put a letter in the [Hull] Daily Mail . . . I do not mean a bold one but one of a mild kind'. Instead, on 15 June, a bold eye-catching notice appeared on page 2 of the *Hull Daily Mail*, drawing readers' attention to a challenge put out by Hohenrein, who offered £500 to be paid to any local charity if any person could prove that the Hohenreins were not English: 'Owing to the erroneous opinion of some of the Public that we are either Germans or Naturalised English'. Hohenrein made reference to 'our consequent unpleasant position' and explained that he had closed the business because of threats, insults, and inconvenience.[25] Then, in August, Charles Hohenrein put another bold notice in the *Hull Daily Mail* drawing attention to his change of surname by deed poll to 'Ross'.[26]

Responses to war, economic decline, industrial action, troubles in Ireland, were all evident in anonymous-letter campaigns of the early twentieth century. Many were in the form of threatening-sounding tip-offs. As a warning letter, the one sent to Hohenrein in 1915 has interesting features. It explains why Hohenrein has been selected for a warning, because of kind treatment when the writer was young. Cryptic details and doodles suggest either hesitancy, or a hope to give disguise to the writing, which is inconsistent, as though not written fluidly; there is variation in the letter slanting. The letter is also nasty; it implies that there was an organized paramilitary group behind the attacks: 'I shall have to carry out my work when I am ordered by my Chief the Captain.' It has similar features to the letters of social protest examined in Chapter 3, but it is also quite different from those letters. Would Hohenrein have felt grateful to receive the letter? Did it tell him things he would have had no inkling of? Was it really a warning, or was it actually a threat? Like the 'Dear Boss' letters sent from 1888, there was a dark edge to these warning notes. Some included casual or flippant details—doodles; colloquialisms like 'ha ha'; suggestions that a band of conspirators was behind the author.

In 1920 threatening letters were sent to a vicar in Pontefract 'and other prominent townsmen'. Each letter began and ended with a sign of the cross. The second letter sent to Reverend A. G. Shipley, the vicar of All Saint's Church, included the line: 'You will no doubt have read my letter. Well, I kept my promise. I had a little fire at your church to-night', signing off 'So bye-bye, my dear Vicar—Yours, Karmo'. On 9 June, some chairs in the church had been doused in paraffin and lit. The damage was not extensive, the stunt seemingly more a minor act of bravado from a desperate man than a serious arson attack. Other letters were signed off 'Great Karmo', 'The Elusive Pimpernel', or 'Great Sydney Carton', the name of a heroic character from Charles Dickens's *Tale of Two Cities*. The writer sprinkled in details about his actual identity: 'I belong to the brave Connaught Rangers at Dover.'[27] William George Crowther, formerly a millhand from Keithley, was arrested in Dover for sending the letters, setting the fire, and other offences, including stealing three billiard balls. He was dressed in the military uniform of a member of the Connaught Rangers. Crowther had joined the army in August 1915, but deserted the following year, and had tramped around after his wife rejected him. Asked why he wrote the letters, Crowther claimed he had been 'wrong in the head' and had not known what he was doing. He got nine months' hard labour.[28]

On the eve of Partition in Ireland, and at a time when Sinn Féin were accused of orchestrating the sending of menacing letters in their cause, there were several episodes of threatening writing connected to this, suggesting copycat cases triggered by newspaper reports and sectarian sympathies.[29] Six men in the east end of Glasgow, the Scottish city most associated with sectarianism, all received threatening letters 'couched in ambiguous terms' in late 1920, one was signed 'Republic', and all the letters were partly printed, partly handwritten, all on plain notepaper.[30] Even beyond Glasgow, Scotland was affected by sectarianism, and, in late 1920, people in Dundee received threatening letters presumed to be from a practical joker, but taken seriously given the context. These letters each took the form of a single slip of paper bearing the words 'You finish existing on New Year's Day' written across the top, then a drawing of skull and crossbones, with 'Sinn Féin. No escape', and then 'Final warning' in 'impressively big' words. The postmark was from a military camp in Dublin, and the letters were sent unstamped, meaning they had to be paid for by the people they were sent to. Their recipients were shopkeepers and shop assistants, people totally unconnected to the Troubles. It was supposed that they were written by a Dundee solider stationed in Ireland, having a 'lark'.[31] In a seemingly unrelated incident, three ladies from Aberdeen were sent threats also hinting at a Sinn Féin connection. Those letters were determined to have been written by a man who had come from a mental asylum.[32]

Other campaigns were more concerted, and directed specifically, with political ends in mind. With the memory of the rail strikes of September 1919 still fresh, Charlie Cramp, the Industrial Secretary to the National Union of Railwaymen, was sent numerous threatening letters in November 1920. The railworkers had declared support for the striking miners, stating: 'these were times…when there should be working-class patriotism'.[33] Over in Rhondda in Wales, A. J. Cook, a miners' agent and trade unionist, received threatening letters in 1923, marked with a skull and crossbones. He received post with postmarks from Tonypandy, Pontypridd, and Cardiff which warned him that he could be killed if another strike took place. One, signed 'Chief B.H.G', mentioned the formation of a secret society. The letters outlined how members would draw lots to see who would kill Cook. Brushing the letters aside as an 'absurd hoax', Cook deduced they were written by people unconnected with the mining industry.[34] It is likely that very many people in positions similar to those of Cramp and Cook also received anonymous letters, but just disregarded them.

Infamous for fifteen minutes

Newspaper reports of crimes and misdemeanours alerted some anonymous letter-writers to potential targets for their pen. In 1943, a doctor with a special interest in anonymous letters suggested that 'few people who figure in the press escape their attentions'.[35] All sections of the newspaper could furnish anonymous pens with victims; some had merely placed an advert in the classifieds. A woman in Heanor became the target of an obscene letter in 1934 after advertising a pedigree puppy.[36] A Methodist preacher, charged with sending an obscene letter in 1923, reasoned that he was simply 'seeking information about a very delicate subject that I felt I could not speak about to any woman. I did not know that there was anything wrong in seeking this information privately by letter.' James Collins Rossiter, described as a 'nurseryman and local preacher' from Radford, near Timsbury in Somerset, enclosed a stamped envelope with his letter to a fifteen-year-old girl in Rotherhithe, for her reply.[37] The recipient attracted Rossiter's attention after her mother placed an advert in a Methodist journal, seeking a position for her daughter. Rossiter denied the charge, supplying the following explanation:

You have heard a good deal of the sexual vice taking place in the country. I have read a good deal on the subject, and I have tried to help some of my own sex by giving information about the subject. I have read books dealing with the matter, but certain points are not clear to me.

In court, attention was drawn to Rossiter's circumstances: his mother was ill, and his father had suffered from 'imbecility' in the years before he died. Rossiter was bound over and made to promise that he would quit talking or writing about sexual matters.[38]

One matter that encouraged many people to put anonymous pen to anonymous paper was a report of cruelty to animals, especially to dogs. In 1931, the receipt of an anonymous letter was raised as a cause of the suicide of a fifty-five-year-old Bournemouth woman accused of cruelty to her pet dog.[39] A sixty-five-year-old Welsh Presbyterian deacon was charged with cruelty to a dog by throwing it into a quarry. The magistrates had dismissed the case, but the deacon was sent anonymous letters. He had already hanged himself by the time they arrived, after hearing that the RSPCA was set to appeal. Two letters came from Manchester and one from Rhyl. The Manchester letter included the words: 'what a callous beast you are'.[40] Three case studies follow, all of which involved cases of perceived harm to an animal or a human; some cases involved both.

Sometime in 1935, seventy-three-year-old Ernest C. and his wife Dorothy, a forty-year-old chemist, were in her shop on Station Road in Longfield near Dartford, smashing a terrier to death with a coal hammer. Dorothy had failed to poison it using prussic acid. Dorothy later testified that she killed about a dozen dogs a year and denied hitting this particular dog many times. Ernest made a statement too: 'I was afraid of it [the terrier] as it had killed 70 chickens. I thought it was dead, I am rather chicken-hearted. I did not want it to bite me.' The RSPCA prosecuted the couple, who were each fined £20.[41] After the case was covered in many newspapers across the country, the couple were subjected to anonymous abuse by letter.[42] Dorothy thought that these letters preyed on her husband's mind. Hundreds of letters arrived, many in the same hand, some advising Ernest to 'Go and take cyanide of potassium.'[43] Dorothy was 'convinced that those letters, which were often scurrilous, broke my husband's heart'.[44]

When Ernest died 'suddenly' six months later, the story became very strange. It was reported that, shortly before he died, Ernest told his doctor that 'this is another Waddingham Case'.[45] Dorothea Waddingham ran a nursing home, and had, a month previously, been executed after being convicted of the murder of patients. 'Nurse Waddingham', like Dorothy C., had also been considerably younger than her first husband.[46] The *Daily Mirror*, covering the story on 18 May, described Dorothy as 'haunted by accusing eyes, tortured by poison-pen letters, a lonely middle-aged widow...bravely fighting a campaign of slander'. Dorothy remained the focus of anonymous abuse, receiving many letters accusing her of murdering Ernest.[47] Dorothy's strange behaviour at this time, as recorded in the press, and in press photographs, attracted more attention.

Dorothy was ready for Ernest's funeral, but it was postponed at the last minute. The coroner wanted to hold an inquest, having heard rumours about the husband of a qualified chemist dying suddenly. Reporters found the 'flaxen-haired middle-aged' Dorothy 'attending to her shop'.[48] It was noted that Ernest, a retired postman, had been much older than his wife. Dorothy complained that Ernest left her nothing; she claimed that his paltry pension stopped when he died. She specu-lated that she might be forced to sell the shop and return to her home city of Birmingham.[49] This she never did. Dorothy remarked:'I intend to continue business in my shop for the present, and trust that the mud thrown will quickly wash off.'[50] A few months after being widowed, and after the coroner reported that Ernest had died of natural causes, Dorothy married Amos, a widower from Burnley who had somehow come into her life. Amos's wife had died in January 1936. Amos came down to Longfield, and lived with Dorothy above the shop, until Dorothy died in 1943.[51]

In 1934, after her husband Arthur Major, a forty-four-year-old lorry driver, died of a seizure, his widow received anonymous letters stating that his death was 'no accident'. The Majors had lived in Kirkby-on-Bain, near Horncastle in Lincolnshire. The day before the inquest into the death in June 1934, the *Nottingham Evening Post* speculated that a 'story of cruel gossip and anonymous letters' would play out, as Major's widow had been 'the victim of anonymous letters which almost drove her to a breakdown'.[52] Not all the letters went to Ethel: one letter, purporting to be from her, went to the council giving notice that she was to quit her cottage.[53] Shortly afterwards the papers were brimming with a different story. Just as with Ernest C., while preparations were being made for Arthur's funeral it was halted. A letter signed 'Fairplay', with a postmark from Horncastle, had been received by the coroner, and it was suggested in this letter that the Majors' neighbour's dog had died of poisoning. It asked, of Arthur, 'Why did he stiffen so quickly', and 'Why was he jerky when dying?'. Neighbours on one side were the Maltbys at Number 1, and the Kettleboroughs at Number 3. The Maltbys had two dogs, and one was seen to have eaten plate scrapings of corned beef put out by Ethel. The dog died, and so was exhumed in response to the anonymous letter to the coroner. Poison was detected. Ethel was arrested.[54]

Standing in the dock in November, 'frail, sallow complexioned' Ethel recalled her life with Arthur. They had married in 1918 and had moved to their new council house. The couple were already unhappy together; they quarrelled often, and Ethel claimed that Arthur drank and assaulted her. Ethel alleged that she had received an anonymous letter 'in block writing accusing her husband of associating with another woman' in May 1934 and found letters which revealed that a relationship formed between Rose Ellen Kettleborough and her husband. Another anonymous letter was sent to the police, claiming that Arthur used his employer's lorry inappropriately and was 'always drunk in charge and is not safe to be on the road', signed with initials F. S. and C. D. (the initials of local parish constables). The letter was in handwriting similar to Ethel's.[55] Ethel Major was hanged on 19 December 1934 in Hull Prison. She had been found guilty of murdering Arthur using strychnine. An appeal had been dismissed.[56] The only woman to be executed in Hull Prison, Major left behind two children, and became known as the 'corned-beef killer'. Although there was evidence that Major endured a very difficult and restrictive life, there was little attention to the stress of her difficult marriage. Focusing on Major within the context of similar stories, Anette Ballinger concluded that Major's case 'demonstrates misconceptions surrounding the battered wife', and that contemporary reactions revealed the harshness meted out to women who defied gender-role expectations.[57] The writer 'Fairplay' was never identified.

The next story involves animal cruelty too, and also recalls the style of letters from Chapter 3 whilst bringing back into focus the Edalji letters from the last chapter. From three days after the Edalji verdict in 1903 there were periodic outbursts of anonymous letters in a new hand, often signed by 'G. H. Darby', or 'Captain G. H. Darby', 'of the Wyrley Gang'. In 1915 the signatory became 'Count von G. H., Darby'—using sign-offs similar to those we saw in letters from the late eighteenth and early nineteenth centuries. 'Darby' then went quiet until 1919. Often the letters appeared to be associated with the animal maimings in the area, which also continued sporadically.[58] 'Darby, Captain of the Wyrley Gang', was actually Enoch Knowles, a labourer in a bolt and nut works in Darlaston. During the Wyrley outrages in the early 1900s, Knowles had been in his mid-twenties and living nearby, but there is no suggestion that he was responsible for the attacks on the animals. Knowles enlisted in 1916, and married Elizabeth Pugh in 1919; both events suppressed his letter-writing urges for a time.[59] He does not seem to have written any further letters until 1931. That same year he was implicated in a county court action. A bailiff in the case received a letter, and from then Knowles spread his attention more generally, mostly triggered by reports in newspapers.[60] Knowles had no personal involvement with most of his victims, or with the cases through which he identified them: he just read about them in the papers, gathered information, and then wrote his 'scurrilous' letters.[61]

Since 1931 the police and Post Office had been monitoring the local post. Some of the 'Darby' letters (written by Knowles) contained death threats, some were obscene. Other letters were written to judges and a journalist.[62] Knowles targeted the licensees of the Railway Hotel in Cannock, bombarding them with fifty-two postcards and five letters, because they had been mentioned as witnesses in a case in the summer of 1934, with details of their names and address included in the newspaper account. One letter, marked 'Death Warning', included the line 'Both your lives is in terrible danger from me every night it is over you being the witness at Stafford against ------ and well in with her.' Knowles picked out Alice R. from newspaper reports in 1932 after her husband was sentenced by Justice Mackinnon for assaulting a girl. Knowles wrote a threatening letter to Mackinnon, pretending it to be from Alice, and he also sent a threatening letter to the organizer of a Christmas Fund, also as Alice, warning the organizer to ensure he looked after her children.[63] Winifred R. became a target of Knowles's campaign after she was a witness in a murder trial in Stafford. Anonymous and 'filthy' letters followed, some threatened stabbing; one, purportedly from a friend of the murderer, threatened that she would be killed that night ('I shall have my revenge'); another that she would be blinded by having petrol thrown in her eyes.[64] In a letter to one woman, Knowles described himself as 'Jack the Ripper of Whitechapel'.[65]

Knowles's guilt was eventually established when a postcard he had addressed to relatives, signed 'Enoch & Lizzie', was compared to the anonymous letters in the post office. A scan through the municipal records found Enoch and Lizzie at an address in Bull Street, which they vacated when they moved into a council house on Park Street, for which Enoch had signed paperwork; the handwriting matched. Knowles was placed under surveillance and observed posting offensive material.[66] Frederick Arthur Balm, an assistant at the Post Office Information Bureau, was involved.[67] The letters from the 1930s were compared with those from 1903–16, and from 1919, when hundreds had been sent. The police were satisfied these were a match.[68] Pleading guilty in November 1934, Knowles was imprisoned for three years. His defence argued that he was 'a teetotaller and almost a non-smoker', and that he had written the letters when he was worried, or ill, when he became a 'man with a disordered mind'. It was claimed that Knowles had a good character, but 'appeared to be simple and childish in many ways', but that he had not intended any actual physical harm.[69] Knowles asked for forgiveness and said that he had 'sent them to folks that I have seen in the newspapers'.[70]

Knowles, along with his younger brother Sidney Ernest, was brought up by his mother, who although always described in the census returns as 'married', was not living with a husband in 1881, 1891, 1901, or 1911 (no father is listed on Sidney's birth certificate).[71] Knowles had escaped suspicion for a long time because he had pretended to be illiterate. It was Enoch, however, who had signed the census return in 1911, when he lived with his mother, in handwriting that would have been familiar to the receivers of the 'Darby' letters, on which he made no attempt to disguise his writing.[72] In 1939, when Knowles was again free, he was still living in his council house in Park Street—but Lizzie had left him.[73]

Clergymen behaving badly

Knowles wrote letters to all sorts of people, including judges and members of the royal family.[74] In 1936 a Scotland Yard detective was reported as stating that 'Most public men, particularly judges and magistrates, are used to the anonymous letter writer', and advising the public to follow his lead and burn letters instead of becoming pre-occupied by them.[75] Clergymen had long been the target of anonymous letters by the 1930s, and they were highly visible characters in their parish. The 1930s saw more attention on the behaviour of individual clergymen, and when stories were reported by the national press, the men of the cloth became the recipients of anonymous letters. These stories show the interplay between the national media and anonymous writers—how each could feed the other. These all focus on the victims of anonymous-letter campaigns. The first case relates to the schism in the Catholic Church in the early twentieth century, reflecting some of the details from the Tractarian letter-writing episodes in Sidmouth that we touched on in Chapter 3. The other two cases centred on scandals created by older clergymen becoming engaged to teenagers.

Reverend Richard O'Halloran's name appeared regularly in the newspapers: he was a thorn in the side of the Catholic Church. His church, St Joseph & St Peter on Mattock Lane in Ealing, in West London, initially operated from the drawing room of Mattock Lodge, a domestic house. An iron structure was eventually constructed to accommodate the growing congregation. In 1896 Archbishop Herbert Vaughan notified O'Halloran that a new mission would be set up in Ealing, under the organization of Benedictine monks: O'Halloran was expected to move on. He refused to quit his mission and was canonically suspended.[76] By 1902 O'Halloran had become a figure of interest for the media, and one of embarrassment for the Catholic Church. His rhetoric becoming increasingly radical, O'Halloran set himself up as the spokesman for the reform of the secular clergy, and gained an ally in 1902 in the form of Arthur Galton, a former Catholic priest who had converted to Anglicanism. Together Galton and O'Halloran

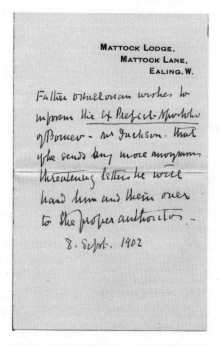

Figure 30. Letter from Father O'Halloran, from Mattock Lodge, Ealing, to Father Thomas Jackson, 8 September 1902, author's own item

pushed the 'Revolt from Rome'.[77] That summer, O'Halloran stated that he had commissioned Galton to write an article for the *Fortnightly Review*.[78] This stance attracted at least one writer of anonymous letters to O'Halloran. On 8 September 1902 O'Halloran wrote to a Reverend Thomas Jackson to ask him to stop sending 'anonymous threatening letters' or else the letters would be handed 'to the proper authorities'.

Father Thomas Jackson was a very different type of Catholic to O'Halloran. A gentle missionary priest, Jackson had garnered much credit during the Afghan War (1878–81) as the chaplain to the forces with the British Army.[79] In 1902 Jackson was part of the St Joseph's Foreign Missionary Society.[80] Jackson and O'Halloran knew each other personally; they had been contemporaries at St Joseph's College, Mill Hill in London (O'Halloran was ordained in 1880, Jackson the year before). The Mill Hill Fathers were founded by Archbishop Vaughan in 1866, who became Archbishop of Westminster in 1892. Fiery O'Halloran clashed often with Vaughan throughout his stormy career, and it came as some surprise when Vaughan offered to O'Halloran a mission in the fashionable district of Ealing.

When O'Halloran wrote to Jackson in 1902 he described him, pointedly, as 'ex Prefect of Labuan & Borneo', a Malaysian mission that Jackson had quit in 1896, 'broken in health', having been sent there in 1881 by Vaughan.[81] The letter was sent to 'St Peter's Apostolic College, Freshfield, nr Liverpool', but it was forwarded to Jackson from there, to 'St Joseph's Home, Patricroft, nr Manchester', an orphanage run by the Missionary Sisters of St Joseph (a Franciscan order) for the Rescue Society. Jackson had been chaplain there since 1900. The little envelope reveals a trip across the country in 1902. When he died in 1916, Jackson, originally from Preston in the north of England, received hagiographic obituaries. The *Lancashire Evening Post* described him as a 'man of extreme simplicity and humility of character, he was beloved by children', and noted that many in the army had believed he ought to have been awarded the Victoria Cross. The two men could not have been more different: Jackson had seen much of the world in his mission to convert. He had accompanied the army, shown bravery and humility, and spent 'fourteen strenuous years of untold hardship and adventure' in Borneo. O'Halloran had threatened schism within the Church and had served some English missions before settling in Ealing, from where he refused to budge, despite orders from the Cardinal.[82] O'Halloran's mission died with him in 1925, and his tin church became a theatre.

Figure 31. Envelope for letter from Father O'Halloran, from Mattock Lodge, Ealing, to Father Thomas Jackson, 8 September 1902, author's own item

O'Halloran's story received relatively little attention outside religious journals and the broadsheets, and Jackson's letters to him were not reported. The tabloid papers were much more taken by another type of clerical scandal—the type which appeared to involve inappropriate relationships. On 18 June 1937 Reverend Stewart B. P., the fifty-five-year-old Rector of Bacton in Suffolk, was looking forward to leaving the country to go on his honeymoon. He had recently married Hilda, who at seventeen was thirty-eight years his junior; only Hilda's parents and a friend of Stewart's attended the wedding. Stewart had been the rector for over a decade, and it was reported that their engagement had 'set the whole neighbourhood agog'. The couple, who met when Hilda was performing in pantomime in Ipswich, had been barraged with insults and innuendoes by mail and telephone. Hilda complained: 'As it is only my husband and myself who can answer the phone—not being able to afford servants—we are compelled to put up with these affronts.'[83] One letter included the line 'You ought to be jolly well ashamed of yourself for marrying a girl of 17.'[84] The *Dundee Courier*, based about 460 miles from Bacton, covered the story, including a strange photograph of 'The Rector and his wife', that showed Hilda perched on the Reverend's chair, pouring tea while her new husband looks on admiringly.[85]

Back in the pulpit in July after his honeymoon, the Reverend was on the defensive: 'While there is much in the country of which we can be proud', he argued, 'there is the danger of getting back to the old pharisaical regard of rules and regulations: the strict observance of the conventions rather than attaining the conditions of love of God, and of one's neighbours.'[86] Gossip continued, and the Reverend was reported to be investigating selling the rectory and moving to a smaller (and presumably more anonymous) property, complaining that 'Many people are still unkind and send insulting messages...But my Hilda is a brave little girl and tries hard not to show the wounds.'[87] The couple eventually moved to the parish of Worsborough Dale, a mining village near Barnsley, where the Reverend appeared to be politically out of step with his parishioners.[88]

One especially tragic campaign of anonymous letter-writing shook the Lincolnshire seaside resort of Cleethorpes in the late 1930s. Events began when a fifty-five-year-old widowed vicar Ralph P. W. met seventeen-year-old Margaret from Grantham, when she was visiting friends.[89] The Reverend's first wife, Elizabeth, had died in 1935, succumbing to septicaemia after scalding her finger while cooking for the Welfare Society. The Reverend had been vicar of Cleethorpes since 1925.[90] Rumours circulated locally, and to settle those, the Reverend announced he was engaged in the parish magazine. The news triggered an influx: 'scores of anonymous, horrible letters' arrived, including one to his fiancée's own home.[91] A censor was employed to deal with the 'filthy and scurrilous' letters: 'Since we announced the engagement almost every post has brought more insults from people too frightened to sign their names.'[92] Some parishioners tried to get the Reverend to resign. One was quoted in the press as saying 'It doesn't appear seemly.'[93]

Inevitably, the national presses picked up the story. A strange article appeared in the *Daily Mirror* which revealed a divided parish and reported that hundreds of 'sightseers' had crowded around the vicarage for a glimpse of the vicar's bride-to-be, 'for the grey-haired canon is very popular'. A Mrs Johnson was quoted: 'When his first wife died we all grieved for him at his loss. Now we can all rejoice for him in his happiness.' Margaret was described in the report as 'a rosy-cheeked brunette...typical English country girl'. It was also noted that she 'sings in Corby church choir', smoked little, and 'does not believe in make-up'.[94] Margaret's mother was reported to say: 'There is not the slightest reason why he and my daughter should not make an ideal married couple. How many young men to day can afford to keep a wife?'[95] A front-page picture accompanied the article, and after this was published, 'horrible anonymous letters' came 'by almost every post'. The Reverend had tried to brush criticisms away: 'No one denied there is a big difference in our ages, but why should that make any difference to our happiness', he remarked.[96] But the anonymous letters preyed on his mind.

On Saturday 29 April 1938, Margaret was cheering on Wolverhampton Wanderers as they were beaten 4–1 by Portsmouth in the FA Cup Final at Wembley Stadium.[97] At home, her fiancé was found dead in his bed, apparently having committed suicide by attaching a tube to a gas fire. The Reverend's daughter, visiting him the day before, found her father 'depressed and worried'.[98] Margaret's father was quoted in the *Sunday Pictorial*: 'It will break the poor child's heart. She was madly in love with him and she did not care two hoots about what people have said . . . They were to have been married in a few weeks' time . . . It was all the poor child could talk about.' The week before, the Reverend had mentioned that anonymous letters were still arriving. Margaret's father stated, 'I know the letters worried him.'[99] Margaret did not attend her fiancé's funeral, but crowds of 'jostling women' did. Two people were rebuked for climbing on the war memorial for a better view. Scores of women 'searched noisily among the many wreaths around the grave until they found [Margaret's] wreath'.[100] Even in death the Reverend was not spared from a morbid rummage through his private life.

Shame is a theme here, and in other anonymous letter campaigns— recipients were informed that they 'ought to be jolly well ashamed of yourself'; that some behaviour thought to be dishonourable had been identified by the writer. Additionally, shame was attached to the lack of signature, indicating that a person was ashamed to sign their own letter, or was a coward for not doing so.

Local responses to national media

The press supplied targets for letter-writers, and also provided them with examples and exemplars by tracing the histories of other campaigns.

In addition, other forms of media pushed the concept of the anonymous letter as one in a range of possibilities for people wanting to pursue issues which had riled them. One man who sent menaces by post in 1935 claimed that he had been inspired by an article ('The Poisoned Pen') in a woman's magazine.[101] The press changed the campaigns. Reports of anonymous-letter cases in the press gave details about detectives' efforts to solve them, and those reports might have made future letter campaigns more difficult to solve by making the writers more ingenious.

This had been going on for a while. Significantly, the letters in the Redhill campaign from the 1910s, perpetrated by Eliza Woodman, were formed of words in printed capitals. There were patterns in the spelling idiosyncrasies: LUNITIC for LUNATIC; RITE for RIGHT; MISIRABLE for MISERABLE. In the letters the words ran right across the paper, without punctuation, broken off at the end of lines and continued on the next.[102] The newspapers added punctuation for ease of reading.[103] A year before the letters started coming, the *London Journal* had identified the tricks used to disguise writing, including changing the spaces between characters and using printed capitals.[104] The Redhill writer appeared to be well informed.

In 1934, a postmistress based on the Isle of Wight was accused of anonymously sending offensive literature and also 'offensive matter' in small boxes marked 'wedding cake', through the post, abusing her position to cover her tracks. She was acquitted.[105] In that case, Gerald Francis Gurrin, a handwriting expert (the son of Thomas Henry Gurrin, whose work was shown to be erroneous in the Beck case, and also in the case against George Edalji), was brought in to examine handwriting. Gerald Gurrin had been consulted on various matters concerning documents, by various authorities, including the Treasury, the Admiralty, the War Office, the Criminal Investigation Department, Scotland Yard, City of London Police, and the Bank of England.[106] On the Isle of Wight, Gerald Gurrin, working for the prosecution, 'produced a bulky bound volume of photographs of numbers of the anonymous letters', and stated that all the letters except two were probably written by the same person: 'the writer of anonymous communications, in attempting to produce a style different from his or her own, usually introduces differences in prominent features and overlooks the minute differences'.[107] Gurrin identified a particular letter as being written by someone else, and remarked that he had often found that, when anonymous letters were circulating, they induced copycat responses: 'another writer emulated the first one'.[108] The defence also called in expert help, consulting Colonel Wladamir Raffalovich Mansfield, from Tulse Hill in London, who stated that it was impossible to consistently alter pen pressure, and that differences in pressure applied by the suspect and by the anonymous letter-writer meant that they were not the same writer.[109] Mansfield was a strange choice of expert witness, having spent most of his career in railway engineering, and then becoming, at the end of his life, interested in photography; there is little about his biography to suppose he had any great insight.[110] In 1936 the *Daily Express*, a daily, national popular newspaper, confidently asserted that 'handwriting experts are seldom able to help in a conviction'.[111] The press did not believe that a woman was capable of writing the letters anyway. The *Portsmouth Evening News* ran the headline: 'Could a woman have written such stuff?', contents deemed so filthy they were likened to something 'concocted by the habitue of a brothel in Buenos Ayres'.[112]

In 'epidemic cases', where there were many letters circulating in a place, the graphologist Robert Saudek assumed the authors to be 'psychopaths, with so-called "hysteric personalities" or with more or less advanced paranoia'. He advised, in such cases, to look out for the recurrence of one person's name—and to consider that person as the prime suspect, as many writers 'include all sorts of evil gossip about themselves to throw the addressees off the scent'.[113] Saudek investigated techniques for disguising handwriting, noting that writers often switched the slant or size of their writing, printed letters, and avoided tell-tale cursives. Some wrote with the less dominant hand, to evade the most common comparative techniques. Others adopted a 'crampy' grasp on the writing tool, and varied the writing pressure from the usual. Writing with a 'badly pointed pencil' or other defective tool gave some writers a head start over the handwriting examiner, making the task of identifying the author more difficult. Others wrote over their words, traced them, adjusted certain parts, and so on—all moves in an increasingly complicated game of obfuscation.[114]

The extent to which anonymous authors consulted works like Saudek's is unknown, but the publication of these books by experts would have made their own jobs harder. Such guides could be used almost as easily by anonymous letter-writers as by those trying to root them out. Nonetheless, handwriting experts were also criticized for not being 'in agreement as to what constitute "important features"' in handwriting. Alfred Lucas, an analytical chemist, dismissed the whole utility of graphology (Saudek's own field), and reminded examiners of anonymous letters of the importance of paying attention not just to words, but also to clues provided by the ink or the paper, even the edges of the flaps of envelopes.[115] C. Ainsworth Mitchell, also a chemist by training, complained that handwriting experts in the recent past 'had not been trained in the principles of science'. Drawing 'dogmatic conclusions from insufficient data' and forging a 'doctrine of infallibility ... resulted in the whole system of the examination of handwriting acquiring a flavour of quackery'. Mitchell described anonymous letters as the types of documents 'on which the opinion is most frequently required, and it will be found that the writing resembles that of the suspected person in some respects and differs from it in others'.[116] Mitchell later moved into forensic science, studying microscopic and chemical qualities of handwriting.[117]

At the same time, some prominent works of fiction might also have helped would-be writers to evade capture. August 1937 saw the theatrical premiere of *Poison Pen*, a play by Richard Llewellyn. It concerned the upset caused when a series of anonymous letters circulate in a small rural community. The show moved to the West End the following year.[118] In *Poison Pen* a handwriting expert, Mr Fullergrave-Rees, discusses habits which give writers away—such as not varying the thickness of their nib or the quality of the stationery and maintaining the same position of the dots over the 'i' and the bar on the 't'.[119] In 1939 the play became the basis of a film starring Flora Robson, Reginald Tate, and Ann Todd: cinema audiences watched the ripples develop in an English village once scurrilous letters alleged various misdeeds, moral, criminal, and sexual. The vicar encourages the parish to ignore the letters, but those targeted find this impossible. Suspicions develop and many people spot a grain of truth in some letters: the writer is well informed. As the letters darken in tone, the villagers become paranoid (the letters bear the local postmark). A shy, local marginal woman becomes the prime suspect—her personality deemed to fit— but her suicide (hanging herself at the village church) does not see an end to the letters. Police mount surveillance, watching the postboxes, but the letters continue to pit the villagers against each other and destroy relationships.

Dorothy L. Sayers' *Gaudy Night*, published in 1935, focused on a tight-knit community, an all-female Oxbridge college. The story is that of a lower-class servant's revenge against a community of higher-status women. Likewise, the play and the film of *Poison Pen* also mirrored contemporary preoccupations with female letter-writers. At the end, the vicar's sister, a highly respected philanthropist, is unmasked as the writer—her excuse in the film is that the letters gave her a feeling of power. She bitterly tells her brother that she was tired of helping others: 'There isn't a thing in the world that's mine!'[120] Llewellyn's key focus is on the consequences of a poison-pen letter campaign wrought on a small community, rather than exploring the reasons why the letters were written. In this way, Llewellyn mirrored the way that newspapers reported the cases at the time.

8

Local reaction

And Winifred Simner sows discontent

British Legion Burgesses of Wimbledon and residents of Kenilworth avenue object against Councillor Russell being appointed mayor see Memorial sent to council by Residents of K[enilworth] A[venue] when he attempted to discharge a Road man & prevented a man to have a fried fish shop & gave his vote to discharge a poor man with Seven children, his disgraceful extortaint [sic] of money to his own use on Flag days Poppy & Lifeboat & all others . . . . Russell must clear out & rob another District . . .[1]

In Wimbledon in 1938 Winifred Ava Simner was charged with publishing defamatory libels—such as this one—about a local councillor, William Henry Russell. The libels were letters sent to the mayor and town clerk. Another letter, sent on the day the local paper speculated that Russell might become the next mayor, stated,

Russell too old & junior member of no brilliance except to cheat all & has no wife. Of no social standing . . . he has no education or building experience is an absolute rotter & up start & not a fit man to be on the council much less a mayor.[2]

Letters claimed there was a shortfall of £48 on Poppy Day collection in 1935, and that '1936 showed eighty-two tins had been taken for his own use and he employed women to collect & not send them to the honest folk at the Town Hall to be included in the total'.[3] Letters had circulated 'spasmodically' for a few years. Some claimed to call out nepotism; some accused the town clerk and the mayor's secretary of accepting bribes to push Russell into the mayoralty; another said that

Russell was a 'bigamist, defrauding liar & not a fit man over 70'.[4] The letters aimed to sow divisions within the Wimbledon Council. One alleged that Councillor Russell had described the mayor, Edwin James Mullins, as an 'old walrus' and his wife as the 'washerwoman of Gladstone Road'.[5] Although other members of the council were targeted in Simner's campaign, the case against her rested on her most consistent victim: Russell. Some of Simner's claims were refutable. Singling out members of the council, Simner identified one as 'a foreigner'. In a letter purporting to come from the 'Ward of St Marys & Burgesses of Wimbledon & British Legion', it was stated: 'We protest his imposing his French ideas upon the Council for wilful waste & theft.' The man in question was born in England, as was his father, and he saw active service in the First World War. In this letter, Simner put forward the names of five men 'of commercial knowledge' as alternatives to the current council members.[6]

Some of Simner's accusations do seem to hold up on the face of it; certainly she saw the letters as a way of exposing truth: 'there is no poison where facts are exposed'.[7] One council member rounded on by Simner was a solicitor who had been cited as a co-respondent in a divorce case in which he had been professionally engaged. That council member had indeed been identified in newspaper articles, as Simner stated in a letter dated 25 June 1938: 'The press have given him a full report of his immorality, so in the interests of all he must resign or be removed at all costs.' Simner's campaign did not stop this man from becoming mayor a few years later.[8] Other council members were described disparagingly, as 'immoral spendthrifts', or criticized for switching their allegiance to the Labour Party; or simply being in 'ill health' and not putting in 'attendances required by Burgesses'.[9] In one extraordinary letter, sent to Mayor Mullins in November 1937, Simner threw dirt at five men, describing them as 'twisters', one for robbing a 'woman Librarian of £500 a year'; one for being 'not above Bribes from Building Trade'; one for living 'with another mans wife'. She added the accusation that the council members called Mullins's wife 'the old char'. 'Beware of them all', she wrote.[10] A long letter sent in July 1938 called attention to the home life of the previous mayor, alleging as an incoherent aside that 'only drink persuaded to elect him as Mayor'. Additionally, off-hand comments are made in this letter about council members making deals to 'fill their own pockets, Cemetery, Electricity, Library'.[11]

Simner's letters also range over other societal issues and it is possible to infer a little about her views. In a letter dated September 1937,

Simner suggested that Lady Emily Roney, who had served as mayor 1933–35, ought to be promoted.[12] One of the councillors was accused of being Catholic, which provides Simner with an opportunity to demand that 'no Roman Catholics be given any important posts [and] that R.C. teachers should not be appointed to Schools to Teach Protestant children as is being done everywhere'. The same letter lists the names of six councillors under the heading 'Vacancies caused', with various reasons that Simner believed they were ineligible for office: immorality, ill-health, poor education, extravagance. Russell appears again at the climax of the list, charged with 'irregularities at Legion & immoral, too old to serve'. The same long letter also accused a councillor of introducing 'cocktails into a committee', appointing 'a drunken caretaker', and 'Allowing a woman teacher to pose as a widow…when she received £2 a week from her husband as separation allowance'.[13] The bitterness of a person who felt marginalized and overlooked comes through quite strongly.

In May 1938 Simner used an anonymous letter addressed to the 'Town Clerk and Councillors', and signed as though coming from 'Labour and Burgess of Wards', to call for the removal of all 'ineligibles from your council, wives of councillors not to serve on committees which their husbands serve, those connected with swindling or having been a corespondent in any divorce suit or a shady solicitor'. This letter was followed up with more details a month later: 'Labour Party demand at all costs it be brought up at once Special Meeting'.[14] In the conclusion to a long letter sent on 11 July 1938, addressed to the town clerk, Simner indulges in a stream of consciousness, ranging through various issues:

Adults going mad, cruel to their children, couples not having children for fear of this Godless A.R.P. curse upon the freedom of the people of England it must be stopped. Keep fit, depriving parents of the pleasure of bringing up their children seized by MOH [Ministry of Health] to drag out teeth and tonsils. Read the Bible, R.C's [Roman Catholics] don't, so must they and Jews clear out of England for they are ignorant of the Scriptures. Roney opened Cinema on Sunday. Print these details and open up the eyes of the Boro. and shut up. Next Mayor Drake Be King Daniel. I challenge you to deny these facts, print in Local paper pass this on and tell them of the heavy damages to be brought against them for calling facts poison. It's time these men resigned…[15]

Pillar-boxes had been watched in the summer of 1937, after the second poison-pen campaign to have struck the community within a few months. The first campaign had largely been ignored because 'the letters attacked only the council policy' and not individuals, but by October

1937, recipients of the letters had combined to ask for protection from the Home Office. The mayor's secretary had explained to them that 'council services have not been attacked and so we are unable to spend Borough funds on investigation'. These perturbing letters were written in block letters and red ink. Each bore a mark showing they were sent with the last post of the day.[16]

Eventually, suspicion alighted upon Simner. Questioned by police, she claimed she was being framed and that Russell was 'her best friend'. Asked if she used buff envelopes, the sort which contained the scurrilous letters, she replied 'never'—but buff envelopes were seen in her room. Simner claimed she had herself received letters, which she had destroyed.[17] The operation to trap Simner and prove her guilt was elaborate. Two women were employed to work behind the counter at the Wimbledon Post Office, and they collaborated with Jean Stratton, a female detective sergeant from New Scotland Yard, and Miss Scott, an employee of the Post Office. On the witness stand, Simner referred to the Post Office clerks, Marjorie Turk and Kathleen Hiscox, as the 'little ladies'. The national newspaper, the *Daily Mirror* preferred 'two blonde girls'. Turk and Hiscox sold to Simner stamps marked with an invisible ink which had been supplied by the Post Office. Stratton wore disguises for a surveillance operation.[18] This is how Winifred Simner was caught. Simner's court appearance at the Old Bailey caught the attention of reporters. Described as a 'rich charity worker', in one appearance Simner wore a 'cape and a straw hat perched high on her head'. Simner claimed she was unable to write with a fine nib, stating that she had written with a thick nib since her college days: 'I used to get in trouble for the blots.' Simner pressed hard with the fine-nibbed pen. Simner was asked, 'Why do you have to bear so heavily on the pen?', to which question she replied, 'It is natural to me.'[19]

In contrast to the fine-nibbed pen, Simner was handled fairly gently by the legal system. Comparing her fate to the harsh punishments meted out to Mary Johnson and Rose Gooding earlier in the century, it may not be irrelevant that both Mary and Rose were of much lower status than Simner. Simner's defence counsel asked that the court pay due regard 'to her respected and honoured life', suggesting that she not be denied opportunity to continue her charitable work. Perhaps such work would allow her, the clever lawyer continued, to 'forget all about this horrible thing'. Judge Beazley more or less echoed this argument, remarking that it 'is a terrible thing that a woman of your position and education should find herself in this position'. Simner was led from the dock, still protesting her innocence, 'with her old-fashioned hat perched horizontally on her head, her wide flowing coat trimmed broadly with fur, and her pince-nez fastened to her dress by a safety pin'. She was placed under the woman probation officer's supervision for three years.[20]

Figure 32. Photograph of Winifred Simner, courtesy of Wendy Roderick

Winifred had once been a woman of importance. At the start of the First World War she had arranged charity appeals for Christmas puddings to be sent to families of soldiers from her home in Isleworth. In a letter to the *Middlesex Chronicle* in November 1914 she revealed her practical nature: 'Experience during the South African War has proved that it is mistaken kindness to send puddings to men at the Front, owing to the illness caused by them.' In September she had sold pedigree ginger short-haired kittens, 'proceeds for Afterneed Parcels'.[21] Having passed the entrance exam for the Civil Service, Simner worked first in the Army Pay Corps in Hounslow, and then had been the head of a pool of 1,600 typists 'engaged in confidential work' for the Permanent Under Secretary for War. Later she worked in the Ministry of Pensions. Presenting herself as a sensible and determined do-gooder, Simner not only supported soldiers' families, but also choirboys and orphans.[22] At the time of the letter campaigns, she was retired, in her sixties. Apparently trapped in a parochial existence, insignificant and overlooked, Simner saw corruption and inefficiency everywhere while men in positions of power around her seemed to live charmed lives. From undertaking confidential work for the Under Secretary to the War Minister in the First World War, Simner now found herself without position as the next war approached. She had not followed the correct career path to slot into an elevated position within local government herself, having never served on a Local Board of Guardians (which administered each Poor Law Union) or been elected as a councillor; instead her efforts had been focused on charity collections and other voluntary work. Other women across the country were being elected to some local roles after 1919, and by 1931 hundreds of women had been elected onto local councils, and some women had served as mayors. In 1928 there were 426 women councillors; by 1937 there were 695. Although this was a tiny percentage of the total, Simner knew at least one of them, Lady Roney, personally.[23]

Against this backdrop of frustrated ambition and stunted potential, a crisis in Winifred's life apparently had a dramatic effect. The letter campaigns had started around 1935, when Winifred's younger sister Eadith May had died. Eadith had been active in charitable works in Dover for over forty years, where she was adored for overworking 'herself for the good of others'. With Eadith dead, Winifred acquired her sister's 'faithful companion', Edith Aves, a widow, who moved in with Winifred.[24] Winifred and Eadith had both been born in India, where their father was stationed. Life for the family had not been as fortunate in India as many later supposed. Looking back on her life for the Brighton paper, the *Evening Argus*, Simner glossed over some of the less glamorous aspects, dwelling instead on her 'illustrious life'. The article covered her link, through her father, to the Indian Mutiny of 1857; her Irish roots, via her mother who was descended from the first Lord Chancellor of Ireland; her grandfather, Abel Simner, a 'city celebrity' known for his Temperance work; and her own work with the army pay staff, amongst whom she was known, affectionately, as 'Auntie'. According to her self-hagiography, Simner had collected £52,000 in charity collections and had been photographed with countless Pearly Kings and Queens happy to be in her circle of acquaintance.[25]

This biography mentions her father, Captain Benjamin of the 76th Foot Regiment. It did not mention the fact that her mother, Francis Mary, had, in 1875, initiated divorce proceedings against him. The divorce was seemingly never finalized, but paperwork survives from 1875, when Frances Mary's account of the marriage makes clear that there were problems. After a dozen years of marriage, with four daughters and one son, Frances Mary wanted escape from the 'great unkindness and cruelty' meted out by her celebrated husband. Benjamin, she claimed, was 'frequently abusing and throwing things at her and striking her and otherwise behaving with great violence towards her', and had been doing so since shortly after the marriage began. In May 1871 he tore off her dress and assaulted her. Three years later he threw 'several severe blows' to her head and face, and since then cohabitation had ceased. Benjamin was reprimanded in a Military Court, but still promoted to major in 1875.[26]

Later shamed by the anonymous letter-writing campaign, Winifred stood in direct contrast to her adored cousin, Captain Percy Reginald Owen Abel Simner, who had become a major in 1916 and worked as a barrister after holding many senior positions in the army.[27] Comparing Winifred's life with Percy's provides some clues about the frustrations experienced by intelligent women in the early twentieth century. Clearly, Winifred idolized Percy. She magnified the grandeur of her own roles in the account of her life in the *Evening Argus*, but essentially she was a female clerk, limited by a glass ceiling. Meanwhile, others enjoyed esteem and responsibility that was always out of her reach. The bitterness and powerlessness of Simner's life seem to have coalesced around members of Wimbledon Council—hence her focus on Russell, a man she thought not entitled to his position.

Winifred's will specifies the clothing to be worn at her funeral, and an elaborate order of service. It features a highly specific and itemized list of objects destined for particular people, with a stern warning: '<u>I STRICTLY REQUEST</u> that nothing be sold or given away to strangers.' Nothing was left to any charity. Her 'dear cousin' Percy was an executor. She was to be buried in a polished solid oak coffin alongside her mother and her sister Eadith in Isleworth Cemetery. The signature to her will appears to be made using a thick-nibbed pen.[28]

A plague of letters, an epidemic of cases

In April 1939, the *Daily Express* reported that 'recent increases in the number of "poison pen" anonymous letters' were 'causing concern to Scotland Yard and the Post Office', and remarked that such writing was an easy crime to commit, but difficult to detect, and 'dastardly in its effects'.[29] Many communities experienced such campaigns in the 1920s and 1930s; the phenomenon is difficult to quantify. Sometimes the letter-writing led on to more serious offences which brought the anonymous communications to light, when otherwise they might never have been recorded. For example, a six-month campaign in Coleford, Somerset, in 1933 culminated in an explosion caused by a quarrying detonator that was connected to the anonymous letter-writer.[30] It is hard to discern the scale of the increase in anonymous-letter campaigns during this period, but a quick review of some cases will explain why so many had the impression of a growing scourge and give a fair impression of how corrosive the everyday effects on individuals and communities could be.

In Hampshire, so many people in the village of Yateley received letters in 1926 (including the vicar, a general, and a colonel) that the press diagnosed an 'epidemic'. Hundreds circulated, all seemingly written in a disguised hand (they look as if they were written with the hand not usually used for writing, by a non-ambidextrous person), and many were 'disgraceful and libellous'.[31] One letter, addressed to a church worker, revealed that the writer carefully watched the comings and goings of the community. The *Daily Mirror* included images of two of the letters. One excerpt from a letter posted in Camberley (four miles from Yateley) read:

... did Sunday evening sermon kit you up a bit. I saw you looked uncomfortable. as you sow so shall you reap. more _____ coming another winter more coal wanted to keep it warm. have you claimed the five pound reward yet[32]

The reward mentioned in this note was offered by the Parochial Church Council for information leading to the unmasking of the writer, who posted most of their work from the village. It was noted that 'a lady who takes the keenest interest in the social life of Yateley' had received more than a dozen letters. Experience from other campaigns might have singled that woman out for scrutiny, but there was no evidence of this in the reports about the campaign. The vicar, Reverend A. J. W. Howell, believed that the writer was a churchgoer. A retired clergyman living in the village also received letters, but Reverend G. H. Oakshott claimed not to take them seriously: 'I treat it as a joke and have burnt most of the epistles', he told reporters.[33]

Canon Feist, the vicar of Leamington, received a letter on the day of his young son's funeral in 1927. It complained about the 'spectacle of illegal ritualism', and callously wondered: 'Would not one clergyman have been sufficient for this ...?' This vicar did note that anonymous letters were relatively uncommon in the town, and that he got fewer in this parish than he had when ministering elsewhere.[34] Many clergymen regarded the receipt of strange letters as an inevitable part of the job. Some letters were obviously from disgruntled members of the congregation, annoyed about the choir, or the seating arrangements, or the quality of the services. Sometimes these letters revealed interpersonal spats. In 1930 Reverend John Macmillian, of St James's in Glasgow, received menacing letters from one of the church office-bearers, an auditor, George Speirs junior, whose writing in the church register was identified as being the same hand as that of the anonymous letters. Speirs was apparently angered by Macmillian's decision to allow the Protestant League to hold their meetings in the church, and threatened action if further meetings took place: 'Dead men tell no tales.'[35]

By 1933, Reverend Henry Brook Young, the rector at Romford, had been receiving obscene anonymous postcards for two years. Young's initial reaction, before reporting the postcards, was to quietly limit his involvement with parish events. At a church meeting in April 1932 he had argued that 'bazaars and sales of work were most unsatisfactory

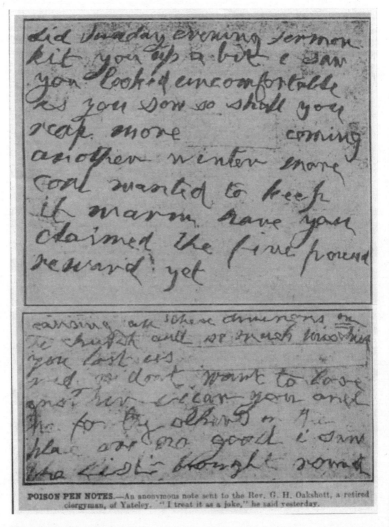

POISON PEN NOTES.—An anonymous note sent to the Rev. G. H. Oakshott, a retired clergyman, of Yateley. "I treat it as a joke," he said yesterday.

Figure 33. Anonymous letter received in Yately, *Daily Mirror*, 25 October 1926, p. 24, permission from Mirrorpix

means of raising money, and that it was not necessary to resort to them'.[36] A year later Young used the parish magazine to draw attention to a campaign of persecution against him and his wife, Emmie, calling it a 'deliberate attempt to besmirch us with the vilest scandal'. In his announcement, Young explained that he had grown to dread parish gatherings. 'Let no one think I am bringing an accusation against the parish', he continued, 'but everyone immediately connected with it knows the little coterie from which these things emanate.' In an attempt to widen the discussion, Young explained how the letters were damaging the welfare of the entire parish by undermining church fundraising: 'The Latin for a crab is cancer, and one who goes about crabbing the church and its work is verily a cancer gnawing at its vitals.'[37] Clearly the affair had rattled him. His predecessor in the parish, Reverend Charles Kempson Waller, had also been hounded with similar postcards; he had only stuck Romford for a year. The parish was described in 1929 as being a 'difficult' one, with 'pitifully few numbers of communicants Sunday by Sunday'. In 1933 Young tried to exchange parishes with a vicar in Gloucestershire. Episcopal permission was granted, but the 'lady patroness' refused. It was reported 'on the spiritualistic side it appeared that his [Young's] aura was not of the right shade of pinkness'.[38] Young's misery deepened. Emmie, his wife, died in early 1934 after a short illness. Young was indisposed in late November 1935, unavailable to open the Christmas market in the church hall. Just over a year later, he died of influenza in the parish he longed to escape. Reports from the time stated that he had been ill for four to five years: that is, roughly since the start of the letter-writing campaign.[39]

Some campaigns were very long. Between 1928 and 1948, many residents in the area around Robin Hood's Bay, a fishing community on the coast of the North York Moors, received anonymous letters, including the vicar of St Stephen's Church, Fylingdales, just a few miles west of the bay. He was called out by letter for shooting at birds; he eventually quit the parish. It was a successor, Reverend Arthur Patrick, who seemed to finally halt the letter campaign and ease local tensions. Until then, people who received letters in the area had kept quiet about them. Reverend Patrick noted in his sermon that, nonetheless, some people had been driven 'almost to suicide' by the letters, which seemed to be written by one person using multiple pen names. There were reports that a local woman, falsely accused by letter of killing her baby, had tried to jump from the cliffs. The letter read aloud by Reverend Patrick included the line: 'You and your wife are nothing but a couple of spivs.'[40] The Director of Public Prosecutions concluded that proceedings should not be taken against the suspected author of these letters because there was insufficient evidence against them. Handwriting experts had failed to firmly establish the source.[41] Handwriting expertise was also called for during a campaign in Bath in 1937–38. A letter to one woman asked, 'Is it true you used weed-killer by mistake for hair restorer? What a face you have got!' Another warned, 'God is watching. You old skinflint, give you a brush and you would be a witch. As you pass, the milk turns sour.' 'You starve your old man. You chapel-dodging old hypocrite.' 'When are your teeth going to be pulled? Your mouth must stink like your gossip.'[42] On and on it went.

Another long but more sporadic campaign in Wellingborough in Northamptonshire started in the late 1920s, and letters were still circulating in 1932. One woman received many letters, some 'scribbled so badly as to be unintelligible'. Some were cryptic. One read: 'A boxer, a ball-slinger, a footballer, and a bandmaster—but you want a runner to catch me.' The woman who received the letter had a nephew who was a boxer; another relative played billiards and football ('ballslinger'); another was a bandmaster. Clearly the writer knew family details, which unsettled the reader. By December 1932 the focus of the campaign had shifted. The latest victim was an undertaker, who was informed by anonymous note that he was a 'parasite of society . . . You thrive on death, but your turn will come.'[43]

Between 1932 and 1934, people of all classes in Stocksbridge near Sheffield received letters. At least fifty were sent. 'The domestic lives of many families have been upset by this wielder of a poison-pen or pencil', noted a local paper.[44] While some campaigns such as this one seemed virtually indiscriminate, in other places letters stigmatized specific groups. In Spondon, Derbyshire in 1932, obscene letters were sent to prominent residents.[45] In the same year, anonymous letters were sent to elderly residents of Horncliffe, a small village in Northumberland, 'dragging up matters that occurred in their families years ago'. The local vicar was also targeted.[46] In 1934, the vicar of Hove was pestered by letters, but these were played down by a churchwarden, who said that a previous vicar had also received 'many scurrilous letters', which he put in the fire. 'Everybody in a public position got them.'[47] In April 1930, people taking principal roles in the West Hartlepool Operatic and Dramatic Society were recipients of anonymous letters and post-cards, a niche campaign which suggested envy and bitterness from a member or former member of the Society.[48] In Bournemouth in the early 1930s, various members of the congregation of the Victoria Park

Methodist Church were sent letters signed 'A Church Member'. Recipients included the Sunday School superintendent and the organist; a female conductor resigned. A 'secret church court' was held, and a report from a London handwriting expert was considered—but things went no further.[49]

While some letters suggested a bitterness directed at particular people through specific grievances, others were indicative of more basic and generalized bigotry. In August 1936, unemployed men living on Enfield Council housing estate got letters—at least a dozen were sent, many suggesting that others had been sent separately to the authorities 'about the unemployed men suggesting that they are working as well as drawing the dole [unemployment benefit]'. In one case an unemployed man who had received letters 'felt compelled to sit in his back garden all day long so that his neighbours could see him and would know that he was not at work'.[50] Justice Rigby Smith spoke out 'in a contemptuous tone' at the Leeds Assizes in May 1936, complaining about the practice of the Inland Revenue to encourage 'the sending of anonymous letters by citizens giving away the secrets of their neighbours'.[51] In 1937, a flood of letters sent to residents in new corporation houses on Crieff Road in Perth caused 'extreme consternation and pain'. The housing scheme had been opposed back in 1933, by '17 occupiers of houses in Crieff Road'. The letters started as soon as new residents moved in. Some were abusive, some even threatened violence against young girls. Letters were also sent to the employers of some residents, 'containing aspersions on the morals and characters of the victims'. One house claimed to receive a couple of letters or postcards a week, and these were 'written in a hand bordering on the illiterate'. One of the residents summed up the situation, fearing for their family members, 'when coming home from work across the Crieff Road bridge...I am in a state of terror every night until they are all safely home'.[52] A man who lived with relatives in one of the council houses was found suffering from head injuries 'received in a scuffle near his home.' At the time no connection was made to the letters, but this must have fuelled anxieties.[53] Long campaigns could lead to pervasive insecurity and anxiety.

These were attacks on community and the things which held it together. The motives of the writers were various, but the effects were similar. During this period there is a sense that the medium of the anonymous letter had become a phenomenon unto itself and that individual psychology was only one dimension of a broader, social problem. The letters sent by Ada Lydia H. (semi-anonymized here, for reasons which will become obvious) are interesting for the way they played on this tension. Ada H. was born in Milton Ernest, a village in Bedfordshire, and had lived there all her life. She was sent to trial at Bedford Assizes on six counts in 1930: two of sending an indecent letter; one of maliciously publishing a defamatory libel; and three of defamatory libel. Many people in the local area had been receiving letters from her: one to a doctor was signed 'Tom', another was found by a schoolboy.[54] Ada H. sent 'packets containing obscene articles through the post' to at least ten people, and also addressed some letters to herself. One letter included the line: 'The head postmaster says the likes of you want setting fire to out of the way.' A letter to one woman, whose husband was a village baker, was described as 'particularly filthy and repellent':

I wonder if you know of the talk that is going on of your husband—that you are trying to poison folks with your bread. You had better mind. She has threatened your well of drinking water also. I won't give you my name just now, but that you should know what is going on and then you can see into things.

Importantly, some of Ada H.'s letters were constructed as though they reflected the voice of the whole community. One sent to a farmer was signed 'Village People' and included these words: 'We are writing to you to ask you if you are aware of the talk that Charlie Graham has to say about you and your wife. It is filthy.' Like those sent in Birdingbury by George Munslowe in 1895 (Chapter 6), the letters were designed to sow discord in the village.[55] Most of the people to whom letters were sent, or who were mentioned in the letters, were of a similar age to Ada H., in their thirties or forties. They included farmers and a kennelman; people she had known all her life.

Ada H. was apparently coerced to confess in the end. Richard Styles, the Bedford Postmaster, was present when she was interviewed by Inspector Arthur Robert Genn at her home—he flicked ominously through a large Bible he had found on her table. Seeking motive, a letter from Ada's husband Henry was highlighted: it had mentioned frustrations surrounding a War Loan that went missing in the post and accusations that the family were claiming they had not received this when they had. Styles, whose expertise was trusted owing to his thirty-eight years of service with the Post Office, claimed that the texture of

Henry H's paper gave it the same feel and appearance as stationery used for some of the anonymous letters.[56] But in court nobody could speak to any bad blood with Ada H.—she seemed to be well liked in the community and was described as inoffensive and quiet, a woman whose language was always clean.[57] With a suspect identified, the community tried to heal its wounds by concentrating on the specific malice and madness of the perpetrator. 'Women tramped miles' to hear the summons in Bedfordshire Police Court, at Sharnbrook, 'but the magistrate ordered them out of court' because the contents of the letters were deemed to be too filthy. Ada H. pleaded guilty at her trial in May 1930. Justice Acton described her letters as 'very vulgar and very senseless. There is no real venom in them. They are nasty, dirty compositions.' Her defence claimed that Ada H. was suffering from 'a mental obsession' and 'an abnormal state of mind' as the result of disease, and that she was under the observation of Dr Charles Montagu Lawrence (a local doctor, not a specialist). Ada H. herself supposed 'it was a case of Satan finding work for idle hands to do'. Medical opinion at the time stated that it was her circumstances which caused her to become aggravated. Justice Acton suggested that she might be moved from her present surroundings but reasoned that this was complicated by her attachment to her husband.[58] It is only too easy to join in with this hunt for motive. For example, looking into Ada H.'s life reveals that before she married, when she was a servant, she had given birth to an illegitimate child. This was perhaps a secret in the village; her son lived with Ada's parents. Ada and Henry did not later have children of their own. When the letters started to circulate, her son, now grown up and living in the village with his wife, had a child of his own. Perhaps Ada H. nursed a hatred towards her community stemming from the way it had forced her to disavow motherhood?[59] At the very least, such speculation indicates that the search for individual reasons might in the end return us to considerations of the wider community and its values.

When in 1938 Marie May F., fourteen years a district nurse at Sidlesham, near Chichester, was charged with publishing three libellous letters, she claimed in her defence that she was motivated by public spirit. Later she retracted this and said she had been dazed— perhaps her legal counsel told her that a 'daze' was more plausible an explanation than 'society', which would be a lesson in itself. Marie F. had posted letters to various local people, including the vicar,

the sanitary inspector, and policemen. The first letter was addressed to
a farm labourer:

What about all the talk in the pubs? Your wife jazzing off to Portsmouth on
Sid's bike. What about Sid's wife's clothes? She was only dead two days when
your old girl carted them away. You will soon have a packet to carry.

Marie F. was bound over for two years, on condition that she entered
a hospital until she was fit for discharge.[60]

Elsewhere, Ethel Florence C. wrote a letter to the wife of a doctor
on the street where Ethel had grown up and still lived. 'We are sorry
we have to write this letter', it began, 'but we think you ought to
know...'. Ethel C. wrote her letters as if they were themselves manifestations of community care. When she was caught in 1934, she was
identified as the sender of anonymous letters and parcels 'of objectionable matter' sent over the best part of a decade to people who lived
nearby. Her activities were detected after the police were called to a
domestic disturbance at her home in Bedminster, a district of Bristol.
Ethel C. was asked to write down her side of the story, and the detective, on seeing her statement, noticed that the writing was similar to the
writing on letters and packages handed in to the police. Ethel C.'s
house was examined, and 'an unusual type of writing pad' was discovered. The letter to the doctor's wife claimed that he was pimp to a
prostitute operating out of his surgery, and also alleged that he had
performed 'an illegal operation' (i.e. an abortion) for the woman. Three
women living on York Road also received parcels, one with a note:
'From Doctor—and his Mistress'. When confronted with the evidence
against her, Ethel C. claimed to have only 'a very faint recollection of
what has happened. I don't remember half of what has occurred.' The
doctor 'has always been a gentleman to me', Ethel C. stated, 'I was not
myself... I don't know what possessed me.' Described by reporters as 'a
pale, thin woman, dressed in a black coat and blue hat', Ethel C. 'trem-
bled violently as she was assisted into the dock'. The case went up to
the Assizes, but there, in February 1935, Ethel C. was deemed unfit to
plead.[61] Once again there is the sense of a phenomenon with roots in
community being transformed into the mystery of individual madness.
People like Marie F., Ethel C., and others appointed themselves *de facto*
moral spokespeople for the community. Others told them how they
should be and how they should behave, so why shouldn't they be
able to participate in this moral community themselves? In this

light, anonymous letters can be seen as forms of participation in communities where moral judgements were applied haphazardly and often unjustly.

The consequences of anonymous-letter campaigns could be devastating, especially in small, tightly knit communities. The secretary of a sports club in Leeds was described by his wife as being a 'changed man' since receiving in 1930 'a cruel anonymous letter' which suggested the club's funds were deficient. The man committed suicide, and in his verdict the deputy coroner admonished not only the writer of the letter which had brought such misery but also 'all writers of such letters'.[62] In November 1931 a retired army major's relationship with his wife was under some strain, and while she was away to try to recover from a nervous breakdown, the major, lonely and depressed, committed suicide. Although they parted 'affectionately', there were unresolved issues stemming from the major's receipt of 'scurrilous anonymous postcards'. The police supposed they were from a woman, but no suspect was named. The major's doctor had suspicions but kept these to himself. On two occasions in the late 1920s the major's windows had been broken by bricks, actions supposed to be 'the act of a woman'. One of the anonymous letters included the cruel line: 'If you were to die to-night not a soul would regret it; you would go unwept, unhonoured and unsung, and most people would say, "a damn good riddance".' His widow explained that shortly after they were married her husband had expressed suicidal thoughts, but that he never talked about his private affairs or his income. The coroner's verdict was suicide 'while of unsound mind'. The postcards as well as the arguments with his wife were cited as affecting his mood.[63] The true nature and cause of such intense private suffering remain inaccessible to the historian as they do to the coroner: perhaps that is for the best. Hurtful communications such as the major received travel through multiple spheres of publicity and privacy, and in a sense they mean different things in each.

As has already been suggested many times, vast numbers of such communications were dealt with in secret by their recipients. Even those which were reported and seemed to lead to unhappiness cannot satisfy our curiosity about how this practice caused harm. But in some cases the cause and effect seem clear. A man from Thirsk in north Yorkshire committed suicide just after Christmas 1938, after receiving letters with a local postmark referring to his time in prison on a rape conviction. The coroner remarked that 'some brute' had sent the letters, which caused more suffering 'than he could reasonably bear'.[64] In this case, but not in those of letters about cases of conviction for dog cruelty, newspaper reports held back on the reason why the man was singled out for anonymous letters. That same year there was a double tragedy, when a couple from Lifton in Devon who had been hounded by anonymous letters both died by suicide a few days apart in May 1938. A bundle of six anonymous letters was found in a drawer. The content of the letters was not revealed—but a local policeman confirmed that they had contributed to the deaths. The couple's solicitor, dismissing rumours about financial problems, stated that the 'real cause of their untimely end is the anonymous letters . . . Whoever wrote them may have it on his conscience that he has brought about these deaths.'[65]

Often, it is impossible to describe the effect of such a letter and whether or not it was significant on its own. A long anonymous letter-writing campaign in Ermington, south Devon, was identified as a motivation behind the suicide of an engaged naval stoker in 1934. Shortly before his wedding, the naval stoker received an anonymous letter posted in Ermington, 'and seemed hurt and upset by it'. The letter suggested that he 'ought to be downright ashamed' of himself, 'getting married and leaving a widowed mother'. He went missing and was later found drowned. The verdict was 'Suicide by drowning while of temporarily unsound mind'. His family insisted they had no objection to the impending wedding. The man's brother said that he had not seemed to make much of the letter. His mother had told him that he was stupid to have burned the letter. The Ermington letter-writer, who was characterized as a 'killjoy', targeted many 'funlovers' with letters.[66] The record, almost certainly incomplete, shows a long campaign with some significant intervals between letters and postcards, sometimes as much as a year. A young man was reprimanded in one from 1933 for 'going about with a girl'. Letters were also sent to the man's employer. The landlord of an inn was targeted, as was one of his female employees. After the stoker's suicide in 1934, the villagers took the letters more seriously: Gardner Hogg, the licensee of the New Inn, handed his letter to the police, stating that 'last year I burnt the letter I had, and thought no more of it'. He hoped clues could expose the writer. The letter-writer stated that Hogg's presence in the 'respectable' village made it a 'living hell'. A farmer from the outskirts of the village received a letter which was written partly in script and partly in ordinary handwriting, with some words 'foolishly mis-spelt in an effort to mislead the reader as to the writer's identity'.[67]

As we have seen, the community's hunt for a suspect was often haphazard and arbitrary, building on and producing stigma which caused its own harm. Accusations of being an anonymous letter-writer could also have damaging emotional effects: 'Poison-pen letters and gossip—menacing the happiness of thousands in Britain's towns and countryside—have claimed another victim', explained a Cornish farmer in 1936. The newspaper report including this quotation continued, 'a wife has died, martyred to the evil that fosters hatred and suspicion so that even families are split by fear'. The farmer, from Lanivet near Bodmin, had recently lost his wife to suicide after their daughter had heard gossip at school about her mother writing poison-pen letters. The farmer's wife's dying words were, 'I never wrote those letters.' Neighbours swore that she could not be the author.[68] A few years later, Richard Llewellyn reflected elements of this story in his play, *Poison Pen*, where Connie Fately, a seamstress, commits suicide after being falsely accused of writing anonymous letters. Such tragedies again highlight the problems involved in making a hard distinction between individual and social stigmatizing behaviour in cases of this kind.

The Ada H. case from Milton Ernest is also interesting for the comments made by Justice Acton in summation. He wondered aloud how 'any intelligent person could pay the slightest attention' to the letters. 'They cannot be as used to getting anonymous letters as some of us are', he said, continuing: 'This is quite a frequent occurrence, and typical of people who are not in good health and at a certain period of life.'[69] The community was effectively censured by Acton for its preciousness or sensitivity. He seems not to have considered the difference between receiving a cruel letter in a public office and receiving one as a private person from a neighbour. Furthermore, many communities in fact showed a significant robustness as well as a perhaps surprising capacity for forgiveness and reconciliation. While Milton Ernest, a small and close-knit community, suffered significant emotional grief as a result of her campaign, it seems that Ada H. was accepted back shortly afterwards.[70]

Cases like Ada H.'s that did make the public record, or became sensations in some way, underwent a kind of transformation. Parochial gossip and local concerns were elevated to the regional or national public domain. As I have repeatedly suggested in this book, these social processes cannot then be separated from the letter-writer's motive, and they often extended and elaborated the psychosocial disturbance they intended. By putting details into her letters, Winifred Simner *has* managed to extend the life cycle of her malicious gossip, through being on public record in official documents and newspaper accounts. Indeed, I have helped Simner to do this, by giving her letters another airing here. Many of these letters were invasions of privacy, and many people would never have alerted anyone to their having received one on the grounds of secrecy. As a method to make people account for themselves and to get justice on her own terms, Simner might have gained some satisfaction, despite the trouble it caused her. In Simner's case, it did not matter that some of what she was highlighting might have been true. From a legal perspective, it was not the truth of her claims that was at issue, but the harm she intended.[71] One can only imagine the extra frustration this caused Simner herself, but perhaps it is wiser not to imagine what she was thinking at all. It may profit us historians more to wonder instead what was going on in Wimbledon before the war.

Conclusion
[unsigned]

What is an anonymous letter? Ought we to place them in some wider perspective, and see them as a competitor for other forms of protest—riot, strike, assault, murder—rather than simply regarding them as the bastard cousin to the signed letter? When anonymous letters were most feared it was because they might damage reputations by exposing secrets or be interpreted as an expression of animosity; a manifestation of hate. But animosity manifests itself in other ways too, and not every angry person wrote anonymous letters. What business would prefer a brick through the window to a stiffly worded, anonymous, letter of complaint? Although follow-up attacks were rare, threatening anonymous letters were seen as harbingers—something worse might follow them into the house. All of the letters in this book share one characteristic: they were not signed by the author, at least not using their own name. This created an asymmetric relationship; the writer knew more about the people involved in the 'correspondence' (perhaps better described as 'unrespondence') than the person they sent the letter to. That the sender knew where the receiver lived, but the receiver did not even know who the sender was, could lead to paranoia.

Previous attempts to discuss anonymous letters have steered the focus onto atypical letters, such as those considered by the historian E. P. Thompson sent in the eighteenth and nineteenth centuries. Fears that the postal system would be abused, that poor people would threaten and abuse richer people, do not appear to have become the main story. Thompson did not consider the likelihood that the style of threatening letters that he examined could be manipulated—used not to express the fears of those with no power, but to further bolster those with power. Anonymous letters were much more nuanced than Thompson allowed them to be. Anonymous letter campaigns were also much more complex than the ways they were used by fiction writers of the early twentieth century.

Pigeonholes

In the previous chapter, I suggested that something like what social psychologists call 'the fundamental attribution error' always pushes us to seek individual psychological explanations for letter-writing campaigns when social contextual explanations may be much better.[1] One of the ways in which we try and make sense of disparate, complex, and partly hidden social and technological phenomena such as anonymous-letter writing is by sorting individuals and their crimes into neat categories. Notice that this is a way of defusing threat and postponing discussion of dynamic social causes. It is instructive to examine one of the only attempts to produce a typology of the anonymous letter, as it will reveal some of the attractions and problems of this approach.

In 1943, Letitia Fairfield gave a paper about anonymous writers to members of the Medico-legal Society. Fairfield categorized writers into four types: informers; persons with a grievance; pathological busybodies; and the writers of the 'libellous missives' familiar in the campaigns from the early twentieth century (the 'poison pen' letter-writers).[2] Some letters considered in this book certainly seemed to conform to this simplistic taxonomy.

Letters from 'informers' comprised Fairfield's largest category. Through all periods, people wrote humdrum letters denouncing wrongdoing and informing on annoying neighbours. The motivations to send these letters are the most obvious. They might have been sent through spite, but they could also have stemmed from compassion, concern, and social rectitude. We do not know which of these motivated the writer of the postcard to the Sanitary Inspector of Hounslow in 1915 that kicked off Chapter 5. This category may (or may not) include the authors of the letters sent informing on the colliery-master partners (Darby & Higgs, and Salter & Raybould), in the 1840s. Alternatively, they could fit into Fairfield's second category—those with grievances. Sent to local authorities and other interested parties, denunciation letters contained specific charges—identifying laws that had been broken and morals that had been flouted. We saw in Chapter 3 the letters about the Poor Law Union in Tynemouth, sent to the Poor Law Commission in 1848–49. There were many similar letters, informing on officials who were transgressing. Other letters tipped off officials, giving information concerning individuals in receipt of poor relief. In March 1812, the Ludlow Overseers of the Poor were sent an anonymous letter from Wells informing them that a man called John Rogers was currently 'at Plymouth Dock in Devonshire with a Company of Commedians' (that is, performing on stage) under the assumed name of 'Howard'. Howard pretended to be single and was 'seducing every young girl he can meet'; one was pregnant. This was despite his wife and child being 'on the Parish [financially supported by the Parish] in Ludlow'.[3] Other authorities could be informed of perceived wrongdoing by unsigned letters. The Scottish Fishery Board received letters in 1936 complaining about sprat boats fishing illegally, and also a letter informing that 'the Boy Andrew' landed undersized haddocks, using illegal nets 'no bigger than a Window Curtain'.[4]

When local authorities, magistrates, coroners, the police, or other officials received anonymous tip-offs, some were followed up, and others were immediately dismissed as written by cranks.[5] Authorities did not have a coordinated response; there were many differences. In 1911 the medical journal *The Lancet* reported that there was 'much discontent' amongst Poor Law officials 'at the practice of the Local Government Board in dealing with anonymous letters'. Treating these with 'the same consideration as properly signed documents' permitted 'any rascal' with a grudge against an official to get publicity. The publication cited a recent case in Banbridge, where the clerk halted an investigation 'concerning the management of the workhouse infirmary', on discovering that it rested on an unsigned letter.[6]

People with real or imaginary grievances were generally motivated by revenge to write anonymously. These were personal vendettas waged by people who had a specific grievance—they had been sacked; not promoted; rejected by a lover; short-changed; disenfranchised; or overlooked. These people had a direct emotional investment in the situation.[7] Ruminating on 'Anonymous Abusive Letters' in 1877, Fyodor Dostoevsky suggested that in periods of time which are 'so unstable, so transitional', not everyone can be satisfied. Many people, Dostoevsky noted, are irritated by always being 'passed over...forgotten or neglected', and, in their frustration, fire off abusive letters.[8] As most of the authors for Fairfield's first two categories were never identified, we can never be certain of their motivations for sending anonymous letters.

Pathological busybodies, who usually wrote to people who were 'temporarily in the public eye', were not (according to Fairfield) triggered by personal grievances. Fairfield asserted that those making up this group were 'predominantly men', and even added (she was writing in 1944), 'they are the very stuff of which anti-semites are made'.[9] Examples of these letters were those sent to people prosecuted for animal cruelty, such as Ernest C. in 1935. Some of Enoch Knowles's letters also fit this category. Would the threatening letter to the Doringtons in 1864 fit here? Probably not. Despite not being personal, these still could have stemmed from envy, and so became entangled with the previous category of grievance. Into which of Fairfield's categories do we put the letters produced with Winifred Simner's fine-nibbed pen?

Writers in Fairfield's fourth category—those who crafted libellous missives—were thought to be spurred by self-loathing or a drive for attention-seeking (especially if they wrote about themselves, like Kathleen O'Brien, Eliza Woodman, and Edith Swan). Fairfield noted that this category was mostly populated by women, and, specifically, women who were generally more educated than those in the other three categories, who were more likely to be male. 'The writers . . . are invariably assumed to be outwardly respectable spinsters of a certain age, of thwarted temperament, and repellent aspect.'[10] Fairfield was careful to add 'assumed', and we have seen that women in this category came in all ages and types of marital status.

Fairfield's four categories obviously fail to encompass all the letter-writers encountered in this book. Where do we put those who wrote the obscene letters from Chapter 4? Where do we put the author who wrote to Hohenrein in Hull in 1915?[11] Elizabeth Sarah Browne's stated motivation to write in 1890—to seek justice on her own terms—was not addressed by Fairfield, but could have triggered other letter-writers also. In 1895 George Munslowe sought to sow the seeds of discord in his community, and focused his attentions on people who owed him money. Ultimately, perhaps, for reasons better known to the writers, many actions boiled down to this: 'I think that *your* behaviour is wrong.' This applied even for the tip-off letters, or those supplying free advice: they suggest, 'You are ignorant of this. I know something that you don't know.' Like the moral economy detailed by E. P. Thompson, managers, officials, bosses, and landlords were *supposed* to know what was happening and *supposed* to protect the people beneath them—when they failed to, they might attract anonymous letters which, outwardly pointing to a problem, simultaneously pointed to an oversight.[12]

Additionally, further categorizations would need to make space for racist letters, which would include the letters sent to the Edaljis, and for other hate crimes too. A further category would encompass hoax and prank letters, like those sent to Edalji and his neighbours in the 1890s, the Ripper letters to the police and press, and the fake tip-off letters sent concerning the death of a Cambridge student in 1931.[13] While some material sent anonymously helped the police to solve crimes by providing vital information, more often anonymous communications hampered investigations.[14] In this light, hoax letters cannot necessarily be discounted as less harmful than those more sensational documents which seem on the face of it to be grievously damaging (we have already noted that often the damage is impossible to measure). Categorizing malicious correspondence according to its importance or harm may be a useless endeavour outside a courtroom.

Letters that come to mind when people think about 'anonymous letters' or 'poison-pen letters' fall mostly into Fairfield's category of 'libellous missives', but, as we have seen, there were many other types. Additionally, some of the letters which fit into that category in terms of their style were not actually considered to be libellous. 'Poison-pen letters' were the focus of police action and legal cases which featured, often sensationally, in newspapers. They are unlikely, however, to have formed the majority of the anonymous letters *sent*.

Grouping the types of anonymous letters as Fairfield did not only excludes much actual writing but fails usefully to capture that which it does categorize, because of the impossibility of clear demarcation. Winifred Simner's letters sent in Wimbledon in the 1930s fit into almost every category. It also involves making assumptions about the actual motivations of the writers. How do we know that the anonymous author of the letter to Ludlow in 1812 referred to earlier only had the intent to inform against their target? Might they have had a personal grudge against Rogers? Might this be a false, libellous, story—quite possibly Rogers had not actually been with any 'company of com-medians'? Might the letter about 'the Boy Andrew' in 1936 have been from one of his fisherman rivals—or was it simply a letter of information from a genuinely concerned person? Letters can only slip neatly into categories if we know the motivations of their authors; usually we do not.

Here it starts to become clear that in taking a rigid forensic approach to the phenomenon we are travelling some well-trodden paths.

Simplistic assumptions about anonymous writers have steered the police down blind alleyways in pursuit of innocent neighbours framed by the actual authors. The anonymity of the letters combined with the judgement of probability to paint entirely false scenarios. This also likely helped Reverend Bingham to evade punishment in 1810 for sending his letters, framed to be from 'the Foresters'. Assumptions in Littlehampton led police to initially overlook the involvement of Edith Swan; the police in Redhill were duped by Eliza Woodman; in Hove, Kathleen O'Brien framed Colonel Gardiner. In all of these cases, the police had assumed that the actual author could not be someone whose reputation had been imputed by the letters. Fairfield's taxonomy creates no pigeonhole into which we can slot such 'decoy' letters. Writing in 1958, the Director of the Home Office Forensic Science Laboratory drew special attention to 'the business man who receives letters which contain certain threats to burgle or set fire to his business premises. They are almost invariably self-written.'[15]

Types of writer

It might seem that a taxonomy of writers might provide more clarity than one of the letters they wrote. This moves us not only towards modern forensic psychology, but possibly down older and more dubious roads leading to the investigation of personality types. The problem is that even at its most respectable, such an effort carries on where the police and courts left off—when the historian might require a broader and looser perspective than the crimefighter. We have seen differences, perceived and real, between writers according to their ages, their social status, and their level of education. Which differences are significant?

Obviously a key fault line is gender, especially when it comes to how writers were represented and treated. Contemporary accounts and literary representations posed the libellous letter-writer as a prickly and uptight spinster. There were numerous, unsubstantiated assertions from 'experts' in the early twentieth century about the likely authors of libellous letters. One declared that these were 'almost invariably . . . the work of a middle-aged woman'.[16] Did women write a certain *type* of anonymous letter (the 'poison-pen letter'), and men other *types* of anonymous letters? This relies on a dilemma: we don't know *who* wrote most of the anonymous letters that were sent. There are many unsolved cases, and many more letters were burned or binned and never investigated. The assumed characteristics of 'poison pen' writers—unmarried, middle-aged women—do not bear scrutiny for very long, as I have shown. Many were married (including Eliza Woodman); many were young (including Kathleen O'Brien). In the twentieth century some examiners of anonymous letters considered the possibility that female writers were affected by 'the mental imbalance which…tends to occur in monthly cycles'.[17] In 1955 an American private detective, claiming to have investigated more than a hundred poison-pen cases, thought the menopause was to blame. Indeed, menopause had been supposed to be behind the letters sent by Diana Langham in Coleford in 1923.[18] Hormonal explanations were less commonly sought when it came to the mystery of why men wrote such letters—despite the fact that some were found guilty of writing obscene letters when their wives were pregnant, and so might have been less inclined to have sex.

Harry Ashton-Wolfe, writing in 1928 about anonymous letters from a legal perspective, dismissed 'anonymous denunciations' (roughly speaking, Fairfield's first two categories) as things unworthy of examination. Instead he focused on poison-pen libels, for which he coined a new term: 'anonymous graphomania'. These he called the 'freakish outpourings of diseased obsessed brains'. Putting these letters entirely down to mania and hysteria, Ashton-Wolfe thought they were 'nearly always' penned by 'a woman or a young girl who has led a life of seclusion; and the mainspring is frankly sexual in every instance'. After claiming that the 'psychology of the anonymous maniac' was 'very complex', he then decided it was basically just 'sex perversion'. Seemingly this only applied when letters were written by women— Ashton-Wolfe had much less to say about obscene anonymous letters written by men, of which I estimate there would have been many more. Somewhat hysterically, Ashton-Wolfe pronounced that urgent steps should be taken to permit habitual writers to be taken straight to mental asylums.[19] An article in the *Daily Express* from 1923 argued similarly: 'Why try these unfortunates at all?' Marginalia on a clipping of that article made by Sir Ernley Blackwell for the Home Office noted that this 'procedure w[ou]ld have led to the certification as insane of Mrs Gooding'. Irate, Blackwell added: 'Simply condemn them unheard to what is far worse for a sane and innocent person...!!'[20]

In other words, the majority of speculation as to the mental dispositions of writers, though not all, hinged on perceptions of respectability and preconceived ideas about the particularity of feminine malice. Prejudices steered detectives investigating anonymous letters, and lawyers in court, and journalists reporting cases, to focus their attentions on specific types of people. At the trial of Annie Dewey, the woman framed by Tugwell in the campaign from 1910, the defence counsel, whilst correctly arguing that Dewey had been framed, posited that the actual letter-writer was a woman. Their reasoning is evocative: the author's gender was, they said, evidenced by the fact that the letters were sent underweight, showing that the writer took 'that small-minded feminine, malicious pleasure in reflecting that the recipients of those letters would have to pay extra post office charges'.[21] If proof were needed that such notions were absurd: George Munslowe, a man, had done exactly the same in 1895, bulking out a letter with a coin to make it overweight.[22]

The overwhelmingly male legal and media systems were highly sensitive to these imagined distinctions of class and breeding when it came to women and accordingly observed female suspects very closely. How the accused women appeared in court attracted much journalistic attention. Annie Dewey was 'dressed in black with gold-rimmed spectacles'.[23] Annie Tugwell, who framed Dewey, was herself later described as 'fashionably dressed in deep mourning'. Like Diana Langham, she wore a veil. Faces were covered; clothes were donned to mourn the loss of respectability in the dock. Female letter-writers were assumed to be the rough types, not the respectable ones—hence Mary Johnson and Rose Gooding were both swiftly (and incorrectly) found guilty, each on more than one occasion, of crimes they did not commit, simply because they seemed more likely to be guilty than their (outwardly) more respectable neighbours. In the summing up at one of Annie Tugwell's trials, the defence counsel asked the jury to imagine how a 'hitherto irreproachable' woman 'suddenly became a woman of the foulest sort, a woman of the beastliest imaginings, and a woman of the cruellest malice—a woman who, in order to saddle a crime upon another woman, had not hesitated to stoop to every kind of forgery and deception'.[24]

The first half of this book's chronological survey is entirely domin-ated by male letter-writers. This could be because the law pursued the types of letters written by men in the nineteenth century, and switched its focus to women in the twentieth century, but it was also the prod-uct of greater male access to writing materials and money for postage stamps, and a slightly higher rate of male literacy in the earlier period. Male anonymous writers were treated differently: there was less focus on their appearance in court; less salacious attention to the content of their letters (even when these were obscene); and they appeared to be pursued less determinedly by the police. Their offences were excused in ways that women's crimes were not.

Take the case of John Archer of Mickleover. He pleaded guilty at the Uttoxeter Police Court to a campaign of letter-writing in Uttoxeter that may have gone on for nearly a dozen years by 1939. Archer stated: 'I am not going to say I am sorry.' The fact that Archer had been to Canada three times was taken as evidence of his respectability. He was fined £10, and threatened with trial if he resumed—and that was that.[25] In Plymouth in 1936, anonymous letters containing scurrilous statements were sent to a widow in Gibbon Street, written on pages torn out of a notebook. The author was traced a few days later but was not named by the *Western Morning News*. There was no prosecution.[26] In London in 1937 a Kenley man accused of anonymously sending libellous material to the parents of a young woman in Thornton Heath had been found in church, pen in hand, with an unfinished letter. The man had been the key suspect since 1936; exercise books had been found at his house that matched the paper used for the letters. These details were considered too slight a basis for a charge, but they certainly seem more robust than evidence brought against some women in court around the same time.[27] Possibly the newspapers were more reticent about reporting as extensively on cases involving men because men generally had more resources to bring in libel actions of their own. But in truth the unbalanced fascination with female letter-writers had more to do with a wider cultural and social fascination with deviant women than with any single practical concern. It is likely that there were more anonymous-letter cases involving female writers in the early twentieth century not because more women wrote them, but because the types of letters that women wrote (in small communi-ties, often to women) were the types of letters that attracted sensational reactions from newspapers.

Obscene letters written by men were more often explained as the consequence of physical or mental disorders or external factors, rather than moral failure. By contrast, women were stereotyped as the 'sex perverts'. Whatever the actual motivations for writing anonymous letters (and sometimes people would have been unsure about their own), all kinds of excuses tumbled out when writers were pressed.[28] William Burke, in 1913, had claimed to be under the influence of hypnosis when he wrote obscene letters; Andrew Dunn Turner, in 1906, blamed a morphine addiction. William Fielden, a clerk living in Rochdale, was deemed to have written abusive letters to women because he had the flu. Fielden was found guilty of writing 'filthy' obscene letters to two women and had been caught after a police entrapment in 1937 when he tried to meet his victims. The judge said to Fielden: 'I am inclined to treat your case as a purely pathological one', after receiving evidence that Fielden had been suffering from 'cerebral influenza'.[29]

'Poison pen' letters were written within neighbourhoods—generally speaking, female domestic territory[30]—but these letters, in content and in motivation, were not always very different from letters men sent to erstwhile employers and workplace colleagues—male public territory. Letters sent to workplaces did not seem to be as threatening as letters sent to homes, perhaps because the material did not travel into private spaces and was received in the course of professional business. A man calling himself 'Doctor Harold' was imprisoned for twelve months at the Liverpool Assizes in 1908 for writing libellous letters to a butcher's coat manufacturer who had employed 'Harold' in 1889 but sacked him for incompetence. The judge noted that 'they seemed to have before them a man who did not know what he was about'. This received little coverage in the press.[31] Letters to employers were more likely to be dismissed, thrown away, or ignored. They could be left at work, not dwelt on. It was more obvious why these letters had been written, since grudges were often well known or at least open secrets—and as such, hardly newsworthy.

When women were accused of writing letters, there was significantly less determination to excuse or explain their behaviour. The letters known as 'poison-pen letters' were sent to people known to the writer, often neighbours, and contained allegations which were either entirely untrue, or had elements of truth mixed with untruths and fantasies. They were, in short, not the letters that these women could be expected to write, or were ever thought capable of writing, to their friends, relatives, and neighbours.[32] Maybe more women were found to be writing 'libellous missives' because those cases followed up were those crafted by women writers who targeted neighbours, and so were seen to be more corrosive to a whole community. Women behaving against type confused the investigators and delighted the reporters. The dirty language used by people like the strait-laced Edith Swan was a fascinating eruption of hidden feelings—where did they come from, how common were they, how far did they go? The mere idea that women could form and use such words seemed to be enough reason to celebrate such cases, but there is sometimes a sense that the community surprise at obscenity was artificial. By stressing the sensation of the discovery, newspapermen and lawyers asserted the abnormality and deviance of a woman thinking of such things and using such words. In 1924, Margaret Jaap, a single woman living in Glasgow, was found guilty of sending letters 'containing words of a grossly offensive character' to a neighbour and others. The court was informed by the prison doctor that Jaap had 'no trace of insanity . . . although she was of low intelligence'. In passing a sentence of six months' hard labour, the Sheriff noted, 'it is said that you are in your right senses', and concluded Jaap was 'an abnormal sexual pervert'.[33] The mother of a girl found to be writing obscene letters in 1924 blamed funfairs as the trigger for her 'unruly behaviour'.[34] For financial reasons, women were less likely to have legal counsel, and so had no professional offering suggestions of mitigating circumstances in court. Having said that, 'funfairs' seems little worse an explanation than 'hypnosis' or 'flu'.

The different ways in which men and women were treated by the legal system and by the media led to some peculiar conclusions about the general phenomenon as it seemed to expand in the twentieth century. In 1958, Wilson R. Harrison, the author of *Suspect Documents: Their Scientific Examination*, stated that 'more than four-fifths of anonymous letters are sent by women'.[35] Colonel Mansfield—the erstwhile railway engineer who became interested in disguised handwriting at the end of his life, and was consulted in the Isle of Wight letter campaign in 1934—believed that all poison-pen letters were written by women aged between thirty and fifty: 'what the public called the poison-pen letter originated from women, whereas from males there was hate, vindictiveness, and revenge'.[36] Such concrete assertions about demographic differences are suspect, not least because the letters available for assessment represent only a fraction of those sent and may have entered the record as a result of various biases and selection processes. Trying to establish exact figures and proportions is meaningless, and thus general pronouncements on the attractions of anonymous letter-writing to specific groups equally so.

It was only rarely considered whether or not life circumstances had contributed to the actions of female letter-writers. By contrast, men could be provoked: 'A slight provocation will excite a hasty and impetuous character; a cautious man, even if he be also a vindictive one, will need a greater incentive', noted Captain Arthur Quirke, a graphologist writing in 1930.[37] Women were thought to be weak, or evil-minded, but were probably actually bored, confused, or frustrated, seeking out alternative lives through their letters; such considerations were almost never aired in public consideration of these cases. Some of the cases we have examined show that in fact women were trying to establish some power, often by wearing the mantle of male authors—by issuing threats or using obscene words. It was only when her husband stood beside her in the dock upon her third appearance in court that the falsely accused Mary Johnson, now with legal counsel for the first time, was actually questioned about *why* she might write such letters, and why she might have taken no steps at all to hide her identity. Quirke—along with many others—declined to speculate on female motives: 'It is impossible to formulate a theory.'[38] In his summing-up in the case against Diana Langham in January 1924, Justice Rowlatt said that there 'can be no excuses whatever, because there is no temptation to it. It is pure wickedness, it is cruel wickedness.'[39] Even the case notes for Kathleen O'Brien shed little light on her motivation to write the anonymous letters that framed her neighbour. As Letitia Fairfield said, it is 'deplorable that we have no analysis' of Edith Swan's mental state. What we do have is much conjecture from the male judges and the reporters, and a lot of rhetoric with words such as weakness, insanity, malice, hormones. Sex mania or sexual repression seemed to be enough for women to put pen to paper: despite all the noise and speculation about their motives, British society was not interested in true or complex explanations. Meanwhile, the historian must be very careful not to replicate this prurience by speculating too much as to mental states. Probably I have crossed this line at times myself out of sheer curiosity.

No doubt some of the writers discussed in this book would have been diagnosed with psychological disorders were they assessed today, but the fact of the matter is that in most cases their mental states were not assessed properly at all and cannot now be reconstructed. Fairfield, devoting the final third of her paper to 'psychoses in anonymous letter writing', noted that the 'most strikingly abnormal feature' of the behaviour of the letter writers 'is its *incongruity*'. According to Fairfield, 'true psychoses do play an important part in all types of anonymous letter writing', but the 'real psychotic' usually wrote rant-ridden, incoherent, or deluded letters. Fairfield, commenting on the Enoch Knowles case, stated that 'he gave no evidence of psychosis while in prison, nor... at any other time'. Edith Swan wrote compulsively, taking risks, putting out more letters when Rose Gooding was locked away. Fairfield remarked that this was certainly an indication of abnormal personality. Whether there was an innate or an environmental cause was beyond Fairfield's remit. Fairfield also cautioned about over-reading letters with obscene content, which marked many of Swan's letters, as this did not necessarily indicate sexual deviance or repression; she (probably rightly) thought the expression was more subtle.[40]

Anonymous-letter writers might not have always understood the reactions they triggered, and I suspect that in many cases letter-writers had only the vaguest idea of the reaction they wanted. Some might have intended their letters to be jokes, which fell flat. Others might not have thought at all about the disruptions they caused. Some may have experienced what is known as dissociative imagination: that is, thinking that the people they wrote to were not real.[41] Clearly, others derived satisfaction from the pain of people they knew could feel and think. Yet it is rarely possible to tell the difference on the basis of text alone. In 2009, Joanna Geary, a reporter for the *Birmingham Post*, asked one of the nastiest 'below-the-line' contributors to the paper's website to meet up with her:

With some considerable trepidation, I invited him for a tour of our offices. The man I met in reception could not have been further from what I expected – polite, erudite, passionate and engaged in local news. For his part, he was oblivious to the image he had been portraying to others online.[42]

Anonymity creates disinhibition—people feel freer to write because they are less likely to be challenged about their words. Many of the letters we have looked at show the author to be play-acting a role—as a member of a gang or even as the moral voice of the community itself. Social psychologists call this 'deindividuation'.[43] In particular it is noticeable that in quite a few of the cases discussed here the writers lived marginalized and often powerless lives within their respective communities. Not signing their names permitted these writers to create entirely new personas for themselves: they became powerful, not powerless; popular, not lonely; racy, not mousy. They had (at least in their own imaginations) a crew, a gang, a village, a street, a housing estate, behind them. Seen this way, anonymous letters have many similarities to online anonymity, apart from the potential size and scope of the audience.

Compared with modern online abuse, the receiver of anonymous letters does not have the option of 'blocking' messages from the sender, and so the decision about what to do once a letter or other item arrives through the door is made later, after a message has been received. There are important differences between anonymous abuse online and in letters, and it can be a little perilous to conflate the two. Crucially, most Twitter abuse is not just readable by the person it is targeted at; it is public. This makes it a much more direct act of shaming than a letter read by only the individual it was sent to. Interestingly, several of the cases I have looked at appear to have led to publicity or legal action only when the letter was inadvertently opened by another or intercepted by the postal service. Meanwhile, hurtful emails or direct messaging certainly bear comparison with anonymous letters—but arguably the effort involved in handwriting a letter, or the arduousness and risk of taking it to a postbox or hand delivering it, for example, makes the intrusion and animus more visceral.

The linguist Claire Hardacker has defined the online troll as a person 'whose real intention(s) is/are to cause disruption and/or to trigger or exacerbate conflict for the purpose of their own amusement'.[44] 'Depending on who you ask', remarks the Internet troll specialist Whitney Phillips, 'the etymology of trolling can be traced either to Norse mythology or to fishing': the former covers the wild-haired snarling trolls who lurk under bridges and thwart billy goats, while trolling in the latter meaning means trawling, dragging, or dangling a lure or bait until something bites.[45] For me the equivocation is important mainly because the first implies passivity and natural malice, the other activity and artifice. Flamers, people who post insults online hoping to inflame readers, also share some characteristics of the anonymous-letter writers, as would the anonymous responders to online memorial pages who enjoy 'LOLing at tragedy' and taunting the bereaved. There is a similarity here to the letter received by Mary Dorothea Cokayne on the death of her son in 1894, from the start of this book. Studying anonymous letters might give clues about how trolling was to develop, and how online abuse can be managed. For instance, just as sensationalized letter campaigns seemed to breed more, so the phenomenon of online hate seems to draw energy from the publicity around it as a social problem. 'Handles', usernames which can conceal identities, make some people feel unaccountable for the bile they spew out online. Online anonymity strips away the social filters and constraints which manage behaviour in face-to-face interactions. This emboldens people to be malicious, or to inflame arguments amongst other Internet users.

As I have already noted, such comparisons of hurtfulness are useless in the end—many people have been emotionally devastated or even killed by digital messages, which can be composed and sent with ease in a few seconds. One of the reasons generalization about this subject seems so unsatisfactory is that specific messages can be so vivid, shocking, and painful. At the beginning of this book, I observed that the actual experience of receiving such a note is very difficult to access without going through it oneself. In a way, the more cases we have looked at, the further we have travelled from the shock of that moment. Perhaps the really useful consideration is what can be done to lessen and mitigate that pain. In the Richard Llewellyn play, *Poison Pen*, Reverend Rainrider advises a parishioner to 'forget you ever received it and burn any others that come your way'.[46] There might be an even better response. When the poet and clergyman George Butt received an 'abusive and threatening' anonymous letter over breakfast one morning in the late eighteenth century, 'in consequence of a loyal sermon...he had preached at Reading', he stayed at the table until he had 'turned it into playful and elegant poetry'.[47] A lesson for us all.

Endnotes

INTRODUCTION

1. Northamptonshire Archives (NA), C 637, Anonymous Letter to Mrs Cokayne Exeter House Roehampton postmarked 10 November 1894, Sutton. Morton died on 8 November.
2. NA, C 1340, 'Diary of George Edward Cokayne 1893–1896', entries for 31 July 1894; 2 August 1894; 13–14 August 1894; 20–1 August 1894; 10 September 1894; 1–18 September 1894; 24–7 September 1894; 2 October 1894; 22–3 October 1894.
3. NA, C 1340, 10 September 1894; 28 October–13 November 1894.
4. 'Charge against a clergyman at Cheltenham', *Swindon Advertiser and North Wilts Chronicle*, 28 July 1877, 6; 'A runaway clergyman', *Sheffield Independent*, 4 August 1877, 6: 'An absconding clergyman', *Leicester Daily Mercury*, 6 August 1877, 3; 'A charge against a clergyman', *Cheltenham Chronicle*, 16 April 1878, 2.
5. NA, C 2287, Cokayne (Ruston) Collection, Miscellaneous, 'Letters & papers relating to Rev George Hill Adams, 1880–1900'; C 2105, 'Miscellaneous letters', one relates to George Hill Adams in prison. George Hill Adams died intestate in Laval Mayenne in France in July 1922.
6. Robert Saudek, *Anonymous Letters: A Study in Crime and Handwriting* (London, 1933), 77.
7. Christopher Hillard's *Littlehampton Libels* (Oxford, 2017) is an excellent case-study monograph about poison-pen letters, and Gordon Weaver focused on letters in his *Conan Doyle and the Parson's Son* (Cambridge, 2006), but the last comprehensive book on (mostly) British anonymous letters, not focused on a single campaign, was Robert Saudek's *Anonymous Letters*. Leon Jackson, 'The spider and the dumpling: Threatening letters in nineteenth-century America', in Celeste-Marie Bernier, Judie Newman, and Matthew Pethers (eds), *The Edinburgh Companion to Nineteenth-Century American Letters and Letter-Writing* (Edinburgh, 2016), 152–68; 'Digging for dirt: Reading blackmail in the Antebellum archive', *Common-Place*, 12:3 (2012), http://commonplace.online/article/reading/ (accessed 22 January 2023). Dr Jackson has kindly shared unpublished work with me also. For a fascinating account of anonymous peer reviewing in the field of geography, see Michael Dear, 'The politics of geography: Hate mail, rabid referees, and culture wars', *Political Geography*, 20 (2001), 1–12.

8. [Frederick Arnold], 'Anonymous letters', *London Society*, 50:300 (December, 1886), 521–31, at 521, 525.

9. Jackson, 'The spider and the dumpling: Threatening letters in nineteenth-century America', 153, plus unpublished work.

10. Wilson R. Harrison, *Suspect Documents: Their Scientific Examination* (New York, 1958), 469.

11. 'I'll catch poison pen—Rector', *Daily Mirror*, 29 January 1962, 5.

12. H. Ashton-Wolfe, 'The scientific side to the detection of crime. No XII—Anonymous letters and graphomania', *London Illustrated News*, 8 September 1928, 416.

13. 'Poison pen letters? Burn them', *Derby Daily Telegraph*, 6 April 1949, 8.

14. Harrison, *Suspect Documents*.

15. E. Thompson, 'The crime of anonymity', in Douglas Hay, Peter Linebaugh, John G. Rule, E. P. Thompson, and Cal Winslow (eds), *Albion's Fatal Tree* (New York, 1975), 255–344. As Jackson has commented, anonymous letters are 'a highly dispersed genre', and are not conveniently gathered into one archive: see 'The spider and the dumpling: Threatening letters in nineteenth-century America', 152.

16. MOA, Diarist 5353, 'Monday night' (1940).

17. Charles Babbage, *A Chapter of Street Noise*, 2nd edn (London, 1864), 17–18.

18. 'Poison pen kills a child: Yard seek writer', *Daily Mirror*, 22 October 1938, 1.

19. MOA, Diarist 5353, 'Monday night' (1940).

20. John Stuart Mill, *On Liberty* (London, 1859), 26.

21. House of Commons, Malicious Communications. A Bill, 28 October 1987, Bill 25; Malicious Communications Acts 1988, 27 July 1988.

22. 'Jacob Henry Burn, deceased', *London Gazette*, 7 January 1870, 159.

23. 'New Place', *Illustrated London News*, 18 September 1847, 186.

24. 'Shakspeare's House', *Dundee, Perth, and Cupar Advertiser*, 17 September 1847, 2.

25. 'New Place', *Carlisle Patriot*, 3 September 1847, 3; 'The sale of Shakspere's House', *Morning Post*, 17 September 1847, 5.

26. John G. Hendy, *History of the Postmarks of the British Isles from 1840 to 1876* (London, 1909), 155.

27. Saudek, *Anonymous Letters*, 78.

28. *Proceedings of the Old Bailey*, Thomas Hellyer, fraud, t18471025-2442; Census returns for 1851 show that Burn was a 'Coal dealer and Literary'. In 1841 he was listed as a bookseller on St Martin's Lane. Census of England, Wales & Scotland, 1841, London, Middlesex Registration District, St Martin in the Fields. Long Acre, St Martin Lane, St Martin in the Fields, TNA, HO 107/740, fo. 17, page 27, schedule number 128; Census of England, Wales & Scotland, 1851, London, Middlesex Registration District, Westminster, Strand, Great Newport Street, Saint Ann's Soho, TNA, HO 107/1510, fo. 377, page 41, schedule number 178.

29. 'Police seek poison pen who called vicar a spiv', *Daily Mirror*, 29 March 1948, 1; '£25 to find poison pen', *Bradford Observer*, 6 April 1948, 1; 'Village

"poison pen" letters', *Guardian*, 22 May 1948, 5; 'Poison pen inquiry fails', *Yorkshire Post and Leeds Intelligencer*, 22 May 1948, 6; 'Robin Hood's Bay poison pen letters', *Bradford Observer*, 22 May 1948, 3; Alan Hynd, 'Crimes of the poisoned pen', *Saturday Evening Post* (11 June 1955), 31, 129–30.

30. Reginald Morrish, *The Police & Crime-Detection Today* (Oxford, 1940), 147.

31. [Arnold], 'Anonymous letters', 522.

32. TNA, SP14/216/2, Secretaries of State: State Papers Domestic, James I 1605, the Monteagle Letter, 1605, reproduced here: https://www.nation-alarchives.gov.uk/education/resources/gunpowder-plot/source-1/ (accessed 11/01/2023).

33. Stewart Evans and Keith Skinner, *Jack the Ripper: Letters from Hell* (Stroud, 2001), see especially 29–30, 33, 55, 82, 218 onwards.

34. 'Mystery of undergraduates' confession', *Nottingham Evening Post*, 16 March 1931, 1; 'Anonymous confession regarded as hoax', *Sheffield Daily Telegraph*, 17 March 1931, 6.

35. 'New "poison pen" wave is baffling police vigil', *Daily Express*, 15 April 1936, 5.

36. Dennis Howitt, *Introduction to Forensic and Criminal Psychology*, 2nd edn (Harlow, 2006), 265; Dominic Watt, 'The identification of the individual through speech', in Carmen Llamas and Dominic Watt (eds), *Language and Identities* (Edinburgh, 2010), 76–85, at 82.

37. WA, 010:18 BA 14908/3/1/1–2, Signalman Edgin[g]ton accused by member of the public, letter and envelope, 11 April 1944.

38. Andrew Sparke, *Bella In The Wych-Elm* (Stourbridge, 2016).

39. WA, 010:18 BA 14908/3/1/6, report by Richard Skerrett, Clent Constabulary, to City Police, Birmingham, 22 April 1944.

40. WA, 010:18 BA 14908/3/1/5, anonymous postcard addressed to Mrs Savage; see also other documents in WA 010:18 BA14908/3/1/1–6.

41. 'Poison pen letters? Burn them', *Derby Daily Telegraph*, 6 April 1946, 8.

42. The Law Commission, 'Criminal law: Report on poison-pen letters', 30 July 1985, 8.

CHAPTER I

1. See Lawrence McNamara, *Reputation and Defamation* (Oxford, 2007), 31–6.

2. TNA, PROB 11/2222/170, Will of William Granville Eliot, 1855; Dictionary of Canadian Biography, 'Gother Mann', http://www.biographi.ca/en/bio/mann_gother_6E.html; E. Walford, *Hardwicke's Annual Biography* (London, 1856), 371–2; 'Lieut.-Colonel William Granville Eliot', *Illustrated London News*, 29 September 1855, 18.

3. The Census for 1881 reveals that Ann was in Ore, in the house Eliot died in, with Eliot's second daughter's family, then in 1891, aged 101, she is living with the family of Eliot's eldest daughter, Census of England, Wales & Scotland, 1881, Sussex, Hastings Registration District, Vale Brook, Stone Stile Lane, Ore, TNA, RG 11/1021, fo. 78, page 4, schedule number 1002;

Census of England, Wales & Scotland, 1891, Sussex, Hastings Registration District, Ivy House, Homefield Terrace, Ore, TNA, RG 12/758, fo. 104, page 15, schedule number 90.

4. Joan Perkin, *Women and Marriage in Nineteenth-century England* (London, 1989), esp. 50–4.

5. 'Court of Chancery Dec 16', *Morning Advertiser*, 17 December 1836, 3; 'Thornton v Bright', in J. W. Mylne and R. D. Craig (eds), *Reports of Cases decided in the High Court of Chancery during the time of Lord Chancellor Cottenham*, 4 vols (New York, 1843), vol. II, 230–56.

6. TNA, PROB 11/2222/170, Will of William Granville Eliot, 1855.

7. David Nordmann and Xavier Dominique, Auctioneers, Paris, Lot 256, Manuscrit—Botanique, Eliot (Anne) Florae, 1830, https://www.ader-paris.fr/en/lot/17302/3332863 (accessed 11/03/2020). The Census returns for 1841 and 1851 both show William occupying his residence in East Sussex alone, except for a handful of servants, Census of England, Wales & Scotland, 1841, Sussex, Hastings Registration District, Vale Brook, Ore, TNA, HO 107/1105, fo. 30, page 13, schedule number 393; Census of England, Wales & Scotland, 1841, Sussex, Hastings Registration District, Vale Brook, Ore, TNA, HO 107/1635, fo. 117, page 28, schedule number 97.

8. R. I. M. Dunbar, 'Gossip in Evolutionary Perspective', *Review of General Psychology* 8:2 (2004), 100–10.

9. Jörg Bergmann, *Discreet Indiscretions: The Social Organization of Gossip* (New York, 1993), esp. 140–54.

10. Margaret G. Holland, 'What's Wrong with Telling the Truth? An Analysis of Gossip', *American Philosophical Quarterly* 33:2 (April 1996), 197–209, at 199, 200; Robert Paine, 'What is Gossip About? An Alternative Hypothesis', *Man* 2:2 (June 1967), 278–85; Richard H. McAdams, 'Group Norms, Gossip, and Blackmail', *University of Pennsylvania Law Review* 144:5 (May 1996), 2237–92; Jörg Bergmann suggests that gossip itself 'possesses a chaotic aspect'. It 'disrupts order, disdains social boundaries, and entices the actors to neglect their social duties' *Discreet Indiscretions*, 134–5.

11. David Vincent, *I Hope I Don't Intrude: Privacy and its Dilemmas in Nineteenth-Century Britain* (Oxford, 2015), 23, 30.

12. Deborah Cohen, *Family Secrets: Living with Shame from the Victorians to the Present Day* (London, 2013), xiii.

13. Worcestershire Archives (WA), 705:73 BA14450/289/18(1), Lady Margaret 'Peggy' Pitches, Countess of Coventry, Correspondence, Letter from 'a well wisher', early nineteenth century.

14. 'News', *Morning Herald and Daily Advertiser*, 23 November 1780, 2. Catherine Gordon, *The Coventrys of Croome* (Chichester, 2000), 141.

15. Other letters, purportedly written and signed by George William Coventry, are in the same hand as this rewritten letter.

16. There are many other examples of reuse, including WA, 705:73 BA14450/292/5 (6) George William Coventry, Viscount Deerhurst and 7th Earl of Coventry, Letters from John Howard.

17. 'Obituary—William Battine, LL.D', *Gentleman's Magazine*, November 1836, 545.

18. 'Insolvent Debtors' Court', *Maidstone Journal and Kentish Advertiser*, 22 November 1831, 3.

19. WA, 705:73 BA 14450/292/11 (2). Bundle of documents relating to agreements regarding William Kitching, the alleged illegitimate child of George William, 7th Earl of Coventry, Solicitor's bill regarding threatened legal action.

20. London Metropolitan Archives (LMA), P89/MRY1/017, Register of Baptisms, St Marylebone, London—Baptism 31 January 1816, 'The R[igh]t Hon[oura]ble George Earl of Coventry' is listed as William's father.

21. WA, 705:73 BA14450/292/11 (2).

22. WA, 705:73 BA14450/292/11 (3). Bundle of documents relating to agreements regarding William Kitching, the alleged illegitimate child of George William, 7th Earl of Coventry, Release and quit claim executed by Joseph Kitching.

23. WA, 705:73 BA14450/292/5 (1) George William Coventry, Viscount Deerhurst and 7th Earl of Coventry, Letters from John Howard, Letter sent from William Kitching to his mother Mary Ann, thanking her for her kindness and the presents received.

24. 'Obituary—William Battine, LL.D', *Gentleman's Magazine*, November 1836, 545.

25. 'The creditors of William Battine', *Cambridge Chronicle & Journal*, 13 August 1819, 1.

26. WA, 705:73 BA14450/291/12 (4), Letter to Lord Coventry from William Battine, 5 July 1822.

27. WA, 705:73 BA14450/289/16 (10), letter from William Battine to Peggy Countess of Coventry, February 1836(?).

28. 'Insolvent Debtors' Court', *Maidstone Journal and Kentish Advertiser*, 22 November 1831, 3.

29. TNA, PROB 11/1871/64, Will of William Battine esq, Doctor of Laws, 1836.

30. WA, 705:73 BA14450/289/7 (2) Letter from Frederick Boyce to Peggy, Countess of Coventry, 23 March 1826.

31. WA, 705:73 BA 14450/289/7 (1) Copy of reply to Frederick Boyce by Peggy, Countess of Coventry, 23 March 1826.

32. WA, 705:73 BA14450/292/2 (1–2), Letters from Ralph Blackiston, 15 Mar 1825–15 Jul 1826.

33. WA, 705:73 BA14450/292/8 (3) Letter from M. Lloyd, 1820s. The issue in 1824/5 centred on the duration of the agreed payments; Blackiston remembered it as being seven years, during which one guinea per week would be allowed for the child. In 1824 these seven years had elapsed, and so the Earl considered himself to be acquitted from all further claims. Joseph Kitching wasn't having this, expressing his surprise at the Earl's 'wish to extinguish the usual stipend', WA, 705:73 BA14450/292/11 (4–5),

notes stating Mr Blackiston's recollections regarding the above release, which 'was to indemnify Lord [Coventry] from being troubled any more by Mr Kitchin[g]'. Five days later, Blackiston recalled how Mr Fraser had drawn up a general release 'which was to indemnify the Lord for being troubled any more by Mr Kitching'. Blackiston's recollections were written on the back of a draft letter, in a hand which looks a little like that of the Countess, who we know was keen to reuse paper in this way.

34. WA, 705:73 BA14450/292/5 (2).
35. Extract from Mr Fraser's letter to Ralph Blackiston, loosely kept with the Coventry household accounts, WA, 705:73 BA14450/173/10 (4), leaf from 15 March 1825.
36. WA, 705:73 BA14450/296/1 (3), letter from Thomas Lloyd to the 7th Earl of Coventry, 10 July 1826.
37. WA, 705:73 BA14450/292/5 (3–7), Letters from John Howard, 1820s; WA, 705:73 BA14450/296/4 (1a), Letter from George Capron [solicitor]; WA, 705:73 BA14450/289/16 (5) Letter to Lady Coventry from William Kitching (at Commercial Coffee House), 25 May 1830; WA, 705:73 BA14450/289/17 (1–2), Letter to and from Coutts and Co [Thomas Coutts and Company, bankers], 29–30 October 1830.
38. WA, 705:73 BA14450/296/4 (2–7), Letters from George Capron [solicitor].
39. WA, 705:73 BA14450/296/4 (8), Letters from George Capron [solicitor].
40. WA, 705:73 BA14450/297/13 (2), letter to the 8th Earl of Coventry from Henry Pytches Boyce, 6 July 1838.
41. Max Gluckman, 'Gossip and Scandal', Current Anthropology 4:3 (June, 1963), 307–16; Vincent, I Hope I Don't Intrude, 167. See above for further discussion of gossip and group norms.
42. On the connection of increasing moralism to educational reform, see Richard Johnson, 'Educational Policy and Social Control in Early Victorian England', Past & Present 49 (November 1970), 96–119.
43. WA, 705:73 BA14450/292/6 (9), letter and flyer from William Hancock, 'Confidential Letter Case', 1830.
44. Gordon, The Coventrys of Croome, 150, 152.
45. WA, 705:73 BA14450/295/11 (1a), a small note signed Mary Deerhurst, 1814.
46. WA, 705:73 BA14450/295/11 (5), letter from Mary Deerhurst to Lord Deerhurst, 1814.
47. Karin Koehler, 'Valentines and the Victorian Imagination: Mary Barton and Far From the Madding Crowd', Victorian Literature and Culture 45 (2017), 395–412.
48. 'Affecting suicide', Stamford Mercury, 3 September 1830, 2.
49. A case involving a mature relationship in 1800: 'Crewe v Crewe', Alexander Wood Renton et al. (eds), English Reports (178 vols) (London, 1900–32), vol. 162, 1104.

50. See Ginger S. Frost, *Promises Broken: Courtship, Class, and Gender in Victorian England* (Charlottesville, VA, 1995); Saskia Lettmaier, *Broken Engagements: The Action for Breach of Promise of Marriage and the Feminine Ideal* (Oxford, 2010); Katie Barclay, 'Emotions, the Law and the Press in Britain: Seduction and Breach of Promise Suits, 1780–1830', *Journal for Eighteenth-Century Studies* 39:2 (2016), 267–84.

51. Wilkie Collins, *The Woman in White* (London, 1871), 55.

52. Lawrence Stone, *The Road to Divorce: England 1580–1987* (Oxford, 1990), 81.

53. *Proceedings upon the Trial of the Action Brought by Mary Elizabeth Smith Against the Right Hon. Washington Sewallis Shirley Earl Ferrers for Breach of Promise of Marriage* (London, 1846), 354.

54. *Proceedings upon the Trial of the Action Brought by Mary Elizabeth Smith*, 352, 358.

55. Lettmaier, *Broken Engagements*, 147.

56. Sometimes his name is written 'Foster'.

57. Mellish's sister.

58. 'Law intelligence', *Bury & Norwich Post,* 3 March 1802, 4; see also 'Law intelligence', *Chester Chronicle,* 5 March 1802, 4. 'Sporting for a wife', *Sporting Magazine; or, Monthly Calendar,* March 1802, 309–22, at 318–22.

59. Isaac Espinasse, *Reports of Cases Argued and Ruled at Nisi Prius in the King's Bench and Common Pleas . . . 1799–1801* (4 vols) (London, 1808), III: 119–21.

60. 'Breach of promise of marriage', *Star,* 8 December 1824, 4; 'Court of King's Bench', *The Examiner,* 12 December 1824, 9.

61. 'Court of King's Bench Dec 6', *Cambridge Chronicle and Journal,* 10 December 1824, 2.

62. 'Court of King's Bench', *The Examiner,* 12 December 1824, 9.

63. Jane Bell, *Bell v. Hill for defamation. Tried before Lord Chief Justice Abbott. Northumberland Assizes. August 9 1822* (North Shields, 1822), 9–10.

64. 'Summer Assizes', *Star,* 13 August 1822, 4; 'Bell v. Hill', *Durham County Advertiser,* 24 August 1822, 4.

65. Bell, *Bell v. Hill for defamation,* 10.

66. *The Cause of Truth Defended; being a Plain Statement of the Facts connected with the Two Trials of the Rev. T. Hill, Methodist Preacher* (London, 1827), iv.

67. Bell, *Bell v. Hill for defamation,* 1.

68. 'Summer Assizes', *Star,* 13 August 1822, 4.

69. *The Cause of Truth Defended,* 20–1.

70. 'Nisi Prius Court', *Sheffield Independent,* 30 July 1825, 4.

71. *The Cause of Truth Defended,* iv, 28.

72. Walter Scott, *The Journal of Sir Walter Scott 1825–32,* (2 vols) (Edinburgh, 1890), vol. I, 101–2.

73. *The Cause of Truth Defended,* 35–6.

74. Bell, *Bell v. Hill for defamation,* 7.

CHAPTER 2

1. Dudley Archives (DA), DRBC/7/8/8, Anonymous letter to Mr Heberard, 1849.

2. M. Sill, 'Landownership and Industry: The East Durham Coalfield in the Nineteenth Century', *Northern History* 20:1 (1984), 146–66, at 149; J. T. Ward, 'Landowners in Mining', in J. T. Ward and R. G. Wilson, eds, *Land and Industry: The Landed Estate and the Industrial Revolution* (Newton Abbot, 1971), 63–116, esp. 71–2; John A. Hassan, 'The Landed Estate, Paternalism and the Coal Industry in Midlothian, 1800–1880', *The Scottish Historical Review* 59:167 (1980), 73–91. A locally relevant exception to this chronology is explored in T. J. Raybould, 'The Development of Lord Dudley's Mineral Estates, 1774–1845', *The Economic History Review* 21:3 (December 1968), 529–44, esp. 541–4. Dudley's policy of 'working his own pits' was reversed only in the mid-1830s. Dudley's estate was 'the largest single economic unit in South Staffordshire': David Brown, 'The industrial revolution, political economy and the British aristocracy: The second Viscount Dudley and Ward as an eighteenth-century canal promoter', *The Journal of Transport History* 27:1 (2006), 1–23, at 19; James A. Jaffe, *The Struggle for Market Power: Industrial Relations in the British Coal Industry, 1800–1840* (Cambridge, 1991), 98. For an analysis of how different mining techniques correlated with different levels of labourer autonomy, see M. J. Daunton, 'Down the Pit: Work in the Great Northern and South Wales Coalfields, 1870–1914', *Economic History Review* n.s. 34:4 (1981), 578–97.

3. 'Our representative system, Dudley', *Daily News* (12 November 1849), 2.

4. J. U. Nef, *The Rise of the British Coal Industry* (London, 1966), 359.

5. J. H. Powell, B. W. Glover, and C. N. Waters, *A Geological Background for Planning and Development in the 'Black Country'* (British Geological Survey, Technical Report WA/92/33) (Nottingham, 1992), 8, 36.

6. Joseph Beete Jukes, *Memoirs of the Geological Survey of Great Britain. The South Staffordshire Coal-Field*, 2nd edn (London, 1859), 18.

7. DA, DRBC/7/1/7, correspondence and legal opinions re mining contract at Moor Lane, notice, from Thos. Honeyborne, forbidding Benjamin and Thomas Brettell and Thomas and John Pidcock from entering lands or mines at Moor Lane and bills, 1808–26.

8. DA, DRBC/7/1/7.

9. DA, DRBC/7/1/7, Notes by Thomas Honeyborne, sent to Thomas Brettell, Summer Hill, 4 April 1809.

10. 'Committal of coalmasters on a charge of felony', *London Daily News*, 18 October 1847, 3.

11. Staffordshire Record Office (SRO), D853/A/2/16D, letter from William Willis Bailey to Earl of Dartmouth, sent from the Heath Colliery, 2 April 1842.

12. SRO, D853/A/2/16C, letter from William Willis Bailey to Earl of Dartmouth, sent from the Heath Colliery, 28 March 1842.

13. SRO, D853/A/2/16D.

14. SRO, D853/A/2/16B, statements, witnessed by William Willis Bailey, signed by Joseph Bird and James Moss, both served as doggy at the colliery.

15. SRO, D853/A/2/16A, signed statement from Richard Peggs, 27 March 1842, witnessed by William Willis Bailey; D853/A/2/16C.

16. SRO, D853/A/2/16A; D853/A/2/16C.

17. SRO, D853/A/2/16C.

18. SRO, D853/A/3/42, letter from a 'well wisher to all parties' to Earl of Dartmouth, 9 August 1847.

19. House of Commons, *Reports from Commissioners 2 Feb–24 Aug 1843*, Vol XIII, 1843, First report of the Midland Mining Commission [508], xxix, xxxiv, xliii, lix–lx, lxx–lxxii, lxxvii.

20. SRO, D853/A/2/13, letter from William Willis Bailey to Earl of Dartmouth, 27 April 1844; D853/A/2/16A. See also D853/A/2/14, letter from William Sandles to Earl of Dartmouth, 17 April 1844.

21. SRO, D853/A/2/13; D853/A/2/16A.

22. See also SRO, D853/A/3/43, letter from William Salter to William Willis Bailey, 18 September 1847; D853/A/3/44, letter from William Willis Bailey to Earl of Dartmouth, 21 September 1847.

23. SRO, D853/A/3/39, unsigned and dated 28 September, but in the same hand as D853/A/3/42, and detailing circumstances from 1847. The letter might be missing a final page.

24. 'Charge of feloniously getting coal', *Staffordshire Advertiser*, 30 October 1847, 4.

25. 'Committal of coalmasters on a charge of felony', *London Daily News*, 18 October 1847, 3.

26. Warington W. Smyth, 'Note on the Mode of Working the Coal and Ironstone of South Staffordshire', in Joseph Beete Jukes, *Memoirs of the Geological Survey of Great Britain*, 219–23.

27. F. G. Bell and I. A. de Bruyn, 'Subsidence problems due to abandoned pillar workings in coal seams', *Bulletin of Engineering Geology and the Environment* 57 (1999), 225–37, at 227.

28. 'Charge of feloniously getting coal', *Staffordshire Advertiser*, 30 October 1847, 4.

29. 'Committal of coalmasters on a charge of felony', *London Daily News*, 18 October 1847, 3; 'Important to owners and lessees of mines', *Wolverhampton Chronicle & Staffordshire Advertiser*, 20 October 1847, 1.

30. 'Frightful colliery accident', *Staffordshire Advertiser*, 12 February 1848, 5.

31. 'Staffordshire', *London Daily News*, 1 November 1847, 3; 'Frightful colliery accident and loss of life', *Bucks Gazette*, 19 February 1848, 3; 'The late mining prosecution', *Staffordshire Advertiser*, 3 June 1848, 5.

32. 'Deaths', *Staffordshire Advertiser*, 22 April 1848, 5. See also TNA, PROB 11/2075/412, Will of William Willis Bailey, 1848; Swannington Heritage Trust, 'Califat Coal Mine', https://swannington-heritage.co.uk/coal-rail/califat-coal-mine.

33. SRO, D853/A/3/52, Letter from William F. Gordon to Earl of Dartmouth, May 1848.

34. SRO, D853/A/2/15, Letter from William Salter to Earl of Dartmouth, 31 January 1850.

35. SRO, D853/A/2/15.

36. 'Election of coroner for the Westbromwich Division', *Staffordshire Advertiser*, 25 September 1852, 7.

37. 'Died', *Wolverhampton Chronicle and Staffordshire Advertiser*, 6 December 1854, 5.

38. Census of England, Wales & Scotland, 1851, Staffordshire, West Bromwich Registration District, High Street, TNA, HO 107/2026, fo. 332, page 7, schedule number 20.

39. DA, DRBC/7/8/8.

40. *Salter's Classified Directory . . . 15 Miles Round Birmingham and Worcester* (Manchester, 1851), 135, 164; 'V. C. Wood's Court', *Law Times Report*, 22:566, 4 February 1854, 253; 'Copy', *Staffordshire Advertiser*, 24 November 1849, 1.

41. TNA, PROB 11/1380/239, Will of Robert Honeyborne, 1802; 'Bankrupts', *The Examiner*, 16 November 1823, 5; 'Bankrupts', *Aris's Birmingham Gazette*, 28 February 1825, 4; TNA, PROB 11/1789/119, Will of Thomas Honeyborne, 1831.

42. David Williams-Thomas, *The Dynasty Builder* (Bath, 2016).

43. DA, DRBC/7/1/6/5, Bundle of miscellaneous papers, Royal Brierley Crystal, letter dated 30 September 1845.

44. 'Stourbridge', *Worcestershire Chronicle*, 28 February 1849, 5.

45. 'Moor Lane, Brierley Hill, *Worcester Journal*, 22 February 1849, 3; 'Break-up of a gang of burglars', *Worcestershire Chronicle*, 28 February 1849, 5; 'Capture of a burglar', *Nottinghamshire Guardian*, 1 March 1849, 2. Census of England, Wales & Scotland, 1851, Staffordshire, Stourbridge Union Registration District, Moor Lane House, Moor Lane, Kingswinford, TNA, HO 107/2036, fo. 329, page 27, schedule numbers 103–4.

46. DA, DRBC/7/1/7, Correspondence and legal opinions about mining, 1808–26.

47. *London Gazette*, 18 March 1845, 893; 'March 7', *Aris's Birmingham Gazette*, 7 April 1845, 4.

48. Darby followed his family trade as a maltster, but also enjoyed a successful side-line as a coalmaster. He owned public houses such as *The Waterloo Inn* near Brierley Hill; the *Traveller's Rest* opposite Oldswinsford Church, and Sugar Loaf Farm in Iverley, TNA, PROB 11/2238/193, Will of Joseph Darby, maltster and coalmaster late of Delph, 1856.

49. DA, DHAR/16/13, letter from Darby & Higgs to Roberts & Eberhardt, 21 August 1847.

50. DA, DHAR/16/10, letter from Darby & Higgs to Roberts & Eberhardt, 28 August 1847.

51. DA, DRBC/7/1/6/5, Bundle of miscellaneous papers, Royal Brierley Crystal, invoice 20 September 1852 from Mr Turner to Mr Silvers.

52. Report for the Oxford, Worcester & Wolverhampton Railway, Kingswinford branch, compiled in February 1845, reproduced in Michael Hale, *Traffic and Transport in Nineteenth Century Kingswinford* (Dudley, 2000), 8.

53. SRO, D695/1/2/17, Report of Mr Leach of his examination of the mines, 1867; Atkinson, Honeyborne's nephew, filed a bill in Chancery against Thomas Crew, then manager of the colliery, claiming that Crew was mining beyond the area permitted according to an indenture from Christmas 1860. Such action both deprived Atkinson and his heirs, and also caused damage requiring compensation. Crew agreed to refrain from his mining activity and pay the legal costs; SRO, D695/1/2/17, Colonel Atkinson and Mr Thomas Crew, Agreement for Compromise, 28 June 1867.

54. H. J. Haden, *Notes of the Stourbridge Glass Trade* (Brierley Hill, 1949), 29.

55. DA, DHAR/34/2, Harward & Evers, Solicitors, Stourbridge, Bundle re: Cooper, Boyle, Standish, 1848–73. For more on the dangers of undermining, see 'Hanley and Shelton', *Staffordshire Advertiser*, 5 May 1849, 4.

56. 'London, April 19', *Derby Mercury*, 20 April 1759, 1.

57. 'Country News', *Derby Mercury*, 17 August 1759, 1.

58. Census of England, Wales & Scotland, 1851, Staffordshire, Stourbridge Union Registration District, Quarry Bank, New Street, Kingswinford, TNA, HO 107/2036, fo. 720, page 45, schedule number 150; *Corporation General and Trades Directory of Birmingham* (Birmingham, 1861), 799.

59. W. F. H. Nicolaisen, 'Names and Narratives', *Journal of American Folklore* 97:385 (1984), 259–72, at 261–2.

60. Cath Edwards, *West Midlands Folk Tales* (Stroud, 2018).

61. *London Gazette*, 18 March 1845 [issue 20454], 893.

62. 'Frightful colliery explosion in south Staffordshire', *The Times*, 26 October 1844, 6.

63. 'Mine accident', *Worcester Journal*, 16 September 1847, 3; 'Fatal colliery accidents', *Birmingham Journal*, 11 December 1847, 5.

64. 'Unreserved sale', *Birmingham Journal*, 15 March 1851, 1; Census of England, Wales & Scotland, 1841, Staffordshire, Stourbridge Registration District, Dudley Road, Kingswinford, TNA, HO 107/ 996, fo. 49, page 23, schedule number 2699; Census of England, Wales & Scotland, 1851, Staffordshire, Stourbridge Union Registration District, Kingswinford, TNA 107/2036, fo. 382, page 36, schedule number 131.

65. 'Deaths', *County Advertiser and Herald for Staffordshire and Worcestershire*, 14 June 1856, 4; 'Dudley Wood Colliery, Rowley Regis', *Birmingham Journal*, 12 July 1856, 7.

66. 'Mines to be let on royalty', *County Advertiser & Herald for Staffordshire and Worcestershire*, 16 May 1857, 1; SRO, D695/1/30/42, Letter from Charles Roberts to the Oxford, Worcester and Wolverhampton Railway Company, 2 December 1854. When Moor Lane Colliery was leased again in 1857 it

was described as being close to both Brierley Hill station and the Stourbridge Canal, and having 35 acres if thick coal, 16 acres of brooch coal, 20 acres of heathen coal, 20 acres of gubbin firestone, and a further 16 acres of pins firestone, with first-rate firebrick clay lying under the whole estate. Pit machinery was included in the lease, as was part of the Moor Lane House, 'The Moor Lane Colliery', *Wolverhampton Chronicle & Staffordshire Advertiser*, 9 September 1857, 4.

67. DA, DRBC/7/8/8.

68. Victor Bailey, 'The Fabrication of Deviance: "Dangerous Classes" and "Criminal Classes" in Victorian England', in John Rule and Robert Malcolmson, eds, *Protest and Survival: Essays for E. Thompson* (London, 1993), 221–56.

69. TNA, MH 12/9158/126, fos 180–1, Anonymous letter to the Poor Law Board from Tynemouth, 9 December 1848; TNA, MH 12/9158/137, fos 193–4, Anonymous letter from North Shields to the Poor Law Board, 20 December 1848; TNA, MH 12/9158/146, fo. 208, Anonymous letter to the Poor Law Board, 18 January 1849; TNA, MH 12/9158/155, fos 221–2, Anonymous letter concerning James L. Barker, Clerk to the Guardians of the Tynemouth Poor Law Union, 1 March 1849; TNA, MH 12/9158/173, anonymous letter received 15 June 1849.

70. TNA, MH 12/10322/197, fo. 283, Letter dated 11 August 1846 from J & W Rees Mogg. See also an anonymous letter from 'a Ratepayer' in October 1845, asking for an audit to be made in Sutton in Ashton and Mansfield, especially focused on the attorney's bills. Annotations on the reverse note that this 'cannot be done', TNA, MH 12/9361/150, fos 233–4, Anonymous letter signed 'a ratepayer' to the Poor Law Board, 11 October 1845.

71. 1849 Deaths in the district of Kidderminster, no. 495, 4 February 1849, Elizabeth Nash [General register Office, Death Certificate]

72. 'The railways for this district', *Worcestershire Chronicle*, 14 May 1845, 4.

73. TNA, MH 12/14019/342, fos 523–5, Anonymous letter to the Poor Law Board, 7 February 1849; 'Awfully sudden death', *Worcester Journal*, 8 February 1849, 3.

74. GRO, COL932305_2019, 1849 Deaths in the District of Kidderminster, Worcestershire, no. 465, Elizabeth Nash, 4 February 1849; TNA, C 202/227/26 Chancery, return of writs, Coroner, Worcester, Ralph Docker to succeed Thomas Halley, 2 December 1837. For a consideration of 'visitation by God', see Pamela Jane Fisher, 'The politics of sudden death: The office and role of the coroner in England and Wales, 1726–1888', Unpublished PhD thesis, University of Leicester, 2007, 186–92. A House of Commons report from 1863 shows that 'Visitation of God' accounted for death in a sixth of the inquests on infants under two years of age conducted by Docker, 'Coroners' inquests on infants under two years of age', in HOC, *Accounts and Papers* (48 vols) (London, 1863), vol. 48, 74.

75. 'Discovery of two human skeletons at Stourbridge', *Manchester Guardian*, 25 March 1848, 9.

76. William Baker, *A Practical Compendium of the Recent Statutes, Cases and Decisions affecting the Office of Coroner* (London, 1851), 23–5; John Leycester Adolphus and Thomas Flower Ellis, *Queen's Bench Reports*, new series (18 vols) (London, 1847), vol. VII, 165–9.

77. Worcester Archives, County of Worcester, Easter Quarter Sessions, 6 April 1857, 'Re: Coroner's Fees and the Expense of Inquests', Worcester, 1857, 6, 8. Docker forwent his fee in 1842, when he supplied a copy of the depositions for a boy who died at Bromsgrove Workhouse that year, noting that he was 'always happy to help'; TNA, MH 12/13905/180 fo. 313, Letter from Ralph Docker to the Poor Law Commission, 7 April 1842, see also TNA, MH 12/13905/153, fos 256–71.

78. TNA, MH 12/14019/342, fos 523–5, Anonymous letter to the Poor Law Board, 7 February 1849. See also a letter from April 1845, when a 'rate payer' wrote, without signing his name, about the sudden death of a 'dumb' girl 'of debauched habits' at the Bromsgrove Workhouse. Thomas Swindell Fletcher, the district surgeon, had been blamed for the death, but the 'rate payer' claimed to know of a complaint the girl had suffered from, and which was not reported to Fletcher, and that she had drunk a large quantity of cold water on the day she died. The 'rate payer' added that Fletcher had enemies in the town, who wanted to cause trouble for him, and asked that the case be properly investigated, TNA, MH 12/13907/53, fos 76–7.

79. Gloucestershire Archives (GA), C01/N/2/B/51, Notice of death, Sergeant James White on inquest for William Strange, 18 November 1856; GA, C01/I/2/D/11, Inquest, William Strange, pit carter, 25 November 1856; GA, C01/N/2/B/55, Anonymous letter about Brandy Bottom Pit Death, 22 November 1856; 'Sodbury Petty Sessions', *Bristol Mercury*, 29 November 1856, 4. See also 'Bristol', *Southern Times and Dorset County Herald*, 7 November 1857, 7.

80. 'Rowley', *Birmingham Daily Gazette*, 22 October 1863, 8; 'The death of Mr Darby—suspicion of poisoning', *Aris's Birmingham Gazette*, 12 December 1863, 8; 'The death of Mr Darby', *Birmingham Journal*, 28 November 1863, 7; see also 'Notice', *Birmingham Journal*, 21 November 1863, 5, for some of the items sold by auction after Darby died.

81. The residue of his property was split instead between various cousins, with the Reverend Augustus George How, vicar of Bromley-by-Bow and husband of his cousin Clara, getting the greatest share 'on account of his large family and being without property', Thomas's will…Lichfield December 1863 [General Register Office, Will]. Despite the advertisement, all the tickets were not claimed, see Birmingham Archives and Collections, HC GH/4/8/1, unused patients' vouchers issued in conformity with the will of Thomas Darby (d. 1863) of Rowley Regis.

82. 'The General Hospital', *Aris's Birmingham Gazette*, 31 October 1863, 7.

CHAPTER 3

1. Gloucestershire Archives (GA), D5334/1, Anonymous letter to the Dorington family of Lypiatt Park, 1864.

2. Mary Rudd, *Historical Records of Bisley with Lypiatt* (first published 1937, reissued, Stroud, 2008), 241.

3. E. P. Thompson, 'The crime of anonymity', in Douglas Hay, Peter Linebaugh, John G. Rule, E. P. Thompson, and Cal Winslow (eds), *Albion's Fatal Tree* (New York, 1975), 255–344, at 273.

4. Thompson, 'The crime of anonymity', 255, 273.

5. E. P. Thompson, 'The Moral Economy of the English Crowd in the Eighteenth Century', *Past & Present* 50 (February 1971), 76–136, at 101; see also 97, 114, 125, 134; E. P. Thompson, *Customs in Common* (London: 1993), 66.

6. Thompson, 'The crime of anonymity', 258, 283.

7. Another seminal contribution to the study of English anonymous letters in this approximate period was *Captain Swing* by Eric Hobsbawm and George Rudé. Like Thompson, they were social historians writing within the tradition of historical materialism. Where Thompson focused on the period 1750–1811, Hobsbawm and Rudé analysed the 'Captain Swing' letters that had attended rural protest movements in the 1830s. As in Thompson's work, in *Captain Swing* threatening pseudonymous or anonymous letters are treated as 'manifestations of discontent' and set alongside acts of arson. Hobsbawm and Rudé go on to include 'threatening (or "Swing") letters' in a list of the 'numerous forms that the labourers' movement assumed'. The list also includes wages meetings, attacks on justices, machine-breaking, etc. Eric Hobsbawm and George Rudé, *Captain Swing* (London, 1969), 84, 97.

8. James C. Scott, *Weapons of the Weak: Everyday Forms of Peasant Resistance* (New Haven, CT, 1985). See especially the discussion of pride in self-identification on p. 229; and p. 334 on anonymous religious circulars. Leon Jackson has more recently described threatening letters as 'an almost unique repertoire of voices from the margins', sent through 'pressing need or dire convictions'; see his 'The spider and the dumpling: Threatening letters in nineteenth-century America', 153.

9. Thompson, 'The crime of anonymity', 278.

10. Thompson, 'The crime of anonymity', 257–8.

11. 'News', *The Monthly Chronologer*, 35 (October 1766), 547; Thompson, 'The crime of anonymity', 280, 328–9. Norfolk Record Office, NCR Case 6h/9.6, Minute of Mayor's court concerning anonymous letter threatening to set fire to James Poole's shop, 1766.

12. 'London', *London Evening Post*, 4 April 1767, 1.

13. Thompson, 'The crime of anonymity', 274.

14. Leon Jackson, researching anonymous threatening letters back to the Middle Ages, finds that written threats have always been made—just less

commonly than verbal ones. There was, according to Jackson, an epidemic of anonymous letters in the 1730s–1760s, especially around 1730–31. Work in progress, kindly shared with me.

15. Jackson, 'The spider and the dumpling: Threatening letters in nineteenth-century America', 155.

16. Carolyn Steedman, 'Threatening letters: E. E. Dodd, E. Thompson and the making of "The crime of anonymity"', *History Workshop Journal* 82 (2016), 50–82, at 71–2.

17. See also Jackson, 'The spider and the dumpling: Threatening letters in nineteenth-century America', 155.

18. Thompson, 'The crime of anonymity', 236; see also Roger Wells, *Wretched Faces: Famine in Wartime England, 1793–1801* (Gloucester, 1988), 90.

19. Hobsbawm and Rudé, *Captain Swing*, 27.

20. See, for example, a letter written anonymously in the late eighteenth century which condemned Thomas Shepherd, the vicar of Basingstoke, for his 'attempt to ruin' his parishioners, in contrast to 'the good Shepherd' who 'layeth down his life for the Sheep'. Shepherd was in favour of enclosure, Hampshire Record Office, Basingstoke Museum miscellanea, 11M94/7, Anonymous letter 'To the worthy inhabitants of the Town of Basin—ke', from 'An Inhabitant', *c*.1780s.

21. Rudd, *Historical Records of Bisley with Lypiatt*, 369, 372.

22. House of Lords, 'Reports from Commissioners: Hand-Loom Weavers', in *The Sessional Papers printed by order of The House of Lords Session 1840* (London, 1840), 213–800, at 519–20.

23. Reports from Commissioners: Hand-Loom Weavers', 520–2.

24. 'Bisley Common inclosure', *Gloucester Journal*, 11 July 1863, 8.

25. 'Bisley Common inclosure', *Stroud Journal*, 11 July 1863, 4.

26. 'John Bravender', *Gloucester Journal*, 28 November 1863, 1.

27. 'On hearing that Bisley Commons were to be enclosed', *Gloucestershire Chronicle*, 7 November 1863, 3.

28. 'News', *Gloucester Journal*, 9 April 1864, 8.

29. 'Churchwarden's orthography', *Birmingham Daily Gazette*, 29 February 1864, 5, and elsewhere.

30. Rudd, *Historical Records of Bisley with Lypiatt*, 157–9.

31. 'Chalford Episcopal Chapel', *Gloucestershire Chronicle*, 18 April 1840, 2. Next, Keble set his sights on Bussage, where he founded St Michaels & All Angels church, consecrated in October 1846, built for a congregation of two hundred following the High Church principles of the Oxford Movement, and 'abounding in stalls, priest's doors, embroidered crosses &c', 'Consecration', *Gloucestershire Chronicle*, 10 October 1846, 3; 'Gloucestershire', *Oxford University & City Herald*, 31 October 1846, 2.

32. 'Chalford Episcopal Chapel', *Gloucestershire Chronicle*, 18 April 1840, 2.

33. According to a note on GA catalogue entry for D5334/1.

34. 'Whitehall', *Gazetteer and New Daily Advertiser*, 25 June 1767, 3; 'Sunday's Post', *Ipswich Journal*, 27 June 1767, 1.

35. David F. Marley, 'The great galleon: The Santisima Trinidad (1750–1765)', *Philippine Studies*, 41:2 (1993), 167–81, at 181.

36. Geoffrey W. Rice, 'Great Britain, the Manila Ransom, and the first Falkland Islands dispute with Spain, 1766', *International History Review* 3:2 (1980), 386–409, 389; David Joel Steinberg, 'The Philippines, 1762–1872', in Steinberg, *In Search of Southeast Asia*, rev edn (Honolulu, 1987), 160–70, at 160–1; Richard H. Dillon, 'The last plan to seize the Manila Galleon', *Pacific History Review* 20:2 (1951), 123–5.

37. 'At Garraway's Coffee House', *Gazetteer and New Daily Advertiser*, 19 June 1765, issue 11,316, 3; 'Public ledger, July 10', *Public Ledger*, 11 July 1765, issue 1,721, 659–60; 'For sale by the candle', *Public Ledger*, 16 July 1765, 675; 'Public ledger, August 1', *Public Ledger*, 2 August 1765, 736; 'London', *Gazetteer and New Daily Advertiser*, 6 August 1765, issue 11,357, 2; 'At Garraway's Coffee House', *Gazetteer and New Daily Advertiser*, 13 September 1765, issue 11,390, 3; 'For sale by the candle', *Public Ledger*, 12 December 1765, issue 1,853, 2087.

38. 'Monday, September 23', *Lloyd's Evening Post*, 20–3 September 1765, issue 1,280, 294; 'London', *Caledonian Mercury*, 15 June 1765, 2.

39. 'Notice is hereby given', *London Gazette*, 13–16 April 1765, issue 10,515, 2.

40. 'For sale by the candle', *Gazetteer and New Daily Advertiser*, 16 January 1766, issue 11,497, 5.

41. 'Many applications', *Gazetteer and New Daily Advertiser*, 25 June 1767, issue 11,952, 3.

42. Thompson, 'The crime of anonymity', 278.

43. See Wells, *Wretched Faces*, 167, 302.

44. 'Threatening letters', *Public Advertiser*, 26 March 1792, issue 18,010, 3; 'Whitehall', *Manchester Mercury*, 27 March 1792, 4; Thompson, 'The crime of anonymity', 274.

45. 'Hired servants', *Manchester Mercury*, 21 February 1792, 4; NB this might well have nothing to do with the fire.

46. 'Factory to let', *Manchester Mercury*, 17 April 1792, 3.

47. *The Universal Magazine*, February 1799, 151; John Higson, *The Gorton Historical Recorder* (Droylsden, 1852), 125.

48. John Harland, *Ballads and Songs of Lancashire*, 2nd edn (London, 1875), 202–3.

49. 'Job White-Bread', *Scarcity of Bread Difficulte Annonae; Or, the Disease Examined, and the Cure Premised* (London, 1795).

50. Clive Emsley, *British Society and the French Wars 1793–1815* (London, 1979), 87; see also Austin Gee, 'British Volunteers Movement, 1793–1807', Unpublished Oxford D.Phil., 1989.

51. TNA, HO 42/49/99 fo. 208, anonymous letter found in a garden of a member of the West Bromwich Volunteer Association.

52. TNA, HO 42/49/99 fo. 206, Letter to Earl Gower, from Richard Jesson, 18 February 1800; HO 42/49/99 fo. 205, Letter from Earl Gower to the Home Office, 21 April 1800.

53. Thompson, 'The crime of anonymity', 278.

54. Essex Record Office, Q/SBb 380/66, Quarter Sessions Bundle, Midsummer 1800.

55. 'Assizes', *Jackson's Oxford Journal*, 15 March 1800, 1.

56. TNA, HO 42/53/172, fos 484–8, Letter from magistrates for the Liberty of Peterborough enclosing seditious letters, 30 November 1800.

57. 'William Hetley's bankruptcy', *Stamford Mercury*, 12 May 1815, 4.

58. 'One hundred pounds reward', *Stamford Mercury*, 5 December 1800, 2.

59. 'August 5', *Historical Chronicle*, 111 (August 1802), 141.

60. 'William Hetley's bankruptcy', *Stamford Mercury*, 12 May 1815, 4.

61. 'Stafford Assizes', *Worcester Journal*, 31 March 1814, 3; 'Provincial intelligence', *The Examiner*, 327, 3 April 1814, 214.

62. Plymouth and West Devon Record Office, Bellamy Papers, PH/178–9; PH/185–6; PH/190; PH/192–3; PH/195–197; PH/276.

63. *London Gazette*, 18 August 1812, 1678. See also 19 September 1812, 1908–9.

64. The History of Parliament, Monmouth Borough, https://www.historyof-parliamentonline.org/volume/1820–1832/constituencies/monmouth.

65. TNA, HO 64/1/19, fos 85–7, letter from T. G. Phillpotts to [Viscount Sidmouth], 16 December 1820; K. E. Kissack, *Monmouth: The Making of a County Town* (London, 1975), 66–7, 83; D. J. V. Jones, *Crime in Nineteenth Century Wales* (Cardiff, 1992), 229.

66. TNA, HO 44/6/20 fo. 57, 20 April 1820 anonymous letter to Sidmouth. See also TNA, HO44/6/16, fos 49–50; Steve Poole, *The Politics of Regicide in England 1760–1850* (Manchester, 2018), 160.

67. TNA, HO 64/19 fo. 241, 'Another fire at Messrs Bellhouses' yard', *Manchester Guardian*, 2 March 1822, 3; 'Disastrous fires', *Lancaster Gazette*, 19 January 1822, 3.

68. Hobsbawm and Rudé, *Captain Swing*, 147.

69. TNA, HO 52/7/252, fos 587–9, a letter to the Home Secretary from John Thomas Huntley, Vicarage House, Kimbolton, 27 November 1830.

70. TNA, HO 52/6, fos 411–13b.

71. *London Gazette*, 12 August 1797, 773.

72. See, for example, Buckinghamshire Archives, D-X 1711/1/163, letter from Charles Baker to Elizabeth Odell, 4 August 1872.

73. Hampshire Record Office, 75M91/P9, Carnarvon of Highclere papers, the Long Family, letter sent to Arthur Atherley, 1 September 1828.

74. Surrey Archives, 9309/3/1/1, Letter to Rev Broderick of Banstead, post-marked Epsom, 27 December 1825.

75. Max Everest-Phillips, 'Protest, poison pen letters and Protestantism in mid-nineteenth century East Devon: The Tractarian crisis at Sidmouth 1859–1865', *Report and Transactions of the Devonshire Association*, 143 (June 2011), pp. 231–81; Rudd, *Historical Records of Bisley with Lypiatt*, 159.

76. 'Conflagration', *Salisbury and Winchester Journal*, 4 February 1811, 4.

77. 'Tuesdays's post', *Hampshire Chronicle*, 11 February 1811, 1.
78. 'Extraordinary case', *Public Ledger & Daily Advertiser*, 5 February 1811, 2; 'Horsham', *Sun*, 27 March 1811, 3; 'Conflagration', *Salisbury and Winchester Journal*, 4 February 1811, 4; David Cox, *Crime in England 1688–1815* (London: 2013), 151–4.
79. 'Horsham', *Sun*, 27 March 1811, 3.
80. 'Horsham', *Sun*, 27 March 1811, 3.
81. 'Extraordinary case', *Public Ledger & Daily Advertiser*, 5 February 1811, 2; 'Horsham', *Sun*, 27 March 1811, 3.
82. 'Home news', *Hampshire Chronicle*, 29 November 1813, 4; 'At Winchester Assizes', *Oxford University and City Herald*, 16 March 1816, 4; 'Hants, Michaelmas', *Hampshire Chronicle*, 20 October 1817, 4; 'Winchester', *Salisbury and Winchester Journal*, 19 January 1818, 4; 'Hampshire', *Hampshire Chronicle*, 22 June 1818, 4; 'The case of Rev. Rich Bingham', *Hampshire Chronicle*, 25 February 1822, 4.
83. Cox, *Crime in England 1688–1815*, 151–2.
84. Robert Bingham, *The Trials of the Rev. Robert Bingham* (London, 1811).
85. 'News', *Stamford Mercury*, 2 August 1811, 3.
86. East Sussex Record Office (ESRO), FRE/2291, Letter from Mary Frewen to John Frewen, Cold Overton, 30 January 1811.
87. Thompson, 'The crime of anonymity', 282.
88. Thompson, 'Moral Economy of the English Crowd', *passim*.
89. For a recent review of how the meaning of 'moral economy' has changed over time, see Norbert Götz, '"Moral Economy": its conceptual history and analytic prospects', *Journal of Global Ethics* 11:2 (2015), 147–62.
90. 'Bisley', *Stroud Journal*, 6 January 1866, 5.

CHAPTER 4

1. Notices, *Loughborough Echo*, 3 November 1916, 1.
2. 'Liberal agent fined', *Sunderland Daily Echo and Shipping Gazette*, 7 February 1917, 5; 'Charge of indecency against John Peer', *Loughborough Echo*, 9 February 1917, 3.
3. Rowland Hill, *Post Office Reform; its Importance and Practicability* (London, 1837), 7.
4. John Wilson Croker, '[Review of] *Post Office Reform: its Importance and Practicability*. By Rowland Hill ', *The Quarterly Review* 64 (1839), 513–74, at 532. See Catherine Golden, *Posting It: The Victorian Revolution in Letter Writing* (Gainesville, FL, 2009), 153; Martin Daunton, *Royal Mail: The Post Office since 1840* (London, 2015), 79.
5. See Golden, *Posting It*, esp. 121–35.
6. See N. Cutmore, 'Development of the Pillar Letter Box 1852–1969', *Proceedings of the Institution of Mechanical Engineers* 184:8 (1969), 202–8; Jean Farrugia, *The Letter Box: A History of Post Office Pillar and Wall Boxes* (New York, 1969).

7. See Christopher Hilliard, *A Matter of Obscenity: The Politics of Censorship in Modern England* (Oxford, 2021), esp. 'Introduction'. Hilliard notes that no one was ever charged under the 1857 Act.

8. Colin Manchester, 'Lord Campbell's act: England's first obscenity statute', *The Journal of Legal History* 9:2 (1988), 223–41, at 225.

9. Manchester, 'Lord Campbell's act', 232.

10. See A. W. B. Simpson, 'Obscenity and the Law', *Law and Philosophy* 1:2 (1982), 239–54, at 239–40, 243. Daunton, *Royal Mail: The Post Office since 1840*, 79.

11. 'News', *Hastings and St Leonard's Observer*, 15 October 1870, 3.

12. Post Office Act 1908, §16.

13. Post Office Act 1908, §63.

14. This point is well made by George Ryley Scott, *Into Whose Hands: An Examination of Obscene Libel in its Legal, Sociological and Literary Aspects* (London, 1945).

15. Colin Manchester, 'A history of the crime of obscene libel', *Journal of Legal History* 12:1 (1991), 36–57, at 45.

16. R v De Montalk (1932) 23 Cr App Rep 182. See discussion in Scott, *Into Whose Hands*, 56–7; Manchester, '. . . the crime of obscene libel', 45.

17. James Fitzjames Stephen, *A History of the Criminal Law of England* (3 vols) (London, 1883), vol. II, 352.

18. Sarah Bull, 'A Purveyor of Garbage? Charles Carrington and the Marketing of Sexual Science in Late-Victorian Britain', *Victorian Review* 38:1 (2012), 55–76, at 55.

19. 'A clergyman charged with writing obscene letters', *Liverpool Mercury*, 13 May 1865, 5; 'Alleged extraordinary conduct of a clergyman', *Durham County Advertiser*, 19 May 1865, 3.

20. TNA, HO140/314, Calendar of Prisoners tried at assizes and quarter sessions in: London, Central Criminal Court (Old Bailey), London (North of the River), London (South of the River) Commencing for the Year 1914, prisoner number, 9.

21. 'Letter Sent to Wrong House', *Bath Chronicle and Weekly Gazette*, 11 July 1914, 12.

22. 'No Bail for Suffragists', *Votes for Women*, 10 July 1914, 10.

23. 'A caution', *Exeter and Plymouth Gazette*, 6 April 1844, 3.

24. Biographical details from: Census of England, Wales & Scotland, 1891, London, Surrey, Lambeth Registration District, Bradford Road, TNA, RG 12/412, fo. 56, page 49, schedule number 265; Census of England, Wales & Scotland, 1901, London, Surrey, Wandsworth Registration District, Elmfield Mansions, 24, Elmfield Road, Streatham, TNA, RG 13/472, fo. 149, page 2, schedule number 13; Census of England, Wales & Scotland, 1911, London, Surrey, Wandsworth Registration District, 24 Elmfield Mansions, Balham, TNA, RG 14/2312, piece number 78, schedule number 71.

25. 'Charge of writing obscene letters', *York Herald*, 7 July 1877, 6.

26. 'Walter Frederic Mason before the magistrates', *Ipswich Journal*, 3 July 1877, 3.

27. On the 'breach of peace' idea, see Stephen, *History of Criminal Law*, vol. II: 300, 307, 312.

28. 'South-eastern circuit', *Times*, 2 August 1877, 11.

29. 'Walter Frederic Mason before the magistrates', *Ipswich Journal*, 3 July 1877, 3.

30. 'Walter Frederic Mason before the magistrates', *Ipswich Journal*, 3 July 1877, 3.

31. 'Ipswich', *Bury and Norwich Post*, 3 July 1877, 8.

32. See for example Croker, '[Review]', 530.

33. Editorial, *London Evening Standard*, 28 March 1877, 5.

34. Cited in 'Whenever', *Ipswich Journal*, 31 March 1877, 5.

35. 'Case goes to Crown Court', *Bury & Norwich Post*, 1 August 1877, 6.

36. TNA, HO140/52, Calendar of prisoners tried at the assizes, Bury St Edmund's, 28 July 1880, prisoner number 13; 'Ipswich', *Bury & Norwich Post*, 20 July 1880, 6.

37. 'Ipswich', *Eastern Daily Press*, 16 July 1888, 3; 'Charge of indecency at Ipswich', *Bury Free Press*, 31 July 1880, 5.

38. Census of England, Wales & Scotland, 1891, London, Surrey, Lambeth Registration District, Bradford Road, TNA, RG 12/412, fo. 56, page 49, schedule number 265; Census of England, Wales & Scotland, 1901, London, Surrey, Wandsworth Registration District, Elmfield Mansions, 24, Elmfield Road, Streatham, TNA, RG 13/472, fo. 149, page 2, schedule number 13.

39. 'Singular charges against a butler', *Cardiff Times*, 21 February 1885, 2; 'Letters at Ivybridge', *Totnes Weekly Times*, 28 February 1885, 4; 'Charge of sending threatening letters', *Exeter & Plymouth Gazette*, 10 April 1885, 2; TNA, HO140/79, Calendar of prisoners tried at the general Quarter Sessions of the Peace, HM Prison Exeter, 1885 (prisoner number 5); 'Trial of John Lee', *Cardiff Times*, 7 February 1885, 5; 'The Devonshire tragedy', *Liverpool Echo*, 25 November 1884, 4; 'Crime and casualties in Devon and Cornwall', *Western Morning News*, 3 January 1885, 5.

40. 'The charge', *Exeter & Plymouth Gazette*, 10 April 1885, 2.

41. Charge of sending threatening letters', *Exeter & Plymouth Gazette*, 10 April 1885, 2.

42. TNA, HO140/79, Calendar of prisoners tried at the general Quarter Sessions of the Peace, HM Prison Exeter, 1885 (prisoner number 5).

43. 'A Wigan divorce suit', *Bolton Evening News*, 8 November 1893, 2; Census of England, Wales & Scotland, 1891, Lancashire, Wigan Registration District, St Thomas Street, TNA, RG 12/3052, fo. 95, page 9, schedule number 43; Census of England, Wales & Scotland, 1901, Lancashire, Wigan Registration District, 12, Hardy Street, TNA, RG 13/3556, fo. 151, page 10, schedule number 56.

44. 'The Britannia', *Era*, 12 November 1887, 14.

45. 'Britannia', *The Stage*, 15 April 1887, 15. See also ' "Queen's Evidence" at the Britannia', *Era*, 20 March 1886, 8.

46. 'Annoying an actress', *Globe*, 26 November 1887, 2; 'Police', *Times*, 26 November 1887, 4; Census of England, Wales & Scotland, 1881, London,

Middlesex, Bethnal Green Registration District, 42, Baroness Road, TNA, RG 11/411, fo. 64, page 45, schedule number 605; Census of England, Wales & Scotland, 1901, London, Middlesex, Bethnal Green Registration District, 42, Baroness Road, TNA, RG 13/285, fo. 127, page 26, schedule number 201.

47. 'Sending objectionable letters', *Manchester Courier and Lancashire General Advertiser*, 17 August 1895, 18; Census of England, Wales & Scotland, 1901, Lancashire, Bolton Registration District, 85, Fletcher Street, TNA, RG 13/3625, fo. 171, page 24, schedule number 133.

48. 'Objectionable letters', *Bolton Evening News*, 14 August 1895, 3; 'Extraordinary conduct of an organist', *Nottingham Evening Post*, 15 August 1895, 2.

49. 'Notice', *Bolton Evening News*, 14 January 1895, 1.

50. 'Letter to authoress', *Derby Daily Telegraph*, 15 November 1913, 2; 'The charge against a barrister', *Times*, 22 November 1913, 4; 'A barrister's delusions', *Evening Mail*, 2 December 1913, 7.

51. 'Public notice', *Hastings and St Leonard's Observer*, 9 February 1907, 5.

52. 'Situations wanted, female', *Hastings and St Leonard's Observer*, 16 June 1906, 11.

53. 'Doctor in the dock', *Hastings and St Leonard's Observer*, 14 July 1906, 5; 'Sussex Assizes', *Hastings and St Leonard's Observer*, 24 November 1906, 10.

54. 'District news', *Birmingham Daily Post*, 27 August 1858, 4; Census of England, Wales & Scotland, 1861, Worcestershire, Staffordshire, Dudley Registration District, Wolverhampton Street, TNA, RG 09/2055, fo. 64, page 39, schedule number 147; Castle Street, TNA, RG 09/2059, fo. 10, page 15, schedule number 70.

55. 'Extraordinary charge against a military officer', *York Herald*, 6 August 1859, 5.

56. 'Extraordinary charge', *Morning Chronicle*, 4 August 1859, 2; 'Latest news', *Hereford Times*, 13 August 1859, 8; 'Assize intelligence', *Bristol Mercury*, 13 August 1859, 4; 'Offences', *Royal Cornwall Gazette*, 26 August 1859, 3.

57. '£50 reward', *Bath Chronicle and Weekly Gazette*, 18 August 1859, 4.

58. 'London, Tuesday October 11', *London Evening Standard*, 11 October 1870, 4.

59. 'Luntley's Invisible Postal Ink', *The Examiner*, 15 October 1870, 7.

60. 'Notes', *Dover Express*, 4 April 1890, 4; Daunton, *Royal Mail*, 40; Golden, *Posting It*, 163.

61. Anon., 'Valentine's Day', *London Review* 10:242 (1865), 195–6, cited in Karin Koehler, 'Valentines and the Victorian Imagination: *Mary Barton* and *Far From the Madding Crowd*', *Victorian Literature and Culture* 45 (2017), 395–412, at 396.

62. 'Percy Farnfield, England', ESPNcricinfo, https://www.espncricinfo.com/england/content/player/13000.html (accessed 12/09/2021).

63. Such calls would grow in prevalence, just as the letters under discussion appear to have responded to expansions of the postal system. By the 1980s up to 10% of women would receive at least one unwanted obscene phone

call a year: see Ken Pease, 'Obscene Telephone Calls to Women in England and Wales', *The Howard Journal* 24:4 (1985), 275–81.

64. 'Obscene postcards to ladies', *Nottingham Evening Post*, 27 May 1918, 2; 'Schoolmaster for trial', *Thanet Advertiser*, 8 June 1918, 4; 'Schoolmaster certified to be of unsound mind', *Dundee Evening Telegraph*, 5 July 1918, 5.

65. Census of England, Wales & Scotland, 1891, Lancashire, Bury Registration District, Hornby Street, Heap, TNA, RG 12/3133, fo. 125, page 8, schedule number 45; Census of England, Wales & Scotland, 1891, Lancashire, Bury Registration District, 14 Princess Street, TNA, RG 12/3135, fo. 96, page 8, schedule number 46.

66. 'Sending libellous letters', *Whitstable Times and Herne Bay Herald*, 27 July 1895, 3.

67. 'Cases at the Quarter Session', *Chelmsford Chronicle*, 22 October 1897, 4; 'Is he a madman?', *Chelmsford Chronicle*, 29 October 1897, 3.

68. 'News', *Stamford Mercury*, 23 December 1904, 2; 'Obscene', *Grantham Journal*, 24 December 1904, 6.

69. 'News', *Stamford Mercury*, 23 December 1904, 2; 'Obscene', *Grantham Journal*, 24 December 1904, 6.

70. Letitia Fairfield, 'The poison pen: A study of anonymous letter writers', *Medico-Legal & Criminological Review* 12:1 (1944), 23–32, 33.

71. Harrison, *Suspect Documents*, 481.

72. 'Postcard nuisance again', *Hull Daily Mail*, 14 February 1898, 4.

73. 'Sensational post card case', *Dover Express*, 4 April 1890, 8.

74. 'Notes', *Dover Express*, 4 April 1890, 4.

75. 'Sensational post card case', *Dover Express*, 4 April 1890, 8; 'Offensive post cards', *Tamworth Herald*, 5 April 1890, 3.

76. 'Charge of sending offensive post cards', *Dover Express*, 3 July 1891, 5.

77. 'Wandering', *Dover Express*, 6 April 1906, 8.

78. Ruth Lewis, Michael Rowe, and Clare Wiper, 'Online Abuse of Feminists as An Emerging form of Violence Against Women and Girls', *The British Journal of Criminology* 57:6 (2017), 1462–81.

79. See in general Emma Alice Jane, '"Back to the kitchen, cunt": speaking the unspeakable about online misogyny', *Continuum* 28:4 (2014), 558–70; Emma Alice Jane, *Misogyny Online: A Short (and Brutish) History* (London, 2017).

CHAPTER 5

1. s.v. 'poison pen' adj. and n. *OED Online*, Oxford University Press, December 2022, www.oed.com/view/Entry/265855 (accessed 22 January 2023).

2. See also Emily Cockayne, *Cheek by Jowl: A History of Neighbours* (London, 2012), 142–4.

3. Item in author's own collection.

4. See, for example, Heston and Isleworth Urban District Council, *1916 Annual Report of the Medical Officer of Health for Heston and Isleworth* [1917], 20.

5. 'Lecture XXIII Sanitary Organization', in E. D. Mapother, *Lectures on Public Health*, 2nd edn (Dublin, 1867), 555–80, at 565.

6. British Library, SPR.Mic.P.432/BL.M.20, England & Wales, Electoral Registers 1910–32, 1913, 1914, pp. 359, 398, Sidney Lawrence, Brentford; Census of England, Wales & Scotland, 1911, Middlesex, Brentford Registration District, 8 Campo Road, TNA, RG 14/6828, schedule number 309, RG78PN340.

7. Cockayne, *Cheek by Jowl*, 36, 162, 177, 189–90, 203, 221.

8. TNA, HO140/284, Calendar of Prisoners tried at the Assizes, Guildford, Surrey, Annie Tugwell, 9 July 1910, number 197004; See also TNA, MEPO 3/189, Office of the Commissioner: Correspondence and Papers, Special Series, Metropolitan Police Office, 'The Sutton Libel Case', 1909–1913.

9. 'A Croydon sensation', *Globe*, 19 March 1909, 3; 'Libel charge fails', *Stamford Mercury*, 2 July 1909, 3; 'Libel suit withdrawn', *Witney Gazette and West Oxfordshire Advertiser*, 3 July 1909, 6.

10. 'Strange case', *Express and Echo*, 21 April 1910, 1; 'Married woman is charged', *Dundee Evening Telegraph*, 28 April 1910, 3; 'The case against a Sutton lady', *Globe*, 28 April 1910, 9.

11. 'Libel suit sequel', *Nottingham Journal*, 29 April 1910, 6.

12. 'Disgusting letters', *Nottingham Journal*, 29 April 1910, 6; 'Secret stamps', *Croydon Chronicle and East Surrey Advertiser*, 30 April 1910, 9; 'Marked stamps', *Croydon Chronicle and East Surrey Advertiser*, 30 July 1910, 13; 'Sutton libel charge', *Croydon Advertiser and East Surrey Reporter*, 30 July 1910, 7; 'Sutton libel charge', *Croydon Guardian and Surrey County Gazette*, 6 August 1910, 4.

13. 'Marked stamps', *Croydon Chronicle and East Surrey Advertiser*, 30 July 1910, 13.

14. 'Jury's puzzle', *Western Times*, 2 August 1910, 8; 'A reign of terror', *Croydon Chronicle and East Surrey Advertiser*, 6 August 1910, 4.

15. The Victorian pioneers index 1837–1888 [electronic resource]: [an index to birth, death, and marriage records held by the Registry of Births, Deaths and Marriages, Victoria], Leslie Warren Tugwell, birth registration number 4698, Melbourne, 1887; 'Offences not otherwise described', *New South Wales Police Gazette*, 4 May 1887, p. 137; Sutton Borough Archives, Water Rate Books, London Borough of Sutton, 1868–1911, various entries for H. Tugwell, 1888–1906; Census of England, Wales & Scotland, 1901, Surrey, Epsom Registration District, 33, Vernon Road, TNA, RG 13/581, fo. 108, page 2, schedule number 14.

16. Annie was working under the name Annie Warren (using part of Harry's name); 'Objectionable letters', *Surrey Mirror*, 9 September 1913, 2; 'Mrs Tugwell', *Globe*, 29 August 1913, 7.

17. 'Alleged offensive postal packets', *Nottingham Evening Post*, 29 August 1913, 5.

18. 'Alleged offensive postal packets', *Nottingham Evening Post*, 1 September 1913, 8; 'Woman in dock', *Dundee Evening Telegraph*, 2 September 1913, 2; 'Libels sent by post', *Western Mail*, 20 October 1913, 5.

19. See Chapter 6.

20. 'Alleged offensive postal packets', *Nottingham Evening Post*, 1 September 1913, 8; 'Woman in dock', *Dundee Evening Telegraph*, 2 September 1913, 2; 'Libels sent by post', *Western Mail*, 20 October 1913, 5.

21. TNA, HO140/306, Calendar Of Prisoners For The Session Commencing For The Year 1913, Central Criminal Court, 7 October 1913 [Annie Tugwell, reference 24489].

22. TNA, BT 334/56, Deaths of seamen reported to the Registrars General, 1912–13, [ship: Talus], E3; BT 334/58, Register of deceased seamen, 1913, [ship: Talus], 18.

23. TNA, MEPO 3/189, Special report signed John Kane, 23 August 1909, 3. For doubts cast on Tugwell's guilt see: 'Allegations of forgery and conspiracy', *Surrey Advertiser*, 17 February 1912, 5; 'A sister's evidence', *Croydon Advertiser and East Surrey Reporter*, 6 August 1910, 8.

24. The Colonel's name was actually Gardner, but he is mostly referred to as Gardiner in documentation, even some official documents.

25. 'Governess's dual personality', *Times*, 29 May 1914, 4.

26. East Sussex Record Office (ESRO), DO/C/6/3632, Hove Building Control conversion into flats, 62 Brunswick Place, by Col Gardiner, 18 March 1912. For disputes caused by spaces shared by neighbours, see Emily Cockayne, *Cheek by Jowl*, 33–4, 96, 100–1, 156–7, 171–2.

27. 'Letters to a governess', *Yorkshire Post & Leeds Intelligencer*, 21 May 1914, 5.

28. 'The charge against a colonel', *Derby Daily Telegraph*, 20 May 1914, 3; 'Retired Colonel charged', *Times*, 21 May 1914, 5.

29. 'Governess's dual personality', *Times*, 29 May 1914, 4.

30. He only stayed for a week before being released on account of his health and old age and instructed to go at least forty miles from Hove. See 'Colonel charged', *Dundee Evening Telegraph*, 12 May 1914, 3; 'Letters to a governess', *Hull Daily Mail*, 13 May 1914, 4; 'Bail for the accused colonel', *Pall Mall Gazette*, 15 May 1914, 5. 'A short story whilst in gaol and on bail from May 11th to May 29th, 1914', appended to C. H. Gardiner, *Soldiers and Civil War* (London, 1914), 53, 55–6, 63, 67.

31. 'Governess's dual personality', *Times*, 29 May 1914, 4; 'Hove libel charge dismissed', *Sussex Agricultural Express*, 4 June 1914, 8; Gardiner, *Soldiers and Civil War*, 68.

32. 'Governess's dual personality', *West Sussex Gazette*, 4 June 1914, 3; 'Two girls in one', *Midlothian Advertiser*, 5 June 1914, 2.

33. 'Psychological obscurities', *Liverpool Daily Post*, 29 May 1914, 6.

34. 'Governess's dual personality', *Times*, 29 May 1914, 4; 'Hove libel charged dismissed', *Sussex Agricultural Express*, 4 June 1914, 8.

35. 'The victim of a girls' mania', *Birmingham Daily Post*, 29 May 1914, 5; 'Dual personality', *Sheffield Evening Telegraph*, 28 May 1914, 5.

36. London Metropolitan Archive (LMA), H64/B/15/002, St Luke's Hospital, Patients' Records: Voluntary Boarders Case Books (indexed), September 1913–October 1916, case 120.

37. LMA, H64/B/16/001, St Luke's Hospital, Patients Records (signed), August 1846–January 1916, entry for 15 September 1914.

38. LMA, H64/B/15/002, case 120. C. N. French, *The Story of St Luke's Hospital* (London, 1951), 13.

39. LMA, H64/B/15/002, case 120; French, *The Story of St Luke's Hospital*, 143.

40. Stephen Hobhouse and A. Fenner Brockway, *English Prisons To-Day* (London, 1922), 5, 12.

41. LMA, H64/B/15/002, case 120.

42. LMA, H64/B/15/002, case 120.

43. LMA, H64/B/06/014, St Luke's Hospital, Patients' Records: New Case Book January 1912–September 1915, Register number 64.

44. LMA, H64/B/15/002, case 120; 'Retired colonel charged with criminal libel', *Manchester Guardian*, 21 May 1914, 6; General Register Office, Probate Registry, Will of Theobald O'Brien, late of 55 Wilton Street, 13 May 1891, Date of Death: 31/03/1891.

45. LMA, H64/B/05/005, St Luke's Hospital, Patients' Records: Register of Discharged and Transfers 1907–1917, 1915, St Luke's Hospital, Patients' Records: Register of Discharged and Transfers 1907–1917, 1915; LMA, H64/B/11/001, St Luke's Hospital, Patients' Records: Medical Register 1907–1916, 1915; https://www.genuki.org.uk/big/eng/DEV/Asylum/Surnames-O (accessed 12/09/2021).

46. 'Dual personality', *The Scotsman*, 27 June 1929, 2; 'A woman's dual personality', *Portsmouth Evening News*, 12 June 1929, 9.

47. Alfred Bucknill, *The Nature of Evidence* (London, 1953), 37–8.

48. 'Alleged threat to kill', *Dorking & Leatherhead Advertiser*, 5 October 1912, 2; 'Threatening letter case', *Dorking & Leatherhead Advertiser*, 27 February 1915, 7.

49. 'Invisible ink clue', *Sheffield Independent*, 5 January 1915, 5; Census of England, Wales & Scotland, 1911, Surrey, Reigate Registration District, 50 St Johns Road, Earlswood, Redhill, TNA, RG 14/3226, Schedule number 171, RG78PN121.

50. Bucknill, *Nature of Evidence*, 38, 48.

51. Detail from Bucknill, *Nature of Evidence*, 37–47.

52. 'Threatening letters', *Surrey Mirror*, 14 August 1914, 5.

53. 'Sending threatening letters', *Dorking & Leatherhead Advertiser*, 19 October 1912, 6.

54. 'Threats to kill', *Dorking & Leatherhead Advertiser*, 24 May 1913, 6; 'Sending threatening letters', *Dorking & Leatherhead Advertiser*, 19 October 1912, 6.

55. 'Alleged threatening letters', *Dorking & Leatherhead Advertiser*, 4 July 1914, p.2.

56. 'Alleged threat to kill', *Dorking & Leatherhead Advertiser*, 5 October 1912, 2; 'One-eyed woman's anonymous letters', *West Sussex Gazette*, 3 October 1912, 12.

57. 'Threats to kill', *Dorking & Leatherhead Advertiser*, 24 May 1913, 6.

58. 'Sending threatening letters', *Dorking & Leatherhead Advertiser*, 19 October 1912, 6.

59. 'Alleged threat to kill', *Dorking & Leatherhead Advertiser*, 5 October 1912, 2; 'Sending threatening letters', *Dorking & Leatherhead Advertiser*, 19 October 1912, 6; Census of England, Wales & Scotland, 1911, Surrey, Reigate Registration District, 56 St Johns Road, Earlswood, Redhill, TNA, RG 14/3226, Schedule number 174, RG78PN121.

60. 'Woman who terrorised another by cruel conduct', *Daily Herald*, 18 October 1912, 9; 'Sending threatening letters', *Dorking & Leatherhead Advertiser*, 19 October 1912, 6.

61. 'Alleged threatening letters', *Dorking & Leatherhead Advertiser*, 4 July 1914, 2; 'Alleged threats to murder', *Daily Citizen*, 23 April 1913, 5; 'Mrs Johnson committed for trial', *Surrey Mirror*, 9 May 1913, 2.

62. 'Threats to kill', *Dorking & Leatherhead Advertiser*, 24 May 1913, 6.

63. 'Threatening letter case', *Surrey Mirror*, 4 July 1913, 5; TNA, HO140/308, 'County of Surrey. A Calendar of Prisoners tried at the Adjourned Session of the Peace holden at Kingston-upon-Thames, 20 May 1913', Case 10; also the register for 1 July 1913, case 1; Bucknill, *Nature of Evidence*, 44.

64. Marguerite A. Sidley, 'A guest of his majesty: a month in Holloway Gaol', www.edithjessiethompson.co.uk (accessed 10/05/2020); TNA, MEPO 6/26, Records of the Metropolitan Police, Habitual Criminals Register 1914, piece 26, page 129.

65. Simon Webb, *The Suffragette Bombers* (Barnsley, 2014), 132.

66. 'Charlwood', *Surrey Mirror*, 9 January 1914, 7.

67. 'Mr & Mrs Johnson charged', *Surrey Mirror*, 26 June 1914, 2; 'Alleged threatening letters', *Dorking & Leatherhead Advertiser*, 4 July 1914, 2.

68. 'Alleged threatening letters', *Dorking & Leatherhead Advertiser*, 4 July 1914, 2.

69. 'Threatening letters', *Dorking & Leatherhead Advertiser*, 15 August 1914, 4.

70. 'Alleged threatening letters', *Dorking & Leatherhead Advertiser*, 4 July 1914, 2.

71. 'Alleged threat to kill', *Dorking & Leatherhead Advertiser*, 5 October 1912, 2.

72. 'Threatening letters', *Surrey Mirror*, 14 August 1914, 5; Bucknill, *Nature of Evidence*, 45.

73. 'Wrongful convictions', *Nottingham Evening Post*, 7 April 1915, 6.

74. '£500 for wrongful conviction', *Daily Express*, 7 April 1915, 3.

75. 'Serious charge', *Surrey Mirror*, 15 December 1914, 2; Serious charges', *Surrey Mirror*, 25 December 1914, 3.

76. 'Serious charges', *Surrey Mirror*, 8 January 1915, 6; 'Invisible ink trap', *Daily Express*, 5 January 1915, 6.

77. 'Threatening letter case', *Dorking & Leatherhead Advertiser*, 27 February 1915, 7; 'Threatening letters by a woman', *The Scotsman*, 25 February 1915, 5.

78. Census of England, Wales & Scotland, 1891, Surrey, Reigate Registration District, High Street, Reigate, TNA, RG 12/578, fo. 73, page 4, schedule number 18 (née Lambert).

79. 'Sending threatening letters', *Dorking & Leatherhead Advertiser*, 19 October 1912, 6.

80. 'Threats to kill', *Dorking & Leatherhead Advertiser*, 24 May 1913, 6.

81. 'Alleged threatening letters', *Dorking & Leatherhead Advertiser*, 4 July 1914, 2; 'Threatening letters', *Dorking & Leatherhead Advertiser*, 15 August 1915, 4.

82. 'Alleged threatening letters', *Dorking & Leatherhead Advertiser*, 4 July 1914, 2.

83. TNA, HO144/2452, 'Notes of Proceedings, Rex v Rose Emma Gooding, High Court of Justice, King's Bench Division, 25 July 1921', fo. 12.

84. For a more detailed narrative see Christopher Hilliard, *The Littlehampton Libels* (Oxford, 2017).

85. Hilliard, *Littlehampton Libels*, 6–10.

86. TNA, HO144/2452, 'Notes of Proceedings, Rex v Rose Emma Gooding, High Court of Justice, King's Bench Division, 25 July 1921', fo. 8; Hilliard, *Littlehampton Libels*, 68.

87. Cited in Hilliard, *Littlehampton Libels*, 87.

88. TNA, HO144/2452, 'Notes of Proceedings, Rex v Rose Emma Gooding, High Court of Justice, King's Bench Division, 25 July 1921', fos 7–8.

89. Hobhouse and Fenner Brockway, *English Prisons To-Day*, 98.

90. TNA, HO144/2452, 416617/3, Note by the Chief Warder Charles Ralph, 15 June 1921; Hobhouse and Fenner Brockway, *English Prisons To-Day*, 211.

91. TNA, HO144/2452, 'Notes of Proceedings, Rex v Rose Emma Gooding, High Court of Justice, King's Bench Division, 25 July 1921', fo. 12. For more on this, see Hilliard, *Littlehampton Libels*, 10–11.

92. Cited in Hilliard, *Littlehampton Libels*, 22.

93. *The Dragon*, [magazine for the Buffs], number 274, September 1922, 314 ('6280121 Pte B. Boxell to complete 12 years').

94. TNA, HO144/2452, 'Notes of Proceedings, Rex v Rose Emma Gooding, High Court of Justice, King's Bench Division, 25 July 1921', fo. 15; TNA, HO144/2452, 416617/6, minutes by Ernley Blackwell, 14 June 1921.

95. 'Threatening letter case', *Dorking & Leatherhead Advertiser*, 27 February 1915, 7; 'Threatening letters by a woman', *The Scotsman*, 25 February 1915, 5.

96. 'Libellous notes to tradesmen', *Globe*, 16 October 1920, 5; 'Strange letters', *Kington Times*, 23 October 1920, 7; 'Anonymous letters', *Lancashire Evening Post*, 20 November 1920, 2.

97. 'Solicitor's wife', *Pall Mall Gazette*, 19 November 1920, 2.

98. '£250 verdict in poison pen case', *Western Daily Press*, 23 July 1924, 3; Electoral Registers for St Nicholas, Brighton, 1922–23.

99. TNA, HO 144/2452, 416617/8, Home Office Minutes [in Sir Ernley Blackwell's hand], 28 July 1921; also 'Compensation in Criminal Case', 416617/10, Letter to Sir Ernley Blackwell from Guy Stephenson, Assistant Director of Public Prosecutions, 4 August 1921.

100. TNA, HO 144/2452, 416617/9, letter from Wannop & Falconer, solicitors, 3 August 1921, to the Home Secretary; TNA, HO 144/2452, 416617/8, Home Office minutes in Ernley Blackwell's hand, 'notice to press issued', 26 July 1921; see also '£250 award for Mrs Gooding', *Daily Mirror*, 9 August 1921, 2.

101. TNA, HO 144/2452, 416617/17, Letter from Sir William Horwood, Metropolitan Commissioner of Police to the Under Secretary of State in the Home Office, 10 October 1922.

102. 'Psychological obscurities', *Liverpool Daily Post*, 29 May 1914, 6.

103. Hilliard, *Littlehampton Libels*, chapter 9.

104. 'Arundel County Bench', *West Sussex Gazette*, 26 April 1934, 3.

105. 1939 Register, TNA, RG101/2637G/005/33 ENNP.

106. Marie Lucinda 'Molly' Lee, gravestone, Hawking Cemetery, Kent.

107. TNA, HO144/2452, 416617/18, Anonymous letter sent to the Home Office, minutes, 11 October 1922.

108. TNA, HO144/2452, 416617/22, Anonymous letter sent to the Home Office on the evening of 6 September 1923, envelope stamped 11 September 192, postmark London E.C.

109. 'Reigate & Redhill', *Surrey Mirror*, 4 June 1937, 9.

110. LMA, H64/B/15/002, case 120; LMA, H64/B/06/014, St Luke's Hospital, Patients' Records: New Case Book, January 1912–September 1915.

111. Hilliard, *Littlehampton Libels*, 21.

112. Hilliard, *Littlehampton Libels*, 34.

113. Maud Pember Reeves, *Round About a Pound a Week* (first published 1913. London, 1979), 174. See also 175, 195.

114. 'Serious charge at Clacton', *Essex Newsman*, 26 December 1903, 3; 'Ex-curate gets twelve months', *Diss Express*, 5 February 1904, 8; 'Charge against a parson', *Barking, East Ham & Ilford Advertiser*, 6 February 1904, 3.

115. TNA, HO 144/2452, 416617/5, Letter from William Gooding to the Home Office, 9 June 1921.

116. Ruth M. Brown, *Littlehampton School Logbook 1871–1911*, Sussex Record Society 95 (Lewes, 2016), 163, 179. Later, Steve wore thick glasses, so they must have relented. In 1902 Edith's younger brother John got into some bother involving a box of gold leaf he claimed to have been given by his father, who was a decorator, Brown, *Littlehampton School Logbook 1871–1911*, 296. Hilliard, *Littlehampton Libels*, 116, 140.

117. Hilliard, *Littlehampton Libels*, 21–2; TNA, HO 144/2452, 416617/5, Letter from William Gooding to the Home Office, 9 June 1921.

118. 'A distressing case at Brixton', *South London Press*, 5 October 1889, 10. Mary married Adam in 1883, after the birth of six of their nine children [General Register Office, England & Wales Marriages 1837–2005, England, Volume 1D, Marriage quarter 1, 1883, page 647].

119. 'Threatening letters', *Dorking & Leatherhead Advertiser*, 15 August 1914, 4; 'Reigate & Redhill', *Surrey Mirror*, 4 June 1937, 9.

120. 'Threats to kill', *Dorking & Leatherhead Advertiser*, 24 May 1913, 6.

121. 'Threats to kill', *Dorking & Leatherhead Advertiser*, 24 May 1913, 6.

122. 'Alleged threatening letters', *Dorking & Leatherhead Advertiser*, 4 July 1914, 2.

123. Harrison, *Suspect Documents*, 481.

124. Hilliard, *Littlehampton Libels*, 25, 33–4, 111; TNA, HO144/2452, 'Notes of Proceedings, Rex v Rose Emma Gooding, High Court of Justice, King's Bench Division, 25 July 1921', fo. 14.

125. Hilliard, *Littlehampton Libels*, 133.

126. Albert Taylor, *The Sanitary Inspector's Handbook*, 4th edn (London, 1905), 50; Albert Taylor, *The Sanitary Inspector's Handbook* (London, 1893), 18. See also 'Office and duties of a sanitary inspector', *Journal of the Royal Sanitary Institute* 29 (1909), 752; Edward F. Willoughby, *The Health Officer's Pocket-Book* (London, 1902), 115.

127. Frank Charles Stockman, *A Practical Guide for Sanitary Inspectors* (London, 1915), 23.

128. Henry Lemmoin-Cannon, *The Sanitary Inspector's Guide* (London, 1902), 111–12; Willoughby, *The Health Officer's Pocket-Book*, 115.

129. For an internal response to a letter sent in 1911 to the sanitary inspector of Northcote in Australia, see Emily Cockayne, 'Social Distancing before Social Distancing', https://www.rummage.work/blog/disgusted, 21 March 2020; Heston and Isleworth Urban District Council, *1910 Annual Report of the Medical Officer of Health for Heston and Isleworth* [1911]; Heston and Isleworth Urban District Council, *1914 Annual Report of the Medical Officer of Health for Heston and Isleworth* [1915], 24; Heston and Isleworth Urban District Council, *1915 Annual Report of the Medical Officer of Health for Heston and Isleworth* [1916], 4.

130. Heston and Isleworth Urban District Council, *1915 Annual Report of the Medical Officer of Health for Heston and Isleworth* [1916], 16. See also Heston and Isleworth Urban District Council, *1914 Annual Report of the Medical Officer of Health for Heston and Isleworth* [1915], 19.

131. When Frank Morgan, a carter living at number 12, was found guilty of working a lame horse in 1914, records show that he kept it on the wasteland, 'Unfit', *West London Observer*, 27 March 1914, 12.

132. Census of England, Wales & Scotland, 1911, Middlesex, Brentford Registration District, 8 Campo Road, TNA, RG 14/6828, schedule number 309, RG78PN340;—Electoral Register, British Library, SPR. Mic.P.432/BL.M.20, 397, 1912—Brentford. Number 14 was not dramatically more overcrowded than many others in the area.

133. *Municipal Engineering & Sanitary Record*, vol. 66 (1920), 471; *Surveyor and Municipal and County Engineer*, 1920, 177.

134. Hilliard, *Littlehampton Libels*, 64, 153.

135. Hilliard, *Littlehampton Libels*, 46, 54.

CHAPTER 6

1. Charles Chabot and Edward Twisleton, *The Handwriting of Junius Professionally Investigated* (London, 1871).

2. Abraham Hayward, *A Review of the Work Entitled The Handwriting of Junius . . .* (Cambridge, 1874), 18.

3. Arthur Conan Doyle, *The Sign of Four* (London, 1917), 24.

4. Rosa Baughan, *Character Indicated by Handwriting* (London, 1880), 12.

5. Arthur Conan Doyle, *The Hound of the Baskervilles* (London, 1902), 65–6.

6. Chabot and Twisleton, *Handwriting of Junius*, lxix.

7. C. Ainsworth Mitchell, *A Scientist in the Criminal Courts* (London, 1945), 74.

8. *Hansard*, 20 February 1809, https://hansard.parliament.uk/Commons/1809-02-20/debates/465c5c1f-4a92-4754-a71f-c938feebafa9/ItWasMovedAndSecondedThatTheEvidenceToHand-WritingAboutToBeProducedBeNotReceivedWhichBeingPutPassedInTheNegativeWithoutADivision (accessed 14/01/2023).

9. 'Some infamous anonymous letters', *Staffordshire Advertiser*, 9 March 1805, 3.

10. 'Death of Mr Chabot', *Dundee Courier*, 20 October 1882, 5.

11. Alexander Wood Renton, 'Phillips v. Martin', *The Law Journal* 2 (1890), 207.

12. Anonymous, 'Experts in handwriting', *Cornhill Magazine* 4:20 (1885), 148–62, at 150–1.

13. Harry How, 'An Expert in Handwriting', *The Strand* 8 (September 1894), 293–300, at 293. Francis Compton Price was one of the last handwriting experts to also be a lithographer, although he was initially described as an 'artist' or a 'water-colour artist' in census returns of 1881 and 1891, a handwriting expert and record agent in 1901, and then a lithographer in 1911, Census of England, Wales & Scotland, 1881, London, Middlesex, St Pancras Registration District, 86 Leighton Road, TNA, RG 11/223, fo. 84, page 13, schedule number 746; Census of England, Wales & Scotland, 1891, London, Middlesex, St Pancras Registration District, Euston Road, TNA, RG 12/122, fo. 67, page 37, schedule number 10; Census of England, Wales & Scotland, 1901, Middlesex, Edmonton, Registration District, 50, Haringey Road, Hornsey, TNA, RG 13/1241, fo. 109, page 10, schedule number 70; Census of England, Wales & Scotland, 1911, London, Middlesex, Islington Registration District, 71 Loraine Mansions, Widdenham Road, Holloway, TNA, RG 14/858, schedule number 196, RG78PN30.

14. Anonymous, 'Experts in handwriting', 150–4.

15. Census of England, Wales & Scotland, 1851, London, Middlesex, St Martin in the Fields Registration District, Adelaide Street, TNA, HO 107/1481, fo. 263, page 32, schedule number 136; Census of England, Wales & Scotland, 1881, London, Middlesex, Holborn Registration District, 7, Theobalds Road, TNA, RG 11/339, fo. 70, page 49, schedule number 563; Census of England, Wales & Scotland, 1891, London, Middlesex, Islington Registration District, Shaftesbury Road, TNA, RG 12/146, fo. 116, page 4, schedule number 18.

16. 'Death of Mr Frederick Netherclift', *Glasgow Evening Post*, 29 March 1892, 5. For Netherclift's involvement in an anonymous-letter case see 'Farringdon Petty Sessions', *Wilts and Gloucester Standard*, 22 August 1885, 5.

17. 'From clubland', *Cheltenham Looker-on*, 2 April 1892, 321.

18. How, 'An Expert in Handwriting', 293.

19. Census of England, Wales & Scotland, 1891, London, Middlesex, Islington Registration District, Hugs Road, TNA, RG 12/144, fo. 65, page 18, schedule number 121; St Pancras Registration District, Patshull Road, TNA, RG 12/139, fo. 117, page 46, schedule number 351.

20. How, 'An Expert in Handwriting', 293, 299.

21. 'Sending threatening letters', *Nottingham Evening Post*, 17 October 1895, 2.

22. 'Extraordinary libel case at Southam', *Leamington Spa Courier*, 13 October 1894, 7.

23. 'Extraordinary libel case from Southam', *Leamington Spa Courier*, 15 December 1894, 9.

24. 'Petty Sessions, Monday', *Rugby Advertiser*, 5 January 1895, 6; 'The Birdingbury Libel Case', *Rugby Advertiser*, 9 March 1895, 5.

25. Census of England, Wales & Scotland, 1881, London, Middlesex, Fulham Registration District, 58, The Grove, Hammersmith, TNA, 11/55, fo. 92, page 4, schedule number 759; Census of England, Wales & Scotland, 1891, London, Middlesex, Fulham Registration District, Comeragh Road, TNA, RG 12/46, fo. 148, page 61, schedule number 374; Census of England, Wales & Scotland, 1901, London, Middlesex, Brentford Registration District, 16 Montpelier Road, Twickenham, TNA, RG 13/1187, fo. 141, page 19, schedule number 98; Census of England, Wales & Scotland, 1911, London, Middlesex, Brentford Registration District, 14 Montpelier Road, Twickenham, TNA, RG 14/6843, schedule number 38, RG78PN341.

26. Henry Dixon: Census of England, Wales & Scotland, 1851, Lancashire, Chorlton Registration District, Dearden Street, Hulme, TNA, HO 107/2221, fo. 515, page 25, schedule number 101; Census of England, Wales & Scotland, 1861, Lancashire, Chorlton Registration District, 14, Church Street, Hulme, TNA, RG 09/2895, fo. 67, page 27, schedule number 166; Census of England, Wales & Scotland, 1871, Lancashire, Chorlton Registration District, Raglan Street, Hulme, TNA, RG 10/4004, fol. 89, page 18, schedule number 106; Census of England, Wales & Scotland, 1881, Lancashire, Chorlton Registration District, 4, Granville Street, Moss Side, TNA, RG 11/3939, fo. 86, page 28, schedule number 747; Census of England, Wales & Scotland, 1891, Lancashire, Chorlton Registration District, Hulton Street, Moss Side, TNA, RG 12/3199, fo.133, page 16, schedule number 106. Others also came through law stationery; see, for examples, Robert Honey, b. 1854, 1939 Register, TNA, RG101/3584F/013/21 Letter Code: KKBS; George Harvey Manton was described as a law stationer in 1851. By 1891, then aged 65 years, Manton was down in the census as 'Expert in Handwriting'. However, in reports of a court case in 1877 (when someone had sent anonymous letters to a judge, threatening murder) Manton was described as 'an expert of 20 years experience', despite being listed in the census as a plan draughtsman in 1861, and then as working in writing 'and illuminating' in 1871, Census of England, Wales & Scotland, 1851, London, Middlesex, Shoreditch Registration District, Briston Street, Shoreditch, TNA, HO 107/1535, fo. 73, page 39, schedule number 44; Census of England, Wales & Scotland, 1861, Lancashire, Manchester Registration District, 56, Fleet Street, TNA, RG 09/2942, fo. 75, page 11, schedule number 57; Census of England, Wales & Scotland,

1871, Lancashire, West Derby Registration District, Canton Street, Everton, TNA, RG 10/3821, fo. 16, page 23, schedule number 123; Census of England, Wales & Scotland, 1891, Lancashire, West Derby Registration District, Rock Street, TNA, RG 12/3000, fo. 87, page 19, schedule number 103. 'Threat to murder Mr Justice Hawkins', *Manchester Times*, 11 August 1811, 6.

27. 'Extraordinary libel on a doctor', *Manchester Evening News*, 7 March 1890, 2; details for Fred Smart see Census of England, Wales & Scotland, 1901, Cheshire, Bucklow Registration District, Craven Lodge, Derbyshire Road, Sale, TNA, RG 13/3325, fo. 157, page 29, schedule number 218; Census of England, Wales & Scotland, 1911, Cheshire, Bucklow Registration District, Craven Lodge Derbyshire Road Sale, TNA, RG 14/21573, schedule number 71, RG78PN1284.

28. 'The village libel case', *Sheffield Daily Telegraph*, 25 October 1911, 9; 'Cheshire libel case', *Daily Telegraph & Courier*, 4 November 1911, 10.

29. Albert S. Osborn, *Photography and Questioned Documents* (Rochester, NY, 1907), 7–8.

30. Albert S. Osborn, *Questioned Documents* (Rochester, NY, 1910), 123, 307. See also Mitchell, *A Scientist in the Criminal Courts*, 74.

31. Chabot and Twisleton, *Handwriting of Junius*, lxi.

32. Mitchell. *A Scientist in the Criminal Courts*, 75.

33. Marcel B. Matley, 'Forensic Handwriting Identification: Is It Legally A Science[?]. A review of court cases which hold handwriting examination to be a science', *International Journal of Forensic Document Examiners* 3:2 (1997), 105–13, at 106; Christopher M. Milroy, 'A Brief History of the Expert Witness', *Academic Forensic Pathology* 7:4 (December 2017), 516–26, at 518–19.

34. Henry Roscoe, ed., 'Folkes Bart v. Chadd and Others', *Reports of Cases Argued and Determined in The Court of the King's Bench in the Twenty-Second, Twenty-Third, Twenty-Fourth, and Twenty-Fifth Years of the Reign of George III* (4 vols) (London, 1813–1831), vol. 3, 157–61.

35. Tal Golan, *Laws of Men and Laws of Nature* (Cambridge, MA, 2004), 44.

36. Roscoe, ed., *Reports*, vol. 3: 160–1.

37. Thomas Sergeant and John C. Lowber (eds), *Reports of Cases Argued and Determined in the English Courts of Common Law . . . Vol. VII* (Philadelphia, PA, 1869), 185–6.

38. Isaac Espinasse, *Reports of Cases Argued and Ruled at Nisi Prius in the King's Bench and Common Pleas . . . 1799–1801* (4 vols) (London, 1808), vol. 3, 119–21.

39. Richard Burn and John King, *The Justice of the Peace, and Parish Officer* (5 vols) (London, 1814), vol. 1, 831.

40. Golan, *Laws of Men*, passim.

41. Alexander M. Burrill, *A treatise on the nature, principles and rules of circumstantial evidence: especially that of the presumptive kind, in criminal cases* (New York, NY, 1856), 662–3.

42. D. Michael Risinger, Mark Denbeaux, and Michael J. Saks, 'Exorcism of Ignorance as a Proxy for Rational Knowledge: The Lessons of Handwriting "Expertise"', *University of Pennsylvania Law Review* 137:3 (1989), 731–92, at 739. See also Ludovic Kennedy, *The Airman and the Carpenter* (London, 1985), 277.

43. 'The anonymous letter fiend', *London Journal*, 25 February 1911, 420.

44. Osborn, *Questioned Documents*, 13, 254, 307, 311, 314.

45. Osborn, *Questioned Documents*, 254.

46. See Rosemary Sassoon, *Handwriting of the Twentieth Century* (London, 1999), 27–53.

47. Osborn, *Questioned Documents*, 318.

48. TNA, HO144/2452, 'Notes of Proceedings, Rex v Rose Emma Gooding, High Court of Justice, King's Bench Division, 25 July 1921', fo. 11.

49. TNA, HO144/2452, includes a letter from Rose to an employer.

50. TNA, HO144/2452, 'Notes of Proceedings, Rex v Rose Emma Gooding, High Court of Justice, King's Bench Division, 25 July 1921', fos 4–5.

51. 'Libel letters', *Daily Mail*, 16 October 1922, 9.

52. TNA, HO144/2452, 'Notes of Proceedings, 25 July 1921', fo. 17.

53. TNA, HO144/2452, copy of letter to Leonard Kershaw by Ernley Blackwell, 6 June 1921.

54. TNA, HO144/2452, 416617/4, copy of the petition from Rose Gooding to the Home Office, sent from HM Prison Portsmouth, 6 June 1921.

55. TNA, HO144/2452, 416617/23, Petition of Edith Swan from Portsmouth Prison, 17 December 1923.

56. 'The Birkbeck Bank', *Observer*, 13 November 1910, 13; 'Birkbeck Bank run', *Sevenoaks Chronicle & Kentish Advertiser*, 18 November 1910, 6; 'The November run', *London Daily News*, 9 June 1911, 1; 'Run on the Birkbeck Bank', *Times*, 12 November 1910, 12.

57. 'The Birkbeck Bank run', *London Daily News*, 17 November 1910, 9.

58. Harrison, *Suspect Documents*, 242–9.

59. 'The November run', *London Daily News*, 9 June 1911, 1; 'Typewriting clues', *Nottingham Evening Post*, 22 November 1910, 3; 'Run on the Birkbeck Bank', *Evesham Standard & West Midland Observer*, 19 November 1910, 7; 'Birkbeck Bank and anonymous letter', *Times*, 22 November 1910, 14; 'Birkbeck Bank', *Daily Mail*, 18 November 1910, 5.

60. See also [Frederick Arnold] 'Anonymous letters', *London Society*, 20:300 (December 1886), 521–31, at 523.

61. 'Secret-office at the General Post-Office', *Illustrated London News*, 29 June 1844, 1; 'A dishonest postman', *Surrey Comet*, 7 October 1899, 3.

62. Christopher Browne, *Getting the Message. The Story of the British Post Office* (Stroud, 1993), 151–2, 155–6.

63. 'Defendant's denials', *Hartlepool Northern Daily Mail*, 21 August 1923, 6; 'Girl and eight offensive cards', *Leeds Mercury*, 22 August 1923, 11.

64. 'Trapped by mirror', *News of the World*, 22 July 1923.

65. 'Littlehampton letter case', *Southern Weekly News*, 18 August 1923. See Hilliard, *Littlehampton Libels*, 152–3.

66. 'Coleford sensation', *Gloucester Citizen*, 13 December 1923, 6; 'Indecent postcards', *Hull Daily Mail*, 14 December 1923, 12; 'Another woman charged', *Dundee Evening Telegraph*, 14 December 1923, 1; 'Anonymous postcards', *Nottingham Evening Post*, 21 December 1923, 5; 'The Coleford sensation', *Gloucester Citizen*, 28 January 1924, 6; 'Anonymous postcards case', *Scotsman*, 29 January 1924, 4.

67. David Vincent, 'The Origins of Public Secrecy in Britain', *Transactions of the Royal Historical Society* 1 (1991), 229–48, at 229–30.

68. 'Strange case', *Express and Echo*, 21 April 1910, 1; 'Married woman is charged', *Dundee Evening Telegraph*, 28 April 1910, 3; 'The case against a Sutton lady', *Globe*, 28 April 1910, 9.

69. 'Disgusting letters', *Nottingham Journal*, 29 April 1910, 6; 'Secret stamps', *Croydon Chronicle and East Surrey Advertiser*, 30 April 1910, 9; 'Marked stamps', *Croydon Chronicle and East Surrey Advertiser*, 30 July 1910, 13; 'Sutton libel charge', *Croydon Advertiser and East Surrey Reporter*, 30 July 1910, 7; 'Sutton libel charge', *Croydon Guardian and Surrey County Gazette*, 6 August 1910, 4.

70. 'Invisible ink used in police trap', *Manchester Courier and Lancashire General Advertiser*, 22 December 1914, 6; 'Serious charges', *Surrey Mirror*, 25 December 1914, 3.

71. 'Invisible ink used in police trap', *Manchester Courier and Lancashire General Advertiser*, 22 December 1914, 6; 'Serious charges', *Surrey Mirror*, 25 December 1914, 3. See also Alfred Bucknill, *The Nature of Evidence* (London, 1953), 46. The Woodman family lived at number 50 and the Whitmores at number 77; it is not clear how these numbering errors crept in.

72. 'Threatening letter case', *Dorking & Leatherhead Advertiser*, 27 February 1915, 7.

73. 'Sutton libel charge', *Croydon Advertiser & East Surrey Reporter*, 30 July 1910, 7.

74. 'Policewoman hides in a shed', *Daily Mirror*, 28 October 1921, 3; 'Women's great triumph', *Worthing Herald*, 6 May 1922, 6; 'Back—but not back on the beat', *Worthing Herald*, 23 August 1957, 11.

75. 'Disgusting letters', *Nottingham Journal*, 29 April 1910, 6; 'Secret stamps', *Croydon Chronicle and East Surrey Advertiser*, 30 April 1910, 9; 'Marked stamps', *Croydon Chronicle and East Surrey Advertiser*, 30 July 1910, 13; 'Sutton libel charge', *Croydon Advertiser and East Surrey Reporter*, 30 July 1910, 7; 'Sutton libel charge', *Croydon Guardian and Surrey County Gazette*, 6 August 1910, 4.

76. TNA, HO144/2452, 'Notes of Proceedings, 25 July 1921', fos 12–13.

77. TNA, HO144/2452, Copy of letter from Ernley Blackwell to Leonard Kershaw, 10 June 1921; Copy of letter from Ernley Blackwell to Archibald Bodkin, 13 June 1921; Copy of letter from Archibald Bodkin to Ernley Blackwell, 13 June 1921; L. S. Brass Telegram to Arthur Shelley, Solicitor,

Littlehampton [n.d.]; also letter to the Clerk of Assize for the South Eastern Circuit, 2 June 1921.

78. 'Alleged threat to kill', *Dorking & Leatherhead Advertiser,* 5 October 1912, 2; 'Sending threatening letters', *Dorking & Leatherhead Advertiser*, 19 October 1912, 6.

79. 'Threats to kill', *Dorking & Leatherhead Advertiser*, 24 May 1913, 6.

80. C. H. Gardiner, *Soldiers and Civil War* (London, 1914), 53–4, 61. Colonel Gardiner also claimed that the police in Hove in 1914 had laid a trap using a decoy letter, which created further distraction and obfuscation.

81. Ashton-Wolfe, 'The scientific side of the detection of crime. No XII—anonymous letters and graphomania', 416.

82. 'Anonymous letters', *Western Gazette*, 1 February 1924, 12; 'Unknown hand', *Daily Mirror*, 7 June 1924, 2; 'Poison pen case retrial', *Dundee Courier*, 7 June 1924, 5; 'Poison pen charges', *Cheltenham Chronicle*, 25 October 1924, 2; 'Poison pen case', *Western Gazette*, 31 October 1924, 11.

83. See, for example, Matt Houlbrook, *Prince of Tricksters: The Incredible True Story of Netley Lucas, Gentleman Crook* (Chicago, IL, 2016), esp. 27.

84. Osborn, *Questioned Documents*, 303.

85. Saudek, *Anonymous Letters*, 84

86. TNA, HO144/2452, 'Notes of Proceedings, 25 July 1921', fo. 16.

87. TNA, HO144/2452, 416617/6, Copy of letter from Superintendent F. J. Peel at Arundel, to Chief Constable A.S. Williams, Horsham Police Station, 8 June 1921.

88. Gardiner, *Soldiers and Civil War*, 61, 68, 71–2.

89. Hilliard, *Littlehampton Libels*, 1. See Mary S. Hartman, 'Crime and the Respectable Woman: Toward a Pattern of Middle-Class Female Criminality in Nineteenth-Century France and England', *Feminist Studies* 2:1 (1974), 38–56.

90. Alfred Bucknill, *The Nature of Evidence* (London, 1953), 42.

91. TNA, MEPO 6/26, Habitual Criminals Register 1914, page 129.

92. Bucknill, *The Nature of Evidence*, 57; Hilliard, *Littlehampton Libels*, 159. See Shamena Anwar, Patrick Bayer, and Randi Hjalmarsson, 'A Jury of *Her* Peers: The Impact of the First Female Jurors on Criminal Convictions', *The Economic Journal* 129:618 (2019), 603–50.

93. Bucknill, *The Nature of Evidence*, 57.

94. Hilliard, *Littlehampton Libels*, 159–60.

95. Gordon Weaver, *Conan Doyle and the Parson's Son* (Cambridge, 2006), 29.

96. Weaver, *Conan Doyle and the Parson's Son*, 30.

97. Weaver, *Conan Doyle and the Parson's Son*, 211; Roger Oldfield, *Outrage: The Edalji Five and the Shadow of Sherlock Holmes* (Cambridge, 2010), 23, 92–3.

98. Weaver, *Conan Doyle and the Parson's Son*, 37. Conan Doyle thought that the 1892–95 letters were the work of various hands, probably two adults and a child. See Oldfield, *Outrage*, 101, 109, 112.

99. Weaver, *Conan Doyle and the Parson's Son*, 56, 65.

100. 'A warning to tradesmen', *Morning Post*, 14 December 1892, 6.

101. 'The Edalji anonymous letters', *Truth*, 16 February 1905, 410–14, at 411.

102. 'The Edalji anonymous letters', *Truth*, 16 February 1905, 410–14.

103. 'Public apology', *Lichfield Mercury*, 10 March 1893, 8.

104. 'Miscellaneous', *Stamford Mercury*, 23 March 1894, 8; see also Oldfield, *Outrage*, 99, 100.

105. 'News', *Cannock Chase Courier*, 21 January 1893, 4; 'A stupid hoax', *London Evening Standard*, 26 July 1895, 6.

106. Weaver, *Conan Doyle and the Parson's Son*, 71.

107. See Oldfield, *Outrage*, 31–50.

108. 'The Edalji anonymous letters', *Truth*, 16 February 1905, 410–14.

109. Weaver, *Conan Doyle and the Parson's Son*, 71–2.

110. Weaver, *Conan Doyle and the Parson's Son*, 67–8.

111. 'Cattle maiming in the midlands', *Gloucester Citizen*, 19 August 1903, 3.

112. Census of England, Wales & Scotland, 1881, London, Middlesex, Holborn Registration District, 33 Great Percy Street, Clerkenwell, TNA, RG 11/349, fo. 52, page 2, schedule number 431; Census of England, Wales & Scotland, 1891, London, Middlesex, City of London Registration District, Holborn Viaduct, St Sepulchre, TNA, RG 12/237, fo. 39, page 18, schedule number 113; Census of England, Wales & Scotland, 1901, Hampshire & Dorset, Christchurch Registration District, The Priory, Priory Road, Bournemouth, TNA, RG 13/1040, fo. 102, page 64, schedule number 76. See also Census of England, Wales & Scotland, 1911, London, Middlesex, Hampstead Registration District, 10 Harley Road, TNA, RG 14/616, schedule number 235, RG78PN22.

113. 'Society slander suit', *Coventry Evening Telegraph*, 9 August 1895, 3.

114. Weaver, *Conan Doyle and the Parson's Son*, 276–781. See also 209–10.

115. 'The Edalji anonymous letters', *Truth*, 16 February 1905, 410–14; Weaver, *Conan Doyle and the Parson's Son*, 120, 208–9, 215.

116. Letter from Arthur Conan Doyle, *Daily Telegraph and Courier*, 11 June 1907, 13.

117. Weaver, *Conan Doyle and the Parson's Son*, 18; Oldfield, *Outrage*, 31–50, 95–6. Weaver, *Conan Doyle and the Parson's Son*, 282–3.

118. 'Arthur Conan Doyle was victim of a police conspiracy', *Guardian*, 18 March 2015, 'Books' section, 4.

CHAPTER 7

1. British Motor Industry Heritage Trust, 'Papers relating to Sir Herbert Austin and the Austin Motor Company', 95/52/14/4, postcard sent from Molesey in Surrey, 11/4/1935.

2. Another anonymous letter sent to Austin is more obscure, written in a haphazard manner, with interjections and words written at right angles to the main text, but appears to be from a disgruntled former employee

demanding 'hush money'. The return address is c/o 131 Steelhouse Lane in Birmingham, which was the location of a firm of solicitors, Philip Baker & Co, see British Motor Industry Heritage Trust, 'Papers relating to Sir Herbert Austin and the Austin Motor Company', 95/52/14/4, letter sent 20/2/1934.

3. 'Austin Motor Co's appeal allowed', *Leamington Spa Courier*, 30 March 1934.

4. *Grace's Guide to British Industrial History*, https://www.gracesguide.co.uk/Edward_Ernest_Lehwess (accessed 20/01/2021).

5. 'Poison pens drive F.A. star from team', *Daily Mirror*, 6 December 1937, 5.

6. 'Soccer star victim of poison pen changes club', *Daily Mirror*, 25 February 1938, 34.

7. 'Dodds goes to Blackpool', *Sheffield Evening Telegraph*, 10 March 1939, 1; 'Revelations by "Jock" Dodds', *Sheffield Evening Telegraph*, 1 April 1939, 9.

8. 'Poison pen at Torquay', *Western Morning News*, 5 November 1937, 6.

9. 'Not all jam being football club president', *Staffordshire Sentinel*, 3 December 1938, 1.

10. Lynn McDonald (ed.), *The Collected Works of Florence Nightingale* (15 vols) (Waterloo, ON, 2001–2012), vol. VIII, 441–2.

11. June Rose, *Marie Stopes and the Sexual Revolution* (London, 1992), 240–1.

12. Wellcome Library PPMCS/A/1/1, Letters to Marie Stopes concerning Married Love: Anonymous and pseudonymous, initialled, with illegible signatures, 1918–c.1950, letter postmarked Finsbury Park, 2 July 1928.

13. 'Dr Marie Stopes wins appeal', *Western Mail*, 21 July 1923, 10. See also 'High Court of Justice', *Times*, 1 March 1923, 5; 'High Court of Justice', *Times*, 16 July 1929, 5.

14. Advert in the *Eastern Morning News*, 23 November 1889, 2; 'Oval and rabbit warren', *Hull Daily Mail*, 6 February 1896, 5; 'International honours for local firm', *Hull Daily Mail*, 5 October 1909, 6.

15. Hull Local Studies Library, L DBHR/2/5/1, Bundle relating to attacks on German shops throughout England, 1914–1918; L DBHR/1/1/13, Anonymous letter to C. Hohenrein, 12 May 1915; and L DBHR/1/1/14, Anonymous warning letter to C. Hohenrein, 13 May 1914.

16. 'War rowdyism in Hull', *Hull Daily Mail*, 5 August 1914, 3; 'Attack on pork butcher's window', *Hull Daily Mail*, 22 October 1914, 4.

17. A. J. L., 'Un-English proceedings', *Hull Daily Mail*, 27 October 1914, 6.

18. 'An unfounded report', *Hull Daily Mail*, 23 November 1914, 1; 'Life in Germany', *Hull Daily Mail*, 12 January 1918, 1.

19. Hull Local Studies Library, L DBHR/1/1/7, Postcard sent 10 November 1914, from 'Fritz' to C. Hohenrein with the message 'Why don't you come and see us? We're not Germans' addressed to 'The English Pork Butcher (I don't think)'.

20. Margrit Sculte Beerbühl, 'Migration, transfer and appropriation: German pork butchers in Britain', *Transfers* 2:3 (Winter 2012), 97–199, at 101–3, 113.

21. 'Anti-German manifestations', *Hull Daily Mail*, 13 May 1915, 2; 'Anti-German demonstrations', *Hull Daily Mail*, 17 May 1915, 3.

22. 'Anti-German demonstrations', *Hull Daily Mail*, 17 May 1915, 3.

23. 'Deaths', *Hull Daily Mail*, 29 September 1902, 2; 'Mail mems', *Hull Daily Mail*, 2 October 1902, 2.

24. 'A curious reflection', *Hull Daily Mail*, 7 June 1915, 3.

25. Notice, *Hull Daily Mail*, 15 June 1915, 2.

26. 'Late advertisements', *Hull Daily Mail*, 4 August 1915, 6.

27. 'From all quarters', *Lancashire Evening Post*, 14 June 1920, 2; 'Pontefract puzzle', *Nottingham Journal*, 14 June 1920, 6; 'Accused man's remarkable letter', *Portsmouth Evening News*, 6 July 1920, 5; 'Quarter Sessions', *Yorkshire Post and Leeds Intelligencer*, 10 July 1920, 13.

28. 'The Pontefract sensation', *Leeds Mercury*, 5 July 1920, 4; 'Quarter Sessions', *Yorkshire Post and Leeds Intelligencer*, 10 July 1920, 13.

29. The total numbers of Sinn Féin letters were regularly totted up by the *Globe*, a Lord Beaverbrook-controlled newspaper. See, for examples, '1,089 outrages', *Globe*, 8 April 1920, 2; 'Bombs again', *Globe*, 19 June 1920, 1.

30. 'Death warrants scare in Glasgow', *Dundee Courier*, 18 November 1920, 5.

31. 'Practical joker at work', *Dundee Courier*, 4 December 1920, 4.

32. 'Sein Fein lunatic', *Aberdeen Press and Journal*, 29 December 1920, 6.

33. 'Standard of life', *Newcastle Journal*, 8 November 1920, 5.

34. 'Miners' agent threatened with death', *Gloucester Citizen*, 28 March 1923, 6; 'Threats to A. J. Cook', *Daily Herald*, 28 March 1923, 1.

35. Fairfield, 'The poison pen', 25.

36. 'Youth fined £10—Obscene letter sent to married woman', *Sheffield Independent*, 10 April 1934, 5.

37. 'Local preacher and girl', *Wells Journal*, 14 December 1923, 7. 'Lay preacher's letter', *Western Daily Press*, 12 December 1923, 6.

38. 'Lay preacher's letter', *Western Daily Press*, 12 December 1923, 6; 'Lay preacher bound over', *Scotsman*, 30 January 1924, 14.

39. Fairfield, 'The poison pen', 26. 'Poison pen letter suicide', *Taunton Courier and Western Advertiser*, 28 October 1931, 8.

40. 'Tragic end to search for Bethesda', *Liverpool Echo*, 2 December 1938, 10; 'Poison pen too late—deacon was already dead', *Daily Mirror*, 3 December 1938, 16.

41. 'Dog beaten to death with hammer', *Hull Daily Mail*, 8 November 1935, 1.

42. Including *Western Gazette, Gloucestershire Echo, Liverpool Echo, Sunderland Daily Echo, Dundee Courier, Yorkshire Evening Post, Daily Herald*.

43. 'Burial stopped for inquest', *Western Mail*, 8 May 1936, 9.

44. 'Tragic widow speaks out', *Daily Herald*, 9 May 1936, 1.

45. 'Dying man feared "Another Waddingham Case"', *Daily Herald*, 9 May 1936, 7.

46. John Rowland, *Poisoner in the Dock: Twelve Studies in Poisoning* (New York, 1960), 137–57.

47. 'Widow fights poison pen', *Daily Mirror*, 18 May 1936, 2.

48. 'Funeral of old man cancelled', *Lincolnshire Echo*, 7 May 1936, 6.

49. 'Tragic widow speaks out', *Daily Herald*, 9 May 1936, 1.

50. 'Sick man's talk of poison', *Dundee Courier*, 9 May 1936, 3.

51. 1939 Register, TNA, RG101/1813D/024/43 Letter Code: DJED; Dorothy was buried in Burnley, alongside Ellen Whittam, Burnley Cemetery, Lancashire, plot NE67.

52. 'A Lincs. poison pen', *Nottingham Evening Post*, 25 June 1934, 8.

53. 'Forged letter mystery', *Daily Herald*, 1 June 1934, 3.

54. 'Allegations of strychnine poisoning', *Boston Guardian*, 3 November 1934, 6; Stephen Wade, *Lincolnshire Murders* (Stroud, 2006), chapter 10; Peter Reynolds and Abby Ruston, 'The incredible story of the unhappy Lincolnshire wife who killed her husband with corned beef', *Grimsby Telegraph*, 5 May 2019, https://www.grimsbytelegraph.co.uk/news/nostalgia/corned-beef-murder-lincolnshire-wife-2827952 (accessed 24/02/2020).

55. 'Allegations of strychnine poisoning', *Boston Guardian*, 3 November 1934, 6.

56. 'Mrs Major executed at Hull Prison', *Boston Guardian*, 22 December 1934, 4.

57. Anette Ballinger, *Dead Women Walking* (Abingdon, 2000), chapter 6; see also p. 352.

58. Oldfield, *Outrage*, 70, 283, 286–7.

59. 'Poison pen activities over 30 years alleged', *Lancashire Evening Post*, 26 October 1934, 7.

60. 'Menacing letters charge', *Times*, 7 November 1934, 13.

61. 'Poison pen charges', *Birmingham Daily Gazette*, 7 November 1934, 4.

62. 'Menacing letters charge', *Times*, 7 November 1934, 13.

63. 'Poison pen activities over 30 years alleged', *Lancashire Evening Post*, 26 October 1934, 7; 'Poison pen charges', *Birmingham Daily Gazette*, 7 November 1934, 4.

64. 'Poison pen charges', *Staffordshire Sentinel*, 30 October 1934, 1; 'Poison pen letters', *Manchester Guardian*, 7 November 1934, 4; 'More poison pen charges', *Dundee Courier*, 31 October 1934, 6.

65. 'Menacing letters charge', *Times*, 7 November 1934, 13.

66. 'Alleged statement to police', *Birmingham Daily Gazette*, 27 October 1934, 5.

67. 'Remarkable poison pen charges', *Hartlepool Daily Mail*, 26 October 1934, 5.

68. 'Poison pen activities over 30 years alleged', *Lancashire Evening Post*, 26 October 1934, 7.

69. 'Poison pen charges', *Birmingham Daily Gazette*, 7 November 1934, 4.

70. Oldfield, *Outrage*, 279.

71. Enoch's father may have been a habitual criminal: Joseph Arnold P. Knowles, possibly alias Rose or Jones.

72. 'Poison pen activities over 30 years alleged', *Lancashire Evening Post*, 26 October 1934, 7; 'Poison pen charges', *Gloucestershire Echo*, 30 October 1934, 8.

73. 1939 Register, TNA, RG101/5394F/011/5 Letter Code: ORND.

74. 'Cruel letters to royal house', *Sheffield Independent*, 7 November 1934, 3.

75. 'New "poison pen" wave is baffling police vigil', *Daily Express*, 15 April 1936, 5.

76. Rene Kollar, *The Return of the Benedictines to London* (London, 1989), 41–3.

77. Rene Kollar, 'Bishops and Benedictines: The case of Father Richard O'Halloran', *Journal of Ecclesiastical History* 38:3 (1987), 362–85, at 365; David M. Cheney, 'Father Thomas Jackson, M.H.M', The Hierarchy of the Catholic Church, https://www.catholic-hierarchy.org/bishop/bjackt. html (accessed 13/03/2020).

78. 'Roman Catholic Church', *Middlesex County Times*, 16 August 1902, 4; 'Father O'Halloran', *Hull Daily Mail*, 3 September 1902, 6.

79. 'General home news', *Newcastle Journal*, 5 April 1916, 8.

80. 'St Bede's College and the late Cardinal', *Tablet*, 11 July 1903, 29.

81. Cheney, 'Father Thomas Jackson, M.H.M'

82. 'Ought to have won V.C.', *Lancashire Evening Post*, 3 April 1916, 5.

83. 'Insults to rector and his girl wife', *Sheffield Independent*, 18 June 1937, 1; 'Rector weds chorus girl', *Dundee Evening Telegraph*, 15 June 1937, 1; 'Bacton', *Diss Express*, 18 June 1937, 9.

84. 'Poison letters to a rector', *Daily Herald*, 18 June 1937, 11.

85. 'Working under sail—Ascot fashions', *Dundee Courier*, 18 June 1937, 10.

86. 'Rector home', *Diss Express*, 9 July 1937, 10.

87. 'Plans stage career for June baby', *Daily Mirror*, 2 February 1938, 2.

88. See, for example, 'Vicar hits out at the squanderers', *Yorkshire Post & Leeds Intelligencer*, 29 October 1949, 6.

89. 'Death of Lincoln Canon recalls engagement protests', *Sheffield Evening Telegraph*, 29 April 1939, 1.

90. 'Death of Cleethorpes vicar's wife', *Nottingham Evening Post*, 2 March 1935, 7.

91. 'Horrible letters sent to canon', *Nottingham Evening Post*, 17 October 1938, 9.

92. 'Vicar has a censor for poison pen letters', *Daily Mirror*, 26 October 1938, 5.

93. 'Canon found dead', *Gloucestershire Echo*, 29 April 1938, 1; 'Women hunt for girl's wreath to canon', *Dundee Evening Telegraph*, 3 May 1939, 7.

94. 'Canon found dead', *Gloucestershire Echo*, 29 April 1938, 1; 'Lincs vicar's romance', *Nottingham Evening Post*, 14 October 1938, 7; 'Vicar has a censor for poison pen letters', *Daily Mirror*, 26 October 1938, 5.

95. 'All day wait for bride of canon', *Daily Mirror*, 15 October 1938, 5.

96. 'Death of Lincoln Canon recalls engagement protests', *Sheffield Evening Telegraph*, 29 April 1939, 1; 'Vicar and his school-girl bride', *Daily Mirror*, 15 October 1938, 1, 5.

97. 'Canon, engaged to girl of 18, is gassed', *Sunday Pictorial*, 30 April 1939, 1.

98. 'Canon's tragic death', *Birmingham Mail*, 1 May 1939, 11.

99. 'Canon, engaged to girl of 18, is gassed', *Sunday Pictorial*, 30 April 1939, 1; 'Death of Lincoln Canon recalls engagement protests', *Sheffield Evening Telegraph*, 29 April 1939, 1.

100. 'Women hunt for girl's wreath to canon', *Dundee Evening Telegraph*, 3 May 1939, 7.

101. 'Menaces inspired by poisoned pen article', *Sheffield Independent*, 5 March 1935, 4.

102. 'Alleged threat to kill', *Dorking & Leatherhead Advertiser*, 5 October 1912, 2; 'Mr & Mrs Johnson charged', *Surrey Mirror*, 26 June 1914, 2; 'Sending threatening letters', *Dorking & Leatherhead Advertiser*, 19 October 1912, 6.

103. 'Threats to kill', *Dorking & Leatherhead Advertiser*, 24 May 1913, 6; 'Sending threatening letters', *Dorking & Leatherhead Advertiser*, 19 October 1912, 6.

104. 'The anonymous letter fiend', *London Journal*, 25 February 1911, 420.

105. 'Postmistress on poison pen charge', *Daily Herald*, 8 June 1934, 7; 'Poison pen in a village', *Daily Mirror*, 17 July 1934, 7; 'Postmistress to return', *Daily Herald*, 26 July 1934, 6.

106. Mixed Claims Commission, United States and Germany, *Opinions and decisions in the sabotage claims handed down June 15, 1939, and October 30, 1939* (Washington DC, 1940), 295.

107. 'Postmistress for trial', *Yorkshire Post & Leeds Intelligencer*, 11 June 1934, 12; 'Resignation question in island case', *Portsmouth Evening News*, 9 June 1934, 9.

108. 'Could a woman have written such stuff?', *Portsmouth Evening News*, 19 July 1934, 14.

109. 'Island postmistress on trial', *Portsmouth Evening News*, 23 July 1934, 12.

110. *Grace's Guide*, 'Wladimir Raffalovich Mansfield (1876–1949)', https://www.gracesguide.co.uk/Wladimir_Raffalovich_Mansfield (21/02/2020). Mansfield delivered a lecture to the Medio-Legal Society in 1942 on the subject of 'Disguise in handwriting', *Medico-Legal Journal* 11:1 (1943), 23–9.

111. 'New poison pen wave is baffling police vigil', *Daily Express*, 15 April 1936, 5.

112. 'Could a woman have written such stuff?', *Portsmouth Evening News*, 19 July 1934, 14.

113. Saudek, *Anonymous Letters*, 84–6.

114. Saudek, *Anonymous Letters*, 80–1.

115. A. Lucas, *Forensic Chemistry and Scientific and Criminal Investigation*, 3rd edn (London, 1935), 131. See also Harrison, *Suspect Documents*, 36, 41, 58. Suzanne Bell, 'Alfred Lucas', *Oxford Dictionary of Forensic Science* (Oxford, 2012), 159–60.

116. C. Ainsworth Mitchell, *The Expert Witness* (Cambridge, 1923), 132, 134.

117. Mitchell, *A Scientist in the Criminal Courts*, 74.

118. 'Embassy "Poison Pen"' by Richard Llewellyn, *Observer*, 23 January 1938, 13.

119. Richard Llewellyn, *Poison Pen* [Samuel French Acting Edition] (London, 1938), 40–1.

120. Llewellyn, *Poison Pen*, 61.

CHAPTER 8

1. TNA, CRIM 1/1033, Central Criminal Court: depositions, Defendant: Simner, Winifred Ava. Charge: Libel, 1938, 'Exhibit 2, copy of letter sent 1 July 1938'.

2. TNA, CRIM 1/1033, 'Exhibit 1, copy of letter sent 1 July 1938'. See also 'Poison pen allegations against woman', *Dundee Evening Telegraph*, 22 July 1938, 6; 'Woman charity worker accused of bigamist letter', *Dundee Courier*, 10 September 1938, 5.

3. 'Poison pen allegations against woman', *Dundee Evening Telegraph*, 22 July 1938, 6; 'Woman charity worker accused of bigamist letter', *Dundee Courier*, 10 September 1938, 5; 'Poison pen trapped woman story', *Daily Herald*, 23 July 1938, 7.

4. TNA, CRIM 1/1033, 'Exhibit 9, copy of letter sent 3 July 1938'. See also 'Poison letter to new mayor', *Daily Mirror*, 23 October 1937, 4; 'Poison pen allegations against woman', *Dundee Evening Telegraph*, 22 July 1938, 6; 'Woman's denial of libel charge', *Times*, 10 September 1938, 7.

5. TNA, CRIM 1/1033, 'Exhibit 1, copy of letter sent 1 July 1938'.

6. TNA, CRIM 1/1033, 'Exhibit 1, copy of letter sent 1 July 1938'; Census of England, Wales & Scotland, 1911, Sussex, Hailsham Registration District, Lime Park Hurstmonceux, TNA, RG14/4858, schedule number 104, RG78PN210; 1939 Register, TNA, RG101/1401G/011/39.

7. TNA, CRIM 1/1033, 'Exhibit 10, copy of letter sent 11 July 1938'.

8. TNA, CRIM 1/1033, 'Exhibit 3, copy of letter sent 25 June 1938'; 'Solicitor's love letters to woman client', *Daily Herald*, 17 July 1936; 'A solicitor in Paddington divorce', *Kensington Post*, 17 July 1936, 5.

9. TNA, CRIM 1/1033, 'Exhibit 4, copy of letter sent 26 September 1937'.

10. TNA, CRIM 1/1033, 'Exhibit 5, copy of letter sent November 1937'.

11. TNA, CRIM 1/1033, 'Exhibit 10'.

12. TNA, CRIM 1/1033, 'Exhibit 1'. See also 'Exhibit 6'.

13. TNA, CRIM 1/1033, 'Exhibit 6'.

14. TNA, CRIM 1/1033, 'Exhibit 7, copy of letter sent 23 May 1938'.

15. TNA, CRIM 1/1033, 'Exhibit 10'.

16. 'Police set pillar-box traps for poison pen writers', *Daily Mirror*, 19 July 1937, 4; 'Poison letter to new mayor', *Daily Mirror*, 23 October 1937, 4; 'Poison pen letters to councillors', *Evening Telegraph*, 17 July 1937, 2.

17. 'Poison pen allegations against woman', *Dundee Evening Telegraph*, 22 July 1938, 6; 'Woman charity worker accused of bigamist letter', *Dundee Courier*, 10 September 1938, 5.

18. 'Blondes set trap for poison pen', *Daily Mirror*, 10 September 1938, 15; 'Poison pen allegations against woman', *Dundee Evening Telegraph*, 22 July 1938, 6; 'Poison pen charges', *Western Morning News*, 23 July 1938, 9.

19. 'Blondes set trap for poison pen', *Daily Mirror*, 10 September 1938, 15; 'Woman's denial of libel charge', *Times*, 10 September 1938, 7.

20. 'Poison pen woman warned', *Daily Mail*, 13 September 1938, 9; 'Judge's poison pen warning', *Daily Mirror*, 13 September 1938, 24.

21. 'Christmas puddings & the war', *Middlesex Chronicle*, 21 November 1914, 7; 'War', *Middlesex Chronicle*, 26 September 1914, 4.

22. 'Isleworth', *Middlesex Chronicle*, 13 May 1916, 8; 'Woman accused of libel', *Liverpool Echo*, 9 September 1938, 9; 'Miss Ava-Simner', *Middlesex Chronicle*, 5 February 1944, 3; 'Isleworth', *Middlesex Chronicle*, 13 May 1916, 8.

23. Anne Baldwin, 'Progress and patterns in the election of women as councillors, 1918–1938', PhD thesis, University of Huddersfield, 2012, 109, 136, 141–2. In 1937 only 8% of councillors across the country were female, and in that year, identified as the best year in this era for female representation, only 6% of the mayors were women; Jaime Reynolds, 'Madam Mayor: The first wave of Liberal women in local government leadership 1819–1939', *Journal of Liberal History* 89 (2015–16), 6–18, at 8.

24. 'Dover town nurses', *Dover Express*, 17 October 1919, 4; 'A Dover Nursing Association', *Dover Express*, 4 October 1935, 7; 'Death of Miss Simner', *Dover Express*, 12 April 1935, 9; findmypast, 1939 Register, TNA, RG101/2515E/010/24 Letter Code: EJGD, 44 Goldstone Villas, Sussex, Hove M.B.

25. 'Miss Ava-Simner', *Middlesex Chronicle*, 5 February 1944, 3. In addition to the various personal crises outlined, Winifred also suffered the death of her fiancé, and the family still possess the wedding dress she never got to wear.

26. TNA, J 77/161/3877, Divorce Court File 3877. Appellant: Frances Mary Simner. Respondent: Benjamin Simner. Wife's petition. 1875.

27. 'Lt Col. P. R. A. O. Simner', *Middlesex Chronicle*, 20 April 1918, 7.

28. Probate, 11 January 1955 [General Register Office, Probate].

29. 'New "poison pen" wave is baffling police', *Daily Express*, 15 April 1936, 5.

30. 'Explosion in village', *Hull Daily Mail*, 27 February 1933, 10.

31. 'Poison pen notes', *Daily Mirror*, 23 October 1926, 22.

32. 'Poison pen notes' *Daily Mirror*, 25 October 1926, 24.

33. 'Poison pen notes', *Daily Mirror*, 23 October 1926, 22; 'Poison pen again', *Nottingham Evening Post*, 23 October 1926, 3.

34. 'Vicar victim of poison pen', *Daily Mirror*, 10 December 1927, 3.

35. 'Dead men tell no tales', *Sheffield Daily Telegraph*, 9 August 1930, 11.

36. 'Poison pen again at work', *Gloucestershire Echo*, 3 May 1933, 1; 'News in brief', *Essex Newsman*, 23 April 1932, 4.

37. 'Persecution', *Hartlepool Northern Daily Mail*, 3 May 1933, 5; 'Reflexion by reflex', *Essex Newsman*, 6 May 1933, 4.

38. 'A Rector's parable', *Chelmsford Chronicle*, 19 July 1929, 7; 'Persecution', *Hartlepool Northern Daily Mail*, 3 May 1933, 5; 'New Rector of St Andrew's, Romford', *Chelmsford Chronicle*, 25 January 1929, 7; 'Patroness puts her foot down', *Gloucestershire Echo*, 16 October 1933, 6.

39. 'Rector bereaved', *Chelmsford Chronicle*, 5 January 1934, 10; 'Romford', *Chelmsford Chronicle*, 29 November 1935, 9; 'Romford Rector's death', *Essex Newsman*, 30 January 1937, 4.

40. 'Police seek poison pen who called vicar a spiv', *Daily Mirror*, 29 March 1948, 1; '£25 to find poison pen', *Bradford Observer*, 6 April 1948, 1; 'Robin Hood's Bay poison pen letters', *Bradford Observer*, 22 May 1948, 3; Alan Hynd, 'Crimes of the poisoned pen', *Saturday Evening Post* (11 June 1955), 31, 129–30, at 130.

41. 'Village "poison pen" letters', *Guardian*, 22 May 1948, 5; 'Poison pen inquiry fails', *Yorkshire Post and Leeds Intelligencer*, 22 May 1948, 6.

42. 'Bath woman summoned at Chippenham', *Bath Chronicle and Weekly Gazette*, 13 August 1938, 3; 'Wives reveal poison pen plague', *Daily Mirror*, 22 September 1938, 5; 'Poison pen charges', *Bath Chronicle and Weekly Gazette*, 15 October 1938, 5.

43. 'Poison pen in village', *Nottingham Evening Post*, 19 January 1929, 8; 'The poison pen', *Hull Daily Mail*, 16 December 1932, 1.

44. 'Town in terror of poison-pen', *Western Daily Press*, 17 September 1934, 6.

45. 'Spondon poison pen mystery', *Derby Daily Telegraph*, 18 January 1932, 1; 'Spondon poison pen again', *Derby Daily Telegraph*, 20 January 1932, 1.

46. 'Poison pen village', *Sheffield Daily Telegraph*, 5 March 1932, 11.

47. 'Vicar and poison pen', *Western Gazette*, 19 January 1934, 13.

48. 'Amateurs and anonymous letter campaign', *Western Daily Press*, 26 April 1930, 11.

49. 'Letters trial', *Daily Herald*, 15 March 1934, 11.

50. 'Poison pen attacks on wives and workless men at housing estate that is a hot-bed of scandal', *Daily Mirror*, 11 August 1936, 5.

51. Cited in 'Taxation is robbery', *The New Age*, volume 59, 1936, 13.

52. 'Protest against Perth housing scheme', *Dundee Evening Telegraph*, 18 August 1933, 3; 'Violence threats to girls', *Evening Telegraph*, 8 October 1937, 4.

53. 'Mystery of Perth man's injuries', *Dundee Courier*, 29 March 1938, 5.

54. 'Poison pen in a village', *Daily Mirror*, 29 March 1930, 2.

55. 'Filthy letters', *Nottingham Evening Post*, 21 March 1930, 11; 'Village disturbed for years', *Yorkshire Evening Post*, 21 March 1930, 9; 'The Milton Ernest case', *Bedfordshire Times and Independent*, 28 March 1930, 7.

56. 'Village disturbed for years', *Yorkshire Evening Post*, 21 March 1930, 9; The Milton Ernest case', *Bedfordshire Times and Independent*, 28 March 1930, 7; 'Boy finds anonymous letter', *Nottingham Evening Post*, 28 March 1930, 4.

57. 'The Milton Ernest case', *Bedfordshire Times and Independent*, 28 March 1930, 7.

58. 'Filthy letters', *Nottingham Evening Post*, 21 March 1930, 11; 'Alleged sending of obscene letters', *Hartlepool Northern Daily Mail*, 21 March 1930, 12; 'Village disturbed for years', *Yorkshire Evening Post*, 21 March 1930, 9; 'The Milton Ernest case', *Bedfordshire Times and Independent*, 4 April 1930, 7; 'Obscene articles', *Hull Daily Mail*, 31 May 1930, 1; 'Victim of circumstances', *Bedfordshire Times and Independent*, 6 June 1930, 10.

59. Certified copy of an entry of birth, application number 10750557-1, birth of [anonymized], 3 October 1903, Milton Ernest, Sharnbrook, Bedford (303), registered on 29 December 1903; Register 1939.

60. 'Poison pen denied by a nurse', *Daily Mirror*, 28 May 1938, 22; 'Poison pen sequel', *Bognor Regis Observer*, 20 July 1938, 8.

61. 'Detective praised by bench', *Gloucester Citizen*, 6 December 1934, 8; 'Bristol poison pen charge', *Western Daily Press*, 6 December 1934, 5; 'Bristol poison pen charge', *Western Daily Press*, 6 December 1934, 5; 'Not fit to plead', *Western Daily Press*, 13 February 1935, 4; Ethel is recorded as living with Herbert in the 1939 register (TNA, RG101/5001F/004/38 Letter Code: OAIH), by which time the couple had moved to Allison Road, Bedminister.

62. 'Anonymous letter leads to suicide', *Sheffield Daily Telegraph*, 20 May 1930, 4.

63. 'Poison pen drives major to suicide', *Sheffield Independent*, 10 November 1931, 5; 'Major abused by postcard', *Dundee Courier*, 10 November 1931, 6; 'Tragic death of Major N. V. S. Pochin, formerly of Market Harborough', *Market Harborough and Midland Mail*, 13 November 1931, 2.

64. 'Letters blamed for suicide', *Yorkshire Post & Leeds Intelligencer*, 'Poison pen kills', *Western Gazette*, 30 December 1938, 16; 'Sentences at York Assizes', *Leeds Mercury*, 12 November 1937, 3.

65. 'Poison pen tragedy', *Western Morning News*, 31 May 1938, 4; 'Did anonymous letter cause double tragedy?' *Western Times*, 3 June 1938, 13. 'Lifton farmer's tragic death', *Western Times*, 27 May 1938, 8.

66. 'Bridegroom who disappeared on wedding eve', *Western Daily Press*, 14 August 1934, 8; 'Died before wedding', *Western Morning News*, 14 August 1934, 3; 'More letters at Ermington', *Western Morning News*, 22 August 1934, 3.

67. 'Writer with poison pen', *Western Morning News*, 22 August 1934, 3.

68. 'Poison-pen gossip kills wife', *Daily Mirror*, 14 April 1936, 1 and back page.

69. 'Obscene articles', *Hull Daily Mail*, 31 May 1930, 1.

70. 'Village disturbed for years', *Yorkshire Evening Post*, 21 March 1930, 9; 1939 Register, TNA, RG101/1996A/009/36 Letter Code: DQDA.

71. A case before Travers Humphreys in October 1936 tested the limits of libel laws. Although there was evidence that Mildred Davis wrote letters defaming two villagers, there was no evidence that she wanted the letters to be shown to other people, and she took no steps to circulate them; and so they were deemed not libellous, and Davis was discharged; 'Poison pen case', *Western Morning News*, 21 October 1936, 9.

CONCLUSION

1. Lee Ross, 'The Intuitive Psychologist and his Shortcomings', *Advances in Experimental Social Psychology* 10 (1977), 173–220.

2. Fairfield, 'The poison pen', at 24–6.

3. Shropshire Archives, P176/L/6/18, anonymous letter to the Overseers for Ludlow, from Wells, 19 March 1812.

4. Dundee City Archives, Letter sent 26/9/1936. See also letter sent 17/2/1936 from 'Old Fisherman'. Viewed on Scran: www.scran.ac.uk/database/record.php?usi=000-000-495-636-C&scache=5w0v435i6p&searchdb=scran; www.scran.ac.uk/database/record.php?usi=000-000-495-635-C&scache=5w0v435i6p&searchdb=scran (accessed 10/02/2023).

5. See, for example, a letter sent to an East Anglian magistrate in October 1917 from a resident of Ditchingham in Norfolk which complains about the activities and behaviour of the local policeman, acting sergeant Howlett. The writer accused Howlett of poaching and neglecting his duties; 'if he can shot rabbits let him go and shot Germans...It is time to have a sharper Policeman'. Signed from 'The Parish of Ditchin[g]ham'..., 'Elizabethjayne2015', Norfolk Record Office blog, 22 January 2017, https://norfolkrecordofficeblog.org/2017/01/12/disgruntled-of-ditchingham-stories-from-the-correspondence-of-w-carr (accessed 29/01/2021).

6. 'The Local Government Board and Anonymous Communications', *Lancet*, 13 May 1911, 1313.

7. The case of William Harold Houghton, from 1933, goes some way to explain the mindset of some letter-writers who responded to their grievances through letters. Houghton had worked for W. & T. Avery Ltd, but had been dismissed, and harboured a grudge about this. In March 1933 Houghton was imprisoned for nine months for writing threatening letters to his erstwhile employers, claiming that 'by his own hand' he would destroy them, and inviting one partner to a duel in Hyde Park. Dr Maurice Hamblin Smith, a specialist in criminology psychology, interviewed Houghton, and concluded that he was a well-educated, intelligent man who had become 'obsessed with a grievance', or an 'imaginary grievance'. He was eccentric, impulsive, and 'got easily excited', see 'Duel challenges', *Gloucestershire Echo*, 16 February 1933, 8; 'Shopbreaking', *Birmingham Daily Gazette*, 9 March 1933, 9.

8. Fyodor Dostoevsky, trans. Kenneth Lanta, *A Writer's Diary Vol. 2 1877–1881* (Evanston, IL, 1994).

9. Fairfield, 'The poison pen', at 24–6.

10. Fairfield, 'The poison pen', at 24–6.

11. See Maureen Casey-Owens, 'The anonymous letter writer—a psychological profile?', *Journal of Forensic Sciences* 29:3 (1984), 816–19.

12. See, for example, letters sent to R. S. Bennett, at Bennett Brothers Ltd. Counterslip Works, Bristol. which pointed out all the failures detected at work—by a worker and 'shareholder', including the behaviour of forewomen and the preponderance of managers; Bristol Archives, 44815/Mgt/St/2, 3 anonymous letters, *c.*1960.

13. 'Mystery of undergraduates' confession', *Nottingham Evening Post*, 16 March 1931, 1; 'Anonymous confession regarded as hoax', *Sheffield Daily Telegraph*, 17 March 1931, 6.

14. 'New "poison pen" wave is baffling police vigil', *Daily Express*, 15 April 1936, 5.
15. Harrison, *Suspect Documents*, 476.
16. Harrison, *Suspect Documents*, 476.
17. Harrison, *Suspect Documents*, 480.
18. Alan Hynd, 'Crimes of the Poisoned Pen', *Saturday Evening Post* (11 June 1955), 31, 129–30.
19. H. Ashton-Wolfe, 'The scientific side of the detection of crime. No XII—anonymous letters and graphomania', 416.
20. TNA, HO 144/2542, 416617/20, clipping of *Daily Express* article, 20 July 1923, plus marginal comments by Ernley Blackwell.
21. 'Disgusting letters', *Nottingham Journal*, 29 April 1910, 6.
22. See also 'Notice to correspondents', *Satirist, or, Monthly Meteor*, 5 October 1809, 384.
23. 'Disguised detective', *Lancashire Evening Post*, 29 July 1910, 3.
24. 'Sutton libel charge', *Globe*, 2 August 1910, 2.
25. Terrible letters', *Staffordshire Advertiser*, 10 June 1939, 8; 'Fined for poison pen letters', *Derby Daily Telegraph*, 6 June 1939, 1.
26. 'Poison pen active', *Western Morning News*, 8 October 1936, 8; 'Poison pen', *Western Morning News*, 17 October 1936, 6.
27. 'Poison pen letter in church', *Daily Mirror*, 14 April 1937.
28. 'Alleged libel on young typist', *Sunday Post*, 23 March 1924; 'Solicitor's libel', *Yorkshire Evening Post*, 27 March 1924, 12.
29. 'Clerk charged with criminal libel', *Dundee Evening Telegraph*, 19 April 1937, 6; 'Libel letters warning', *Sunderland Daily Echo*, 28 April 1937, 5.
30. Cockayne, *Cheek by Jowl*, 131–2, 189–90.
31. '12 months for libel', *Manchester Courier & Lancashire General Advertiser*, 5 March 1908, 9.
32. Fairfield, 'The poison pen', 26.
33. 'Amazing revelations in case against woman', *Evening Telegraph*, 9 June 1924, 7; 'Poison pen in Glasgow', *Dundee Evening Telegraph*, 9 June 1924, 7; 'An abnormal pervert', *Western Daily Press*, 10 June 1924, 3; Census of England, Wales & Scotland, 1901, Lanarkshire, Gorbals Registration District, 197, Thistle Street, Glasgow, Govan, TNA, RG 13, schedule number 70.
34. 'Fun fairs blamed', *Western Morning News*, 13 May 1942, 3.
35. Harrison, *Suspect Documents*, 60.
36. Cited in Fairfield, 'The poison pen', 32.
37. Arthur Quirke, *Forged, Anonymous and Suspect Documents* (London, 1930), 218.
38. Ibid., 218.
39. 'The Coleford sensation', *Gloucester Citizen*, 28 January 1924, 6.
40. Fairfield, 'The poison pen', 26m 29.
41. See John Suller, 'The online disinhibition effect', *Cyberpsychological Behaviour* 7:3 (2004), 321–6.

42. Cited in Martin Belam, 'All the trolls out there—come out and explain yourself', *Guardian*, 14 September 2011.

43. See for example E. Diener et al., 'Effects of deindividuation variables on stealing among Halloween trick-or-treaters', *Journal of Personality & Social Psychology* 33 (1976), 178–83.

44. Claire Hardacker, 'Trolling in asynchronous computer-mediated communication: From user definitions to academic definition', *Journal of Politeness Research* 6:2 (2010), 237.

45. Whitney Phillips, *This Is Why We Can't Have Nice Things: Mapping the Relationship between Online Trolling and Mainstream Culture* (Cambridge, MA, 2015), 15.

46. Llewellyn, *Poison Pen*, 19.

47. 'Art. XII. Poems, Odes, Prologues and Epilogues spoken on public occasions at Reading School. To which is added some account of the Lives of the Rev. Mr. Benwell and the Rev. Dr. Butt', *The British Critic*, volumes 25–6, 1805, 412.

Bibliography

MANUSCRIPT SOURCES

Bristol Archives
44815/Mgt/St/2, Records of Bennett Brothers Limited of Counterslip, three anonymous letters, c. 1960.

British Library
Electoral Registers, Brentford – SPR.Mic.P.432/BL.M.20, 1910–32.

British Motor Industry Heritage Trust
95/52/14/4, Papers relating to Sir Herbert Austin and the Austin Motor Company.

Buckinghamshire Archives
D-X 1711/1/163, Letter from Charles Baker to Elizabeth Odell, 4 August 1872.

Dudley Archives
DHAR/16 and DHAR/34, Harward & Evers, Solicitors, Stourbridge.
BDRC/7, Royal Brierley Crystal and the Williams-Thomas Family, Family Papers.

East Sussex Record Office
FRE/2291, Letter from Mary Frewen to John Frewen, Cold Overton, 30 January 1811.
DO/C/6/3632, Hove Building Control conversion into flats, 62 Brunswick Place, by Col Gardiner, 18 March 1912.

Essex Record Office
Q/SBb 380/66, Quarter Sessions Bundle, Midsummer 1800.

General Register Office
Marriage, Birth & Death certificates, various

Gloucestershire Archives
C01/N/2/B/51 & 55, County Coroner, Lover Division, Inquest Papers, Notices of Death, 1856.

C01/I/2/D/11, County Coroner, Lover Division, Inquest Files, 1856.

D5334/1, Dorington family of Lypiatt Park, threatening letter about Bisley Common enclosure, 1864.

Hampshire Record Office

75M91/P9, Carnarvon of Highclere papers, the Long Family, anonymous letter sent to Arthur Atherley, 1 September 1828.

11M94/7, Basingstoke Museum miscellanea, anonymous letter 'To the worthy inhabitants of the Town of Basin—ke', from 'An Inhabitant', c.1780s.

Hull Local Studies Library

L DBHR/2/5/1, Bundle relating to attacks on German shops throughout England, c.1914–18.

L DBHR/1/1/7, Postcard from 'Fritz' to C. Hohenrein, 10 November 1914.

L DBHR/1/1/13, Anonymous letter to C. Hohenrein, 12 May 1915.

L DBHR/1/1/14, Anonymous warning letter to C. Hohenrein, 13 May 1915.

London Metropolitan Archive

H64/B/05/005, St Luke's Hospital, Patients' Records: Register of Discharged and Transfers 1907–1917, 1915.

H64/B/06/014, St Luke's Hospital, Patients' Records: New Case Book, January 1912–September 1915.

H64/B/11/001, St Luke's Hospital, Patients' Records: Medical Register 1907–16, 1915.

H64/B/15/002, St Luke's Hospital, Patients' Records: Voluntary Boarders Case Books (indexed), September 1913–October 1916.

H64/B/16/001, St Luke's Hospital, Patients' Records (signed), August 1846–January 1916.

P89/MRY1/017, Register of Baptisms, St Marylebone, London.

Mass Observation Archive

Diarist 5353, (1940).

[The] National Archive

BT 334/56, Deaths of seamen reported to the Registrars General, 1912–13.

BT 334/58, Register of deceased seamen, 1913.

C 202/227/26, Chancery, return of writs, Coroner, Worcester, 2 December 1837.

CRIM 1/1033, Central Criminal Court: depositions, Defendant: Simner, Winifred Ava. Charge: Libel, 1938.

HO 42, Home Office: Domestic Correspondence, George III, Letters & Papers, 1800.

HO 44, Home Office: Domestic Correspondence, 1773–1861.

HO 52, Home Office: Counties Correspondence, 1820–1850.

HO 64, Home Office: Criminal (Rewards and Pardons) Correspondence and Secret Service Reports, 1820–1840.

HO 107, Census Returns for England, Wales & Scotland, 1841, 1851.

HO 140, Home Office: Calendar of Prisoners, 1868–1971.

HO 144/2452, File relating to the cases of Rosa Emma Gooding and Edith Emily Swan, 1921–1923.

J 77, Court for Divorce and Matrimonial Causes, later Supreme Court of Judicature: Divorce and Matrimonial Causes Files, 1852–2002 (1875).

MEPO 3/189, Metropolitan Police: Office of the Commissioner: Correspondence and Papers, Special Series, 'The Sutton Libel Case', 1909–13.

MEPO 6/26, Habitual Criminals Register 1914.

MH 12/10322, Ministry of Health, Local Government Board and predecessors: Correspondence with Poor Law Union: Clutton.

MH 12/13905–7, Ministry of Health, Local Government Board and predecessors: Correspondence with Poor Law Union: Bromsgrove.

MH 12/14019, Ministry of Health, Local Government Board and predecessors: Correspondence with Poor Law Union: Kidderminster.

MH 12/9158, Ministry of Health, Local Government Board and predecessors: Correspondence with Poor Law Union: Tynemouth.

MH 12/9361, Ministry of Health, Local Government Board and predecessors: Correspondence with Poor Law Union: Mansfield.

PROB 11/1380/239, Will of Robert Honeyborne, 1802.

PROB 11/1789/119, Will of Thomas Honeyborne, 1831.

PROB 11/1871/64, Will of William Battine esq, Doctor of Laws, 1836.

PROB 11/2075/412, Will of William Willis Bailey, 1848.

PROB 11/2222/170, Will of William Granville Eliot, 1855.

PROB 11/2238/193, Will of Joseph Darby, 1856.

RG 9, Census Returns for England, Wales & Scotland, 1861.

RG 10, Census Returns for England, Wales & Scotland, 1871.

RG 11, Census Returns for England, Wales & Scotland, 1881.

RG 12, Census Returns for England, Wales & Scotland, 1891.

RG 13, Census Returns for England, Wales & Scotland, 1901.

RG 14, Census Returns for England, Wales & Scotland, 1911.

RG 101, 1939 Register.

SP14/216/2, Secretaries of State: State Papers Domestic, James I 1605, the Monteagle Letter, 1605.

Norfolk Record Office

NCR Case 6h/9.6, Minute of Mayor's court concerning anonymous letter threatening to set fire to James Poole's shop, 1766.

Northamptonshire Archives

C 637, Anonymous Letter to Mrs Cokayne Exeter House Roehampton postmarked 10 November 1894, Sutton.

C 1340, 'Diary of George Edward Cokayne 1893–1896'.

C 2287, Cokayne (Ruston) Collection, Miscellaneous, 'Letters & papers relating to Rev George Hill Adams, 1880–1900'.

Plymouth and West Devon Record Office

Bellamy Papers, PH/178–9; PH/185–6; PH/190; PH/192–3; PH/195–7; PH/276.

Shropshire Archives

P176/L/6/18, Anonymous letter to the Overseers for Ludlow, from Wells, 19 March 1812.

Staffordshire Record Office

D695/1/30/42, Letter from Charles Roberts to the Oxford, Worcester and Wolverhampton Railway Company, 2 December 1854.

D695/1/2/17, Papers in Chancery case Atkinson v Crew concerning mines at Moor Lane, Kingswinford, 1845–1867.

D853/A/2, Papers relating to the Dartmouth estates in South Staffordshire, correspondence and accounts.

D853/A/3, Papers relating to the Dartmouth estates in South Staffordshire, correspondence mainly between Robert Dawson (and later R. Murchison) and Lord Dartmouth.

Surrey Archives

9309/3/1/1, Letter to Rev Broderick of Banstead, postmarked Epsom, 27 December 1825.

Wellcome Library

PPMCS/A/1/1, Letters to Marie Stopes concerning Married Love: anonymous and pseudonymous, initialled, and illegible signatures, 1918–c. 1950, letter 33/36.

Worcestershire Archives

010:18 BA 14908/3/1/1–6, Signalman Edgin[g]ton accused by member of the public, letter and envelope, 11 April 1944; anonymous postcard addressed to Mrs Savage; report by Richard Skerrett, Clent Constabulary, to City Police, Birmingham, 22 April 1944.

705:73 BA14450/173/10 (4), Croome Collection—the family and estate papers of the Earls of Coventry, household account book, leaf from 15 March 1825.

705:73 BA14450/289/1 -19, Croome Collection—the family and estate papers of the Earls of Coventry. Letters received and sent by Lady Margaret 'Peggy' Pitches, c. 1801–1 Apr 1831.

705:73 BA14450/291–292, Croome Collection—the family and estate papers of the Earls of Coventry. Letters sent and received by George William, 7th Earl of Coventry, 29 Jul 1788–7 Jun 1830.

705:73 BA14450/295–299, Croome Collection—the family and estate papers of the Earls of Coventry. Letters received by George William Coventry, Viscount Deerhurst and 8th Earl of Coventry, 2 Jan 1812–29 Aug 1841.

PRINTED PRIMARY SOURCES

Aberdeen Press and Journal, 1920
Aris's Birmingham Gazette, 1825, 1845, 1863
Barking, East Ham & Ilford Advertiser, 1904
Bath Chronicle and Weekly Gazette, 1859, 1914, 1938
Bedfordshire Times and Independent, 1930
Birmingham Daily Gazette, 1863–64, 1933–34
Birmingham Daily Post, 1858, 1914
Birmingham Journal, 1847, 1851, 1856, 1863
Birmingham Mail, 1939
Bognor Regis Observer, 1938
Bolton Evening News, 1893, 1895
Boston Guardian, 1934
Bradford Observer, 1948
Bristol Mercury, 1856, 1859
British Critic, 1805
Bucks Gazette, 1848
Bury & Norwich Post, 1802, 1877, 1880
Bury Free Press, 1880
Caledonian Mercury, 1765
Cambridge Chronicle & Journal 1819, 1824
Cannock Chase Courier, 1893
Cardiff Times, 1885
Carlisle Patriot, 1847
Chelmsford Chronicle, 1897, 1929, 1934–35
Cheltenham Chronicle, 1878, 1924
Cheltenham Looker-on, 1892
Chester Chronicle, 1802
Cornhill Magazine, 1885
County Advertiser & Herald for Staffordshire and Worcestershire, 1856–57
Coventry Evening Telegraph, 1895
Croydon Advertiser and East Surrey Reporter, 1910
Croydon Chronicle and East Surrey Advertiser, 1910
Croydon Guardian and Surrey County Gazette, 1910
Daily Citizen, 1913
Daily Express, 1915, 1936
Daily Herald, 1912, 1923, 1934, 1936–38
Daily Mail, 1910, 1915, 1921–22, 1927, 1936, 1938
Daily Mirror, 1921, 1924, 1926, 1930, 1934, 1936–38, 1948, 1962
Daily News, 1849
Daily Telegraph & Courier, 1907, 1911
Derby Daily Telegraph, 1913–14, 1932, 1939, 1946, 1949
Derby Mercury, 1759

Diss Express, 1904, 1937

Dorking & Leatherhead Advertiser, 1912–15

Dover Express, 1890–91, 1906, 1919, 1935

Dundee Courier, 1882, 1920, 1924, 1931, 1934, 1936–38

Dundee Evening Telegraph, 1910, 1913–14, 1918, 1923–24, 1933, 1937–39

Dundee, Perth, and Cupar Advertiser, 1847

Durham County Advertiser, 1822, 1865

Eastern Daily Press, 1888

Eastern Morning News, 1889

Era, 1886–87

Essex Newsman, 1903, 1932–33, 1937

Evening Mail, 1913

Evening Post, 1931

Evening Telegraph, 1924, 1937

Evesham Standard & West Midland Observer, 1910

Exeter & Plymouth Gazette, 1844, 1885

Express and Echo, 1910

Gazetteer and New Daily Advertiser, 1765–67

Gentleman's Magazine, 1836

Glasgow Evening Post, 1892

Globe, 1887, 1909–10, 1913, 1920

Gloucester Citizen, 1903, 1923–24, 1934

Gloucester Journal, 1863–64

Gloucestershire Chronicle, 1840, 1846, 1863

Gloucestershire Echo, 1933–34, 1938

Grantham Journal, 1904

Grimsby Telegraph, 2019

Guardian, 1948, 2015

Hampshire Chronicle, 1811, 1813, 1817–18, 1822

Hartlepool Daily Mail, 1934

Hartlepool Northern Daily Mail, 1923, 1930, 1933

Hastings and St Leonard's Observer, 1870, 1906–07

Hereford Times, 1859

Historical Chronicle, 1802

Hull Daily Mail, 1896, 1898, 1902, 1909, 1914–15, 1918, 1923, 1930, 1932–33, 1935

Illustrated London News, 1844, 1847, 1855

Ipswich Journal, 1767, 1877

Jackson's Oxford Journal, 1800

Journal of the Royal Sanitary Institute, 1909

Kensington Post, 1936

Kington Times, 1920

Lancashire Evening Post, 1910, 1916, 1920, 1934

Lancaster Gazette, 1822

Lancet, 1911
Law Times Report, 1854
Leamington Spa Courier, 1894, 1934
Leeds Mercury, 1920, 1923, 1937
Leicester Daily Mercury, 1877
Lichfield Mercury, 1893
Lincolnshire Echo, 1936
Liverpool Daily Post, 1914
Liverpool Echo, 1884, 1938
Liverpool Mercury, 1865
Lloyd's Evening Post, 1765
London Daily News, 1847, 1910–11
London Evening Post, 1767
London Evening Standard, 1870, 1877, 1895
London Gazette, 1765, 1797, 1812, 1845, 1870
London Journal, 1911
Loughborough Echo, 1916–17
Maidstone Journal and Kentish Advertiser, 1831
Manchester Courier & Lancashire General Advertiser, 1895, 1908, 1914
Manchester Evening News, 1890
Manchester Guardian, 1822, 1848, 1914, 1934
Manchester Mercury, 1792
Manchester Times, 1811
Market Harborough and Midland Mail, 1931
Middlesex Chronicle, 1914, 1916, 1918, 1944
Middlesex County Times, 1902
Midlothian Advertiser, 1914
Monthly Chronologer, 1766
Morning Advertiser, 1836
Morning Chronicle, 1859
Morning Herald and Daily Advertiser, 1780
Morning Post, 1847, 1892
Municipal Engineering & Sanitary Record, 1920
Newcastle Journal, 1916, 1920
New South Wales Police Gazette, 1887
News of the World, 1923
Nottingham Evening Post, 1895, 1910, 1913, 1915, 1918, 1923, 1926, 1929–31, 1934–35, 1938
Nottingham Journal, 1910, 1920
Nottinghamshire Guardian, 1849
Observer, 1910, 1938
Oxford University & City Herald, 1816, 1846
Pall Mall Gazette, 1914, 1920
Portsmouth Evening News, 1920, 1929, 1934

Public Advertiser, 1792
Public Ledger, 1765
Public Ledger & Daily Advertiser, 1811
Royal Cornwall Gazette, 1859
Rugby Advertiser, 1895
Salisbury and Winchester Journal, 1811, 1818
Satirist, or, Monthly Meteor, 1809
Saturday Evening Post, 1955
Sevenoaks Chronicle & Kentish Advertiser, 1910
Sheffield Daily Telegraph, 1911, 1930–32
Sheffield Evening Telegraph, 1914, 1939
Sheffield Independent, 1825, 1877, 1915, 1931, 1934–35, 1937, 1939
Southern Times and Dorset County Herald, 1857
Southern Weekly News, 1923
South London Press, 1889
Sporting Magazine; or, Monthly Calendar, 1802
Staffordshire Advertiser, 1805, 1847–49, 1852, 1939
Staffordshire Sentinel, 1934, 1938
Stamford Mercury, 1800, 1811, 1815, 1830, 1894, 1904, 1909
Star, 1822, 1824
Stroud Journal, 1863, 1866
Sun, 1811
Sunday Pictorial, 1939
Sunday Post, 1924
Sunderland Daily Echo, 1937
Sunderland Daily Echo and Shipping Gazette, 1917
Surrey Advertiser, 1912
Surrey Comet, 1899
Surrey Mirror, 1913–15, 1937
Surveyor and Municipal and County Engineer, 1920
Sussex Agricultural Express, 1914
Swindon Advertiser and North Wilts Chronicle, 1877
Tablet, 1903
Tamworth Herald, 1890
Taunton Courier and Western Advertiser, 1931
Thanet Advertiser, 1918
The Dragon [magazine for the Buffs], 1922
The Examiner, 1814, 1823–24, 1870
The Law Journal, 1890
The New Age, 1936
The Scotsman, 1915, 1924, 1929
The Stage, 1887
The Times, 1844, 1877, 1887, 1910, 1913–14, 1923, 1929, 1934, 1938
The Universal Magazine, 1799

Totnes Weekly Times, 1885
Truth, 1905
Votes for Women, 1914
Wells Journal, 1923
Western Daily Press, 1923–24, 1930, 1934
Western Gazette, 1924, 1934, 1938
Western Mail, 1913, 1923, 1936
Western Morning News, 1885, 1936, 1936–38, 1942
Western Times, 1910, 1938
West London Observer, 1914
West Sussex Gazette, 1912, 1914, 1934
Whitstable Times and Herne Bay Herald, 1895
Wilts and Gloucester Standard, 1885
Witney Gazette and West Oxfordshire Advertiser, 1909
Wolverhampton Chronicle & Staffordshire Advertiser, 1847, 1854, 1857
Worcester Journal, 1814, 1847, 1849
Worcestershire Chronicle, 1845, 1849
Worthing Herald, 1922, 1957
York Herald, 1859, 1877
Yorkshire Evening Post, 1924, 1930
Yorkshire Post & Leeds Intelligencer, 1914, 1920, 1934, 1948–49

Adolphus, John Leycester and Thomas Flower Ellis, *Queen's Bench Reports*, new series (18 vols) (London, 1847), vol. VII
[Arnold, Frederick], 'Anonymous letters', *London Society* 50:300 (1886), 521–31
Ashton-Wolfe, H., 'The scientific side to the detection of crime. No XII – Anonymous letters and graphomania', *London Illustrated News*, 8 September 1928
Babbage, Charles, *A Chapter of Street Noise*, 2nd edn (London, 1864)
Baker, William, *A Practical Compendium of the Recent Statutes, Cases and Decisions affecting the Office of Coroner* (London, 1851)
Baughan, Rosa, *Character Indicated by Handwriting* (London, 1880)
Beete Jukes, Joseph, *Memoirs of the Geological Survey of Great Britain. The South Staffordshire Coal-Field*, 2nd edn (London, 1859)
Bell, Jane, *Bell v. Hill for defamation. Tried before Lord Chief Justice Abbott. Northumberland Assizes. August 9 1822* (North Shields, 1822)
Bingham, Robert, *The Trials of the Rev. Robert Bingham* (London, 1811)
Brown, Ruth M., *Littlehampton School Logbook 1871–1911*, Sussex Record Society 95 (Lewes, 2016)
Burn, Richard and John King, *The Justice of the Peace, and Parish Officer* (5 vols) (London, 1814), vol. I
Burrill, Alexander M., *A treatise on the nature, principles and rules of circumstantial evidence: especially that of the presumptive kind, in criminal cases* (New York, 1856)
Chabot, Charles and Edward Twisleton, *The Handwriting of Junius Professionally Investigated* (London, 1871)

Collins, Wilkie, *The Woman in White* (London, 1871)

Conan Doyle, Arthur, *The Hound of the Baskervilles* (London, 1902)

Conan Doyle, Arthur, *The Sign of Four* (London, 1917)

Corporation General and Trades Directory of Birmingham (Birmingham, 1861)

Croker, John Wilson, '[Review of] *Post Office Reform: its Importance and Practicability*. By Rowland Hill', *The Quarterly Review* 64 (1839), 513–74

Dostoevsky, Fyodor, trans. Kenneth Lanta, *A Writer's Diary Vol. 2 1877–1881* (Evanston, IL, 1994)

Espinasse, Isaac, *Reports of Cases Argued and Ruled at Nisi Prius in the King's Bench and Common Pleas . . . 1799–1801* (4 vols) (London, 1808), vol. 3

Gardiner, C. H., *Soldiers and Civil War* (London, 1914)

Harland, John, *Ballads and Songs of Lancashire*, 2nd edn (London, 1875)

Hayward, Abraham, *A Review of the Work Entitled The Handwriting of Junius* (Cambridge, 1874)

Heston and Isleworth Urban District Council, *1910 Annual Report of the Medical Officer of Health for Heston and Isleworth* (London, 1911)

Heston and Isleworth Urban District Council, *1914 Annual Report of the Medical Officer of Health for Heston and Isleworth* (London, 1915)

Heston and Isleworth Urban District Council, *1915 Annual Report of the Medical Officer of Health for Heston and Isleworth* (London, 1916)

Heston and Isleworth Urban District Council, *1916 Annual Report of the Medical Officer of Health for Heston and Isleworth* (London, 1917)

Higson, John, *The Gorton Historical Recorder* (Droylsden, 1852)

Hill, Rowland, *Post Office Reform; its Importance and Practicability* (London, 1837)

Hill, Thomas, *The Cause of Truth Defended; being a Plain Statement of the Facts connected with the Two Trials of the Rev. T. Hill, Methodist Preacher* (London, 1827)

Hobhouse, Stephen and A. Fenner Brockway, *English Prisons To-Day* (London, 1922)

House of Commons, 'Samuel Johnson, examined' *Hansard*, Volume 12: debated on Monday 20 February 1809, column 856, https://hansard.parliament.uk/Commons/1809-02-20. Accessed 11/1/2023

House of Commons, *Reports from Commissioners 2 Feb–24 Aug 1843*, Vol. XIII (London 1843)

House of Commons, *Accounts and Papers* (48 vols) (London, 1863), vol. 48

House of Commons, Malicious Communications. A Bill, 28 October 1987, Bill 25

House of Commons, Malicious Communications Acts 1988, 27 July 1988

House of Lords, 'Reports from Commissioners: Hand-Loom Weavers', in *The Sessional Papers printed by order of The House of Lords Session 1840* (London, 1840), 213–800

How, Harry, 'An Expert in Handwriting', *The Strand* 8 (September 1894), 293–300

Lemmoin-Cannon, Henry, *The Sanitary Inspector's Guide* (London, 1902)

Llewellyn, Richard, *Poison Pen* [Samuel French Acting Edition] (London, 1938)

Lucas, A., *Forensic Chemistry and Scientific and Criminal Investigation*, 3rd edn (London, 1935)

Mapother, E. D., 'Lecture XXIII Sanitary organization', *Lectures on Public Health*, 2nd edn (Dublin, 1867)

McDonald, Lynn (ed.), *The Collected Works of Florence Nightingale* (15 vols) (Waterloo, ON, 2001–2012), vol. VIII

Mill, John Stuart, *On Liberty* (London, 1859)

Mixed Claims Commission, United States and Germany, *Opinions and decisions in the sabotage claims handed down June 15, 1939, and October 30, 1939* (Washington DC, 1940)

Mylne, J. W. and R. D. Craig (eds), *Reports of Cases decided in the High Court of Chancery during the time of Lord Chancellor Cottenham* (4 vols) (New York, 1843), vol. II

Osborn, Albert S., *Photography and Questioned Documents* (Rochester, NY, 1907)

Osborn, Albert S., *Questioned Documents* (Rochester, NY, 1910)

Pember Reeves, Maud, *Round About a Pound a Week* (London, 1979) [first published 1913]

Quirke, Arthur, *Forged, Anonymous and Suspect Documents* (London, 1930)

Renton, Alexander Wood et al. (eds), *The English Reports* (178 vols) (London, 1900–32), vol. 162

Roscoe, Henry (ed.), 'Folkes Bart v. Chadd and Others', *Reports of Cases Argued and Determined in The Court of the King's Bench in the Twenty-Second, Twenty-Third, Twenty-Fourth, and Twenty-Fifth Years of the Reign of George III* (4 vols) (London, 1813–31), vol. 3, 157–61

Scott, Walter, *The Journal of Sir Walter Scott 1825–32* (2 vols) (Edinburgh, 1890), vol. I

Sergeant, Thomas and John C. Lowber (eds), *Reports of Cases Argued and Determined in the English Courts of Common Law... Vol. VII* (Philadelphia, PA, 1869)

Slater, Isaac, *Slater's Classified Directory... 15 Miles Round Birmingham and Worcester* (Manchester, 1851)

Smyth, Warington W., 'Note on the Mode of Working the Coal and Ironstone of South Staffordshire', in Joseph Beete Jukes, *Memoirs of the Geological Survey of Great Britain. The South Staffordshire Coal-Field*, 2nd edn (London, 1859), 219–23

Stephen, James Fitzjames, *A History of the Criminal Law of England* (3 vols) (London, 1883), vol. II

Stockman, Frank Charles, *A Practical Guide for Sanitary Inspectors* (London, 1915)

Taylor, Albert, *The Sanitary Inspector's Handbook* (London, 1893)

Taylor, Albert, *The Sanitary Inspector's Handbook*, 4th edn (London, 1905)

Walford, E., *Hardwicke's Annual Biography* (London, 1856)

White-Bread, Job, *Scarcity of Bread Difficulte Annonae; Or, the Disease Examined, and the Cure Premised* (London, 1795)

Wightman, Justice, *Proceedings upon the Trial of the Action Brought by Mary Elizabeth Smith Against the Right Hon. Washington Sewallis Shirley Earl Ferrers for Breach of Promise of Marriage* (London, 1846)

Willoughby, Edward F., *The Health Officer's Pocket-Book* (London, 1902)

SECONDARY SOURCES

Ainsworth Mitchell, C., *A Scientist in the Criminal Courts* (London, 1945)

Ainsworth Mitchell, C., *The Expert Witness* (Cambridge, 1923)

Anwar, Shamena, Patrick Bayer, and Randi Hjalmarsson, 'A Jury of Her Peers: The Impact of the First Female Jurors on Criminal Convictions', *The Economic Journal* 129:618 (2019), 603–50

Bailey, Victor, 'The Fabrication of Deviance: "Dangerous Classes" and "Criminal Classes" in Victorian England', in John Rule and Robert Malcolmson, eds, *Protest and Survival: Essays for E. Thompson* (London, 1993), 221–56

Ballinger, Anette, *Dead Women Walking* (Abingdon, 2000)

Barclay, Katie, 'Emotions, the Law and the Press in Britain: Seduction and Breach of Promise Suits, 1780–1830', *Journal for Eighteenth-Century Studies* 39:2 (2016), 267–84

Belam, Martin, 'All the trolls out there—come out and explain yourself', *Guardian*, 14 September 2011

Bell, F. G. and I. A. de Bruyn, 'Subsidence problems due to abandoned pillar workings in coal seams', *Bulletin of Engineering Geology and the Environment* 57 (1999), 225–37

Bell, Suzanne, 'Alfred Lucas', *Oxford Dictionary of Forensic Science* (Oxford, 2012), 159–60

Bergmann, Jörg, *Discreet Indiscretions: The Social Organization of Gossip* (New York, 1993)

Brown, David, 'The industrial revolution, political economy and the British aristocracy: The second Viscount Dudley and Ward as an eighteenth-century canal promoter', *The Journal of Transport History* 27:1 (2006), 1–23

Browne, Christopher, *Getting the Message: The Story of the British Post Office* (Stroud, 1993)

Bucknill, Alfred, *The Nature of Evidence* (London, 1953)

Bull, Sarah, 'A Purveyor of Garbage? Charles Carrington and the Marketing of Sexual Science in Late-Victorian Britain', *Victorian Review* 38:1 (2012), 55–76

Casey-Owens, Maureen, 'The anonymous letter writer—a psychological profile?', *Journal of Forensic Sciences* 29:3 (1984), 816–19

Cockayne, Emily, *Cheek by Jowl: A History of Neighbours* (London, 2012)

Cohen, Deborah, *Family Secrets: Living with Shame from the Victorians to the Present Day* (London, 2013)

Cox, David, *Crime in England 1688–1815* (London, 2013)

Cutmore, N., 'Development of the Pillar Letter Box 1852–1969', *Proceedings of the Institution of Mechanical Engineers* 184:8 (1969), 202–8

Daunton, M. J., 'Down the Pit: Work in the Great Northern and South Wales Coalfields, 1870–1914', *Economic History Review*, new series. 34:4 (1981), 578–97

Daunton, Martin, *Royal Mail: the Post Office since 1840* (London, 2015)

Dear, Michael, 'The politics of geography: Hate mail, rabid referees, and culture wars', *Political Geography* 20 (2001), 1–12

Diener, E. et al., 'Effects of deindividuation variables on stealing among Halloween trick-or-treaters', *Journal of Personality & Social Psychology* 33 (1976), 178–83

Dillon, Richard H., 'The last plan to seize the Manila Galleon', *Pacific History Review* 20:2 (1951), 123–5

Dunbar, R. I. M., 'Gossip in Evolutionary Perspective', *Review of General Psychology* 8:2 (2004), 100–10

Edwards, Cath, *West Midlands Folk Tales* (Stroud, 2018)

Emsley, Clive, *British Society and the French Wars 1793–1815* (London, 1979)

Evans, Stewart and Keith Skinner, *Jack the Ripper: Letters from Hell* (Stroud, 2001)

Everest-Phillips, Max, 'Protest, poison pen letters and Protestantism in mid-nineteenth century East Devon: The Tractarian crisis at Sidmouth 1859–1865'. *Report and Transactions of the Devonshire Association*, 143 (June 2011), pp. 231–81

Fairfield, Letitia, 'The poison pen: A study of anonymous letter writers', *Medico-Legal & Criminological Review* 12:1 (1944), 23–32

Farrugia, Jean, *The Letter Box: A History of Post Office Pillar and Wall Boxes* (New York, 1969)

French, C. N., *The Story of St Luke's Hospital* (London, 1951)

Frost, Ginger S., *Promises Broken: Courtship, Class, and Gender in Victorian England* (Charlottesville, VA, 1995)

Gluckman, Max, 'Gossip and Scandal', *Current Anthropology* 4:3 (June 1963), 307–16

Golan, Tal, *Laws of Men and Laws of Nature* (Cambridge, MA, 2004)

Golden, Catherine, *Posting It: The Victorian Revolution in Letter Writing* (Gainesville, FL, 2009)

Gordon, Catherine, The *Coventrys of Croome* (Chichester, 2000)

Götz, Norbert, ' "Moral Economy": Its conceptual history and analytic prospects', *Journal of Global Ethics* 11:2 (2015), 147–62

Haden, H. J., *Notes of the Stourbridge Glass Trade* (Brierley Hill, 1949)

Hale, Michael, *Traffic and Transport in Nineteenth Century Kingswinford* (Dudley, 2000)

Hardacker, Claire, 'Trolling in asynchronous computer-mediated communication: From user definitions to academic definition', *Journal of Politeness Research* 6:2 (2010), 215–42

Harrison, Wilson R., *Suspect Documents: Their Scientific Examination* (New York, 1958)

Hartman, Mary S., 'Crime and the Respectable Woman: Toward a Pattern of Middle-Class Female Criminality in Nineteenth-Century France and England', *Feminist Studies* 2:1 (1974), 38–56

Hassan, John A., 'The Landed Estate, Paternalism and the Coal Industry in Midlothian, 1800-1880', *The Scottish Historical Review* 59:167 (1980), 73–9

Hendy, John G., *History of the Postmarks of the British Isles from 1840 to 1876* (London, 1909)

Hilliard, Christopher, *The Littlehampton Libels* (Oxford, 2017)

Hilliard, Christopher, *A Matter of Obscenity: The Politics of Censorship in Modern England* (Oxford, 2021)

Hobsbawm, Eric and George Rudé, *Captain Swing* (London, 1969)

Holland, Margaret G., 'What's Wrong with Telling the Truth? An Analysis of Gossip', *American Philosophical Quarterly* 33:2 (1996), 197–209

Houlbrook, Matt, *Prince of Tricksters: The Incredible True Story of Netley Lucas, Gentleman Crook* (Chicago, IL, 2016)

Howitt, Dennis, *Introduction to Forensic and Criminal Psychology*, 2nd edn (Harlow, 2006)

Hynd, Alan, 'Crimes of the Poisoned Pen', *Saturday Evening Post*, 11 June 1955

Jackson, Leon, 'Digging for dirt: Reading blackmail in the Antebellum archive', *Common-Place* 12:3 (2012), http://commonplace.online/article/reading/

Jackson, Leon, 'The spider and the dumpling: Threatening letters in nineteenth-century America', in Celeste-Marie Bernier, Judie Newman, and Matthew Pethers (eds), *The Edinburgh Companion to Nineteenth-Century American Letters and Letter-writing* (Edinburgh, 2016), 152–68

Jaffe, James A., *The Struggle for Market Power: Industrial Relations in the British Coal Industry, 1800–1840* (Cambridge, 1991)

Jane, Emma Alice, '"Back to the kitchen, cunt": Speaking the unspeakable about online misogyny', *Continuum* 28:4 (2014), 558–70

Jane, Emma Alice, *Misogyny Online: A Short (and Brutish) History* (London, 2017)

Johnson, Richard, 'Educational Policy and Social Control in Early Victorian England', *Past & Present* 49 (November 1970), 96–119

Jones, D. J. V., *Crime in Nineteenth Century Wales* (Cardiff, 1992)

Kennedy, Ludovic, *The Airman and the Carpenter* (London, 1985)

Kissack, K. E., *Monmouth: The Making of a County Town* (London, 1975)

Koehler, Karin, 'Valentines and the Victorian Imagination: *Mary Barton* and *Far From the Madding Crowd*', *Victorian Literature and Culture* 45 (2017), 395–412

Kollar, Rene, 'Bishops and Benedictines: The case of Father Richard O'Halloran', *Journal of Ecclesiastical History* 38:3 (1987), 362–85

Kollar, Rene, *The Return of the Benedictines to London* (London, 1989)

Lettmaier, Saskia, *Broken Engagements: The Action for Breach of Promise of Marriage and the Feminine Ideal* (Oxford, 2010)

Lewis, Ruth, Michael Rowe, and Clare Wiper, 'Online Abuse of Feminists as An Emerging Form of Violence Against Women and Girls', *The British Journal of Criminology* 57:6 (2017), 1462–81

Manchester, Colin, 'Lord Campbell's act: England's first obscenity statute', *The Journal of Legal History* 9:2 (1988), 223–41

Manchester, Colin, 'A history of the crime of obscene libel', *The Journal of Legal History* 12:1 (1991), 36–57

Mansfield, W. W., 'Disguise in handwriting', *Medico-Legal Journal* 11:1 (1943), 23–9

Marley, David F., 'The great galleon: The Santisima Trinidad (1750–1765)', *Philippine Studies* 41:2 (1993), 167–81

Matley, Marcel B., 'Forensic Handwriting Identification: Is It Legally A Science? A review of court cases which hold handwriting examination to be a science', *International Journal of Forensic Document Examiners* 3:2 (1997), 105–13

McAdams, Richard H., 'Group Norms, Gossip, and Blackmail', *University of Pennsylvania Law Review* 144:5 (1996), 2237–92

McNamara, Lawrence, *Reputation and Defamation* (Oxford, 2007)

Milroy, Christopher M., 'A Brief History of the Expert Witness', *Academic Forensic Pathology* 7:4 (2017), 516–26

Morrish, Reginald, *The Police & Crime-Detection Today* (Oxford, 1940)

Nef, J. U., *The Rise of the British Coal Industry* (London, 1966)

Nicolaisen, W. F. H., 'Names and Narratives', *Journal of American Folklore* 97:385 (1984), 259–72

Oldfield, Roger, *Outrage: The Edalji Five and the Shadow of Sherlock Holmes* (Cambridge, 2010)

Paine, Robert, 'What is Gossip About? An Alternative Hypothesis', *Man* 2:2 (1967), 278–85

Pease, Ken, 'Obscene Telephone Calls to Women in England and Wales', *The Howard Journal* 24:4 (1985), 275–81

Perkin, Joan, *Women and Marriage in Nineteenth-century England* (London, 1989), esp. 50–4

Phillips, Whitney, *This Is Why We Can't Have Nice Things: Mapping the Relationship between Online Trolling and Mainstream Culture* (Cambridge, MA, 2015)

Poole, Steve, *The Politics of Regicide in England 1760–1850* (Manchester, 2018)

Powell, J. H., B. W. Glover, and C. N. Waters, *A Geological Background for Planning and Development in the 'Black Country'* (British Geological Survey, Technical Report WA/92/33) (Nottingham, 1992)

Raybould, T. J., 'The Development of Lord Dudley's Mineral Estates, 1774–1845', *The Economic History Review* 21:3 (1968), 529–44

Reynolds, Jaime, 'Madam Mayor: The first wave of Liberal women in local government leadership 1819–1939', *Journal of Liberal History* 89 (2015–16), 6–18

Rice, Geoffrey W., 'Great Britain, the Manila Ransom, and the first Falkland Islands dispute with Spain, 1766', *International History Review* 3:2 (1980), 386–409

Risinger, D. Michael, Mark Denbeaux, and Michael J. Saks, 'Exorcism of Ignorance as a Proxy for Rational Knowledge: The Lessons of Handwriting "Expertise"', *University of Pennsylvania Law Review* 137:3 (1989), 731–92

Rose, June, *Marie Stopes and the Sexual Revolution* (London, 1992)

Ross, Lee, 'The Intuitive Psychologist and his Shortcomings', *Advances in Experimental Social Psychology* 10 (1977), 173–220

Rowland, John, *Poisoner in the Dock: Twelve Studies in Poisoning* (New York, 1960), 137–57

Rudd, Mary, *Historical Records of Bisley with Lypiatt* (Stroud, 2008) [first published 1937]

Ryley Scott, George, *Into Whose Hands: An Examination of Obscene Libel in its Legal, Sociological and Literary Aspects* (London, 1945)

Sassoon, Rosemary, *Handwriting of the Twentieth Century* (London, 1999)

Saudek, Robert, *Anonymous Letters: A Study in Crime and Handwriting* (London, 1933)

Scott, James C., *Weapons of the Weak: Everyday Forms of Peasant Resistance* (New Haven, CT, 1985)

Sculte Beerbühl, Margrit, 'Migration, transfer and appropriation: German pork butchers in Britain', *Transfers* 2:3 (2012), 97–199

Sill, M., 'Landownership and Industry: The East Durham Coalfield in the Nineteenth Century', *Northern History* 20:1 (1984), 146–66

Simpson, A. W. B., 'Obscenity and the Law', *Law and Philosophy* 1:2 (1982), 239–54

Sparke, Andrew, *Bella in the Wych-Elm* (Stourbridge, 2016)

Steedman, Carolyn, 'Threatening letters: E. E. Dodd, E. Thompson and the making of "The crime of anonymity"', *History Workshop Journal* 82 (2016), 50–82

Steinberg, David Joel, 'The Philippines, 1762–1872', in Steinberg (ed.), *In Search of Southeast Asia*, rev. edn (Honolulu, 1987), 160–70

Stone, Lawrence, *The Road to Divorce: England 1580–1987* (Oxford, 1990)

Suller, John, 'The online disinhibition effect', *Cyberpsychological Behaviour* 7:3 (2004), 321–6

Thompson, E. P., 'The Moral Economy of the English Crowd in the Eighteenth Century', *Past & Present* 50 (February 1971), 76–136

Thompson, E. P., 'The crime of anonymity', in Douglas Hay, Peter Linebaugh, John G. Rule, E. P. Thompson, and Cal Winslow (eds), *Albion's Fatal Tree* (New York, 1975), 255–344

Thompson, E. P., *Customs in Common* (London: 1993)

Vincent, David, 'The Origins of Public Secrecy in Britain', *Transactions of the Royal Historical Society* 1 (1991), 229–48

Vincent, David, *I Hope I Don't Intrude: Privacy and its Dilemmas in Nineteenth-Century Britain* (Oxford, 2015)

Wade, Stephen, *Lincolnshire Murders* (Stroud, 2006)

Ward, J. T., 'Landowners in Mining', in J. T. Ward and R. G. Wilson (eds), *Land and Industry: The Landed Estate and the Industrial Revolution* (Newton Abbot, 1971), 63–116

Watt, Dominic, 'The identification of the individual through speech', in Carmen Llamas and Dominic Watt (eds), *Language and Identities* (Edinburgh, 2010), 76–85

Weaver, Gordon, *Conan Doyle and the Parson's Son* (Cambridge, 2006)

Webb, Simon, *The Suffragette Bombers* (Barnsley, 2014)

Wells, Roger, *Wretched Faces: Famine in Wartime England, 1793–1801* (Gloucester, 1988)

Williams-Thomas, David, *The Dynasty Builder* (Bath, 2016)

UNPUBLISHED SOURCES

Baldwin, Anne, 'Progress and patterns in the election of women as councillors, 1918-1938', PhD thesis, University of Huddersfield, 2012

Catholic-Hierarchy.org, http://www.catholic-hierarchy.org

Cockayne, Emily, 'Social Distancing before Social Distancing', https://www.rummage.work/blog/disgusted

David Nordmann and Xavier Dominique, Auctioneers, Paris, Lot 256, Manuscrit—Botanique, Eliot (Anne) Florae, 1830, https://www.ader-paris.fr/en/lot/17302/3332863

Dictionary of Canadian Biography, http://www.biographi.ca/en/index.php

'Elizabethjayne2015', Norfolk Record Office blog, https://norfolkrecordofficeblog.org/2017/01/12/disgruntled-of-ditchingham-stories-from-the-correspondence-of-w-carr 22 January 2017

ESPNcricinfo, https://www.espncricinfo.com/england/content/player/13000.html (accessed 12/09/2021)

Fisher, Pamela Jane, 'The politics of sudden death: The office and role of the coroner in England and Wales, 1726–1888', PhD thesis, University of Leicester, 2007

Gee, Austin, 'British Volunteers Movement, 1793-1807', D.Phil. thesis, University of Oxford, 1989

Grace's Guide to British Industrial History, www.gracesguide.co.uk

Grace's Guide to British Industrial History, https://www.gracesguide.co.uk/Edward_Ernest_Lehwess (accessed 20/01/2021)

History of Parliament, Monmouth Borough, https://www.historyofparliamentonline.org/volume/1820-1832/constituencies/monmouth

Proceedings of the Old Bailey, 1674–1913: https://www.oldbaileyonline.org

SCRAN, Learning Cultural Heritage, part of Historic Environment Scotland, https://www.scran.ac.uk/

Sidley, Marguerite A., 'A guest of his majesty: a month in Holloway Gaol', Edith Jessie Thompson website, www.edithjessiethompson.co.uk

Swannington Heritage Trust, https://swannington-heritage.co.uk

Index

Alwalton (Huntingdonshire) 79–80
anonymous letters, defined 34,
   209–10
Anson, George Augustus 161–2
Archer, John 217
Arnold, Frederick 4, 14
arson 76
   after threats 77, 79, 82, 86–8, 172
   threatened by letter 7, 67–8,
      76–80, 82, 122, 124, 202, 214
Ashton-Wolfe, Henry 6, 215
Austin, Herbert 163–5

Bacton (Norfolk) 182–3
bail, granted 95, 116, 170
   skipped 3, 96, 97–8, 103
Bailey, William Willis 48–54, 59
Balm, Frederick Arthur 178
Banbridge (County Down) 211
Bath (Somerset) 79, 103
Battine, William 29, 32–3
Baughan, Rosa 140
Beck, Adolf 115, 131, 185
Bedminster (Bristol) 204
Bell, Jane 37–43
Bingham, Robert 85–8, 214
Birdingbury (Warwick) 144–5, 202
Birkbeck Bank 151–2
Bishop, Arthur 153
Bisley Commons 64–7, 70–4
Bisley (Gloucestershire) 64–7, 70–4,
   85, 89
Black Act (1723) 67
blackmail 4, 23–33, 67, 94; *see also*
   extortion; Battine, William
Blackwell, Ernley 150, 215–16

blasphemy 9, 160
block writing
   capitals 17, 149, 185
   letters 16, 165, 177, 192, 206
blotting paper 153, 155
Bodkin, Archibald 114, 128, 157
Bolton (Greater Manchester) 100–1
Boston, Jane 145–6
Bournemouth 174–5, 200–1
Bowler, Walter Edward 153
Boyce, Frederick 28–9, 32
Boyle, William 105
Brierley Hill (West Midlands) 44–8,
   55–60
Brighton (East Sussex) 19–22, 130
Brown, Elizabeth Sarah 104,
   106–8, 212
Brown, Frederick M. 105
Bucknill, Alfred 120–1, 158
Burke, William 101, 218
Burn, Jacob Henry 10–14, 226n.28
Bury (Greater Manchester) 105
Butt, George 223

Caddick, Elisha 52–4, 56
Captain Darby letters 177–9
Captain Swing letters 82–3, 84,
   238n.7
Carshalton (Surrey) 1–3, 113
Cartwright, Frederick C. 152–3
Catholic priests, letters sent to 132,
   179–81
Catholicism 85, 113–14, 115, 118,
   179–81, 191
Chabot, Charles 139, 142, 146
Christie, Agatha 17

church congregation
  member, writing
    anonymously 197
  members targeted 38–43, 100, 113,
    152, 157, 200–1
Cleethorpes (Lincolnshire) 183–4
clergymen
  anonymous letters sent to 83–8,
    152, 159–60, 172, 179–84,
    196–200, 203, 223; see also
    Catholic priests, letters sent to;
    Tractarianism
  writing anonymously 85, 94,
    180–2; see also Bingham,
    Robert; Hill, Thomas; Jackson,
    Thomas
coal mining
  Rhondda, Wales 173–4
  undermining 52–3, 55–7
  West Midlands 45–60, 232n.2;
    see also Moor Lane Colliery
    (Brierley Hill); Heath Colliery,
    (West Bromwich)
Cokayne, George Edward 1, 3
Cokayne, Mary Dorothea 1–3, 85,
  115, 223
Cokayne, Morton Willoughby
  1–3, 115
Coleback, Thomas 36, 141–2, 148
Coleford (Gloucestershire) 153–4, 215
Coleford (Somerset) 196
Collins, Wilkie 23, 34
Communications Act (1988) 8
compensation
  for libel 37–43, 131
  for miscarriage of justice 131, 162
complaints, see tip-offs
Conan Doyle, Arthur 140–1, 162
  Sherlock Holmes 140–1, 156
Cook, A. J. 173–4
copycat cases 100, 173, 185–6
coroners 54, 62, 176, 205–6, 236n.74;
    see also Docker, Ralph
  letters sent to 62, 176, 211
corruption 9, 189–90, 194

Coventry, 7th Earl, George
    William 23–8, 30–3
  blindness of 24, 27, 30, 32
Coventry, 8th Earl, George 31, 32–4
Coventry, Countess Peggy 23–5,
    27–9, 32–3
  handwriting of 24–5, 29, 228n.15
Coventry, Mary Beauclerk 33–4
Cramp, Charlie 173–4
Crowther, William George 172–3
cryptic details 168, 172, 200; see also
    doodles
Customs Act (1846) 92

Darby, Joseph 56–9, 62, 210, 234n.48
Darby, Thomas 62–3, 237n.81
Dartmouth, Earl of 48–52
death threats 9, 64–89, 99, 120,
    159–60, 178
decoy writing 4, 113–38, 156–7, 214
defamation 9, 101–2, 109
  defamatory libel 95, 113, 116, 130,
    145, 189, 202
  slander 17, 103–4, 130–1, 162, 175
deindividuation 221–2
detection 10, 13–14, 93, 101, 139–62,
    185, 192, 204, 216; see also
    evidence; surveillance
Dewey, Annie 113–14, 120, 155,
    157, 216
disinhibition 221
Dixon, Henry 145–6
Docker, Ralph 61–3, 237n.77
document examination 106, 145;
    see also handwriting, analysis
  photographic enlargement 146,
    155, 162
Dodd, Edward 69, 79
doodles 168, 172
doorsteps, things left on 120, 124, 126
Dorington, Lord John Edward 64–7,
    73–4, 89, 212
Dostoevsky, Fyodor 211
Dover 106–8, 172, 194
Dudley, Lord 47

Dudley (West Midlands) 50, 102–3
Dundee (Scotland) 173

Eaton, James 49–50, 51–2
Eberhardt, Henry 44–6, 55–7, 59
Edalji, George 159–62, 177,
    185, 213
Edalji, Shapurji 158–61, 177, 213
Eliot, Anne 21–2
Eliot, Major William Granville
    19–22, 23
employers 9, 97, 98, 116–17, 138, 177
    letters to current 130, 152, 201,
        206, 218
    letters to erstwhile 9, 113, 218,
        270n.7, 270n.12
enclosure 67, 70–3, 86, 239n.20
envelopes 74, 151, 159, 169, 174,
    181–2, 187, 192
    watermarked 154
    wrappers 12, 25, 31
Ermington (Devon) 206
evidence
    circumstantial 26, 87, 105, 115, 123,
        125, 128, 148, 161
    handwriting, see handwriting;
        handwriting, analysis
    material 122, 154–5, 157; see also
        blotting paper; envelopes; ink;
        paper; pen; pencil; stamps,
        marked
    extortion 8, 33, 67, 82, 84, 125, 189;
        see also blackmail

Fairfield, Letitia 106, 210–14, 215,
    220–1
Farnfield, Percy Hamilton 104–5
Fielden, William 218
football clubs 165
Forbes, John Alexander 103
Forster, Joseph 35–6, 148
framed (falsely implicated) as
    anonymous writers, see Dewey,
    Annie; Gardiner, Charles
    Henry; Gooding, Rose;

Johnson, Mary; see also
    neighbours, falsely framed
fraud 12–13, 59, 85–7, 119–20

Garbett, William 100–1, 144
gardens, letters left in 78, 79, 120
Gardiner, Charles Henry 115–17,
    120, 127, 137, 155, 158, 214,
    248n.24
gendered expectations 106, 113,
    214–15
    not conforming to 108, 132, 177,
        216–17
Giles, Cecilia 152–3
Glasgow 173, 197, 219
Gooding household,
    Littlehampton 136, 138
Gooding, Rose 127–9, 157–8,
    192, 216
    compensation 131
    framed (falsely implicated)
        127–9, 216
    handwriting 150
    imprisoned 127–9, 221
    lasting animosity against 133
    reported to NSPCC 127
gossip 19–43, 99, 105, 109, 115,
    182–4, 201–8, 228n.10
graphology 3–4, 140, 187; see also
    Baughan, Rosa; Saudek,
    Robert; Quirke, Arthur
Great Wyrley (Staffordshire)
    158–62, 177
Grimshaw brothers 77–8
grooming 94, 102–3
Gurrin, Gerald Francis 185–6
Gurrin, Thomas 113, 115, 162

Hagley murder 15–17
halfpenny post 103–4, 106
handwriting 17, 35–6, 40, 52, 55, 79,
    101, 116, 118, 144–6, 149
    analysis 86–7, 95–7, 100, 139,
        147–8, 150, 154, 254n.13,
        255n.26; see also Chabot, Charles;

handwriting (*cont.*)
    Dixon, Henry; Gurrin, Gerald
    Francis; Gurrin, Thomas; Inglis,
    George Douglas; Inglis, George
    Smith; Mansfield, Wladamir
    Raffalovich; Netherclift,
    Frederick G.; Netherclift,
    Joseph; Schooling, John
    Holt; Smart, Fred
   cursive 186
   disguised 8, 86, 130, 140, 145, 147,
    151, 152, 156, 186, 219; *see also*
    block writing
   in non-dominant hand 144, 196
   mimicked 120, 160
   not analysed 122, 128
   not disguised 66
   recognized 94, 178, 204
Hanley (Staffordshire) 141–2
Hardacker, Claire 222
Harrison, Wilson R. 219
Hartlepool (County Durham) 220
Hastings (East Sussex) 101–2
Heath Colliery (West
   Bromwich) 49–52, 62
Hellmuth, Andrew 102–3
Hereford 68
Higgs, Joseph 56–8, 59, 210
Hill, Rowland 91
Hill, Thomas 38–43
Hilliard, Christopher 131, 225n.7
Hobsbawm, Eric 82–3, 238n.7
Hohenrein, Charles 167–72, 212
Home Office 70, 131, 150, 155, 191–2,
   215–16
   letters to 78–9, 133
   specialists 106, 214
Honeyborne, family 55, 57,
   235n.53
Honeyborne, Thomas 47–8, 55–6
Horncliffe (Northumberland) 200
Hove (East Sussex) 115–20, 129, 155,
   158, 200, 214
Hull 31, 38, 167–71, 212
Hume, Joseph 147

illiteracy and semi-literacy 58,
   124–5, 201
   feigned 149–50, 179, 207
indecent letters 8–9, 92–3, 114–15,
   125; *see also* obscene letters
Inglis, George Douglas 144
Inglis, George Smith 99, 143–5, 146
ink 124, 146, 149, 187
   invisible 104, 154, 156, 192
   red 14, 192
Internet 4, 6, 17, 91, 100, 108,
   222–3
   social media 222; *see also* Twitter
   trolling 222–3
Ipswich (Suffolk) 96–7
Isle of Wight 185, 219
Ivybridge (Devon) 98–9

Jaap, Margaret 219
Jack the Ripper, hoax letters 14, 95
Jackson, Leon 4, 225n.7, 238n.8,
   238n.14
Jackson, Thomas 180–2
Johnson, Mary 120–2, 123, 135–6,
   158, 192
   appeal 123
   compensation 131
   framed (falsely implicated) 120–5,
   126–7, 155–7, 216, 220
   lasting animosity against 125, 133
judges 158, 178, 179, 220
   Acton, Edward, Justice 203, 207
   Avory, Horace, Justice 158
   Beazley, Hugh Loveday, Justice
   192–3
   Best, William Draper, Justice 148
   Brett, William Baliol, Justice 98
   Dallas, Robert, Justice 80–1
   Humphreys, Richard Somers
   Travers, Justice 114, 126,
   269n.71
   MacKinnon, Frank Douglas,
   Justice 178
   Rowlatt, Sidney Arthur Taylor,
   Justice 220

Scrutton, Thomas Edward, Justice 167
Swift, Rigby Philip Watson, Justice 201
justice, miscarriage of 13, 157, 162; *see also* compensation, for miscarriage of justice; framed (falsely implicated) as anonymous writers
justice system
    court appearances 114, 125, 153, 158, 192–3, 216
    Director of Public Prosecutions 128, 157, 199–200, 214; *see also* Bodkin, Archibald
    jury composition 128, 158
    jury decisions 36, 114, 123, 125, 126, 145, 148, 158
    King's Bench 35, 37, 81
    perjury 125, 129, 147

Keble, Thomas 73, 85, 239n31
Kidderminster (Worcestershire) 15–17, 46, 60–1
Kirkby-on-Bain (Lincolnshire) 176–7
Kitching, Joseph 26, 30–2, 229n.33
Kitching, Mary Ann 25–6, 28, 30, 32
Kitching, William George 26, 28, 30–2
Knowles, Enoch 177–9, 212, 221

Lancet, The 94, 211
Langham, Diana 153–4, 155, 215, 216, 220
Lanivet (Cornwall) 207
Last, Nella 6, 7–8
Lazarus, Philip 100
Lee, 'Molly' Marie Lucinda 129–31, 132, 135, 156
legislation, *see* Black Act (1723); Communications Act (1988); Customs Act (1846); Libel Act (1843); Obscene Publications Act (1857); Post Office Act (1908); Post Office Protection Act (1884); Vagrancy Act (1838)
Lennard, George 98–9
letter case, confidential 33
Lettmaier, Saskia 35
Libel Act (1843) 144
libel, legal definitions 8–9, 38, 108, 208; *see also* Libel Act (1843)
libellous letters 105, 109–38, 144–5, 150–3, 157, 196, 203, 210–15, 217–19
libellous postcards 92
libellous publication 93–5
literacy; *see also* illiteracy and semi-literacy
    gender differences 112, 217
    increasing rates of 68, 92
lithography 141–4, 254n.13
Littlehampton (West Sussex) 127–9, 131, 150, 153
    policing in 155, 157, 214
    Western Road 127–9, 135–8
livestock, injury to 161–2
Llewellyn, Richard 187–8, 207, 223
local government, women in 194, 267n.23
Lomax, Albert 105, 106
London
    Bromley 104–5
    Croydon 124–5, 133, 152–3, 217
    Hounslow 109–12, 137–8, 194, 210
    Romford 197–9
    Sidcup 104–5
    Willesden Green 130
    Wimbledon 9, 189–92, 195–6, 208, 213
Long Benton (Northumberland) 84–5
Loughborough (Leicestershire) 90–1
Lucas, Alfred 187
Ludd, Ned 79, 80
Ludlow (Shropshire) 211, 213
Lusitania (ship) 170–1

Major, Ethel 176–7
Malvern (Worcestershire) 17
Manchester 77, 82, 145
Mann, General Gother 19–21
Mansfield, William Murray 147–8
Mansfield, Wladamir
    Raffalovich 186, 219
Maresfield (East Sussex) 85–8
marriage, breach of promise of 34–7
Mason, Walter Frederic 95–8
Mellish, Esther 35–6, 148
Men of Secrets, see Post Office,
    Investigations Branch
Methodist congregation members,
    targets of anonymous letters
    38–43, 100, 200–1
Methodist minister, writing
    anonymously 38–43
Mill, J. S. 8
Milton Ernest (Bedfordshire)
    202–3, 207
Mitchell, C. Ainsworth 187
Monmouth (Wales) 81–2
Monteagle, Lord 14
Moor Lane Colliery (Brierley Hill)
    44, 46–7, 56–9, 61, 235n.66
Moor Lane Glassworks (Brierley
    Hill) 44, 46–8, 55–7
moral economy 67, 70, 74, 83, 88,
    212, 242n.89
morality, corruptibility of 92, 96,
    103, 132
Morpeth (Northumberland) 6
Morrish, Reginald 13–14
Moss, Gladys 155
motivations 10, 82, 93, 98, 108, 153,
    210–14, 218–20
    anger 144, 218
    anxiety 179
    dazed 203
    economic grievance 76, 82
    funfairs 219
    hypnosis 101, 218–19
    influenza 218
    jealousy and envy 98, 129, 135–6

menopause 153–4, 215
morphine 102
misogyny 95, 108, 165–6
paranoia 186
public spiritedness 82, 203, 210
quest for suffrage 131
racism 158–62, 213
revenge and spite 34, 82, 98,
    210–11, 218
seeking justice 107, 208, 212, 218
sexual perversion or mania 105–6,
    215, 219
sexual repression 129, 132, 220–1
Munslowe, George 144–5, 146, 202,
    212, 216
murder 58, 98, 175, 176–7, 178, 209;
    see also Hagley murder;
    poisoning

Nash, Elizabeth 60–2
neighbours 60–1, 69, 91, 109, 137–8,
    160, 201, 207
    as recipients of letters 5–7, 69,
    102–3, 130–1, 219
    at risk in arson cases 74, 76
    falsely framed 120–9, 214, 216, 220
    feminine expectations of
    good 135, 183, 218–19
    tip-offs 61–2, 109–12, 201, 210
Netherclift, Frederick G. 143
Netherclift, Joseph 143–4
newspapers
    below-the-line contributors 221
    classified messages 76, 90, 100,
    171–2
    Daily Express 186, 196, 215
    hoax classified messages 161
    Hull Daily Mail 170–1
    Ipswich Journal 96, 97–8
    London Gazette 66–8
Nicholls, George 128–9, 131, 134,
    135, 151
Nightingale, Florence 116, 140, 165
North Shields (Tyne & Wear) 37–43
Norwich (Norfolk) 68

O'Brien, Kathleen 115–20, 127, 132,
     133, 214, 215
  fraudulent activity 119–20
  in Hove 115–17, 137, 155
  in St Luke's Asylum 117–19, 125
  supposed motivations 131, 156,
     212, 220
O'Halloran, Richard 180–2
obscene letters 3–4, 8–9, 85, 90–108,
     109, 165, 200, 212; see also
     indecent letters
  carrying threats 98–9, 178
  targets identified 99–102, 174
  written by men 9, 90–103, 105–8,
     215, 217–18
  written by women 106–8, 152–4,
     155, 202–3, 219–20
obscene postcards 103–7, 197–8
Obscene Publications Act (1857)
     92–3, 243n.7
Old Bailey 13, 130, 192
Oxley, William 38, 42–3

paper 30, 102, 125, 132, 143, 149,
     154, 158, 173, 203, 217; see also
     blotting paper
  watermarks 38, 87, 102, 149, 154
paranoia 5, 82, 158, 186, 187, 209
parliamentary reports 17, 51, 70
Peer, John 90–3
pen 146
  nibs 187, 192, 196, 212
  stylographic 122, 155
pencil 17, 149, 150, 165
  badly pointed 186
Penny Post 34, 91, 97
Perth (Scotland) 201
Peterloo Massacre 81, 82
pillar boxes 8, 91, 104
  watched 156, 191
Plymouth (Devon) 81, 217
poison-pen letters, defined 8,
     109, 210
poisoning 109, 120, 126, 176
  accusation 62, 175

police
  Birmingham City 15–17
  hoax communications from 162
  hoax communications to 14,
     15–17, 213
  Metropolitan 13–14, 128, 155, 179,
     185, 192, 196
  plain clothes 96, 156
  Redhill 120, 122–4, 126–7, 129,
     136, 157, 214
  Staffordshire 161–2
  surveillance, see surveillance
  undercover 155, 156
  West Yorkshire 14–15
Pontefract (West Yorkshire) 172
Poor Law Union, Clutton 60
Poor Law Union, Tynemouth 60,
     210–11
Poor Law, tip-offs 60, 62, 210–11, 213
pornography 92–4
post boxes, see pillar boxes
post marks 2, 12, 15, 25, 102, 115, 151,
     173, 176, 187, 205
Post Office
  Bath 103
  Bedford 202
  Inspector of Franks 36, 141–2,
     147–8; see also Coleback,
     Thomas; Hume, Joseph
  Investigations Branch 152; see also
     Balm, Frederick Arthur; Bishop,
     Arthur; Bowler, Walter Edward;
     Cartwright, Frederick C.
  Littlehampton 153
  Nottingham 106
  Wimbledon 192
Post Office Act (1908) 92–3, 152
Post Office Protection Act
     (1884) 106–7
postcards, anonymous 146, 152, 156,
     165, 178, 200, 201, 205, 206
  indecent 93, 104, 105, 152–3,
     197–9
  readable by postal workers 92,
     103–4

Postmaster General 106–7
prisons; *see also* punishments for
    writing anonymous letters,
    imprisonment
    Holloway 115, 120, 123–4, 126
    King's Bench 27, 28, 77
    Lewes 116, 129
    Portsmouth 127, 128, 150
pseudonyms 3, 44, 47, 67, 83, 95, 139
    'A friend' 3, 151
    'A nark' 162
    'Curiosity' 171
    'Fairplay' 176–7
    'Fritz' 170
    'Mulberynose Snooks' 10–13
    'Veritas' 44–5, 47, 55, 59
    'Well-wisher' 23–4, 26, 28, 37, 50,
        52, 59
punishments for writing anonymous
    letters
    fines 91, 98, 100, 105, 106, 217
    imprisonment with hard
        labour 98, 99, 105, 115, 126, 128,
        131, 145, 173, 219
    imprisonment without hard
        labour 114
    transportation 67, 82

Quirke, Arthur 220

Raybould, William 49–55, 210
recipients of anonymous letters 5–6,
        18, 106, 108, 156, 173, 205; *see also*
    church congregation, members
        targeted; clergymen, anonymous
        letters sent to; employers;
        football clubs; neighbours, as
        recipients of letters
    people convicted of crimes and
        misdemeanours 205–6, 212
    pork butchers 105, 167–71
    prominent residents 38, 172,
        189–92, 200, 202
    relatives of prominent
        residents 204
    residents of a housing estate 201
    sanitary inspectors 109–12, 137–8,
        204, 210

Redhill (Surrey) 120–7, 129, 133, 136,
        154, 157
responses, emotional, to receiving an
        anonymous letter 6, 34, 101,
        145, 197, 206, 215, 223; *see also*
        paranoia; shame; suicide as a
        response to accusations; suicide,
        attempted
riots 4, 78–9, 209
    Hull 171
    Swing 82–3
Robin Hood's Bay (North Yorkshire)
        199–200
Robinson, Enoch 105–6
Rochdale (Greater Manchester) 218
Rossiter, James Collins 174
Rowley Regis 50, 58, 62–3
Rudé, George 82, 238n.7

Saffron Walden (Essex) 79
Salter, William 49–55, 210
sanitary inspectors 107
    as letter recipients 109–12, 137–8,
        204, 210
    guidelines 137–8
Santissima Trinidada (ship) 75–6
Saudek, Robert 3–4, 186–7
Sayers, Dorothy L. 187–8
Schooling, John Holt 145
Scott, James C. 68, 238n.8
Scott, Walter 42–3
sectarianism 173
self-harm 105, 119, 125
shame 6, 34, 91–2, 184, 195, 206
Sheringham (Norfolk) 156
Sidlesham (West Sussex) 203–4
Sidmouth (Devon) 85, 179–80
Sidmouth, Viscount 82
Sidney Sussex College,
        Cambridge 14
Simner, Winifred Ava 194–6, 267n.25
    court appearance 192–3
    letters of 189–93, 208
    supposed motivations 9, 190–1,
        195–6, 208, 212, 213
Sinn Féin 173, 262n.29
Sissison, William 38–40, 43
Skerrett, Richard 15

Smart, Fred 146
Smith, Mary 35
Spain, James 124, 126–7
Spondon (Derbyshire) 200
Springfield (Essex) 105
stamps 12, 91, 217; *see also*
    under-stamped mail;
    unstamped mail
    marked 96, 125, 153–4, 156, 192
stationery, *see* blotting paper;
    envelopes; ink; paper; pen;
    pencil; stamps
Steedman, Carolyn 69
Stevens & Williams Glassworks 44,
    46–7, 55–7
Stocksbridge (Sheffield) 200
Stonell, Bertram 94–5
Stopes, Marie 165–7
Stourbridge (West Midlands) 44–7,
    55–7
suffragettes 108, 124, 131
    conditions of imprisonment 95,
        116, 123–4
suicide 77, 135, 160, 199
    as a response to receiving letters
        7, 34, 174–5, 184, 187, 199, 205–7
    as a response to accusations 207
    attempted 119, 199
surveillance 152, 154–6, 178, 187,
    191–2; *see also* police, plain
    clothes
Sutton (Surrey) 1–2, 113–15,
    129, 154
Swan, Edith Emily 127–32, 133
    decoy letters of 128–9, 212
    framing a neighbour 127–9, 214
    supposed motivations 129, 131–2,
        134–7, 138, 219–21
Swan, household 127–9, 135–8,
    252n.116

telegram communication 17, 152
telephone communication 17, 105,
    182, 245n.63
Thompson, E. P. 6, 66–70, 76, 79, 88,
    209–10, 212

threatening letters, *see* arson,
    threatened by letter; death
    threats
tip-offs 4, 44–63, 172, 211, 212
    hoax 14, 213
Tractarianism 73, 85, 179–80
Tugwell, Annie 115, 135
    decoy letters 113–15, 120, 131, 132
    framing another 113–15, 120, 128,
        154–5, 157, 216
    imprisoned 122–4
    supposed motivation 115
Tugwell, Harry Warren 114, 115
Turner, Andrew Dunn 101–2, 218
Twisteton, Edward 139–40, 141, 146
Twitter 6, 165, 222
typed letters 17, 90, 101, 151–2
typewriters 151–2

Underhill, Evelyn 101, 165
under-stamped mail 144
unstamped mail 138, 173
Uttoxeter (Staffordshire) 217

Vagrancy Act (1838) 92
Valentine's Day messages 34, 104, 143

Warburton, John 141–2
watermarks 38, 87, 102, 149, 154
Wellingborough
    (Northamptonshire) 200
West Bromwich Volunteer
    Association 78–9
West Bromwich (West Midlands)
    48–55
Wharton, Amelia Ann 37
Woodman, Eliza 121–2, 215, 258n.71
    decoy letters of 120–7, 128, 131–3,
        154–5, 157, 185, 212, 214
    possible motivations 135–6
    sentenced 126, 129
Wyrley Gang, *see* Captain Darby
    letters

Yateley (Hampshire) 196–7, 198
Yorkshire Ripper 14–15